Conversion and Apostasy in the L ‑‑‑‑‑‑

The commonly accepted wisdom is that nationalism replaced religion in the age of modernity. In the nineteenth-century Ottoman Empire, the focus of Selim Deringil's book, traditional religious structures crumbled as the empire itself began to fall apart. The state's answer to schism was regulation and control, administered in the form of a number of edicts in the early part of the century. It is against this background that different religious communities and individuals negotiated survival by converting to Islam when their political interests or their lives were at stake. As the century progressed, however, and as this engaging study illustrates with examples from real-life cases, conversion was no longer sufficient to guarantee citizenship and property rights as the state became increasingly paranoid about its apostates and what it perceived as their "de-nationalization." The book tells the story of the struggle for the bodies and the souls of people, waged between the Ottoman state, the Great Powers, and a multitude of evangelical organizations. Many of the stories shed light on current flash-points in the Arab world and the Balkans, offering alternative perspectives on national and religious identity and the interconnections between the two.

Selim Deringil is Professor of History at Boğaziçi University in Istanbul, Turkey. He is the author of *The Well-Protected Domains: Ideology and the Legitimation of Power in the Ottoman Empire 1876–1909* (1999).

Conversion and Apostasy in the Late Ottoman Empire

SELIM DERINGIL
Boğaziçi University

CAMBRIDGE
UNIVERSITY PRESS

32 Avenue of the Americas, New York NY 10013-2473, USA

Cambridge University Press is part of the University of Cambridge.

It furthers the University's mission by disseminating knowledge in the pursuit of
education, learning and research at the highest international levels of excellence.

www.cambridge.org
Information on this title: www.cambridge.org/9781107546011

First published 2012
First paperback edition 2015

A catalogue record for this publication is available from the British Library

Library of Congress Cataloguing in Publication data
Deringil, Selim, 1951–
Conversion and apostasy in the late Ottoman Empire / Selim Deringil, Bogazici University.
pages   cm
Includes bibliographical references and index.
ISBN 978-1-107-00455-9
1. Religion and state – Turkey – History – 19th century.   2. Islam and state –
Turkey – History – 19th century.   3. Turkey – History – 19th century.
4. Turkey – Religion – 19th century.   5. Conversion – Islam – History – 19th century.
6. Apostasy – Islam – History – 19th century.   7. Islam – Turkey – History –
19th century.   8. Christianity – Turkey – History – 19th century.   I. Title.
DR557.D47   2012
297.5´74095609034–dc23   2011052381

ISBN 978-1-107-00455-9 Hardback
ISBN 978-1-107-54601-1 Paperback

To Alev

Contents

Plates follow p. xii.

Acknowledgements

When you set out to remember the people who helped you along the way, you realize what a long road it has been. Many friends and colleagues have been kind enough to offer suggestions, material, criticism, and support along the way. I will try to remember them all and offer thanks where it is due. I humbly apologize in advance for any I may forget.

Special thanks to Sinan Kuneralp, who provided so many of my references that I feel particularly grateful to him. I am also particularly indebted to Kevork Bardakjian for his generosity with time and sources regarding providing and translating bibliographical material in Armenian that I would otherwise have not had access to. Similarly, Yorgos Tzedopoulos and Eleni Gara shared their insights on the crypto-Christians of Anatolia. I am also very grateful to Ussama Makdisi for reading the manuscript and providing insightful detailed comments, as well as to the two anonymous readers.

As usual, at my intellectual and professional home, Boğaziçi University in Istanbul, my "alter ego" friend and colleague, Edhem Eldem, provided material, criticism, and humour. Cem Behar was generous with his time and expertise, particularly regarding the deciphering of difficult Ottoman documents and providing invaluable advice on things demographic and cultural. Faruk Birtek has a special place in friendship and esteem, and I can never thank him enough for his interest and support. I also owe Nadir Özbek thanks for his insightful criticism and particularly for his patience and understanding with a computer illiterate as he set up the databases for my archival material. Special thanks are also due to my friends and colleagues in the History Department and to the "driving engine" of our department, Oya Arıkan.

At the level of international institutional as well as intellectual support, I am particularly indebted to my dear friend and esteemed colleague Paschalis Kitromilides and the Asia Minor Institute in Athens. Similarly, I am indebted to Abdul-Rahim Abu Husayn and the American University of Beirut for inviting me on three occasions and to all the students and colleagues there who came to my talks and offered valuable comments. In the same context, I must fondly remember the late Professor Kamal Salibi for his gracious hospitality. François Georgeon was kind enough to invite me to his seminar at the Ecole des Hautes Etudes en Sciences Sociales, and the Ecole was very generous in its support during my stay in Paris. My thanks also to Anthony Grafton for inviting me to present a preliminary outline of the work on this book at the Davis Center of Princeton University and for the very useful comments and critiques of the graduate students and colleagues. I thank Amy Singer and Ehud Toledano of the University of Tel Aviv and Dror Ze'evi and the other colleagues at the University of the Negev at Ber Sheba for their generous invitations to teach at their institutions and present papers related to my project. At the University of Michigan, Ann Arbor, I owe thanks to Müge Göçek, Ron Suny, and Gerard Libaridian. I also thank the Collegium Budapest for its generous support and Rector Gabor Klaniczay and Director Fred Girod for inviting me, for it was at the Collegium that I began this book. At the Central European University in the same city I owe special thanks to my friends and colleagues Andras Kovacs, Maria Kovacs, Ayşe Çağlar, Arif Çağlar, Szabolcs Pogonyi, Michael Miller, Lazslo Kontler, and Constantin Iordachi. Finally, at the level of institutional support, I am very grateful to the European University Institute in Florence for offering me the Fernand Braudel Fellowship, and particularly to Anthony Molho for his friendship and stimulating conversation. Also at the EUI, I have greatly benefited from the knowledgeable and erudite conversation of Rainer Baubock and Antonella Romano. Many thanks also to Clare Tame for her valuable editorial support.

I also thank the staff of the Başbakanlık Osmanlı Arşivi, particularly the director, Mustafa Budak, for their professionalism, as well as the staff of the Library of Boğaziçi University, particularly the head librarian, Hatice Gür.

My thanks also to the following: Engin Akarlı, Taner Akçam, Ayhan Aktar, Gülen Aktaş, Dilek Akyalçın-Kaya, Marc Baer, Bahar Başer, Aylin Beşiryan, Geza David, Ahmet Ersoy, Selçuk Esenbel, Caroline Finkel, Dan and Carolyn Goffman, Don Handelmann, Milos Jovanović, Vangelis Kechriotis, Macit Kenanoğlu, Raimond Kevorkian, Cengiz Kırlı, Niyazi Kızılyürek, Rober Koptaş, Claire Mouradian, Dennis Papazian,

Kahraman Şakul, Ariel Salzman, Ara Sarafian, Irvin Cemil Shick, Dejan Stjepanović, Yücel Terzibaşoğlu, Maria Todorova, Fernando Veliz, Gültekin Yıldız, and Eric Jan Zürcher.

Last, but by no means least, I offer my greatest thanks to Alev and Begüm for their patience, love, and support.

Needless to say, all the errors, oversights, exaggerations, bad jokes, and the like are entirely my own.

Ras Beirut
21 November 2011

PLATE I. Richard Guyon/Hürşid Paşa's gravestone in the British Military Cemetery in Haydarpaşa, Istanbul. The inscription in Hungarian reads: "Here lies Count Richard Guyon. Turkish Paşa, Son of France, Born in England, Hungarian Nationalist. Deceased 1856". (Photograph courtesy of Ahmet Boratav)

PLATE 2. The inscription on the headstone reads as follows: "George Kmetty (İsmail Paşa) 1813–1869. Lieutenant-General of the Ottomans. Defender of Kars. Chief of the forces in Syria. In whom Hungary mourns a brave commander in her National War 1848–49. This granite covering his mortal remains is erected by the command of The Sultan". (James Stuart Curl, *Kentsal Green Cemetary: The Origins and Development of the General Cemetery of All Souls, Kentsal Green, London, 1824–2001* [London, 2003], p. 259. (Photograph and reference courtesy of Tom Garnett)

PLATE 3. "L,Univers Illustré, 20 May 1876. "The assasination of the Consuls of France and Germany, Salonica." The obviously orientalized depiction of the scene of the murders nonetheless comprises some accurate details, such as the metal bars torn from the windows of the mosque that were used as murder weapons. (Edhem Eldem Collection)

PLATE 4. "L'assiette au beure Turc", 16 August 1902. "Le grand saigneur..."
The vicious satire of the wording and the depiction of Abdülhamid II as a ruthless
slayer of Christians is typical of his image in the West. (Edhem Eldem Collection)

PLATE 5. Statue of Joseph Bem on the Duna Rackpart in Budapest. The legend at the base of the statue reads: "I will take that bridge or fall!", referring to the critical battle that took place on 9 February 1849 between the Hungarian national army (the *honvéds*) and Habsburg imperials in Piski, Transylvania. The bridge in question was the bridge spanning the river Sztrigy. (Photograph courtesy of Szabolcs Pogonyí)

PLATE 6. Grand Vizier Reşid Paşa,
circa 1848. (Edhem Eldem Collection)

PLATE 7. Sultan Abdülmecid I. (Edhem
Eldem Collection)

SALONIQUE. — Cour de la mosquée où a eu lieu le massacre.
Les consuls ont été entraînés dans la maison à gauche et tués au premier étage, sur le balcon. (Croq. de M. J. Viaud.)

PLATE 8. Drawing of the actual mosque, the "clocktower mosque", in which the consuls of France and Germany were murdered in Salonica in May 1876. The caption reads: "The consuls were dragged into the building on the left and murdered on the terrace." The drawing was made by Pierre Loti. The "clocktower" appears to be a sundial on the tower. (Edhem Eldem Collection)

PLATE 9. Stratford Canning's official seal and signature in Ottoman script. He signs himself as: "Your servant, pure of heart, Stratford Canning, Ambassador of the State of England at The Gate of Felicity". The date is 1826. (From a letter by Stratford Canning to Mehmed Reşid Pasha, 4 June 1826, in Edhem Eldem, "From Blissful Indifference to Anguished Concern: Ottoman Perceptions of Antiquities, 1799–1869", in Zainab Bahrani, Zeynep Çelik, and Edhem Eldem (eds.), *Scramble for the Past: A Story of Archaeology in the Ottoman Empire, 1753–1914* [Istanbul, 2011]).

PLATE 10. Portrait of Stratford Canning. (Stanley Lane-Poole, *The Life of the Right Honourable Stratford Canning*, vol. 2 [London, 1888], frontispiece)

Introduction

A Bosnian or a Herzegovinian Turk is a Turk by law, but as far as language and kinship are concerned, whatever his grandfathers were so will the last of his descendants be: Bosnians and Herzegovinians, until God decrees the end of the world. They are called Turks while the Turks rule the land; and when the real Turks return to their homeland where they came from, the Bosnians will remain Bosnians, and will be like their ancestors were.[1]

THE SPECIFIC NATURE OF CONVERSION AND APOSTASY IN THE NINETEENTH-CENTURY OTTOMAN STATE: NATIONALISM AND DE-NATIONALISATION.

Nationalism is like mercury. You put a drop in your palm, it has mass, weight, and colour; yet when you try to seize it, it seeps out between your fingers, and you know that it will kill you if you swallow it.

The basic question to be asked in this book is: how were nineteenth-century cases of conversion and apostasy in the Ottoman Empire different compared to earlier cases of conversion and apostasy? Why would people join a faith that was on the retreat? Why was the conversion of a goatherd in Macedonia in, say, 1657 very different from the conversion of a goatherd in the same geographic area in 1876? What makes conversion and apostasy different in the nineteenth-century Ottoman context is that they overlap with the rise of ethnic nationalism and the age of National Revival

---

[1] Dositej Obradović, "Letter to Haralampije", in Balćzs Trencsényi and Michael Kopećek (eds.), *Discourses of Collective Identity in Central and Southeast Europe: Texts and Commentaries* (Budapest and New York, 2006), Vol. 1, p. 128. Dositej Obradović (ca. 1740–1811), "Orthodox monk, writer, teacher and politician … is considered the most prominent figure of the Enlightenment in Serbia".

MAP I. The Balkan provinces of the Ottoman Empire, circa 1870. (Map courtesy of Ömer Emre)

movements that swept across Europe. Everyone felt special; moreover, everyone felt more special than his or her neighbour. Let us hear the voice of Joakim Vukić, a Serbian educator, writer, and theatre impresario: "During my stay in Serbia I also observed some other folk superstitions and customs which were taken over by the Serbs from the Turkish people, for they had lived with the Turks continuously for a period of 437 years; and the Turks are up to their ears in their superstition and nonsense." [2]

I believe that nationalism is primarily a product of the last two centuries. Together with Benedict Anderson, I believe it to be a "cultural construct". Like Eric Hobsbawm, I find that it "invents traditions"; and I agree with John Breuilly that it is "primarily political". [3]

Conversion and/or apostasy were seen as particularly dangerous in the nineteenth-century Ottoman Empire because they were perceived as

---

[2] Joakim Vukić, "Characteristics of the Serbian People (1828)", *In Discourses of Collective Identity*, p. 116.

[3] Benedict Anderson, *Imagined Communities: Reflections on the Origins and Spread of Nationalism* (London, 1991); Eric Hobsbawm and Terence Ranger (eds.), *The Invention of Tradition* (Cambridge, England, 1983); Eric Hobsbawm, *Nations and Nationalism since 1780* (Cambridge, England, 1990); Selim Deringil, "Invented Tradition as Public Image in the Ottoman Empire 1808–1908", *CSSH* 35 (1993), 3–29; John Breuilly, *Nationalism and the State* (Manchester, 1993).

de-nationalisation. Although almost all the literature on nationalism, and on that even more slippery concept, national identity, is focused on how they are *acquired*, whether they are "perennial", "invented", "imagined", or "ancient", much less attention has been lavished on the implications of and fear caused by their actual or potential *loss*. The fear of and hatred for the apostate in this context is quite important in understanding the process of a potential loss of national identity or the loss of a member of the flock or *ethnie*. The fear that the apostate evokes because "he knows our secrets" or the hatred of which he or she becomes the object is focused on the apostate/convert because they establish a *precedent*; they are potential *unravellers*. The nationalist canon usually focuses on the good examples, the role models for emulative purposes, the hero, the martyr; but nobody wants to talk about the bad apple, the turncoat, the quisling. When they do have to be talked about, it is only by way of focusing emotive hatred that, again, works to bond the healthy apples ever more firmly together.

What do I mean by "de-nationalisation"? I take this to mean the loss of a soul and a body from an increasingly "nationally imagined" community. This loss was also seen as a symbolic rape of the community's honour if the convert/apostate was a woman or a child. As such, the negative symbolism of the convert/apostate can be seen as a transgression of what Smith refers to as the "symbolic realm" of the community, or, by extension, the violation of the "inner world" of the ethnic community or nation.[4]

Benedict Anderson states that it is the power to convert and assimilate that gives the Old World religions their extraordinary force and validity, particularly through what he calls "becoming adepts in the truth language". He goes on to explain:

And, as truth languages imbued with an impulse largely foreign to nationalism, the impulse towards conversion. By conversion I mean not so much the acceptance of particular religious tenets, but alchemic absorption. The barbarian becomes 'Middle Kingdom' the Rif Muslim the Ilongo Christian. The whole nature of man's being is sacrally malleable. . . . It was after all, this possibility of conversion through the sacred language that made it possible for an 'Englishman' to become Pope and a 'Manchu' Son of Heaven.[5]

It is at this point that I disagree with Anderson; conversion was by no means "largely foreign to nationalism". When one studies religious conversion in

---

[4] Anderson, *Imagined Communities*; Anthony Smith, *Ethno-symbolism and Nationalism: A Cultural Approach* (Abingdon and New York, 2009), pp. 55, 64.

[5] Anderson, *Imagined Communities*, p. 15.

the Ottoman Empire over time, one finds a very different evolution. Religion does not fade away with the advance of nationalism, but rather becomes yoked to it through the process of conversion and apostasy. In the earlier centuries, the sixteenth, seventeenth, and even the eighteenth, conversion was seen as an undesirable development. Priests and other members of the community or congregation saw it as a bad thing because it reduced their numbers and demoralized them. Yet when we come to the nineteenth century, religious identity is linked to national identity to such an extent that conversion to Islam and, after 1844, potential conversion from Islam to Christianity were seen as a loss of identity, a harbinger of greater catastrophe, that is, potential de-nationalization. It was perceived not as an individually reprehensible act, but as an affront to the whole (more or less amorphously imagined) community, a deadly threat and an insult to a self-conscious group.

In his seminal article on the concept of "imagined communities" in a Balkan context, Paschalis Kitromilides points to the vital role of national churches in the process of "nation-building" in the Balkans, a process begun by the unilateral declaration of autonomy from the Istanbul Patriarchate of the Greek National Church in 1833, which "spearheaded all nationalist initiatives in the latter part of the nineteenth and throughout the twentieth century".[6] Fikret Adanır concurs: "[T]he dominance of ethnic nationalism should not lead us to underrate the importance of religion. More often than not religion dominated all other elements in Balkan nationalism. The wars of liberation during the nineteenth century were at the same time wars of religion".[7]

Similarly, Mark Mazower underlines the fact that with the advent of nationalism, "Religion became a marker of national identity in ways not known in the past, and therefore more sharply marked off from neighboring religions".[8]

In such a context, in which religion and nationality were so entangled, the apostate from a given religious community could be seen as a traitor (if the apostasy was ostensibly voluntary), as a martyr to the national cause (if he or she was subsequently killed by the other side), or as national

---

[6] Paschalis Kitromilides, "'Imagined Communities' and the Origins of the National Question in the Balkans", in Paschalis Kitromilides, *Enlightenment, Nationalism, Orthodoxy: Studies in the Culture and Political Thought of South-Eastern Europe* (Aldershot, 1994), pp. 149–152.

[7] Fikret Adanır, "The Formation of a 'Muslim' Nation in Bosnia-Hercegovina: A Historiographic Discussion", in Fikret Adanır and Suraiya Faroqhi (eds.), *The Ottomans and the Balkans: A Discussion of Historiography* (London, Boston, and Köln, 2002), p. 303.

[8] Mark Mazower, *The Balkans* (London, 2001) p. 76.

symbolic terrain to be re-conquered (in the case of actual or supposed abduction of women). As put by Irvin Cemil Schick: "As a *metaphor*, however, sexual violence also provides a symbolically dense representation of territorial appropriation and of the inability of men to defend their territory and their manhood".[9] In a historical conjuncture of almost continuous tension and upheaval, half-understood nationalist slogans, and abundant rumour presaging this or that impending disaster, the occurrence of something as minor as the conversion of an obscure peasant could achieve international dimensions.

Fear of de-nationalisation did not have to be articulated as such; very often it was not. Usually the people who took to the streets or went after each other with stones and knives had only a hazy awareness of the broader political implications. Sometimes, by word of mouth, rumour, or even the occasional newspaper, they had more precise information about real or imagined dangers.

The extent to which conversion and/or apostasy was seen as de-nationalisation is admirably examined in an article by Zoran Milutinović in which he discusses the works of four writers of Slovene, Croatian, Serbian, and Bosnian literature during the period of National Revival in the early nineteenth century.[10] In all four works, the enemy "Other" is not a foreign conqueror but an apostate who collaborates with the conqueror by adopting his faith.[11] In Milutinović's own words: "[The] culprit is never the Other, it is always an apostate, a renegade, someone ambiguously placed between us and them, by being one of us, but siding with them nevertheless".[12]

---

[9] Irvin Cemil Schick, "Christian Maidens, Turkish Ravishers: The Sexualization of National Conflict in the Late Ottoman Period", in Amila Baturović and Irvin Cemil Schick (eds.), *Women in the Ottoman Balkans: Gender, Culture, and History* (New York, 2007), pp. 274–304. Emphasis in original. It is hard to disagree with David Nirenberg when he claims that "competition for women and competition for converts are related". David Nirenberg, *Communities of Violence: Persecution of Minorities in the Middle Ages* (Princeton, 1996), pp. 128, 185.

[10] Zoran Milutinović, "Sword, Priest and Conversion: On Religion and Apostasy in South Slav Literature in the Period of National Revival", *Central Europe* 6 (2008), 17–46. My thanks to Fernando Veliz for bringing this reference to my attention.

[11] Ibid. The works in question are: the poem of the Croat writer, poet, and statesman Ivan Mazuranić, *Smrt Smail- agea Čengića* (Smail –aga Cengic's death) (1846); the Slovene poet France Prešern and his epic *Krst pri Savici* (Baptism on the Savica) (1836); the prince-bishop of Montenegro Petar II Petrović Njegos's epic poem *Gorski vijenaj* (The Mountain Wreath) (1847); and the Bosnian statesman and president of the Diet of Bosnia Safvet Bey Basagić and his play *Abdullah Pasa* (1900).

[12] Ibid., p. 41.

In an insightful recent study of Serbian historiography, Bojan Aleksov points out that the issue of conversion to Islam by Serbs has always been at the crux of Serbian nationalism. He mentions the term "religious nationalism", whereby "In the minds of the ordinary people, every neighbour who professed a different religion belonged to the 'enemy' civilization."[13] In the early nineteenth century, religion and nation were so closely linked in nationalist Serbian history that one historian, Georgije Magarašević, actually declared in 1827 that "Islamised Serbs, blinded by fanaticism, are much worse than the Turks".[14] Another Serbian historian, Jaša Ignjatović, writing in the late nineteenth century, very clearly identified conversion with de-nationalisation: "A Serb without religious rites and customs is not considered a Serb. A dissident from the faith is considered by the people as a lost son, as one who has lost the sense of the importance of Serbhood. Religious ideas are still more important than nation-building ideas".[15]

A similar situation prevailed in Bulgaria, where, Maria Todorova tells us, "Conversion to Islam as a historiographical trope can be interpreted as serving a particular internal social and political function". This function served as the legitimation for the forcible name-changing campaign enforced on the Bulgarian Muslims in the late 1980s.[16] It is interesting that the basic function of the discipline of history, and within that discipline, the study of conversion, remained virtually the same from the early nineteenth to the end of the twentieth century. In the case of socialist Bulgaria, what Carsten Riis observes to be the function of historiography, "the formation and maintenance of national consciousness", would also have held true in the early days of Bulgarian nationalism.[17]

When religion in the Balkans was parcelled out among various national churches, questions of the acquisition, loss, or betrayal of nationality were ultimately played out in the secular national arena even if the struggle was expressed in religious terms. A paradoxical result of this, as far as the Ottoman government was concerned, was what I will call the

[13] Bojan Aleksov, "Adamant and Treacherous: Serbian Historians on Religious Conversions", in Pal Kolstø (ed.), *Myths and Boundaries in South-Eastern Europe* (London, 2005), pp. 158–190. Aleksov points out that the term "religious nationalism" itself was coined by Milorad Ekmečić, *Stvaranje Jugoslavije 1790–1818* (Belgrade, 1989).
[14] Ibid., p. 164.
[15] Ibid., p. 171.
[16] Maria Todorova, "Conversion to Islam as a trope in Bulgarian Historiography, Fiction and Film", in Maria Todorova (ed.), *Balkan Identities* (London, 2004), pp. 129–157.
[17] Carsten Riis, *Religion, Politics, and Historiography in Bulgaria* (New York, 2002), p. 22.

bureaucratization and ultimate secularization of the conversion process as part of the Tanzimat reforms.

Another specific aspect of the nineteenth century was the fact that the non-Muslim subjects of the Ottoman Empire who were involved in conversion and apostasy disputes could claim the protection of one or the other of the Great Powers, beginning with the Russian claim to protect the Orthodox subjects of the empire, supposedly granted by the Treaty of Küçük Kaynarca of 1774.[18] For the Muslims, on the other hand, as the dominant *ethnie*, the apostasy of a Muslim, already a mortal offence by religious law, now became a double insult because it flew in the face of centuries of assumed superiority. If the offender in question was backed by a foreign power, the representatives of that power could also become the targets of the Muslims' vengeance. The social and political tensions caused by conversion and apostasy cases led ultimately to their being perceived as an "Imperial Headache".

The nineteenth century saw what can only be described as the "cracking of the shell" of the traditional religious structure in the Ottoman Empire as schism followed schism and the state tried to regularize and regulate. In many ways the dates speak for themselves. In 1830 the Armenian Catholics were recognized as a separate community or *millet*. In 1831 the Armenian Patriarch excommunicated the Armenian Protestants, yet the Protestants were formally recognized as a separate *millet* in 1846. In 1833 the Greek kingdom was recognized as an independent state, and in the same year the National Greek Church was established. In 1839 the Tanzimat Edict was declared. In 1844 the Sultan Abdülmecid I promised to ban the legal execution of apostates from Islam, theoretically (or so the missionaries thought) opening the way for Muslims converting to Christianity. In 1849 there was an influx of Hungarian and Polish asylum seekers and their (in most cases) highly dubious conversions to Islam. In 1856 the Reform Edict officially declared the freedom of religion. In 1870 the Bulgarian Exharchate was created, and Bulgarian Orthodoxy broke away from the Ecumenical Orthodox Patriarchate of Istanbul. In 1876 the Ottoman Constitution was declared, and religious freedom was guaranteed. This is the process that Lucette Valensi traced in Jerusalem, Damascus, and Aleppo.: "These back and forth movements expressed a powerful religious agitation. . . . The nineteenth century inaugurated a new

---

[18] J. C Hurewitz, *Diplomacy in the Near and Middle East: A Documentary Record 1535–1914* (Toronto, London, and New York 1956), Vol. 1, p. 54. This claim was based on "a liberal (and questionable) interpretation of Articles 7 and 14 of the 1774 instrument".

competition between diverse religious groups who attempted to reform their methods and to improve the training of their clergy to better resist the pressures of missionaries from all orders".[19]

This historic specificity of nineteenth-century conversion and apostasy is better understood when contrasted with earlier periods. It is interesting to compare the conversion process at the time when the Ottoman Empire was at the apex of its power in the sixteenth century, on the one hand, and the situation in the nineteenth century when Ottoman power was at its nadir, on the other. Tijana Kristić's brilliant study of high-profile converts in the sixteenth and seventeenth centuries has shown us that the careers of figures such as the Hungarian convert Murad b. Abdullah (c. 1509–86) unfolded at a time when Sultan Süleyman was "engaged in an acute struggle with both the Habsburg Emperor Charles V and the Safavid Shah İsmail for the title of the prophesied messianic Last Emperor (*sahib-kıran*)".[20] It was in this context that Murad wrote his polemical treatise *The Guide for One's Turning towards God*, attacking Christianity and upholding Islam as the one true faith. Kristić points out that in the intense political competition among Ottoman, Austrian, and Persian rulers, the conversion of a learned Orthodox priest such as Mehmed b. Abdullah constituted a "symbolic victory". Such symbolic victories are notably absent in the nineteenth century. The conversions of General Joseph Bem and General Ladislas Czartoryski at mid-century were hardly touted as symbolic victories over the Austrians or Russians. In some ways they were almost an embarrassment, and their usefulness as military experts had to be weighed against the diplomatic cost of protecting them. Similarly, the conversion of the Armenian Bishop Harutyun was kept very low-profile, and he was set to work translating Armenian newspapers.[21]

In her study of the last Ottoman conquest, that of Crete in 1669, Molly Greene pointed out that most of the island's Muslims were Greeks who had converted during the protracted campaign and joined the Ottoman

---

[19] Lucette Valensi, "Inter-Communal Relations and Changes in Religious Affiliation in the Middle East, Seventeenth to Nineteenth Centuries", *Comparative Studies in Society and History* 39 (1997), 268, 269.

[20] Tijana Kristić, "Illuminated by the Light of Islam and the Glory of the Ottoman Sultanate: Self-Narratives of Conversion to Islam in the Age of Confessionalisation". *Comparative Studies in Society and History* 51 (2009), 35–63. See Chapters 3 and 4 of this volume.

[21] See Chapter 4 of this volume.

janissary corps: "Conversion in Crete did not automatically create a fierce and brutal divide between the two communities".[22] It is actually possible that "conversion was part of the mechanism that maintained connections between groups and kept the network of intergroup relations well oiled."[23]

Mixed marriages were quite common in seventeenth- and eighteenth-century Crete. Nuri Adıyeke, working on the basis of the court records (*sicils*) of Crete, found that there were many instances of a Muslim father leaving his children in the care of his still-Christian wife and her family when he went away on campaign, sometimes never to return. Evidently, the administrators became concerned that the religious faith of these children would become perverted as a result of being brought up in a Christian household. As a result, on two occasions, in 1707 and 1727, they ordered that these children be registered and brought to Candia and placed temporarily with pious Muslims. There were also frequent complaints, registered by the court, that a certain person, ostensibly a Muslim, had been seen going to church. Another issue was circumcision. In 1658, it was brought to the courts' attention that most of the men who had converted were not circumcised. The *kadis* were ordered to ensure that all new converts be circumcised. Adıyeke concludes:

In conclusion many people ... converted to Islam in Crete from the seventeenth to the nineteenth century. In this context ... certain problems ... directly arising from conversion were experienced. ... However it should be noted that these complications did not produce a social trauma caused by conversion. ... Problems arising from conversion to Islam did not give rise to greater social conflicts in Crete where social transformation problems were experienced rather as daily problems which were to be resolved by legal means.[24]

Considering what a flashpoint of nationalist agitation Crete became in the nineteenth century, the relative containment of tensions related to conversion and apostasy is remarkable. In fact, this apparent containment had to be explained away by Greek nationalist historiography in the nineteenth century. One way of doing this was to claim that the numerous early converts in the seventeenth century had not been Greeks at all, but Venetians who had converted in order to save their property. Yet

---

[22] Molly Greene, *A Shared World: Christians and Muslims in the Early Modern Mediterranean* (Princeton, 2000), p. 107.

[23] Karen Barkey, *Empire of Difference: The Ottomans in Comparative Perspective* (Cambridge and New York, 2008), p. 128.

[24] Nuri Adıyeke, "Multi-Dimensional Complications of Conversion to Islam in Ottoman Crete", in Antonis Anastosopoulos (ed.), *Crete and the Eastern Mediterranean 1645–1840* (Rethymno, 2008), pp. 203–209.

when it came to those who had ostensibly remained crypto-Christians, declared their Christianity during the Greek War of Independence of 1820, and been executed, they were declared glorious national martyrs: "[Thus] while the historiographers do not regard the locals converting to Islam as Greeks, those who apostatize during the [war] are announced as martyrs".[25]

Marc Baer's important book on conversion during the reign of Mehmed IV (r. 1648–87) sheds further light on the specificity of conversions in the later period. Examining the revival of piety spearheaded by the Kadızadeli movement and the influence wielded by the charismatic Vani Mehmed Efendi on the sultan, his mother Turhan Sultan, and his Grand Vizier Fazıl Ahmed Paşa, Baer notes that this was the high point of Ottoman power, when "The broadest circle of conversion reached deep into central Europe and the Mediterranean accompanying the greatest extension of Ottoman boundaries". Mehmet IV himself was depicted in the sources of the time "as a warrior of the faith against the infidels".[26] The sultan actively sought to convert people during his hunting expeditions, and his mother made a point of demolishing the Jewish commercial quarter and converting it into the sacred Muslim space that was to become the massive Yeni Cami complex in the centre of the old city.[27]

The glaring contrast between the period depicted as a time of triumphant and triumphalist Islam, when the sultan himself was, in Baer's words, an active "convert maker", and the nineteenth century is indeed striking. In the time frame of this book the Ottoman Empire is very much on the defensive; it is in fact fighting for survival. When reading the documents from the Tanzimat State period, it seems unclear whether the Ottomans even *wanted* conversions at all.

Johann Strauss, in his textual analysis of seventeenth- and eighteenth-century Greek chronicles of the Ottoman period, points out that "the basic antagonism between 'Christians' on the one hand and 'Turks' on the other runs throughout the chronicles". However, relating to the controversial issue of conversion, he notes that "The subject plays an important role. ... It should be stressed however, that in these texts conversion is seen mainly as a problem of faith, of apostasy, and not as

---

[25] Nükhet and Nuri Adıyeke, "Myths and Realities on Ottoman Crete", paper presented at the conference The Mediterranean of Myths, the Myths of the Mediterranean, 3–4 June 2010, Istanbul. Cited with permission of the authors.

[26] Marc Baer, *Honored by the Glory of Islam: Conversion and Conquest in Ottoman Europe* (Oxford, 2008), pp. 10–11.

[27] Ibid., pp. 81–104.

a method of denationalization".[28] Even in cases of gross transgression, as in the case of men who actively sought martyrdom in the eighteenth century, the sword was slow to emerge from its sheath. Take the case of the monk Damascinos from Mount Athos, who was an apostate from Islam and was brought before the *kadi* to allow him the opportunity to repent: "[The *kadi*] offered him coffee which he proceeded to throw in the official's face and started declaiming against Islam as a false religion. He seemed to want to attract the worst punishments the Turks could inflict upon him. But he was taken for a madman and simply given a severe beating." Yet he kept trying, and after publicly insulting Islam three times in front of Turkish soldiers, he was executed.[29]

A similar case, unearthed from the kadı *sicils* of Kara Ferye by Eleni Gara, was recorded in 1627 in Veria in northern Greece. A Janissary calling himself Ömer Çavuş committed apostasy and declared that he was an "infidel" named İstati. He was asked three times to repent, and when he refused, he was handed over to the authorities for punishment, technically becoming material for neo-martyrdom. The interesting thing is, Ömer/İstati does not appear in the vitae of neo-martyrs that became a standard basis for latter-day Greek nationalism. Eleni Gara's observation is quite accurate:

[I]t appears that the Church and its clergymen at that time and place did not feel any urgent need to keep a record of all neomartyr-like deaths nor to compose vitae in honour of executed Christians. ... In short, as long as there was no agenda for which such cases could be of use, there was no need to record every single case of execution and proclaim the victims neomartyrs.[30]

Compared to stories like the above, the cases referred to in the subsequent chapters can be much more minor transgressions, but they acquired explosive symbolic power in a tense historical conjuncture.

Another tendency in Balkan and Turkish historiography has been to project the prejudices and preconceptions of nationalism back into the past. Paschalis Kitromilides's warning is well taken:

---

[28] Johann Strauss, "Ottoman Rule Experienced and Remembered: Remarks on Some Local Greek Chronicles of the Tourkokratia", in Fikret Adanir and Suraiya Faroghi (eds.), *The Ottomans and the Balkans: A Discussion of Historiography* (Leiden, 2002), p. 206.

[29] Michel Balivet, *Romano Byzantine et Pays de Rum Turc. Histoire d'une espace d'imbrication Greco-turque* (Istanbul, 1994), p. 187.

[30] Eleni Gara, "Neomartyr without a Message", *Archivum Ottomanicum* 23 (2005/06), pp. 155–175.

[T]he fact that since the late 19th century national and ethnic conflicts in the Balkans were fought out in the religious domain should not be allowed to colour our understanding of phenomena in a pre-nationalist era such as the 18th century.[31]

The first time the Ottoman Empire confronted full-fledged nationalism was during the Greek War of Independence (1821–26). Hakan Erdem's fascinating (and tantalizingly brief) article is very instructive in this regard. The Ottomans intercepted and translated correspondence from the Greek leadership, including a critical letter by Alexander Ypsilantis calling on all Hellenes to rise to defend the "motherland". What is most interesting is that this letter and others like it were translated into Turkish, which meant that concepts such as "motherland" (*vatan*), "freedom and independence" (*serbestiyet ve istîklâl*), and compatriots (*hemvatan*) came to be understood for the first time as the new vocabulary of a new creature, and an extremely dangerous creature at that. As pithily put by Erdem:

> The real importance of the Greek War of Independence for the Ottomans was that it brought nationalism home. ... The Ottoman administrators could no longer afford to treat nationalist ideas as distant curiosities of the French Revolution. Inescapably, they came to realize that nationalism was a potent force to fight against, usually by the adoption of the same tools used by their opponents.[32]

As the brushfire of nationalism spread in Ottoman Rumeli, conversion and apostasy became highly symbolic political issues.

Today, conversion and apostasy are still highly politicized issues in the Balkans and in Turkey. The very terminology used is politically charged. Even in what is otherwise a quite moderate scholarly work, it is possible to come across statements such as: "No doubt many non-Muslims melt into the Turkish population in time and become Turkified. Yet we should still remember the ethnic origins of many Muslims who live in Bursa".[33] Similarly, the term *dönme* (he or she who has been "turned"), meaning convert, as in "Armenian *dönme*" (*Ermeni dönmesi*), has negative connotations, whereas "*muhtedi Ermeni*," simply meaning "Armenian

---

[31] Paschalis Kitromilides, "Orthodox Culture and Collective Identity in the Ottoman Balkans during the Eighteenth Century", in *An Orthodox Commonwealth: Symbolic Legacies and Cultural Encounters in SouthEastern Europe* (Aldershot, 2007), pp. 131–145.

[32] Hakan Erdem, " 'Do Not Think of the Greeks as Agricultural Labourers': Ottoman Responses to the Greek War of Independence", in Faruk Birtek and Thalia Dragonas (eds.), *Citizenship and the Nation-State in Greece and Turkey* (London, 2005), pp. 67–88.

[33] Osman Çetin, *Sicillere Göre Bursa'da Ihtida Hareketleri ve Sosyal Sonuçları 1472–1909* (Conversion movements in Bursa according to the court records and their social consequences) (Ankara, 1994), pp. 3–5.

convert", does not.[34] Moreover, even today in parts of Anatolia when one wishes to express disdain regarding someone who is somewhat "new money" or *parvenu*, the saying is "Johnny-come-lately turned from infidel" (*sonradan görme gâvurdan dönme*). Even in modern works on issues dealing with conversion and apostasy, a remarkably strident tone sometimes creeps into the discourse. In an article that is otherwise a solid piece of archival research (and will be cited as such *in extenso* later), regarding the apostate, Selahittin Özçelik declares:

Because the concepts of Islam and citizenship are considered identical, he who turns away from this can be said to be committing the crime of *treason to state and fatherland*. He who abandoned his faith was also disrupting public order and as such could not be allowed to circulate freely among Muslims. . . . For this reason the punishment for this crime had to be extremely severe . . .[35]

Although ostensibly the author is speaking about Islam in the age of the Prophet, his tone and vocabulary are entirely modern; "treason to state and fatherland" are not concepts that can be deduced from works on classical Islam.

Thus the conversion issue is certainly not yet "history" in that part of the world. In a sense, this book is the pre-history of these issues.

CONVERSION AND APOSTASY IN OTTOMAN ISLAM: LEGALITY AND REALITY

The official position regarding conversion in Islam is that forced conversion is not acceptable. Conversion must be voluntary, an act committed "of the free will and conscience", (*bit'tav ver'-rızâ*) of the convert, and access to the faith must be freely accorded.[36] This was the official position,

---

[34] The term *dönme* was originally applied to the followers of Sabbatai Zvi, a Jewish mystical rabbi of the seventeenth century who declared himself the Mesiah, was persecuted by the authorities, and was forced to convert to Islam. Many of his followers also converted but continued to remain crypto-Jews. I have deliberately omitted any discussion on this topic as there is a considerable amount of literature on it, and it is not directly germaine to the period. On the Sabbataist movement, see Leyla Neyzi, "Remembering to Forget: Sabbateanism, National Identity and Subjectivity in Turkey", *Comparative Studies in Society and History* 44 (2002), 137–158; Marc Baer, "The Double Bind of Race and Religion: The Conversion of the Dönme to Turkish Secular Nationalism", *Comparative Studies in Society and History* 46 (2004), 682–708.

[35] Selahittin Özçelik, "Osmanlı İç Hukukunda Zorunlu bir Tehir (Mürted Maddesi)", *OTAM* 11 (2000), 350. Italics in original, "*devlete ve vatana ihanet*".

[36] The appropriate *sura* in the Qur'an is II: 256: "There is no compulsion in religion. The right direction is henceforth distinct from error. And he who rejecteth false deities and

yet the reality on the ground could be very different. The spectrum of "voluntary" and "forced" could be very broad, as was any notion of "free will". The act of conversion could range from the proverbial "conversion at the point of the sword" to the sincerely accomplished act of a spiritual athlete who saw Islam as the one religion ensuring salvation. The gradations of conviction and motivation were almost infinite. They could range from the conscious act of a Polish aristocrat-cum-revolutionary who took refuge in the Ottoman Empire in 1848 and converted in order to avoid being handed over to his enemies who would hang him, to an Armenian Bishop who converted out of love, to the inveterate French gambler who converted hoping to escape his gambling debts. People converted to save their lives, like the Armenians during the pogroms in late nineteenth-century Anatolia. But there was also that grey area, the small insults of everyday life – being referred to as *mürd* (dead, but used only for animals) rather than *merhum* (having attained God's peace) when you die, not being allowed to wear certain colours or clothes (green was for Muslims only), or not being allowed to ride certain animals (horses, camels); these little barbs, endured on a daily basis, must have been the reason for many a conversion to Islam.[37]

In this regard what Richard Bulliet has referred to as "social conversion" in the medieval context is still applicable in the modern age:

> [L]eaving aside ecstatic converts, no one willingly converts from one religion to another if by virtue of conversion he markedly lowers his social status. More starkly put, if an emperor converts to a religion of slaves, he does not become a slave; the religion becomes a religion of emperors.[38]

Ottomans were not inquisitional. Nobody particularly cared if *Macar* (Hungarian) Ismail Paşa drank wine in private or even if he was never known to fast during Ramazan. What mattered was that he could beat the Russians. The ruling class in the Ottoman Empire was not unduly occupied with the sincerity of the conversion. There were no dark sentinels constantly on the alert to catch someone out in heresy. Their attitude was distinctly pragmatic, particularly when it came to employing converts with

---

believeth in Allah hath grasped a firm handhold which will never break. Allah is Hearer, Knower".

[37] The definition of *mürd* in the *Redhouse Turkish English Lexicon* is "dead (not said of Muslims)". A more explicit definition is given in Şemseddin Sami, *Kamus-u Turki*: "croaked, kicked the bucket, used for animals" (*Gebermiş. Hayvanat için kullanılır*). *Merhum* is defined in *Redhouse* as "deceased and admitted into God's mercy".

[38] Richard W. Bulliet, *Conversion to Islam in the Medieval Period: An Essay in Quantitative History* (Cambridge, Mass., and London, 1979), pp. 34, 36, 37, 41.

specialist skills, such as shipwrights, gunmakers, and later on, cartographers and census takers.[39] The interesting thing was that in the nineteenth century, these "foreign experts", as they would now be called, were not required to convert, yet many did.

Ottoman pragmatism may be merely another application of the general Islamic attitude to conversion, which is not based on miraculous experiences; indeed, Islam has little room for miracles.[40] Islam was never a "missionary religion" where the primary objective is to save souls. "It was not a missionary movement in which the chief objective of the Muslim warriors was the conversion of men and women to the Islamic faith".[41]

To invite someone to embrace Islam individually was an auspicious act, and great merit accrued to the person doing it in the event of a successful conversion: "A convert to Islam is not unnaturally regarded as a person specially illuminated by God, being thus enabled to see the true faith in spite of the errors of his upbringing".[42] Yet there were no Muslim equivalents of the Franciscans or Dominicans or Jesuits, or, for that matter, of the Presbyterians or Congregationalists. Muslim *derviş* orders were indeed instrumental in the spread of Islam, particularly during the expansion of the empire in the Balkans, but they sought to convert more by example than by overt proselytizing. Ömer Lütfi Barkan, in his classic article on the "colonizing *dervişes*" in the Balkans, makes the point that the primary duty of the *dervişes* was to provide hospitality and security in remote areas. Barkan does allow a triumphalist note to creep into his narrative when he claims that the *dervişes* prepared the ground for the later arrival of Ottoman armies and had "already conquered the other side spiritually"

---

[39] This was a canonically endorsed position. See Ömer Nasuhi Bilmen, *Hukuku İslamiyye ve İstilahatı Fıkhhiyye Kamusu* (The encyclopedia of Islamic law and *Fıkh* rulings) (Istanbul, 1969), Vol. 4, pp. 5–6, 8: " [A Muslim is one who] proclaims the true religion in words and externally, submits to all its orders, whether or not there is true belief. Therefore by the pronouncing of the holy formula, abstaining from acts forbidden by the holy law, observing the prescribed external forms the person achieves the legal status of a Muslim, personal belief in [one's] conscience is not sought out". As to questions of apostasy, " A person is only declared an apostate if he openly declares his doubts and hesitations, it is not possible to look into anyone's heart".

[40] Larry Poston, *Islamic Da'wah in the West: Muslim Missionary Activity and the Dynamics of Conversion to Islam* (Oxford, 1992), p. 158.

[41] Ibid., p. 13. The one very obvious case of forced Islamization that will be omitted from the present study is the child levy (*devşirme*) that was the basis for the recruitment of the elite Janissary corps. The best source on this is still Halil İnalcık, *The Ottoman Empire: The Classical Age*.

[42] William Hasluck, *Christianity and Islam under the Sultans* (Oxford, 1929), Vol. I, p. 44.

when they arrived. He also notes the zeal of the newly converted; "[i]t is clear that *dervişes* who had been Christians would carry out more zealous and impassionate religious propaganda". However, the people who converted tended to be the servants in their hospices or others who were attracted to their exemplary piety. As to mass conversion, Barkan is quite unequivocal: "In truth in Ottoman history, until the conquest of Istanbul we cannot speak of mass Islamization or the cosmopoliticization of the state".[43] Victor Menage also takes note of the "proselytizing zeal" of the *ghazis* and the "missionizing zeal" of the *babas*, yet points out that once the actual apparatus of state was in place, "In the Balkans the rapid introduction of an efficient state apparatus ensured the protection of the new *dhimmis* against the illegal pressures to embrace Islam".[44]

Halil Inalcık's pioneering work on the spread of Islam in the Balkans draws attention to the fact that mass immediate forced conversion to Islam was hardly ever practiced among the Albanian, Serbian, or Bulgarian aristocracies immediately after the Ottoman conquest. Among these classes Islamization was a gradual process that lasted from the mid-fourteenth to the sixteenth century.[45]

More recent research has also drawn attention to the fact that "even if zealous local administrators applied pressure [on *rea'ya*] to convert, mass Islamization was prevented and those who attempted to practice it were punished".[46]

Conversion, when it did occur, tended to be spread over time: "The process of Islamization progressed and matured over decades and centuries largely as the result of the creation of an Islamic ambiance and the development of religious and communal institutions".[47] There was also a

[43] Ömer Lütfi Barkan, "Osmanlı İmparatorluğu'nda bir iskan ve kolonizasyon metodu olarak Vakıflar ve Temlikler I: Istila Devrinin Kolonizatör Türk Dervişleri ve Vakfiyeler" (The Vakif and Temlik as a method of colonization in the Ottoman Empire: The colonizing Turkish Dervişes and the Vakfiye of the expansion period), *Vakıflar Dergisi* 2 (1942), 282, 283, 284, 303, 304.

[44] Victor Menage, "The Islamization of Anatolia", in Nehemiah Levtzion (ed.), *Conversion to Islam* (New York, 1979), p. 67. This volume still remains the seminal work on this topic. A *ghazi* is a warrior in holy war; a *baba* is a dervish leader, usually of the Bektaşi order; *dhimmis* are protected "people of the Book", that is, Christians and Jews in the Ottoman state.

[45] Halil Inalcik, "Ottoman Methods of Conquest", *Studia Islamica* 2 (1954), 103–129.

[46] Nükhet Adıyeke, "Osmanlı millet sistemi uygulamasında gelenekçiliğin rolü" (The role of traditionalism in the application of the Ottoman millet system), *Düşünen Siyaset*, (1999), 161–162.

[47] Nehemiah Levtzion, "Toward a Comparative Study of Islamization", in Levtzion (ed.), *Conversion to Islam*, pp. 1–23.

solid economic logic behind the lack of a systematic policy of forced conversion. The *dhimmis* paid the "head tax" or *cizye*, which was one of the major sources of income of the treasury.[48] "In the decades following Ottoman conquest of Cyprus from the Venetians (1571)", Ronald Jennings notes, "many of the island's Christians converted to Islam. Contemporary observers and modern scholars have usually attributed that conversion to official compulsion, but no contemporary local sources substantiate that view".[49] Jennings believes that the Christian population was "proselytized carefully" by the sufi Mevlevi order; "conversion to Islam was common in Cyprus between 1580 and 1637. Several instances of individual conversions occurred but nothing was found involving small groups."[50]

At the level of humbler folk, in remote areas of the Balkans and Anatolia before the advent of the nation-state, there occurred what Mark Mazower has referred to as "slippage between religions". Peasants who were asked whether they were Christian or Muslim might reply, "We are Muslims but of the Virgin Mary". In those areas where religion and supernatural beliefs met and intertwined, "practice mattered more than dogma".[51] William Hasluck pointed out all those years ago that

For the illiterate whether Moslem or Christian, doctrine is important mainly as embodying a series of prohibitions: their vital and positive religion is bound up with the cult of the saints and demands for concrete objects of worship, especially graves and relics, and above all miracles, to sustain its faith.

He also traced the ways in which Christian and Muslim "sanctuaries" could become "ambiguous", this ambiguity allowing them to be used as numinous sites by the people of both confessions.[52] John Fine has also remarked that the religion of the peasantry in the Balkans and elsewhere was "practice oriented" and dealt "primarily with this world. It has little or

---

[48] Hasluck, *Christianity and Islam under the Sultans*, p. 469. "Under the Ottoman Turks at least there is very little historical evidence for conversion on a large scale in Asia Minor. So long as the *rayahs* [sic] were not dangerous, they could be 'milked' better than True Believers, and conversion *en masse* was to no-one's interest". See also Mark Mazower, *The Balkans: A Short History* (New York, 2002), p. 48: "If the Balkans did not become another Islamic land, one reason was that the sultans had no interest in making this happen. Christians paid higher taxes, and mass conversions would have impoverished the empire".

[49] Ronald Jennings, *Christians and Muslims in Ottoman Cyprus and the Mediterranean World 1571–1640* (New York and London, 1993), pp. 137–143.

[50] Ibid. Jennings's sources consist of the *kadi* court records (*sicil*).

[51] Mazower, *The Balkans. A Short History*, pp. 58, 59.

[52] Hasluck, *Christianity and Islam under the Sultans*, p. 570.

no doctrine and its emphasis is chiefly or even entirely upon practices that aim at worldly goals: at the health and welfare of the family, crops and animals".[53] H. T. Norris drew attention to the phenomenon of "superficial conversion" to Islam among Balkan women, many of whom continued to adore local saints, so much so that a Balkan proverb was coined: "Saint Ilia up to mid-day and after mid-day Alia". Once converted, the peasantry usually would not be exposed to any sound Muslim doctrine, with the exception of those who joined a local *tekke* (derviş lodge). There was also a tacit unspoken agreement among priests, rabbis, and imams to seek some "religious common ground".[54]

While on the subject of common ground, people who were in need of daily religious guidance could switch from one religion to the other. This was why conversion to Islam occurred more often in badly churched areas. People were actually known to tell the religious authorities that if they were not provided with a priest, they would go over to Islam. The lack of a priest was often compensated for by the presence of a *hoca*. This was the case of the Catholic Albanians in the village of Mat around 1700. The villagers told a passing missionary that they would convert if the archbishop in Durrës did not regularly send them a priest. The archbishop managed to send missionaries twice a year. "The villagers, however, were not satisfied and threatened to call a *hodja* if they could not have a regular priest".[55] Similarly, a factor contributing to the conversion of the Hemşin Armenians in the Pontic mountains of the Black Sea in the eighteenth century may have been the lack of priests: "The thirty-six villages of Karadere were served by only one priest. . . . the weakness of the church may have played a significant role in the conversion process."[56]

My intention here is not to contend that the *pax ottomana* was some kind of utopia where everyone knew their place and lived in peace and harmony. Beliefs, syncretic as they may be, are still beliefs, and even the most "syncretic" of Christians could violently object to any forced Islamization. Also, one should not nourish any illusions about the oft-cited phenomenon of "Ottoman tolerance" of the non-Muslim confessions. As elegantly put by Maria Todorova:

[53] John Fine, *The Early Medieval Balkans: A Critical Survey from the Sixth to the Twelfth Century* (Ann Arbor, Michigan, 1987), p. 171.
[54] H. T. Norris, *Islam in the Balkans* (Columbia, South Carolina, 1993), p. 264.
[55] Stavro Skendi, *Balkan Cultural Studies* (New York, 1980), p. 154.
[56] Hovan H. Simonian, "Hemshin from Islamization to the End of the Nineteenth Century", in Hovan H. Simonian (ed.), *The Hemshin: History, Society and Identity in the Highlands of North East Turkey* (New York, 2007), p. 62.

For all the objections to romanticized heartbreaking assessments of Christian plight under the infidel Turk, a tendency that has been long and rightly criticized, the Ottoman Empire was, first and foremost, an Islamic state with a strict religious hierarchy where the non-Muslims occupied, without any doubt, the back seats. The strict division on religious lines prevented integration of the population, except in cases of conversion.[57]

There was also an almost traditional folkloric aspect to the assumption that non-Muslims constitued a lower order: "One of the aspects of Ottoman traditionalism that was very closely adhered to was the understanding that the non-Muslims were second class. This was not just so because of Islamic law, according to the Ottomans, this was in keeping with their nature".[58]

On two occasions, in 1517 and in 1647, the sultans Selim I (r. 1512–20) and Ibrahim I (r. 1640–48) seriously considered enforcing Islamization on the Balkans, but both were dissuaded by the Şeyhülislams of the time on Qur'anic grounds; "In general there was no Muslim analogue to the widespread Christian impulse to drive out the infidel and the heretic".[59] Nor was there an Ottoman equivalent to the periodic mass expulsion of non-Christian populations as seen in the Latin west.[60]

Mass forced conversion did indeed occur in the western Rhodope mountains in Bulgaria in the seventeenth century, when during the period from June 1679 to May 1680 there were altogether 339 converts (193 men and 146 women).[61] The seventeenth century does indeed seem to be an exceptional period when the pietist movement of the Kadızadeli, led by the sultan's preacher, Vani Mehmed Efendi, gained influence and counted not

---

[57] Maria Todorova, "The Ottoman Legacy in the Balkans", in Carl L. Brown (ed.), *Imperial Legacy: The Ottoman Imprint on the Balkans and the Middle East* (New York, 1996), p. 47.

[58] Nukhet Adıyeke, "Osmanlı Millet Sistemi uygulamasında gelenekçiliğin rolü", p. 162.

[59] Mazower, *The Balkans: A Short History*, p. 48. The office of the Şeyhülislam was an Ottoman innovation. It was during the period that the famous Ebu's Su'ud Efendi held the office (1545–74) that the post would take on the definitive character it would hold until the nineteenth century. I. H. Uzunçarşılı, *Osmanlı İmparatorluğu'nun İlmiye Teşkilatı* (The scholarly establishment in the Ottoman Empire) (Ankara, 1988).

[60] Ariel Salzmann, "Is There a Moral Economy of State Formation? Religious Minorities and Repertoires of Regime Integration in the Middle East and Western Europe 600–1614", *Theory and Society* 39 (2010), 299–313.

[61] Maria Todorova, "Conversion to Islam as a Trope in Bulgarian Historiography, Fiction and Film", in Maria Todorova (ed.), *Balkan Identities: Nation and Memory* (London, 2004), pp. 129–157. I would like to thank Maria Todorova for her many insightful comments on these issues.

only the sultan himself but also the Grand Vizier Fazıl Ahmed Paşa among its supporters. Marc Baer indeed refers to it as a "unique historical epoch".[62] The perceptions of external threat, such as Russian advances in the eighteenth century, also provoked outbursts of persecution and forced conversion, often accompanied by heavy taxation to offset the ruinous costs of recent wars.[63] Stavro Skendi mentions mass conversion in the seventeenth century, although he concurs that mass forced conversion was not the rule and that mass conversion did not occur before the end of the reign of Süleyman the Magnificent in 1566.[64] Also, force in the form of extortionate taxation and forced conversion campaigns was used against the Armenian population of the northeast Black sea region in the mid-seventeenth and early eighteenth centuries in an effort to create a buffer zone against eventual Russian encroachment.[65]

As to the matter of apostasy from Islam, the story is more complicated. It has been firmly believed that the punishment for someone who abandoned Islam was death.[66] The apostate is called a *murtadd* in Arabic, a *mürted* in Turkish, and he or she is committing the crime of *ridda*, "a turning away from Islam".[67] Islamic law has two basic sources, the Qur'an and the Sunna, the acts and traditions of the Prophet Muhammad. On top of this there are the *hadith* (Turkish *hadis*), which are legal interpretations of the Prophet's sayings or acts, pronounced over the centuries by famous scholars.[68] The Qur'an deals with the topic of apostasy in seven *suras*. None of these specify the death penalty for the apostate, but they all talk of the apostate in damning terms.[69] The death penalty for the apostate is

[62] Baer, *Honoured by the Glory of Islam*, p. 6.

[63] Hasluck, *Christianity and Islam under the Sultans*, p. 471.

[64] Stavro Skendi, "Crypto Christianity in the Balkan Area under the Ottomans", *Slavic Review* 26 (1967), 227–246.

[65] Claire Mouradian, "Aperçus sur l'Islamization des Arméniens dans l'Empire Ottoman: le cas des Hamchentsi/Hemşinli", paper presented at the conference Conversion to Islam in the Mediterranean World, Rome, 4–6 September 1997, p. 11. Cited with permission of the author.

[66] Samuel M. Zwemer, *The Law of Apostasy in Islam: Answering the Question Why There Are So Few Moslem Converts, and Giving Examples of Their Moral Courage and Martyrdom* (London, 1924), pp. 80–81.

[67] Heffening, "Murtadd", in *Encyclopaedia of Islam* (Leiden, 1965), Vol. 3, pp. 736–738.

[68] "*Hadith*: Being an account of what the Prophet said or did, or of his tacit approval of something said or done in his presence. Hadith came to be recognized as a foundation for Islam second only to the Kur'an", *The Encyclopaedia of Islam* (Leiden, 2004).

[69] İrfan İnce, "Ridde", *İslam Ansiklopedisi*, Vol. 35 (İstanbul, 2008), pp. 88–91. *Holy Qur'an*. el-Bakara 2/108,217; Âl-i Imran3/86, 90–91; el-Maide 5/54; et-Tevbe 9/66,74; en-Nahl 16/106; el-Hac 22/11; Muhammed 47/24–26.

based on various *hadith*.[70] Although there has always been some debate among scholars about the application of the death penalty, until the nineteenth century apostasy was seen as a crime in both civil and criminal law. The doctrine remained valid until 1844, and the death penalty fell into desuetude but was never formally abolished.[71]

The highly respected Şeyhülislam of the sixteenth century, Ebu's Su'ud Efendi, was unequivocal in his *fetva* on this matter: "Question: What is the Şer'i ruling for a *dhimmi* who reverts to infidelity after having accepted Islam? Answer: He is recalled to Islam, if he does not return he is killed".[72] A major study on Ebu's Su'ud has also drawn attention to his strictness in this regard: "The penalty for the male apostate is death. Before the execution ... jurists grant a three day delay. If during this period, the apostate repents and accepts Islam he is reprieved. ... An apostate in fact lives in a legal twilight. If he migrates and a judge rules that he has reached the realm of war, he becomes legally dead".[73] For women the punishment was less severe; they were beaten and imprisoned, but very rarely were they executed.[74]

Upon closer inspection, however, it appears that the death penalty was not widely imposed, and even when it was, it was seen as a last resort. One source goes so far as to say, "[A]s far as we can see there is no certain evidence that the death penalty was applied to apostates in the classical age of the Ottoman Empire".[75] Yet the belief remained that the punishment for apostasy was death. As late as October 1843 we come across the last case of a formal, official execution of an apostate by beheading in the capital, Istanbul. The American missionary Cyrus Hamlin noted in his memoirs that the issue caused severe divisions in Ottoman ruling circles: "The old Mussulman party had triumphed in the most disgraceful manner. The act

---

[70] Ibid., "Ridde": Some of these are Buhari, *İstitatabetü'l mürteddin* 2, where it is said that the Prophet ordained "Kill those who change their religion"; Buhari *Diyat 6*, "where the Prophet ordained that a Muslim who abandons his religion and community is committing one of the three cardinal crimes requiring the death penalty"; and various *hadith* dealing with the waging of war against the apostates in the time of the Caliph Ebubekir.

[71] Rudolph Peters and Gert J.J. De Vries, "Apostasy in Islam", *Die Welt des Islams* 17 (1975–76), pp. 1–25. See Chapter 2 of this volume.

[72] Ertuğrul Düzdağ, *Ebussud Efendi Fetvaları Işığında 16. Asır Türk Hayatı* (Sixteenth-century life in Turkey in the light of the Fetvas of Ebussuud Efendi) (Istanbul, 1972), p. 90.

[73] Colin Imber, *Ebu's Su'ud: The Islamic Legal Tradition* (Stanford, 1997), pp. 70–71.

[74] Ömer Nasuhi Bilmen, *Hukuki Islamiyye ve Istilahati Fikhiyye Kamusu* (Istanbul, 1969), p. 10.

[75] Selahittin Özçelik, "Osmanlı İç Hukukunda Zorunlu bir Tehir (Mürted Maddesi)".

divided Turkish sentiment and feeling; the old Turks commending it, the young Turkish party, already forming, cursing it as a needless insult to Europe and a supreme folly of old fools".[76]

Yet, as will be seen in the subsequent pages of this book, apostasy was a quite frequent occurrence in the nineteenth-century Ottoman Empire. People could move in and out of religions, or indeed, as in the case of the crypto-Christians to be discussed later, be "a people of two religious faiths".

It should also be recalled that one man's conversion was another man's apostasy. Ussama Makdisi's very perceptive remarks on the stigmatization of the convert can apply equally to the apostate:

Conversion was a sin, a treachery that far surpassed that of secular betrayal, for secular betrayal could be justified and rationalized, even forgiven and forgotten. Conversion marked an absolute break with the past, a rejection of heritage and history and a new beginning. Moreover, it indicated an intrusion by others into a private, sacred sphere of life – a theft that undermined the very basis of the social order, which depended on a quiescent and theoretically unchanging religiosity.[77]

The apostate was therefore seen as the "traitor within the gates", somewhat akin to the witch in medieval society in Europe; "the witch is the figure of a person who has turned traitor to his own group. . . . The witch is the hidden enemy within the gate. He eats away like the maggot in the apple".[78]

At times when Islam was weak, apostates from Islam were considered particularly dangerous because they could infect others by their example.[79] Perceptions of weakness and threat on the part of the Muslims after the Tanzimat Edict of 1839 and the Reform Edict of 1856 may well have made them more violent and radical in their reactions to apostasy. It may also be the case that feelings of insecurity caused people to seek "scapegoats" as defined by Rene Girard: "A scapegoat is identified, differentiated from the

---

[76] Cyrus Hamlin, *Among the Turks* (New York, 1878), pp. 80–81. See Chapter 2 of this volume.

[77] Ussama Makdisi, *The Culture of Sectarianism. Community: History and Violence in Nineteenth Century Ottoman Lebanon* (Berkeley, 2000), p. 36. Although Lebanon was the very place where people shifted religious allegiances, or at least where the members of the ruling classes could profess one religion in public and practice another in private. See Engin Akarli, *The Long Peace: Ottoman Lebanon 1861–1920* (Berkeley, 1993), p. 21.

[78] Philip Mayer, "Witches", inaugural lecture, Rhodes University, 1954, in Max Marwick (ed.), *Witchcraft and Sorcery: Selected Readings* (Bungay, 1982), pp. 54–70. My thanks to Gabor Klaniczay for this reference.

[79] Ahmet Yaşar Ocak, *Osmanlı Toplumunda Zındıklar ve Mülhidler* (Istanbul, 1998), p. 94.

group and attacked so that insiders feel united as they never did before. The alien threat displaces everything else."[80]

ABOUT THE BOOK

This book began some ten years ago with the publication of an article that represented the first fruits of my research into conversion and apostasy in the late Ottoman Empire.[81] It will examine the politics of conversion and apostasy at a time when the Ottoman Empire was undergoing critical changes. It is my belief that the handling of apostasy and conversion cases follows the political climate and discourse of the time. From 1839 to the end of the century, the Sublime State underwent profound transformations in its conceptions of ruler and subject. The Tanzimat reforms were a sincere effort to win the hearts and minds of its non-Muslim subjects to a project of modern state formation, ultimately culminating in the first constitution of 1876. However, after the loss of the most valuable Balkan provinces, the Hamidian state found itself obliged to fall back on its Muslim population. In this context the outbreak of Armenian nationalism in Anatolia, the last stronghold, was seen as a deadly threat. On the other hand, the Ottoman decision-makers faced intense pressure from the foreign powers. Although the Ottoman governments retained ultimate political agency to the very end, foreign pressure was a constant reality in their political decision-making.

In the first chapter I discuss the beginning of the Tanzimat process, which was the process of general reforms and profound changes in Ottoman state and society; this I treat as a discrete period that I call the Tanzimat State. An important point that must be stressed is that the spirit of the Tanzimat reforms was internalized by the Ottoman elite themselves. This was not just some smoke screen or window dressing for the benefit of foreign observers. The Ottoman ruling classes took the Tanzimat State seriously. Although the beginning of the Tanzimat is usually dated from the proclamation of the Edict of the Rose Chamber (*Gülhane Hat-ı Hümayunu*) of 1839, and although it is clearly possible to trace the origins of the reform process to earlier periods, the fact that the Gülhane Edict was a critical watershed is undeniable. The issuance of decrees guaranteeing the

---

[80] Rene Girard, "Generative Scapegoating", in R. G. Hammerton-Kelly (ed.), *Violent Origins: Ritual Killing and Cultural Formation* (Stanford, 1987), pp. 73–148.

[81] Selim Deringil, "'There is No Compulsion in Religion': On Conversion and Apostasy in the Late Ottoman Empire", *Comparative Studies in Society and History* 42 (2000), 547–575.

security of life, honour, and property of all of the sultan's subjects was a common practice often carried out by newly enthroned sultans.[82] What made the Gülhane different was that it made *promises*. Sultan Abdülmecid I (r. 1839–61) swore a solemn oath, in the holiest of sanctuaries, the Chamber of the Sacred Relics, to uphold the guarantees that were granted in the edict. Contrary to popular belief, there is no specific declaration of the equality of Muslim and non-Muslim subjects in the actual document; the edict simply declares that all the sultan's subjects will benefit from the Tanzimat. The other important document that is enshrined as a basis of the Tanzimat is the Reform Edict of 18 February 1856. This was a document issued shortly before the Treaty of Paris (30 March 1856) ending the Crimean War that guaranteed the territorial integrity of the Ottoman Empire and accepted it as a member of the Concert of Europe. The Reform Edict is entirely concerned with the rights and privileges of the non-Muslim subjects of the Ottoman Empire. Although the two documents are usually lumped together, they are in fact very different. The Gülhane Edict was mostly "homegrown" and the result of long deliberations among members of the Ottoman secular and religious bureaucracy, whereas the Reform Edict of 1856 was largely the result of foreign pressure. Another critical development that has gone virtually unnoticed in the grand narrative was the sultan's official declaration of a ban on the execution of apostates from Islam (1844). This is critical because it gives us an insight into the dilemma facing the Ottoman rulers and their bureaucracy. On the one hand, the ban was the result of foreign pressure, but it came to be upheld because the Ottoman elite sincerely believed that such executions were not in keeping with the spirit of the Tanzimat State. On the other hand, for the Caliph of All Muslims to be seen to be failing to defend Islam would have a seriously de-legitimizing effect in the eyes of the sultan's Muslim subjects. Therefore, some sort of solution had to be negotiated. The solution was to send out an imperial order (*irade*) to the provinces decreeing that apostates were no longer to be executed, but to instruct them not to make the order public.

   The story of this book unfolds at the time when Great Power imperialism was at its peak and the discourses of the "White Man's Burden" and "*Mission Civilizatrice*" ruled the international agenda. This is the historical context of the second chapter, which provides the diplomatic dimension of the story told in the previous one. Although I firmly believe that the fate of the Ottoman state was ultimately decided by the Ottomans

---

[82] "*Adaletname*", *Encyclopedia of Islam*.

themselves, we cannot deny that they operated under severe constraints, the main constraint being the claim of the Great Powers to be the protectors of the Christians in the Ottoman Empire. This claim made the representatives of the Great Powers major actors in the domestic affairs of the Ottoman state and was also reflected in the cases of conversion and apostasy. Very often a convert/apostate would claim foreign power protection. When that happened, an additional dimension was added to the conversion procedure: the local consul of the power concerned or his representative had to be present at the conversion ceremony. In fact, the ban on the execution of apostates (1844) was the result of an intense diplomatic crisis involving the Porte, the British ambassador, Stratford Canning, and the French ambassador, Borkine. The issue was the conversion and subsequent apostasy of an Armenian who was publicly executed by beheading in 1843. Moreover, the fact that it came so soon after the declaration of the Tanzimat Edict of 1839, and that the executed person was dressed in Western clothes, caused a scandal. It also cleared the way for the ascendancy of the "reform party" at the Porte, who felt that if they were to join the modern world, such a practice was totally unacceptable. In fact, the main point of the British and French diplomats was that the execution of apostates "was not in keeping with civilization". The word thus made its way into Ottoman diplomatic parlance as "*sivilizasyon*".[83]

The developments discussed in the previous two chapters, particularly the declaration of religious freedom after 1856, were to be the cause of the surfacing of a whole spate of crypto-Christianity throughout the empire, which is discussed in Chapter 3. These people declared that they had secretly been Christians all along but had pretended to be Muslims for various reasons. One reason was the avoidance of the *cizye* (a poll tax levied on Christians). Now they were taking the state at its word as it had officially declared religious freedom, and they were "coming out". However, the phenomenon of crypto-Christianity appears to be much more complicated when subjected to closer scrutiny. The two spectacular cases dealt with in this volume are those of the Kromlides, a Pontic Greek community living in a mountainous zone on the Black Sea coast, and an offshoot of that community called the Stavriotes living in the region of Ak Dağ Maden in the province of Ankara in central Anatolia. Both communities were crypto-Christian, claiming that they had practiced Christianity in secret ever since their conversion to Islam in the seventeenth century.

---

[83] Selahittin Özçelik, "Osmanlı İç Hukukunda Zorunlu bir Tehir (Mürted Maddesi)", p. 375.

The Kromlides openly declared that they were Christians in 1857, after the declaration of the Reform Edict. Although they trusted the Sublime Porte's declaration of religious freedom, it turned out that the Ottoman state was quite worried that this would be the thin end of the wedge and that the Kromlides would be followed by other people, ostensibly Muslims, making the same claim. The obvious advantage of claiming Christianity was the avoidance of military service. Although the Ottoman government instituted universal military service for Muslims and non-Muslims alike in 1843, this was not actually put into practice until 1910.

An interesting aspect of this crypto, or secret, Christianity is that in some cases it was not secret at all, or was at best a "public secret". The Kromlides and the Stavriotes were not obscure sects hidden away in their mountain fastness; they were the notables and some of the richest men and women in the area. Therefore, it is also brought out by the archival documentation that their so called secret faith was quite well known and that they were locally called, pejoratively of course, "a people of two religions".

A very interesting insight into how the late Ottoman Empire saw conversion in the late nineteenth century can be gained from the examination of people who can be called latter-day renegades or "career converts", which is the focus of Chapter 4. Also, these conversions forced the state to consider just who qualified as an Ottoman subject, as subjecthood became something very close to citizenship, as defined by the Ottoman Citizenship Law of 1869. The nineteenth century was the century of the professional revolutionary or freedom fighter. Figures ranging from Lord Byron to General Joseph Bem adopted a cause, usually national independence, but not necessarily the independence of their own nation. Byron died fighting for the Greeks, and General Joseph Bem, originally a Pole, became a leader of the Hungarian Nationalists, commanding the Hungarian armies fighting against the Austrians and Russians in 1848–49. The Hungarians were badly defeated, and thousands of them, including General Bem and many of his close aids, sought asylum in the Ottoman Empire. The Ottoman Empire had extradition treaties with Austria and Russia. The only way the Hungarians could avoid extradition was by converting to Islam. Many of them did. There were many others like Bem who entered the service of the Ottoman Empire throughout the nineteenth century. At the other end of the social spectrum, many of these career converts were of humble origins, technicians, railway workers, even brigands turned policemen in Ottoman service. Far from being actively encouraged to convert, in the increasingly unstable political milieu of the nineteenth century such people came to be considered a security risk.

As the relatively more tolerant atmosphere of the Tanzimat State gave way to the more sternly Muslim rule of Sultan Abdülhamid II (r. 1876–1909), one of the greatest crises of the nineteenth century was to unfold in eastern Anatolia: the Armenian massacres of 1894–97. The mass conversions of Armenians seeking to save their lives during this crisis is the subject of Chapter 5. What happened in Anatolia during these critical years throws into relief much of what was discussed in the previous chapters regarding conversion and apostasy. None of the meticulous regulations regarding the "proper procedure" of conversion were applied to the Armenians. Sometimes entire villages converted in order to save their lives from the attacks of the Kurdish Hamidiye Regiments and the local population, who took the occasion to plunder Armenian property. The "Armenian Question", as it came to be called in diplomatic parlance, also highlighted the weakness of the Ottoman state at that time as compared to earlier centuries, as international public opinion became a major consideration. Abdülhamid II was to gain world opprobrium as the "Red Sultan" as the result of his Armenian policies.

What determined the attitude of those holding power towards those who had left the fold? Although the accepted wisdom was that execution was religiously permitted, indeed ordained, the historical record shows that this dictum was often deliberately disregarded. Was it simply a matter of the degree of the state's coercive power? Was it the presence of the vigilant foreigners? Or was there an increasingly prevalent notion that "this was not the done thing anymore"? Most importantly, how does the study of the politics of conversion and apostasy in the late Ottoman Empire contribute to concepts such as ethnic nationalism, citizenship, inclusion and exclusion from the imagined community, and the social politics of identity formation?

I

"Avoiding the Imperial Headache"

Conversion, Apostasy, and the Tanzimat State

The History of the Tanzimat era is neither dramatic, nor grotesque, nor
splendid. It is a tragedy in the true sense of the term. It was a time of tragic
irresolution which simmered as history moved on. It was a time when a
society; with its institutions, traditions, and statesmen, moved towards its
inevitable end. It was a time of darkness and treason, as well as an epic era,
when legends of virtue and vision were wrought. It was a century during
which progress and decline danced their deadly dance. It was the Longest
Century of the Ottoman Empire.

> İlber Ortaylı, *İmparatorluğun En Uzun Yüzyılı* (The longest
> century of the Empire), p. 13 (my translation)

THE "TANZIMAT STATE" AND "TANZIMAT MAN"

The nineteenth century began disastrously for the Ottoman Empire. What
started as a revolt of Serbian *knez* (chieftains) in 1805 ended as a proto-
nationalist movement backed by Russia.[1] The Greek War of Independence
(1821–29) seemed to presage a whole series of similar uprisings throughout the empire.[2] Worst of all, the sultan's erstwhile vassal, Mehmet Ali
Paşa Kavalalı of Egypt, developed into a regional potentate who was able
to inflict disastrous defeats on the Ottoman armies.[3] His son Ibrahim Paşa

---

[1] Selim Aslantaş, *Sırp İsyanları 19. Yüzyılın Şafağında Balkanlar* (The Serbian uprisings: The
Balkans at the dawn of the nineteenth century) (Istanbul, 2007). This very interesting
monograph marks the first time that the issue has been dealt with through a contrapuntal
reading of both Ottoman and Serbian sources.
[2] See Hakan Erdem, "Do Not Think of Greeks as Agricultural Labourers".
[3] For a revisionist view of Mehmed Ali as an Egyptian ruler, see Khaled Fahmy, *All the
Pasha's Men: Mehmed Ali, History and the Making of Modern Egypt* (New York, 1997).

was poised to strike at Istanbul itself by 1839 and was stopped only by the intervention of the British, French, and Russians. Ironically, the empire had been brought to the very brink of collapse not by Russia or by any Christian power but by a Muslim army commanded by a man who was himself very much an Ottoman.[4] In this context, it became necessary, and even imperative, for the remaining Christian subjects of the empire, the *reaya*, particularly those in Rumeli, to be integrated into a new schema of governance.[5] The Tanzimat State was thus primarily the first, and last, attempt of the Ottoman ruling class to extend an invitation to its non-Muslim subjects to become true citizens, as the term *reaya* (subject) increasingly came to mean "subject" as in "British subject", eventually to be replaced by *teba*, meaning "citizen".

There are actually indications that the Tanzimat was a project launched by Mahmud II (r. 1808–39). Although he was notorious as an iron-fisted ruler, when Mahmud visited Rumeli in 1837, this was projected as "a beneficent gesture to show his benevolence towards the *reaya*". The sultan's speech to the population was later published in the official Ottoman newspaper, the *Takvim-i Vekayi*:

Our greatest desire is the preservation well being and order of our Muslim and *reaya* subjects in all of our Well-Protected Domains. We have undertaken this inconvenience [of the journey] solely to improve the conditions of our domains and with the munificent aim of assuring the protection of our people and of our *reaya (himayeyi ahali ve reaya).*[6]

In the critical years between the Tanzimat Edict of 3 November 1839, the Reform Edict of 3 February 1856, and the Constitution of 1876, the Ottoman state embarked upon a project that was nothing less than the quest to establish a new mechanism of consent for its rule.[7] It is this time frame that I propose to consider as the "Tanzimat State". Just what was the Tanzimat State? How does one justify considering it as a discrete period? What sets it apart from the periods preceding and following it? Who were the "Tanzimat Men" responsible for designing and

---

[4] On the Kavalalı dynasty as Ottomans, see Ehud Toledano, *State and Society in Mid-nineteeth Century Egypt* (New York, 1990).

[5] The term *reaya* actually means "tax-paying subject"; after the Tanzimat, it came to mean exclusively non-Muslims, as in "*reaya* and Muslims" (*reaya ve Muslimin*).

[6] Halil İnalcık, *Tanzimat ve Bulgar Meselesi* (The Tanzimat and the Bulgarian question) (Istanbul, 1992), p. 27.

[7] On this, see Roderic H. Davison, "Turkish Attitudes Concerning Christian-Muslim Equality in the Nineteenth Century", in his *Essays in Ottoman and Turkish History 1774–1923* (Austin, Texas, 1990), pp. 112–31.

implementing it? It will be the purpose of this chapter to give some spec-
ulative answers to these questions, and particularly to see them through
the prism of the religious politics of the period, more specifically, in the
context of state attitudes towards conversion and apostasy. In these years,
when the old order had been displaced, but the new one that would replace
it was still unclear, conversion and apostasy came to occupy a very strategic location in the relations between the rulers and the ruled. In all the
archival documentation pertaining to conversion, the concern, bordering
on obsession, is that the conversion should not muddy the waters and
risk causing ill-feeling and mistrust between Muslim and Christian, and
above all, between the subjects and the Tanzimat State. The most important aspect of the documentation is that it illustrates quite conclusively
that the issues of conversion and/or apostasy were seen as key issues in
domestic politics, and it became a point of honour to "avoid the Imperial
Headache," which became the catch-all phrase for anything likely to incur
the sultan's or his government's displeasure. Indeed, the documentary
evidence shows that the Ottoman authorities did not care very much at
this time about swelling the ranks of the faithful.

To approach the last question first: Who was "Tanzimat Man"? In the
words of İlber Ortaylı:

> The Tanzimat Man (*Tanzimatçı*) responds to the cautious conservatism of a tradi-
> tional society and the impositions of the modern world. He does not believe in
> democracy and does not think about it, but he knows that he cannot accomplish
> much if he distances himself too far from the masses of the ruled.[8]

Although the Tanzimat Man may not have been too concerned about
democracy as such, there is no doubt that he was concerned about the
idea of law. Even in the eyes of the conservative Cevdet Paşa, "the primary
duty of the state official should be to act in accordance with the aim of
bringing the rule of law (*ikrah-ı hukuk*) into execution."[9]

THE GÜLHANE EDICT AND THE PROMISES
OF THE TANZIMAT

Although Halil İnalcık has tended to see the Gülhane Edict as a continuation of the *adaletname* genre, whereby each new sultan ascending the

---

[8] İlber Ortaylı, *İmparatorluğun en Uzun Yüzyılı*, p. 12.
[9] Cristoph K. Neumann, *Araç Tarih amaç Tanzîmat. Tarih-i Cevdet'in Siyasi Anlamı* (History as
a tool, Tanzimat as the aim: The political meaning of Cevdet's history) (Istanbul, 1999), p. 194.

throne promised to rule justly, the Gülhane Edict is categorically different.[10] Again, in the words of Ortaylı,

The 'nation' (*millet*) to whom justice and prosperity was being promised was the entire subject population of the empire. This was the difference between the Edict and its predecessors. The dominant principles in the Edict were not the direct copies of the principles of the French Enlightenment. Nor were they the result of the pressure of a newly arisen class pushing forward their world view. But, this 'principle of equality' [of Muslim and non-Muslim] was adopted out of practical considerations seeking to find a solution for the crises created by the structural changes in the empire. These considerations were primarily the nationalist revolts and regional uprisings which had shaken the empire since the beginning of the century [particularly those] of the Balkan peoples provoked by the foreign powers.[11]

A major consideration in the aims of the Tanzimat State was the mobilizing of the population as an efficient productive force, the security of the conditions of production being the first priority. It was in accordance with this concern that the Tanzimat Men established the local representative councils (*Eyalet Muhhassıl Meclisleri*) in the provinces. The Tanzimat reformers were hardly interested in democracy as such; their aim was more a shift from sultanic despotism to a legal authoritarian regime, similar to that of the Habsburg Empire.[12] The most significant aspect of these councils was that they would systematically include non-Muslim members of the community. Councils in major centres were to have thirteen members. Of these, six would be appointed government officials. The others would be representatives of the local population, Muslim and non-Muslim. The latter would usually be represented by the leading cleric and the *kocabaşı* (headman).[13] These councils will feature prominently in the cases of disputed conversion to be discussed later.

Despite the good intentions of the Porte, in some places the actual application of the Tanzimat yielded results opposite to those intended. In 1841, in Niş, the *reaya* rebelled because their tax burden actually increased due to the corruption and malpractice of the tax collectors (*muhassıl*). When the revolt was put down brutally by the use of Albanian irregulars, many villages were burnt, and some of the Bulgarian peasantry took refuge

---

[10] Halil İnalcık, "Sened-i İttifak ve Gülhane Hatt-ı Hümayunu", *Belleten* 128 (1964), 109–112.

[11] İlber Ortaylı, *Tanzimat'dan Sonra Mahalli İdareler* (Local government after the Tanzimat) (Ankara, 1974), p. 1.

[12] Ibid., pp. 4–5.

[13] Roderic Davison, "The Advent of the Principle of Representation in the Government of the Ottoman Empire", in *Essays in Ottoman and Turkish History 1774–1923*, pp. 96–111.

in autonomous Serbia. This was the last thing the Porte wanted; the officials responsible were sternly admonished, and the sultan declared an official amnesty, promising financial compensation to the escaped *reaya* if they returned to their villages. The actual wording of the *ferman* read to the *reaya* by the Porte's envoy, Yakup Paşa, is indicative of the mentality of the Tanzimat State: "We know that like your homes, your hearts are also scorched. . . . The Sublime State has sent me here with the sole purpose of seeking the comfort of the poor".[14]

In one of the now-classic works on the application of the Tanzimat, Halil İnalcık has drawn attention to the instructions given to Ali Rıza Paşa, who was sent to Vidin to quell the 1850 rising. These instructions are important as they illustrate the attitude of the Tanzimat statesmen towards peasant rebels:

The first duty of the Paşa is to settle the matter without bloodshed and violence using firm but gentle language . Only if this does not yield results, the rising is to be crushed quickly using regular troops. Because if this is not done there is a very real danger that the rebellion will spread throughout the province. Even if force has to be used you are to spare innocents who have been duped by trouble makers. You are to exert the utmost care so that not even a nose bleeds unnecessarily . . .[15]

Wishing to distance himself from the draconian rule of his father, Mahmud II, Abdülmecid I (r. 1839–61) sought a new legitimacy for his rule and found it in the stance of a just and compassionate monarch. Although the Tanzimat Edict has often been evaluated as an imposition of the foreign powers – more specifically, of the British Ambassador Stratford Canning via the intermediary of the Grand Vizier, Mustafa Reşid Paşa – an important article by Butrus Abu Manneh has put an entirely new face on the matter.[16] In this article Abu Manneh persuasively argues that much of the Tanzimat Edict was actually the result of the inner dynamics operating at the Sublime Porte. He focuses on two memoranda compiled by a committee including prominent *ulema* (religious scholars), Reşid Paşa being in Paris at the time. Abu Manneh particularly draws our attention to an *irade*

---

[14] Ahmet Uzun, *Tanzimat ve Sosyal Direnişler, 1841 Niş İsyanı Üzerine ayrıntılı bir İnceleme* (The Tanzimat and social resistance: A detailed study of the 1841 Niş uprising) (Istanbul, 2002), p. 76.

[15] İnalcık, *Tanzimat ve Bulgar Meselesi*, p. 52. In the event, there were plenty of "nosebleeds" as the state was unable to avoid bloody reprisals by Albanian irregulars. For a more recent study of the Niş uprising, see Uzun, *Tanzimat ve Sosyal Direnisler*.

[16] Butrus Abu Manneh, "The Islamic Origins of the Tanzimat Edict", *Die Welt des Islams* (1994), 173–203.

(imperial decree) issued on 17 July 1839, some two months before the actual declaration of the Gülhane Rescript:

This *irade* of Sultan Abdülmecid was issued to his own ministers meeting in council and was concerned not with specific abuses but with general principles. This is what makes it of special interest to us here because it contains basic principles that were to appear afterwards in the Gülhane, for example, that the *shari'a* should be applied, that justice and righteousness should prevail, and that care should be given to 'all' subjects of His Majesty, as well as the required guarantees for their well-being.

What differentiates this from the previous *adaletname* genre is, again according to Abu Manneh, that "these decrees differ from Abdülmecid's *irade* in that they were normally addressed to governors, judges or military commanders in the provinces and concerned with the abuses of authority committed by them or by their subordinates there."[17]

Indeed, in a recent evaluation Caroline Finkel states unequivocally: "The prominence of Reşid Paşa as a conduit for British influence subsequently manifested in Ottoman legislation has tended to overshadow the home grown aspects of the Edict."[18] The very wording of the Tanzimat Edict is self-consciously within the framework of Islamic jurisprudence, the very first article stating, "[A]ny state not ruled by the Şeriat cannot prevail" (*Kavanin-i şer'iyye tahtında idare olunmıyan memalikin payidar olamıyacağı*).[19] The edict clearly states that "when a person is in danger of losing his life, honour and property he has no other recourse than to rebel".[20] Indeed, we can speculate that the formulators of the edict allowed a deliberate double entendre to seep into the text, because *şeriat*, in addition to meaning şeriat *qua* Şeriat, "Islamic canon law", may also mean, generically, "law or law code". Indeed, the standard English translation of the edict begins by stating, "All the world knows that in the first days of the Ottoman monarchy, the glorious precepts of the Koran and the laws of the empire were always honoured", and the paragraph ends with, "[A]n empire in fact loses all its stability so soon as it ceases to observe its laws".[21]

---

[17] Ibid., p. 190.
[18] Caroline Finkel, *Osman's Dream: The Story of the Ottoman Empire 1300–1923* (London, 2005), p. 449.
[19] *Düstur* (Register of Ottoman Laws) 1. Tertip. Istanbul Matbaa-i Amire 1299 (Istanbul Imperial Press, 1872), vol. 1, pp. 4–7.
[20] Ibid.
[21] *Redhouse Sözlüğü, Türkçe-İngilizce* (1979) "şeriat", and *Redhouse Turkish-English Lexicon* (Beirut 1974) also includes a secular definition: "A law, a code of law; legislation; especially the divine laws". J. C. Hurewitz, *Diplomacy in the Near and Middle East*, vol. 1 (Princeton, 1956), pp. 113–16.

Another indication that a new era had dawned heralding the rule of law was the wording of the new Criminal Code of 1840. This forbade arbitrary punishment, physical abuse, and verbal insults. The law stated quite unequivocally, "even if a Minister of the state were to kill a shepherd, he will be punished according to the law".[22]

The most striking aspect of the Tanzimat Edict was that it made *promises*. It has usually been thought that these promises were made to the foreign powers with a view to assuaging their pressure to defend the non-Muslim subjects of the Porte. Although there is no denying the reality of foreign intervention and pressure, as will be seen in the next chapter, it will be the purpose of this chapter to stress that those very promises were meant entirely sincerely and were aimed primarily at the local population. As elegantly put by Abu Manneh,

Indeed the declaration in the Gülhane Rescript that the decline of the state resulted from not observing the *Shari'a* and *kanun* (temporal law), and that henceforth, the life honour and property of all subjects would be guaranteed, were not slogans, but fundamental principles to which the Sultan and the Porte adhered throughout most of the Tanzimat period.[23]

The Gülhane Rescript actually spelled it out in so many words:

In testimony of our promises we will, after having deposited these presents in the hall containing the Glorious Mantle of the Prophet, in the presence of all the *ulemas* and the grandees of the empire, make oath thereto in the name of God, and shall afterwards cause the oath to be taken by the ulemas and grandees of the empire.[24]

During the early days of the Serbian uprising in the first decade of the nineteenth century, the Serbian rebels prepared two petitions to send to Istanbul, putting forward their demands. The first petition, prepared in April 1805, was relatively modest, dealing mostly with demands for fair taxation, collected by a chief *knez* (notable) who would represent all the *knez* to the sultan. Belgrade would be under the control not of a military commander but of a tax *emin*. The more radical group also prepared a second petition that was much more extreme in its demands, including an autonomous Serbia similar to other autonomous areas in the empire like the Ionian Islands or the

---

[22] Cengiz Kırlı, *Sultan ve Kamuoyu* (The sultan and public opinion) (Istanbul, 2009), p. 74.

[23] Butrus Abu Manneh, "The Sultan and the Bureaucracy: The Anti-Tanzimat Concepts of Grand Vizier Mahmud Nedim Paşa", in *Studies on Islam and the Ottoman Empire in the 19th Century 1826–1876* (Istanbul, 2001), pp. 161–80.

[24] Hurewitz, *Diplomacy in the Near and Middle East*, vol. 1, p. 115. The reference to the Prophet's Mantle etc. refers to the Chamber of Sacred Relics, where various items attributed to the Prophet are kept.

Romanian Principalities. Ottoman soldiers would leave the Serbian *sancaks*, and these would be defended by Serbian troops. Encouraged by Russia, the *knez* presented the second petition.[25]

The first petition had been much more moderate, stressed loyalty to the sultan, and made requests that boiled down to basic rights and freedoms that would later be formulated in the Tanzimat Edict of 1839.[26] Although there is no hard evidence, it is quite possible that petitions like these were remembered in ruling circles in the Porte and had some effect on the formulators of the actual edict.

İnalcık has pointed out that there was every indication that the *reaya* took the Tanzimat Men at their word and held them to their promises:

Now let us listen to the *reaya* themselves. In 1850 the people of Vidin, in a petition sent to the sultan, state the following: 'Although we have heard it said that an Auspicious Tanzimat (*Tanzimat-ı Hayriyye*) has been put into application in the Well Protected Domains, we have not seen even the slightest application of it to our humble persons'.[27]

Declaring their grievances against the exploitation of the local strongmen, the Bulgarian subjects of the Sultan declared, "And we thought that there was a Tanzimat".[28]

Milen Petrov has recently shown us that during the pilot project of the Danube Vilayet of Midhat Paşa, in Bulgaria, the *reaya* would learn to "speak Tanzimat" and make use of the new secular (*nizamiye*) courts to pursue their own aims. Both Christian and Muslim subjects showed that they fully understood how they could use the Tanzimat State to further their specific interests.[29]

Yet it is important to realize that there was nothing in the Tanzimat Edict that specifically stated the equality of Muslim and non-Muslim.[30] Indeed, in the matter of the wearing of the *fez* by Muslim and non-Muslim officials alike there was a certain anxiety that the matter of equality might

---

[25] Aslantaş, *Sırp İsyanlari 19*, pp. 95–7.

[26] Ibid., p. 99.

[27] İnalcık, *Tanzimat ve Bulgar Meselesi*, p. 37.

[28] Ibid., p. 99: "*Biz zannederiz ki Tanzimat vardır*".

[29] Milen V. Petrov, "Everyday Forms of Compliance: Subaltern Commentaries on Ottoman Reform, 1864–1868", *Comparative Studies in Society and History* 46 (2004), 730–59.

[30] Roderic Davison, "Turkish Attitudes Concerning Christian-Muslim Equality in the Nineteenth Century", *Essays in Ottoman Turkish History 1774–1923*, pp. 112–131. See also Hurewitz, *Diplomacy in the Near and Middle East*, pp. 113–16: "The Hattı Şerif of Gülhane".

be taken too far. Nearly two years to the day after the proclamation of the Tanzimat Edict, the minister of war (*Serasker*) received a *ferman*:

[It has come to our attention that] lately the non-Muslim servants of the Sublime State have taken to concealing the ribbon on their *fezes* [indicating non-Muslim status] with the tassel and thus reducing the difference between themselves and the Muslims. . . . thus the number of *reaya* who go about in the previous manner has been much reduced . . .[31]

Another indication of the spirit of the times was the proposal put forward by Admiral of the Fleet Halil Rifat Paşa in 1847, that on religious high days, priests be allowed to board Ottoman naval vessels to perform the religious services as most of the crews were Christians. He went so far as to propose that priests be permanently assigned to ships where a special cabin would be set aside as a chapel and decked out with icons donated by the Patriarchate. For this the crews had thanked the admiral. On 18 September 1847 Sultan Abdülmecid issued an *irade* decreeing that priests were to be permitted to board the ships while they were at anchor, but he had to consult the Şeyhülislam on the matter of priests being present while the ship was sailing.[32] The matter was referred to the Şeyhülislam Arif Hikmet Efendi, who ruled that it was out of the question to allow services to take place aboard ship as "this was tantamount to building a new church on each ship". He did allow the crew to go ashore for masses, but only under escort in order to discourage desertion.[33]

Istanbul has always suffered from disastrous fires. Cevdet Paşa recounts that when a great fire broke out in 1850 in the Muslim quarter of Laleli, there was an attempt to raise money for the victims by public collection: "The Istanbullus are used to fires and not used to charity so only some eighty thousand *kuruş* was raised", Cevdet commented. The same year another big fire broke out, this time in the Christian quarter of Samatya. Again, Cevdet's

---

[31] Başbakanlık Osmanlı Arşivi (Prime Ministry, Ottoman Archives, Istanbul herafter BOA). A. MKT 5/67, 14 Şevval 1258 / 18 November 1842, the Sublime Porte to the Minister of War. Order repeated to Imperial Armoury (*Tophane*), Admiralty (*Kapudan Paşa*), Imperial Guard (*Asakir-i Hassa*). The fez had been adopted during the reign of Mahmud II as the official headgear of all government officials. As a head covering that became the symbol of "Turkishness", it was very much an "invented tradition". For a discussion of the fez as an invented tradition, see Selim Deringil, "The Invention of Tradition as Public Image in the Late Ottoman Empire", *Comparative Studies in Society and History* 35 (1993), 3–29.

[32] Ufuk Gülsoy, *Osmanli Gayri-Müslimlerinin Askerlik Seruveni* (The military service adventure of Ottoman non-Muslims) (Istanbul, 2000), p. 45. It must be borne in mind that the majority of the crews in naval ships at the time would have been Ottoman Greek Orthodox.

[33] Ibid., p. 46. Although we will meet Arif Hikmet Efendi again as a committed advocate of the Tanzimat, there were evidently some limits to his tolerance.

tongue-in-cheek observation was, "It would not do to omit to start a collection for the Samatya fire as it would give rise to mutterings of 'no one cares about the Christians' (*Hıristiyanlar aranmıyor*) but remembering how hesitant people were to contribute to the previous [Muslim] fire the matter was dropped".[34]

There is little doubt that the Tanzimat was intensely unpopular among the general Muslim population. Many thought that it was the end of their privileged status and felt deeply threatened. A fascinating article by Cengiz Kırlı, based on hitherto unused spy reports, provides us with an insight into how the Tanzimat was seen in the Istanbul streets in the early 1840s.[35] In an atmosphere where news of another uprising in the Balkans arrived every day and rumour and counter-rumour were rife, many Muslims feared that the breakup of the empire was imminent. There was also the feeling that the Tanzimat fostered a general lawlessness. A prominent view was that the Tanzimat had done away with the death penalty. In Salonica, according to one such rumour, the Greeks had killed two Jews, but the Paşa had let them go because their crimes "could not be proved according to the Tanzimat reforms". Another Muslim was heard to say, "These Croats have been plundering our villages, because they have no fear of death [penalty]. Look at what I am going to do! I am going to fight a *reaya*, and I am going to kill him. If anyone asks me why I did it, I will say I did it, because there is no death penalty in the Tanzimat." According to another report a spy had overheard two Muslims discussing the ringing of church bells, a practice hitherto forbidden:

These infidels are ringing bells and the palace is right here. Oh God! Give us a chance and we are going to make them sorry to have been born. And look, they have their kids wear green headscarves. It seems the rule has passed to them.

As news of uprisings continued to pour in, two Muslims were heard to say, "We hear of *reaya* uprisings all over. Do you think this could have happened previously? But it is not the fault of the *reaya*. It is our fault. Since they invented the Tanzimat, even the fear of the police had vanished. This

[34] Cevdet Paşa, *Tezakir* no. 7, "The Events of the Year 1271" (1855), p. 53. On the Istanbul fires, see Zeynep Çelik, *The Remaking of Istanbul: Portrait of an Ottoman City in the Nineteenth Century* (Berkeley, 1993).

[35] Cengiz Kırlı, "Balkan Nationalisms and the Ottoman Empire: Views from Istanbul Streets", in Antonis Anastasopoulos and Elias Kolovos (eds.), *Ottoman Rule and the Balkans, 1760–1850: Conflict, Transformation, Adaptation.* Proceedings of an international conference held in Rethymno, Greece, 13–14 December 2003, pp. 249–63.

is the result". In such a political milieu rumours were not simply "anxiety-provoking" but "anxiety-confirming".[36]

The Tanzimat also had its enemies among the highest ranks of the Ottoman elite. The most formidable among them was Mahmud Nedim Paşa, who would become Grand Vizier after Âli's death in 1871. Mahmud Nedim was a virulent critic of the Tanzimat.[37]

CONVERSION AND APOSTASY AS THE
"IMPERIAL HEADACHE"

The issues of conversion and apostasy had been particularly thorny ones, since the old religiously sanctioned execution of apostates from Islam was no longer enforced.[38] It became a matter of official policy to prevent the execution of apostates. This was for two reasons. First, after the "apostasy crisis" of 1844 there was increasing pressure on the part of foreign powers to prevent the practice because it was "uncivilised". This will be discussed in the next chapter.[39] Second, and more significantly, there was an increasing awareness among the Ottoman elite that if a new social consensus between rulers and subjects was to be achieved, anything that was likely to heighten tension and make the already difficult task of building the new society even more difficult was extremely undesirable. The Tanzimat statesmen tried to shift from a system that George Augustinos has called "coordinated inequality" to a more equitable system:

As matters settled out after the Tanzimat however individual instances of forbidden actions took place infrequently between the confessional communities. Cases of conversion or apostasy, depending on one's viewpoint, were among the most dramatic if not sensational of such incidents. Because the highest most sacred laws of a community were involved, these episodes had a great potential to produce destructive outbursts of fanaticism between confessional groups.[40]

As will be seen later, conversion and/or apostasy cases were by no means "individual instances" or "infrequent", and the "confessional communities"

[36] Ibid., pp. 254, 255. In relation to the function of rumour, Kırlı is citing P. Lienhardt, "The Interpretation of Rumour", in J. M. H. Beattie and R. G. Lienhardt (eds.), *Studies in Social Anthropology: Essays in Memory of E. E. Evans-Pritchard* (Oxford, 1975), p. 115. Green was a colour reserved for Muslims.
[37] Butrus Abu Manneh, "The Sultan and the Bureaucracy", pp. 161–80.
[38] See my "There Is No Compulsion in Religion."
[39] On this, see Chapter 2 of this volume, "Conversion as Diplomatic Crisis".
[40] Gerasimos Augustinos, *The Greeks of Asia Minor: Confession, Community and Ethnicity in the Nineteenth Century* (Kent, Ohio & London, 1992), p. 203.

that Augustinos mentions were coming to see themselves more and more as "nationally imagined communities", making the clashes all the more "dramatic". The immediate aftermath of the Tanzimat Edict saw an anxious Sublime Porte walking a tightrope between the need to establish the "reordering" on a firm footing, neutralize foreign pressure, and, more importantly, preserve social equilibrium while at the same time safeguarding its legitimacy in the eyes of its Muslim subjects. The repeated orders to the provinces reflect this anxiety.

Yet there is a significant additional dimension that seems to have escaped the attention of historians. The Porte was following a two-tier policy here. The ambassadors were to be given these assurances, that the execution of apostates was outlawed forthwith and that no force or coercion was to be used in the process of conversion, but nowhere in the Ottoman provinces was this to be proclaimed publicly. Document after document mentions verbatim that what was desired above all was "avoiding the Imperial Headache" (*tasdî -i Âliyi mucib olmamak*).[41] The "headache" would probably have consisted of overbearing diplomats going on about the "promises of the Turks", non-Muslim communities anxious about any claim of forced conversion, clamouring *millet* clergymen all too ready to cry forced conversion, and most of all, some elements in the Muslim population that might take the law into their own hands at any moment. In most of the cases of apostasy discussed in this chapter, the apostate is a recent convert to Islam. In this context, conversion to Islam, although an auspicious act religiously, became politically inconvenient.

The following acknowledgement of an order received by the Kaimakam of Filibe (Plovdiv) is one of many similar documents:

The Imperial Order (*Irade-i Seniyye*) pertaining to the future treatment of one who commits apostasy has been received and understood. As ordered, [such persons] will not be executed and they will not be brought up before the local courts but sent directly to Istanbul. It has also been understood that it is not necessary to mention this order here and there and to avoid unnecessary public mention of it. (*Bunun şuna buna beyan ve ifadesine hacet olmadığı.*[42]

In a similar vein the Vali of Akka (Acre) in Palestine was to write:

The order pertaining to the prevention of forced conversions has been received and understood. Particularly the forcing or importuning of children in this regard is

---

[41] Sir James Redhouse, *A Turkish and English Lexicon* (Beirut, 1974): "*tasdî*: a giving one a headache figuratively, by a request or importunity".

[42] BOA Sadaret Mektubî (A/MKT) 10/52–1 9 Rebiyulevvel 1260 / 29 March 1844, the Kaimakam of Filibe, Abdulahad.

contrary to regulation and *berats* (privileges) issued to the Metropolitans. The *ferman* relating to this has been transmitted *secretly* (*hafiyyen*) from predecessor to successor in this office.[43]

These two documents furnish some important clues. First, the injunction not to bring apostates before the local courts indicates a desire to avoid publicity and possible provocation of local resentment, Muslim and non-Muslim alike. Second, the aspect of secrecy can be understood as a desire to avoid offending Muslim sensibilities and possibly a desire to avoid intervention on the part of meddling foreign consuls, missionaries, and so forth. The need for secrecy is also stressed in the document pertaining to the undesirability of the conversion of *reaya* children, where accusations of forced conversion, abduction, rape, and abuse could be made. Yet this order too was to be kept secret, not to be "announced here and there", because the Muslim population would be mortally offended if the officials of the Islamic government refused a conversion.

The officials are quite plainly being asked to proceed on a "need-to-know basis". The *Mutasarrıf* of Akka, Mehmed Said, actually mentions that the order was secretly transmitted from predecessor to successor, implying that this was a general standing order to all provinces. This is also borne out by the almost standardised replies received from each province. Similarly, a few days later the *kaimakam* of Kastamonu was to declare: "According to the just laws now in force . . . It has been understood that apostates are not to be executed but are to be sent directly to Istanbul".[44]

As in so many of these cases, to issue an order was one thing, to actually enforce it was another. This is borne out by the fact that some six years later similar orders were still being sent out. On 9 September 1850, the Vali of Üsküp (Skopje Macedonia) acknowledged receipt of the *irade* dated 16 Şevval 1266 (25 August 1850) to the effect that "when people from other *millets* want to come to Islam they should be adequately questioned in the local council to make sure that no sort of force or coercion was being used". The Vali informed the Porte that he had issued the appropriate instructions to all localities in his province.[45] The capsule phrase, "no sort of force or coercion" (*bir güna cebr ve ikrah*), is repeated verbatim in all of these acknowledgements.

---

[43] BOA HR. MKT. 3/65, 16 Rebiyulahir 1260 / 5 May 1844, Mutasarrıf of Akka Mehmed Said to the Sublime Porte. My emphasis.
[44] BOA A.MKT 10/61, 13 Rebiyülevvel 1260 / 2 April 1844, Kaimakam of Kastamonu, Esseyid Mehmed Salih to the Sublime Porte.
[45] BOA A.MKT. UM 33/46, 2 Zilkade 1266 / 9 September 1850, the Vali of Üsküp İsmail Paşa to the Sublime Porte.

In what was clearly the acknowledgement of the order circulated to all the provinces, the Vali of Salonica replied on 12 September 1850 that the *irade* had been "received and understood". The Vali fully admitted that "such irregularities are reported from outlying districts, particularly involving *reaya* girls and boys, and these are clearly contrary to the Holy Law and the wishes of our August Master".[46]

The acknowledgement received from far-off Crete is interesting in its detail:

Although it is not permitted to apply force or coercion in bringing non-Muslims to Islam some have been carrying off *reaya* girls to the mountains, there doing what they want with them, and then taking them to their home villages, claiming that they have become Muslims. Others frighten *reaya* servants who serve in their homes and bring them before the local courts, claiming that they want to become Muslims. These latter then repeat the *Shahada* that they have been made to memorize without understanding what it is to become honoured with the glory of Islam. Also some [Christian] children fearing punishment at the hands of their parents run away and declare that they want to become Muslims. Some irresponsible officials, out of ignorance, hastily accept their conversions. [These children] when questioned later admit that they accepted Islam unknowingly and unwillingly. . . . In matters such as these [as ordered in the *irade*] in order to avoid future complications, if the convert is young, it is imperative to carry out the conversion in the presence of the parents and in front of witnesses to dispel all doubt.[47]

Province after province reported that they had received the order. The acknowledgments all follow a similar pattern: the admission that such untoward acts were occurring "in outlying areas", promises to stop any recurrence, the required presence of next of kin during the conversion procedure, and the required presence of the local priest or *desbot* (lower-ranking secular head of the non-Muslim community), all of this being carried out in the presence of the local administrative council.[48]

[46] BOA A.MKT UM 32/71, 4 Zilkade 1266 / 11 September 1850, the Vali of Salonica, Yakub Abduh Paşa to the Sublime Porte.

[47] BOA A.MKT.U M 31/60 9 Zilkade 1266 / 16 September, 1850 Müşir of Crete Mustafa Naili Paşa to the Sublime Porte.

[48] BOA A.MKT UM 34/92, 9 Zilhicce 1266 / 16 October 1850, Vali of Sayda Vamık Paşa to the Sublime Porte; A.MKT UM 32/39, 29 Zilkade 1266 / 6 October 1850, the Vali of Ankara Mehmed Vecihi Paşa to the Sublime Porte (my thanks to Edhem Eldem for helping me decipher the signature seal); A.MKT UM 32/73, 9 Zilkade 1266 / 17 September 1850, the Vali of Vidin El-Seyyid Ali Rıza Paşa to the Sublime Porte; A.MKT UM 32/55, 6 Zilkade 1266 / 13 September 1850, the Müşir of Aydın Halil Mazhar Paşa to the Sublime Porte; A.MKT UM 33/8, 5 Zilkade 1266 / 12 September 1850, Mutasarrıf of Rumeli Hasan Hüsnü Paşa to the Sublime Porte. My thanks to Gültekin Yıldız for these references.

There are repeated references to a "council of advisors made up of famous *ulema*" who sat in Istanbul and deliberated on the matter and determined what course of action was to be followed. It was also determined by the same council that if the contested conversion case were to occur in the capital, it should be brought before no lesser a body than the Higher Council for Judicial Affairs (*Meclis-i Valayı Ahkam-ı Adliye*).[49]

Strife caused by conversions between Christian confessions also came to be considered part of the "Imperial Headache". On 1 June 1855 the Armenian Catholic Patriarch wrote to the Porte complaining that Armenian Catholics in Kütahya, Eyalet of Bursa, were being victimised by the local Apostolic Armenian Metropolitan and the *Kocabaşis* (senior head of non-Muslim community):

It is not necessary to recall to Your Excellency that this sort of thing is entirely against the principle of the freedom of religion and can cause injury and headache as [acts of this nature] are entirely contrary to the spirit of justice and mercy of this age.[50]

The Porte replied in the same spirit: "It is not necessary to remind you that thanks to the Wellspring of Justice his Imperial Majesty all peoples of the Sublime State are to be protected and ... anyone changing religion of their own free will is not to be interfered with".[51] "Avoiding the Imperial Headache" and "spirit of the age" had also become by-words in the non-Muslim communities of the Tanzimat State.

CONVERSION PROCEDURE

The conversion cases usually follow a broad pattern. The potential converts declare that they want to be "honoured with the Islamic religion" (*Islam ile müşerref olmak*); they are then brought before the religious court of the judge, the *kadi*. Each potential convert has a spiritual guide, a sort of

[49] BOA A.MKT UM 34/30, 10 Zilkade 1266 / 18 September 1850, the Vali of Sıvas Mehmed Münir Paşa to the Sublime Porte; A.MKT 31/60 9 Zilkade 1266 / 16 September 1850, Müşir of Crete, Mustafa Naili Paşa, to the Sublime Porte. On the *Meclis-i Vala*, see İlber Ortaylı, *İmparatorluğun En Uzun Yüzyılı*, p. 148: "The *Meclis-i Vala-i Ahkam- Adliye* was the highest ranking advisory body in the empire and also functioned as the council of appeal". By the same author, *Tanzimattan Sonra Mahalli İdareler*, p. 36: "[After the Reform Edict of 1856] each non-Muslim community was to be represented in the *Meclis-i Vala* by their religious chiefs and lay members who would be appointed for one year". The deliberations of this council will be discussed in the following chapter.
[50] BOA HR.MKT 95/24, 15 Ramazan 1271 / 1 June 1855, the Armenian Catholic Patriarchate to the Sublime Porte.
[51] Ibid., 21 Ramazan 1271 / 7 June 1855, the Sublime Porte to *vilayet* of Hüdavendigar (Bursa).

'sponsor', who guides him or her through the conversion process. This person was of critical importance because very often he or she was the object of accusations of forcible conversion or pressure. They were often wealthy or powerful Muslims who had been employing the potential convert as a servant in their household.[52] In the presence of the judge and witnesses, the potential converts declared openly that they were converting with "free will and conscience" (*bil tav ve ul rıza*) and that they had not been pressured in any way (*bir gûna ibram ve ilhah olunmadığı*). The converts had to declare that they were of sound mind (*akîl*) and had reached the age of legal responsibility (*bülüğ*). The converts then repeated the sacred formula "There is no God but Allah and Muhammed is his Prophet" "in their own words" (*kelimeteyni şehadeteyni kendi lisaniyla tekellüm ederek*), at which point they were given an Islamic name. The procedure was then repeated in the secular local administrative council (*meclisi idare*) of the province (*eyalet/ vilayet*), prefecture (*sancak*), or district (*kaza*).[53] At this point the parents of the convert or next of kin were to be present together with the highest local religious functionary (priest or community leader), who would be given the opportunity to dissuade the convert.[54] There is frequent reference to conversion being carried out "according to the proper procedure" (*usul ve nizamına tevfiken*). The documents testifying to the act of legitimate conversion were to be signed and sealed by Muslim and Christian officials alike. The procedure was not to be hurried, and if a few days' delay was required for the priest or the next of kin to arrive, the conversion was to be postponed. Only those children who had reached the age of puberty were allowed to convert. Also, in the case of girls who came to the

---

[52] Eyal Ginio, "Childhood, Mental Capacity and Conversion to Islam in the Ottoman State", *Byzantine and Modern Greek Studies* 25 (2001), 90–119.

[53] BOA Dahiliye Nezareti Hukuk Müşavirliği (DH-HMŞ) 13/47; 23 Haziran 1320 / 6 July 1904, general no. 244, file no. 62570 (Ministry of the Interior Legal Advisors Bureau). In the catalogue of the documents of the Ministry of the Interior Legal Advisors Bureau there is a special category entitled *ihtida*, "conversion". Although the regulations cited above date from 1904, they are the updated formulations of earlier practices.

[54] The element of attempted dissuasion seems to be a survival from earlier practices. George Arnakis claims that it was part of the earlier *berats* (privileges) accorded to the Orthodox Church after the Ottoman conquest: "The religious head of his community had the right to try to dissuade him in the presence of his parents or relatives. During the long Ottoman rule this stipulation was violated repeatedly in actual practice, but nonetheless its inclusion in the *berats* saved thousands of Christians from forceful Islamization". See George Arnakis, "The Greek Church of Constantinople and the Ottoman Empire", *The Journal of Modern History* 24 (1952), 235–50.

ceremony veiled, the veil had to be lifted to ascertain identity.[55] At the end of all this, the convert was accepted as a Muslim and registered as such, being given a "certificate of conversion" (*ihtida ilamı*).[56]

What makes this procedure even more significant is that according to traditional Islamic practice, there is no stipulation that the act of conversion be witnessed by a *kadı*, let alone by secular authorities. Conversion is purely personal and can be carried out alone. A recent authoritative source clearly states: "The only requirement for conversion is the *shahada*, the acceptance of the oneness of Allah and of Muhammad as his prophet. This does not have to be carried out with any ceremony or in the presence of any religious authority".[57]

Marc Baer has cited *fetwas* from the *fetwa* collections of seventeenth-century Şeyhülislams Minkârizade and Çatalcalı Ali Efendi, where "Valid conversions for men might be as simple as wrapping their head in a Muslim turban, saying the Muslim credo and declaring themselves to be Muslims in the presence of other Muslims".[58] Only if the converts wanted to have an official record for legal purposes did they go to the *kadı* court – in order to prove, for instance, that they were Muslims and hence exempt from the capitation tax (*cizye*).[59] The procedure outlined here was therefore

---

[55] BOA A.MKT 114/35, 7 Ramazan 1264 / 7 August 1848. Account of the conversion ceremony of a woman, Metka, daughter of Mulacu, from the *kaza* of Şehrikoy near Niş; evidently Metka had shown up veiled.

[56] Osman Çetin, *Sicillere Göre Bursa'da Ihtida Hareketleri ve Sosyal Sonuçları 1472–1909* (Ankara, 1994), pp. 3–5.

[57] Ali Köse, "İhtida", *Islam Ansiklopedisi* (Istanbul, 2000): Türk Diyanet Vakfı, vol. 21, p. 555.
   There is actually a website that instructs potential converts, called "How to Convert to Islam and Become a Muslim", where the potential convert is told, "One may convert alone in privacy, or he/she may do so in the presence of others". There is also a "Live Help" link that asks: "Have a question or need help about converting? Click here to chat now or to request a call back". The site talks the potential convert through the *Shahada* and gives basic information on Islam, making sure to stress that when a person converts, "all of a person's previous sins are forgiven". The site ends with: "We welcome you to Islam, congratulate you on your decision, and will try to help you in any way we can". See www.islamreligion.com/articles/204/; click on "How to convert to Islam and become a Muslim".

[58] Marc Baer, "Islamic Conversion Narratives of Women: Social Change and Gendered Religious Hierarchy in Early Modern Istanbul", *Gender and History* 16 (2004), 425–58.

[59] Eyal Ginio, "Childhood, Mental Capacity and Conversion to Islam in the Ottoman State", *Byzantine and Modern Greek Studies* 25 (2001), 90–119, particularly 97: "[O]ne was not obliged to have recourse to a court order in order to articulate one's conversion. Muslim religious treatises speak of the simple utterance of the confession of faith, known as the *Şehadet*, the defining characteristic of Islam. There was no requirement that such a religious declaration should be pronounced in court". See also Macit Kenanoğlu, *Osmanlı Devletinde Fikir ve İnanç Hürriyeti* (Freedom of thought and religion in the Ottoman Empire), unpublished paper. Also personal communication from Macit Kenanoglu dated

an innovation of the Tanzimat State. Later in the nineteenth century it also became accepted practice to announce the conversions in the press in special columns marked "conversion" *(ihtida)*, much like an obituary column. Here is a typical example:

Kevork Efendi, a member of the Armenian millet and a notable of Diyarbakır, has made it known that he has been honoured by accepting Islam. He has duly presented a petition to the governorate for the application of the *Şeriat* procedures. When questioned according to accepted procedure he firmly said I have presented this petition with complete freedom of conscience and because my conversion is the result of divine salvation. The above mentioned is a person of considerable wealth, of some sixty years of age, sound of mind and body and is in no way needy or destitute. Therefore his petition was accepted and he was offered the faith. According to his own wish he took the name of Ali.[60]

At all points the procedure was in appearance extremely bureaucratic and straightforward, with the main aim being that the conversion be proven to be voluntary. Another interesting aspect to the procedure just mentioned is that at no point does it mention circumcision. This may be because circumcision is in fact a *sunat al-fitra*, a practice that is recommended but not obligatory:

there is an expectation in some quarters that males should undergo circumcision, should this be necessary. . . . although recommended, this is not considered obligatory, and older people becoming Muslim may well decide not to go ahead with this operation.[61]

25 October 2005. See also Akif Erdoğru, "Osmanlı Kıbrıs'ında İhtida Meselesi, 1580–1640" (The matter of conversion in Ottoman Cyprus) (İzmir, 1999), pp. 164–71.

[60] *Tercüman-I Hakikat* no. 3028, 14 Zilkade 1305, p. 3. For similar announcements, see *Tercüman-I Hakikat* no. 3045, 1 Agustos / 3 Zilhicce 1305, dealing with the conversion of "Catholic Ibrahim Yusuf Mu'man from Jabal Lubnan" and "Meryem daughter of Mardiros from the Armenian community" of the *vilayet* of Aleppo. They converted "voluntarily and of their own free will" and took the names Ibrahim and Vasfiye. Note that Ibrahim already had a Muslim name, by no means an uncommon occurrence in Lebanon. The newspaper announced that both cases had been duly reported to the Ministry of Justice and Religious Sects. The same newspaper regularly gave news of conversions from all corners of the empire, ranging from Dedeagaç in Thrace to Lebanon; see *Tercuman-ı Hakikat* nos. 3025, 15 Zilkade 1305, and 3031, 17 Zilkade 1305 / 26 July 1888. My thanks to Gülçin Tunalı for finding these references.

[61] See Yasin Dutton, "Conversion to Islam: The Qur'anic Paradigm", in Christopher Lamb and M. Darrol Bryant (eds.), *Religious Conversion: Contemporary Practices and Controversies* (London and New York, 1999), pp. 151–66. See also *The Encyclopaedia of Islam* (Leiden, 2004), *khitan*: "Not mentioned in the Kur'an but in old poetry and *hadith*. . . . Must have been a common practice in early Arabia . . . It is further recognized in *hadith* that circumcision belongs to pre-Islamic institutions. . . . In traditions which enumerate the features of natural religion (*al fitra*) circumcision is mentioned together with the clipping of the nails, the use of the toothpick, the cutting of the moustaches, and the more profuse length of the beard".

This is all the more surprising as there was a specific Ottoman law dating from the seventeenth century clearly setting forth the regulation pertaining to circumcision. The law is called the "Statute Regarding New Muslims" (*Kanun-u Nev Müslim*) and is quite explicit:

> If an infidel wants to become a Muslim in the Imperial Council (*Divan*) in the presence of the Grand Vizier he must be made to pronounce the Şehadet. The Treasurer (*Defterdar*) will then be ordered to give him a purse and a new set of clothes. Then he will be given into the custody of a poursuivant (*çavuş*) who will take him to one of the state surgeons of the court where the surgeon on duty that day will take him to the place set apart for this and perform his circumcision forthwith. It is an old law that a surgeon is on duty every day in the Imperial Divan and in the palace of the Grand Vizier.[62]

The Statute Regarding New Muslims was formulated in an earlier era and continued to be used in the nineteenth century.[63]

There are registers (*defters*) in the Ottoman archives dating from the mid-nineteenth century that contain short entries regarding the conversion records. Here is a typical entry: "One who was originally of the Armenian *millet* has presented himself wishing to be honoured with the glory of Islam. He had the religion presented to him was given the name Ali and sent to the official hospital (*bimarhane*) for his circumcision."[64] Another entry reads as follows:

> One who was originally an Austrian subject has been presented by the Foreign Ministry and wishing to be honoured by the glory of Islam had the religion presented to him was given the name of Mehmed and sent to the official hospital for his circumcision.[65]

Yet another entry concerns a Jew: "One who was originally from the Jewish millet has presented himself stating that he wished to be honoured with the glory of Islam he had the religion presented to him and was given

---

[62] *Milli Tetebbu'lar Mecmuasi*, vol. 1, no. 3, Temmuz–Agustos (July–August) 1331 (1915). My thanks to Yasemin Umur for this reference.

[63] Baer, *Honored by the Glory of Islam*, p. 191. This has indeed been indicated by Marc Baer, who points out that the statute was the work of Abdi Paşa, who was imperial chancellor and official chronicler between 1669 and 1678. Grand Vizier Kara Mustafa Paşa ordered him to "codify the statute outlining correct procedure while compiling all known Ottoman statutes into a single collection of Ottoman Law. ... This became the Statute of the New Muslim". Abdi Paşa finished the statute in 1677.

[64] BOA. Bab-ı Ali Evrak Odası (BEO) A 592. Sadaret Nezaret ve Devair (ANZD) 634. 27 Safer 1265 / 22 January 1849. There are 341 entries in this *defter* that runs from 1265 to 1268. My thanks to Dilek Akyalçın Kaya for this reference.

[65] Ibid., 22 Safer 1265 / 17 January 1849.

the name Mehmed Hidayetullah, he was then sent to the hospital for his circumcision".[66]

There are several interesting aspects to these entries. We are not given the original name of the convert, only his original community (*millet*) or nationality (*tabiyet*). Very often these entries will provide information as to the "channel" the convert came from, as in the case of the Austrian subject just mentioned who was "presented" by the Foreign Ministry. In other cases the "sponsor" of the convert is mentioned, and he or she is returned to them after the ceremony. It is interesting that in all of the cases of Jewish male converts, despite the fact that they were Jewish and there-fore supposedly already circumcised, the convert is still sent to the hospital for circumcision (*hitanı icra için*). Presumably this was in order to check that he was in fact circumcised.

The potential convert would present a petition in standard formulaic language, of which the following is an example. The petition is addressed to the Grand Vizier:

May God grant long life to our Glorious merciful and bounteous Sultan, Amen. I the humble petitioner am originally from the Armenian millet and had hitherto been in the state of infidelity and ignorance. I have now reached salvation through being honoured with the glory of Islam and have left the false religion and have understood that the only true religion is that of Muhammed. I have wholeheartedly believed this and clearly stated it with my own tongue. I seek the mercy of pronouncing the *shahada* in the presence of your Excellency on this auspicious day and wish to be circumcised and to don the robe of honour (*kisve*). As in all things this is for his August Majesty to order.[67]

As late as 1911, there was a report of a case where a convert "claimed to have converted years before but his circumcision had not yet been carried out". This was the case of the convert Mehmed, originally a Christian from the village of Kara Göl, *sancak* of Canik. Mehmet had been serving his time in prison on a murder charge and had submitted a petition to the Grand Vizier requesting that his circumcision be carried out. The Ministry of Interior duly ordered that his circumcision should be carried out as "if this is not done it will be a bad example".[68]

[66] Ibid., 7 Safer 1266 / 23 December 1849.
[67] BOA Cevdet Tasnifi: Adliye 2083 H1257 M1841. The other examples of petitions in this source are almost verbatim repetitions, replacing "Armenian" with "Jew" or "Rum".
[68] BOA DH.ID 116/16, 16 Nisan 1327 / 29 April 1911, Mutasarrıf of Canik to the Ministry of the Interior.

CONVERSION CASES

On 30 January 1846, the Prefect (*müdir*) of the prefecture of Silistre (Bulgaria) wrote to the Grand Vizier's Chancery that a young Armenian boy had been encouraged to convert to Islam by a certain Hüseyin Ağa, a lieutenant in the local military band. His parents had applied to the authorities asking that that their son be removed to Istanbul. The *müdir* testified that the boy had sworn in his presence that he "had not been forced or importuned in any way" and that "his conversion was entirely a result of his desire for salvation". The matter was taken extremely seriously at the highest level, and the commander of the Army of Rumelia in Silistre reiterated that in keeping with his orders from the Grand Vizier, he was entrusting the boy to a loyal officer and was sending him to Istanbul. He requested that the Grand Vizier's Chancery inform him of the boy's safe arrival. In due course he was so informed.[69]

The document mirrors several themes that will continue to come up in this context. First, the convert always repeats on these occasions that he or she has chosen Islam freely and without being subjected to any compulsion whatsoever. Second, the fact that a matter as ostensibly marginal as the conversion of a small boy should be taken up to the highest reaches of the state indicates that conversion had become a critical issue. Third, the convert was removed from the local setting and almost always sent to Istanbul.

The pattern can be discerned in case after case: the elaborate ceremony of conversion, in religious and secular councils, with the presence of Christian clergy and next of kin, leading to an ostentatious show of the sincerity of the conversion.[70] On 22 June 1846, the Vali of Silistre was instructed in no uncertain terms that conversions were not to be accepted "unless it became clear that [the person] was entering Islam purely as the result of the promptings of his conscience". The Vali, Mehmed Said Paşa, referred to an *irade* that he had recently received to that effect and acknowledged that he had "forwarded the auspicious orders to all the officials of the district".[71] The

---

[69] BOA Bab-'Ali Evrak Odası Sadaret Evrakı Mektubi Kalemi, Secretariat of the Sublime Porte Chancery A.MKT 59/24, 2 Safer 1262 / 30 January 1846.

[70] BOA A.MKT 59/54. Report of the meeting of the Administrative Council of Silistre, 27 Cemaziyelahir 1262 / 22 June 1846. Signed by Hamparsum, leader of the Armenian millet of Silistre; Haci Mehmed Emin, keeper of the local community savings chest (*emin- i sandik*); Haci Mehmed Tahir, attendant of the public bath; El Hac Süleyman Şükrü, the Kadi's representative (*naib*); and Numan the scribe. The document is also interesting as it gives us a profile of the sort of people who could be on a local council.

[71] BOA A.MKT.UM 171/14, 19 Safer 1271 / 11 November 1854, the Vali of Silistre to the Sublime Porte.

irade that the Vali was referring to was almost certainly the circulating order mentioned earlier.

On 10 February 1846 the *mutasarrıf* of Rumeli reported that a boy from Manastır, "a grocer's apprentice named Nikola, about nine or ten years of age", had declared that he had become Muslim. He had been duly entrusted to the care of a guardian, Halil Bey, a member of the local council. The matter had immediately been referred to Istanbul, and the tone of the communication bears the clear indication of some anxiety as to the propriety of the conversion:

> [Although] he had declared that he was accepting Islam of his own free will, as he is very young and may not be able to tell right from wrong, this may cause loose talk among his kin and community. This should be avoided if at all possible. If it transpires that everything remains calm and there is no lamentation things should be left as they are. This is the line of action ordered by the August Grand Vezirate in keeping with the requirements of the times.[72]

Several important recurrent themes stand out here. First, the concern over "loose talk" (*kîl-u kâl*) is constantly at the forefront of the official mind. The second is that the convert, being underage, could somehow be rumoured to have been led astray or tricked into accepting Islam. This is a concern emanating from the Christian community. Third, if there is no "loose talk", things should be left as they are. This is a concern emanating from the Muslim community, which could potentially be offended if the boy were to become an apostate. Fourth, it is stated that this line of conduct is official policy, as detemined by the historical conjuncture.

The various instances of dubious conversions, and the Porte's reactions to them, show that the Ottoman authorities did not actually *want* Christians to convert at this time, but could not openly say so. Any such untoward event could only have destabilizing consequences.

This historical conjuncture forms the setting for a letter from the Greek Patriarch in Istanbul dated 9 August 1846, protesting the dubious conversion of a young Greek boy as the result of the efforts of a certain Halil Ağa, who had "promised him many rewards and blessings" if he should convert. The Patriarch protested, "[T]his sort of thing is not in keeping with peace and harmony and may cause the festering of ill will and enmity between communities" (*milleteyn beyninde burudet ve husumeti mucib*).

---

[72] BOA A MKT 37/61 13 Safer 1262 / 10 February 1846, the Mutasarrif of the *eyalet* (province) of Rumeli to the Grand Vezirate. Manastir is present-day Bitola, the capital of the Republic of Macedonia. A/MKT 34/24, 19 Muharrem 1262 / 17 January 1846, memorandum of the meeting of the Council of Manastir.

The authorities were duly instructed to release the boy and to entrust him to a guardian, who would bring him to Istanbul. Here again, we catch a further whiff of the spirit of the times as the Patriarch actually warns the Grand Vizier that such untoward events may cause "ill will and enmity between the communities".[73] Although not involving any sort of conversion, another case evoking the new spirit of the era occured in Bandırma on the coast of the Marmara Sea. The Greek Patriarch in Istanbul reported on 18 August 1850 that a twelve-year-old Greek boy had been set upon by two Muslims, raped, and very badly beaten. The culprits had been apprehended, but the *naib* (representative) of the *kadı* court in Erdek had released them and had "uttered words that would encourage such rabble". The Greek community had sent a petition of protest to the Patriarchate. The Patriarch stated that "as honour is as precious as life if the culprits are not punished this will be extremely damaging to the trust and confidence of the people (*emniyet-i ahali ez her cihet meslub olub*)."[74]

Similar cases appeared all over Anatolia. On 20 June 1846 the Vali of Diyarbekir reported that an Armenian girl, "approximately ten-years-old", had converted to Islam in the *kaza* of Divrik. The Vali outlined his options as either giving the girl back to her father, "in keeping with the delicacy of the times and conditions (*nezaket-i vakt ve hal icabınca*)", or, if she persisted, sending her to Istanbul under escort. The Vali's assesment of the situation makes clear just what he meant by the "delicacy of the times":

"Since the Auspicious Tanzimat, in all the posts in which I served, when matters like this came up, in order to avoid causing headache for our August Benefactor [the sultan], I sought to avoid exaggerating the issue and tried, in keeping with the times and conditions to quietly put the matter to rest (*sessizce hüsn-ü indifa'ına*)".[75]

"Avoiding the Imperial Headache" becomes something of a recurring motif in these matters. On 28 July 1846, the Vali of Silistre was to apologize to the Grand Vizier that he had been unable to avoid "causing headache to His Excellency" over a case that had come up in his province. The Vali felt

---

[73] BOA A.MKT 50/3, 18 Ramazan 1262 / 9 August 1846, letter from the Greek Patriarch to the Grand Vezirate. Encloses a petition signed and sealed by thirteen leading Greeks of Inebolu. The Greek Patriarch at this time was Anthimos VI, who served twice as Patriarch, 1846–52; see www.patriarchate.org.

[74] BOA HR.MKT 35/72, 9 Sevval 1266 / 18 August 1850, memorandum from the Greek Patriarch of Istanbul.

[75] BOA A.MKT 44/30, 25 Cemaziyelahir 1262 / 20 June 1846, the Vali of Diyarbekir, Ahmed Izzed, to the Grand Vezirate.

duty-bound to make his apologies: "Your strict instructions that this sort of thing which would cause headache is to be avoided and settled without undue hubub are being dutifully obeyed".[76]

We must also bear in mind that all of these cases of dubious conversions of *reaya* were occurring against a background of a Rumeli in turmoil. The 1841 rising in Niş was fresh in mind, and the region was far from being tranquil.[77] The *reaya* involved were mostly children, giving rise to the suspicion of untoward persuasion at the very least. Even though the documents talk about the conversions eventually being carried out according to due process, there is a very real danger that they could have caused some sort of conflagration or at least embarrassment, hence the constant reference to "the delicacy of the times and circumstances".

A case definitely involving official embarrassment was reflected in a report by the *kaimakam* of Köstendil, a *kaza* of Niş. The official reported that while he had been absent in Niş, a ten-year-old girl, Istinyo, daughter of Çuka, had converted to Islam. Subsequently, under pressure from her mother, she had apostatised and had been brought before the local council. The mother was claiming that as she was under the age of legal responsibility, she should be allowed to go back to her former religion. It is at this point that the *kaimakam*'s report becomes interesting:

Although I am fully aware of the secret order (*irade-i hafiyye*) whereby measures should be taken to ensure that young Christians do not come to Islam, this case is a difficult one. As the girl is technically of legal age and she has declared that she has become a Muslim before a Şeriat court, to openly allow her to commit apostasy would be religiously reprehensible. Also, as I was away in Niş when the matter came up, no one knew about the secret order.

The *kaimakam* therefore had to let the matter rest and ask for instructions.[78]

What is striking here is a direct reference to an order emanating from Istanbul that "secretly" instructed local officials to discourage conversion to Islam by young children. The obvious discrepancy lies between the "secret order" and the very numerous references to the conversion (and often subsequent apostasy) of such children. The order is, however, in

---

[76] BOA A.MKT 49/41, 6 Ramazan 1262 / 28 July 1846, the Vali of Silistre, Mahmud Said Izzed, to the Grand Vezirate.

[77] Davidson, "The Advent of the Principle of Representation in the Government of the Ottoman Empire".

[78] BOA A/MKT 40/1, 19 Rebiyulahir 1262 / 16 April 1846, the Kaimakam of Köstendil to the Grand Vezirate.

keeping with the order referred to earlier instructing provincial officials to avoid the execution of apostates, but not to announce this publicly.[79]

As in all the instances where officials were instructed to assuage local sectarian passions and thus avoid the "official headache", here too it appears that there were official instructions that had to be kept secret because the Caliph of Islam could not openly discourage conversion to the One True Religion.

Another reference to such a secret order is found in a communication dated 5 May 1844, from the *kaza* of Akka (Acre) in Palestine. The *müdür* of the *kaza*, Mehmed Said, declared: "[T]he order pertaining to the prevention of the importuning of young children to accept Islam has been secretly handed on from predecessor to successor of this office in accordance with the *ferman*." The issue came up in connection with a young Christian girl who purportedly had converted to Islam, but whose conversion was being challenged by her parents and relatives. When summoned before the *Şeriat* court, she recanted, saying that she had been forced into the act. The court duly ordered that because she was a minor, she should be given back to her parents.[80] The orders state in no uncertain terms that "No subject of the Sublime State shall be forced by anyone to convert to Islam against their wishes". It had come to the Foreign Ministry's attention that "There are many cases reported where the said person is a child who has been importuned by an insistence to accept Islam. ... In no way is this to be admitted as it is entirely in contravention of current laws and regulations as set down in the letters of patent (*berat*) given to the various Archbishoprics".[81]

A similar case was reported in Salonica on 18 June 1844. A ten-year-old Armenian girl, having secured her father's permission, was taken to the local bathhouse by a Muslim woman, their neighbour. When she did not return home at the appointed hour, her parents went to the Muslim home, only to be told that their daughter had converted to Islam and that they should go away. The girl's parents, after failing to secure justice locally, had arrived in Istanbul to lodge a formal complaint with the Patriarchate stating that the girl was underage and that she had converted under duress. The Porte, using the formula quoted earlier, "although nothing can be said, etc.",

---

[79] BOA HR.MKT 3/65, 16 Rebiyülahir 1260 / 5 May 1844, the Müdür of Acre, Mehmed Said, to the Grand Vezirate.

[80] BOA HR.MKT 3/65, 16 Rebiyülahir 1260 / 15 May 1844, Foreign Ministry to the Commanders of Akka and Sayda. The fact that the Foreign Ministry was involved suggests that she may have been a foreign subject.

[81] Ibid. The phrase used is "*arz-˘ Islamiyet'le ibram ve ilhah*".

ordered that the local authorities determine the sincerity of the conversion and the age of the girl, and stated very clearly that "if the illegal use of force has occurred, this is very damaging for the confidence of the Christian subjects and can cause disruption of the order of the state" (*insilab-ı emniyet-i reayayı mucib ve ihlal-i nizam-i memleketi müstevcib*).[82]

Ottoman Rumeli seems to have been rife with cases of disputed conversions at this time. In early summer 1847, again in Niş, a certain Sefrika, daughter of Nikola, converted in dubious circumstances. Her parents contested the conversion, protesting that "she had been bewitched (*musahhar edilmiş*) and was not responsible for her actions". Sefrika died soon after under very suspicious circumstances, and foul play was suspected. What is interesting about this case is that it was commented on by the highest religious authority in the empire, the Şeyhülislam, Arif Hikmet Efendi, who, addressing the Grand Vezirate, gave his personal opinion on the case:

I have had the honour to receive the memorandum from Your Exalted Person enclosing the memorandum from the *kaza* council of Şehriköy in the *eyalet* of Niş. Because this is a strange affair I have referred it to the office of the Şeyhülislam. The Şeriat answer (*fetva*) has been returned and enclosed in my answer to your Exalted Office. The *naïb* of the *kaza* of Şehriköy has been immediately dismissed, and the remainder of the measures to be taken are entirely up to your Exalted Personage. [Yet] some thoughts have lately occurred to me. If it is ascertained how or why the aforementioned deceased died, or who was responsible for her death, and if you order an investigation and inquest to this end, this will save the honour of the Sublime Sultanate (*tekmil-i namus-u Saltanat-ı Seniyye*) and Your August Personage will acquire much merit and praise, as I am sure you know, but I wanted to remind you just the same.[83]

---

[82] BOA HR.MKT 4/10, Gurre-i Cemaziyelahir 1260 / 18 June 1844, the Sublime Porte to the Muşir of Salonica.

[83] BOA A.MKT 86/42, 21 Cemaziyelahir 1263/6 June 1847; 26 Receb 1263 / 11 July 1847, memorandum from Şeyhülislam Arif Hikmet Efendi to the Sublime Porte. Arif Hikmet Efendi was one of the leading lights of the early Tanzimat and stands out as one of the most distinguished representatives of the *ulema*. He served as Şeyhülislam from 21 November 1846 to 11 March 1854. He had a reputation as an accomplished scholar and poet "who was famous for speaking well". He also founded a library in Mecca. See *Sicil-i Osmani*, vol. 1, p. 311. See also Mahir Aydın, "Arif Hikmet Beyefendinin Rumeli Tanzimat Müfettişliği ve teftiş defteri" (The ledger of the Tanzimat inspectorate of Arif Hikmet Beyefendi, inspector of Rumeli), *Belleten* 48 (1992), 102–21. He had also composed a *Divan* in which he had written laudatory verses concerning the Gülhane Rescript and Sultan Abdülmecid. See Bilal Kemikli, *Şair Şeyhülislam Arif Hikmet Beyefendi. Hayatı Eserleri ve Şiirleri* (The poet Şeyhülislam, Arif Hikmet Efendi: His life works and poetry) (Ankara, 2003). My thanks to Osman Koyunoğlu for these two references.

It is important to note that Arif Hikmet Efendi was one of the two *ulema* inspectors sent to the provinces to examine the implementation of the Tanzimat. He was appointed inspector for Rumeli. As put by Abu Manneh, "Thus on the occasion of sending the aforementioned two senior *ulema* to Rumeli and Anatolia, it was stated that, 'the basic purpose of the Tanzimat was the application of the foundations of justice ... and the guaranteeing of the good order of land and people'."[84] It must also be recalled that this issue arose very soon after the uprisings at nearby Vidin and that the area was still unsettled. The document refers to "loose talk among the *reaya*", which may well have been an oblique reference to the affair being followed in the Serbian press, many of the Ottoman Serbs having relatives in autonomous Serbia.[85]

Although the Porte had made its point regarding forced conversion and had particularly stressed that forced conversion of minors was forbidden, it was one thing to issue an order and quite another to enforce it. Three years after the proclamation of the Reform Edict, the Ministry of Justice and Religious Sects felt obliged to issue another circulating order stating that "although the necessary orders have been sent to all officials regarding the regulations for the conversion of non-Muslims to Islam, some malpractices have been reported from certain places".[86] The order stated in quite stringent language that "some misguided and ignorant people who know nothing of their religion have been forcing Christians to come to Islam through force and fear." This was causing "wagging of tongues" and was to be stopped. The order then repeated the stages of the conversion procedure, that is, that the highest religious functionary of the convert and their parents or next of kin had to be present. They were to be closely questioned by the local administrative council. There was also a provision that had not appeared before: the convert and his or her next of kin should be put in a separate room where the next of kin would be given the

---

[84] Butrus Abu Manneh, "The Islamic Roots of the Gülhane Rescript".

[85] My thanks to Milos Jovanović, who pointed out to me that the Serbian official newspaper, the *Srpska Novina*, which had began publication in 1841, closely followed developments among Ottoman Serbs. Developments in the Ottoman Empire were followed by the press across the Balkans. Events such as the Battle of Grahovo (August 1836), where the Bosnian commander Ali Paşa burned and razed the town of Grahovo in Herzegovina, received "immediate and loud publicity. Newspapers across Dalmatia, Croatia, Slavonia and Serbia published extensive reports of the event." See Zoran Milutinović, "Sword, Priest and Conversion: On Religion and Apostasy in South Slav Literature in the Period of National Revival".

[86] BOA YEE 31/18, 7 Muharrem 1276 / 6 July 1859, the Ministry of Justice and Religious Sects, Circulating order.

opportunity to dissuade the convert. Only after all this, and only if the convert still declared that the conversion was of his or her own free will and conscience, would the procedure be carried out. The entire process was to be duly put in a report (*mazbata*), which was to be signed and sealed by the Muslim and non-Muslim members of the council. If any converts were determined to be underage, even if they insisted on their conversion, they were to be handed over to their next of kin. The order made it quite clear that the whole aim of the process was "to banish the doubts and suspicions of all parties".[87]

Nearly all of these cases of conversion involve children or adolescents. There is a marked contrast between the way the Ottoman state dealt with the conversion of minors in the previous century and its attitude toward the converts here. Eyal Ginio has shown on the basis of the study of the eighteenth-century *kadi sicils* (court records) of Salonica that the conversion of children over the age of ten was usually uncontested by the religious authorities: "Generally speaking, when considering the conversion of adolescents above the age of ten, the *kadi* apparently assumed that they had fully understood the meaning of their religious act. The discerning minors could adopt Islam, their conversion was acknowledged without further questioning".[88] Furthermore, there was no question in the eighteenth century of the involvement of any outside parties as conversion "can be performed without the permission of the child's custodian as conversion to Islam benefits the child and the process must therefore be regarded as receiving a gift or alms-both of which are legally permissible for a minor."[89] The historical context of the Tanzimat State had strengthened the legal position of non-Muslims to a degree unimaginable in the previous century. Nonetheless, the fact that such legal safeguards were deemed necessary, linked to the repeated secret orders that children not be brought to Islam, strongly implies that serious social tensions were at issue here and that forced conversion was quite widespread.

The age of puberty was essential to the legitimacy of the conversion. Although traditional practice specified only "puberty" (*büluğ*), this was a matter that could be contested.[90] In the years before the obligatory

---

[87] Ibid., "*asıl maksad her tarafın eşkal ve şübhatını def' etmek*".

[88] Ginio, "Childhood, Mental Capacity and Conversion to Islam in the Ottoman State", p. 110.

[89] Ibid., p. 104. Ginio is referring here to a treatise by Ibrahim al-Halabi (d. 1549), *Majma al-anhar bi-sharh multaqa al abhar*, vol. 2, pp. 11–19.

[90] Ibid. Ginio points out that the essential for Muslim jurists was "the age of discernment", p. 99: "While puberty (*büluğ*) is recognized following physical changes, mental capacity (*rüşd*) is harder to distinguish as objective criteria do not exist."

registration of births, it was often the visual testimony of the local council or the *kadı* that determined whether a particular convert was mature. Despite official papers proving minority, the official on the spot could sometimes allow a conversion to take place. Accordingly, on 6 April 1906 the Kaymakam of Biga decided in the case of a certain Arpina: "Although according to her identity papers she is underage, she seems strong in body".[91] For parties contesting the conversion, such as the family of the convert, the age of maturity was the make-or-break criterion because there was very little they could do legally if the convert insisted on remaining in Islam.

The age of the convert keeps cropping up as the critical issue. In one such case it had been reported from Yanya (Ioannina, Greece) that a notable of the region, a certain Süleyman ibn Ibrahim, had "lured a ten-year-old Greek boy with certain promises and forced him to become a Muslim". The boy, Nikola, was brought before the *kadı*, where he declared that he was "leaving the false faith and embracing Islam". An enquiry was then held by the local council, where, in the presence of the *kocabaşıs* and the local *desbot*, Nikola declared that he was converting "purely because of his love of the purity and brilliance (*nezafet ve revnak*) of the Islamic religion". Although the council declared that "it was clear to us that he was at least fourteen years of age", the *despot* still demanded that Nikola be sent to Istanbul, where a proper investigation could be carried out to determine his age. The council agreed, but stated that because he had denied any pressure or coercion he should be released into the custody of Süleyman Ağa, "who returned two days later bearing the news that the boy had escaped".[92]

The case raises several questions. First, how does a fifteen- (or ten)-year-old boy, who was more than likely an uneducated peasant, become aware of the "purity and brilliance" of a religion? As in other cases, the presentation of formulaic answers such as "I was struck by the purity of Islam" or "I had been attracted by the Islamic faith for some two (or more) years" or "I want to convert purely to save my soul (*mücerred hidayete ermek saikasiyla*)" suggests that these were capsule phrases that would give a veneer of legality to a very dubious conversion. In this particular case, the fact that the boy is said to have "escaped" is also suspect.[93]

[91] BOA DH.ID 63/38, 24 Mart 1332 / 6 April 1906, the Kaymakam of Biga to the Mutasarrif of Kil'a I Sultani.
[92] BOA A/MKT 113/8, 26 Receb 1264 / 28 June 1848, report of the meeting of the Administrative Council of Yanya signed by all the members present.
[93] For another sample of a similar case, see BOA Irade Dahiliye 4627, 17 Şevval 1260 / 30 October 1844. The *kaimakam* of Yanina was to write to the Vali of Üsküp (Skopje Macedonia) that the report that two underage Greek boys had been pressured into

The question of minimum age was to be a continuing bone of contention between the Christian Patriarchates and the Ministry of Justice and Religious Sects. In May 1879 the issue came up once again as the Greek Orthodox Patriarchate was now asking for a definite minimum age for conversions. The matter had come before the Council of State, and it had been decided that "the request of the Patriarchate is out of order because the establishment of a definite age contravenes the right of freedom [of religion]." The Patriarchate had countered by refusing to send the priests who had to be present to ensure that the conversion was legitimate. The Armenian Patriarchate had sent a similar memorandum insisting that the minimum age be twenty.[94] The interesting thing about this exchange is that the council was actually turning the tables on the Patriarchates, who would usually be the ones to insist on the principle of religious freedom; by claiming that fixing a definite age would curtail the religious freedom of the potential convert, the council was leaving the entire issue up to the visual confirmation of puberty. After the establishment of birth certificates, the Greek Patriarchate insisted that baptism certificates be the definitive document for determining whether the convert was of age, whereas the Ottoman authorities maintained that the legal basis for all such matters was the Ottoman birth certificate.[95] By 1913 the minimum age for conversion for both genders was increased from fifteen to twenty.[96]

Conversion of Women as a Test of the Tanzimat State

There is also a gender aspect to the conversion stories and the way they apply to the Tanzimat State. Conversion was also about negotiating the practice of quotidian survival for women. How do I get rid of this husband who gets drunk all the time and beats me? How do I marry Ali, whom I love, but who happens to be of a different faith? What will happen to my children if I do? How can I get out of an arranged marriage to a man whom I do not love and who is old enough to be my father? According to Islamic law, a Muslim woman may not be married to a non-Muslim man,

accepting Islam was unfounded. They were "fifteen and eighteen years of age, in possession of their mental faculties (*akil*) and at the age of legal responsibility (*baliğ*)."

[94] BOA YEE 31/18, memorandum of the Ministry of Justice and Religious Sects. The memorandum is undated, but the response of the Greek Patriarchate is dated 7 Cemaziyelahir 1296 / 30 May 1879.

[95] BOA DH.HMŞ 13/47, 30 Tesrin-I Sani 1327 / 12 November 1911, general directives of the Ministry of the Interior relating to the verification of the age of converts, no. 503, file 3.

[96] BOA DH.HMŞ 13/49, 25 Mayis 1329 / 7 June 1913. Ministry of the Interior no. 79107; DH.HMS 13/50, 3 Agustos 1329 / 16 August 1913.

although the reverse is possible, the lineage of religion passing down the male line.[97] As divorce was very difficult if not impossible for Christian or Jewish women, particularly if the husband was not prepared to grant it, sometimes they converted to Islam as a way of procuring an "automatic divorce". Marc Baer's very useful study illustrates that in the case of Jews, "only a husband could grant a divorce", and if he did not, there was not much the wife could do about it. Also, obtaining a divorce in order to marry someone else was not permitted. In these conditions, "Conversion to Islam would free these women from forced, arranged or failed marriages, and abusive and undesirable husbands". The husband would be asked three times if he also wanted to convert, if he refused, the marriage was declared null and void.[98] This was seen as a "trick" by some jurists who disapproved of it, and more often than not the female partner had to have a ready Muslim husband-to-be waiting in the wings.[99]

An added incentive for a woman to take such a step was the Islamic injunction that in the case of a divorce where one of the parties becomes a Muslim, that party acquires custody of the children, as "the child is dependent on the auspicious parent".[100] Later in the century this was changed, and the documents tell us time and again that the official position was that the children should be able to choose which religion they wanted to belong to upon reaching maturity.[101]

In 1860, Grand Vizier Kıbrıslı Mehmed Emin Paşa was sent on a tour of inspection in Rumeli. This was in response to continuing complaints that

---

[97] Reuben Lewy, "The Social Structure of Islam", in *Orientalism: Early Sources* (London & New York, 2004), p. 123.

[98] Marc Baer, "Islamic Conversion Narratives of Women: Social Change and Gendered Religious Hierarchy in Early Modern Ottoman Istanbul", *Gender and History* 16 (2004), 425–58 . See also Ahmed Shukri, *Mohammedan Law of Marriage and Divorce* (New York, 1966).

[99] Rudolph Peters and Gert J. J. De Vries, "Apostasy in Islam", *Die Welt des Islams* 17 (1975), 1–4, 1–25, particularly 9: "Only the Malikite and the Hanafite schools give provisions for the case of a woman apostatizing in order to free herself from the bonds of matrimony, a legal trick still resorted to in countries where there is hardly any social stigma and no penal consequences attached to apostasy." For a fascinating study of Coptic Christian *men* converting to Islam in order to divorce their Christian wives, because, according to Coptic law a Coptic woman may not be married to a Muslim man, see Mohamed Afifi, "Reflections on the Personal Laws of Egyptian Copts", in Amira El Azhary Sonbol (ed.), *Women, the Family and Divorce Laws in Islamic History* (Syracuse, NY, 1996), pp. 202–15.

[100] Ömer Nasuhi Bilmen, *Hukukı İslamiyye ve Istitlaat-i Fikhiyye Kamusu*, vol. 4 (Istanbul, 1969), p. 22 .

[101] BOA DH.MKT 431/68, 28 Rebiyülevvel 1313 / 19 September 1895, the Ministry of Justice and Religious Sects to the Ministry of the Interior; BOA DH.MKT 571/68, 16 Ağustos 1901 / 29 August 1901, the Sublime Porte. Ministry of the Interior to Ministry of Justice and Religious Sects.

non-Muslims were being forcibly converted and otherwise mistreated. This tour of inspection by the highest authority in the land after the sultan was another manifestation of how seriously the Tanzimat State took the complaints of the *reaya*.[102] The tribunal sat as the Grand Administrative Council of the eyalet of Niş (*Meclis-i Kebir-i Eyalet*). Fourteen women and related witnesses were summoned to the court. All of the women except one declared that she had converted "of her own free will and desire" and had married a Muslim man. The dates of conversion ranged from one to sixteen years previous to the date of the inquest.[103] Some of the women seem to have been particularly forthright in their declarations of sincerity. One actually declared, "[W]ho can force me to become a Muslim, of course I converted of my own free will". Another declared, "[O]f course we all became Muslims of our own free will, who can force anyone to change their religion? You are disturbing us." The vehemence in her tone was put down to the fact that "she was heavily pregnant and that it was actully difficult for her to attend the court, therefore no umbrage was taken".[104] One woman, Istanka, declared that she had been forced. Istanka had been converted in the administrative court of *kaza* of Leskofça. She stated that the Leskofça court had first turned her away, and only after several trips had she been able to convert. The members of the *kaza* court of Leskofça were summoned before the Court of Inquiry at Niş. There the delegate of the Metropolitan and chief religious authority in Leskofça, the priest Mito, declared that "all of the Christian girls who came before us declared that they were converting of their own free will and desire. I have never heard of force being applied in any case".[105] In the end, Istanka admitted that she had made up the story that she had been forced, "because she had tired of her husband and wanted to go back to her family", and that she was determined to go back to her original (Christian) faith. This part of Mehmed Emin Paşa's proceedings concluded by declaring that all thirteen of the women had been questioned in the presence of their husbands and relatives as well as separately and had actually declared, "[W]ho can force anyone to leave their religion?" Accordingly, the court declared that the various reports of forced conversion were baseless. The "most highly respected and eldest of the members of

---

[102] Yonca Köksal and Davut Erkan, *Sadrazam Kıbrıslı Mehmed Emin Paşa'nın Rumeli Teftişi* (The tour of inspection of Grand Vezier Kıbrıslı Mehmed Emin Paşa in Rumeli.) (Istanbul, 2007). This is a very useful volume that consists of archival documents dealing with the proceedings of the various commissions of enquiry presided over by the Grand Vezier.
[103] Ibid.
[104] Ibid., p. 436.
[105] Ibid., p. 435.

the Grand Council", a Jew by the name of Eşer Efendi, declared "in a totally neutral manner that he had never heard of anyone in the environs being forced to change their religion, all the other members unanimously agreed with him".[106]

APOSTASY (*IRTIDAD*)

Many of the conversion cases are also cases of subsequent apostasy. The commonly held belief was that apostasy from Islam was punishable by death. This is not in the Qur'an, but it had become a recognized and accepted part of Islamic jurisprudence. Even in a standard modern reference work published in 1969, authored by Ömer Nasuhi Bilmen, one of Turkey's leading *fikh* experts, the death penalty is seen as a standard procedure:

[A man] who commits apostasy has adopted a belligerent position towards the Islamic community. ... To kill such a belligerent is always legitimate. For the general good such a punishment is necessary.

Even the language used is emotional and provocative:

For those who commit the sin of apostasy, thereby depriving themselves of the eternal happiness of Islam, such a severe punishment as the death penalty is needed in order to prevent the spread of such harmful tendencies. ... The Islamic community will hate anyone who becomes an apostate, even his own family and relatives will hate him.[107]

The apostate is very much the enemy within; according to Bilmen, "The person who has fallen into the crime of apostasy is most likely to harm the Islamic community. He is a very dangerous (*muzir*) person who will try to damage the Islamic community he comes from. Because he will have knowledge as to the ways and mysteries of Islam it is highly likely that he will serve other powers as a spy".[108]

Compared to such stringent language found in a modern reference work, official practice in the nineteenth century was considerably more lenient. As we have seen, the official policy was that the old religiously sanctioned execution of apostates from Islam was no longer enforced. Yet in the days before the Reform Edict of 1856, there was considerable uncertainty as to what the actual procedure should be. Despite official assurances of religious

---

[106] Ibid., pp. 436–7.
[107] Ömer Nasuhi Bilmen, *Hukukı İslamiyye ve Istitlaat-i Fikhiyye Kamusu*, p. 14.
[108] Ibid., p. 15.

freedom, apostasy was still very much a matter that raised social hackles among the population at large.

Some of the cases of conversion and apostasy could also become the occasion for the settling of private scores between officials, as one side blamed the other for not carrying out the proper procedure. Such a case occurred in the province of Tekfurdağı (Tekirdağ) in the *kaza* of Gelibolu (Gallipoli) on 19 June 1848.[109] A twelve-year-old Greek boy, Fratendi, son of Ashdrenuz, declared that he wanted to convert. He was duly brought before the *kadı* court by his patron, Hafız Mahmud, and there, in the presence of numerous witnesses, he declared that he had not been forced and "that for some two years he had been driven by a desire for salvation". His father, who was a sharecropper on Hafız Mahmud's land, claimed that Mahmud had forced his son, and appealed to the local Greek Metropolitan to put the case before the authorities. The boy became a bone of contention between the *kadı*'s representative (the *naib*) and the *mudir*, Ahmed Münih Bey. Each side accused the other of incorrect behaviour, and at one point the *mudir* openly declared that the boy, as far as he was concerned, was not a Muslim; he refused to give him up to his patron, Hafız Mahmud, and kept him in his own dwelling. The interesting thing about this case is that the local Christian (Greek and Armenian) and Jewish community leaders drew up a petition, signed and sealed by over one hundred of their number, declaring to the governor of Tekfurdağı that Ahmed Münih Bey was very popular in their communities:

Ahmed Münih Bey has always upheld the letter and the spirit of the Auspicious Tanzimat and has never offended any of us in any way. Thanks to his selfless efforts we are at peace here and the affairs of the poor subjects prosper and we pray constantly for the long life and health of our August Master the Sultan.[110]

The important aspect of this statement is the fact that Ahmed Münih Bey is being praised by non-Muslims according to the criteria of a new order claiming to protect Muslims and non-Muslims equally.

What was involved in most cases seems to have been a mutual saving of face. On the one hand, the non-Muslim community of the convert was pacified to some extent by the bodily removal of the offending party to Istanbul. On the other, particularly in contested cases where there was

---

[109] BOA A.MKT 113/39, 17 Receb 1264 / 19 June 1848, the Muhassıl of the Liva of Tekfurdağı, Şakir Bey, to the Sublime Porte. Letter from Naib Hüseyin Efendi to the Office of the Şeyhülislam. Petition signed by 120 members of the Greek, Armenian, and Jewish communities.

[110] Ibid.

the possibility that the convert might become an apostate or had already become an apostate, the same solution pacified the Muslim community, which no longer had to tolerate the presence of a person who flagrantly flouted its religious rules.

In at least one instance, the official policy of the state was stated very clearly in terms that can only be described as, "You are instructed to look the other way". On 30 October 1844 the *Muşir* of the Army of Rumeli, Reşid Paşa, was given instructions regarding his request for guidance about what to do with the apostates in the region of Noveberde. He was told in no uncertain terms that "In offensive matters (*madde-i mekruhe*) such as these, [the offenders] should be sent to Istanbul, without being officially referred to the local *kadı* court". It was deemed essential that the apostates be removed from their locality with a minimum of fanfare, for, "if the case is announced in the court, then they are shipped off to Istanbul, the matter will still come to the attention of the foreign embassies and cause useless loose talk". Therefore, "the abovementioned [apostates] should be put in prison, and then after some time, when the affair had quietened down, they should be made to appear to have escaped from jail and speedily sent on their way (*habishaneden firar edmişcesine haki-mane def'lerine*)". As a second option they were to set out on their exile to Istanbul under escort but "be made to appear to have escaped during the journey" (*esnayı rahda bir tarafa savuşturulmak*).[111]

Apostates seem to have become a public embarassement for all concerned. On 12 March 1845 the vilayet of Bursa reported that an Armenian woman had converted "of her own will", and subsequently "as the result of the deceptions of her mother and the community" she had reneged on her word and declared herself a Christian. The matter was resolved after the local authorities decided that "she was not quite in command of her faculties" and had her shipped off to Istanbul.[112]

A typical case was reported on 10 February 1853 from Tekirdağ, where a Greek woman was said to have converted to Islam and then declared for Christianity before the local council. She had been kept in the dwelling of the local *kocabaşı* until she was abducted by a Muslim mob who claimed

[111] BOA Irade Dahiliye 4627, 17 Şevval 1260 / 30 October 1844, the Sublime Porte to the Müşir of Rumeli, Reşid Paşa. It is highly unlikely that what was meant here was that the apostates in question were to be killed en route. As will be seen in the subsequent chapter, the state, foreign powers, and the apostates' community kept close tabs on what happened to the person(s).
[112] BOA A.MKT 37/51, 14 Rebiyülevvel 1262 / 12 March 1845, Vilayet of Bursa to the Sublime Porte.

she was a Muslim. The Patriarchate had remonstrated with the Porte, demanding the removal of the woman to Istanbul "for questioning".[113]

By the twentieth century the official position of the Ottoman state regarding the matter of apostasy had become clear. Not only was the official execution of apostates a thing of the past, but cases of apostasy had become a matter of bureaucratic routine. On 30 March 1910 an Armenian Catholic woman from the *vilayet* of Ankara, Lisa, daughter of Agop, declared that she had converted to Islam some six years previously, but now wanted to go back to her old faith. She was brought to Istanbul for questioning at the Ministry of Police. In the presence of the chief scribe (*Kapıkethüdası*) of the Patriarchate, the priest Andon, she declared: " I want to go back to my old faith. I say this with a free will and conscience. I have not been brought under pressure from any quarter. My real name is Elizabet. My father's name is Agob." The *vilayet* of Ankara was told:

[If] a member of a non-Muslim community appears to have lived for some time as a Muslim but later wants to return to their old faith, the current procedure is, if there is a serious objection to their remaining in their original location, that they simply be moved to another location.

In the event, Elizabet was set free of police custody and walked away a Catholic. The deposition signed by the police official and the representative of the Patriarchate ends rather pitifully: "[S]he could not sign as she is illiterate".[114]

CONCLUSION

Even someone like the Rev. Edwin Munsell Bliss, every inch the devoted missionary, and no friend of the Ottomans, had to admit that

During the remainder of the reign of Abd-ul-Medjid and that of Abd-ul Aziz (1861–1876) the conditions of the Christians throughout the empire generally improved. For the most part the situation was far better than it had been at any time ... On the whole, the situation of the Christians was far better when Abd-ul Hamid II came to the throne in 1876, than it had been at any time since the establishment of the Ottoman dynasty.[115]

---

[113] BOA HR.MKT 56/65, 26 Cemaziyelevvel 1269 / 8 March 1853, Greek Orthodox Patriarch to the Sublime Porte.

[114] BOA DH.EUM.THR 30/78, 17 Mart 1326 / 30 March 1910, the Ministry of Justice and Religious Sects to the Department of Police; written deposition signed by police official Zakreb Macit and the priest Andon.

[115] Edward Munsell Bliss, *Turkey and the Armenian Atrocities, The Reign of Terror: From Tatar Huts to Constantinople Palaces* (Philadelphia, 1896), p. 279.

In the spring of 1863, Sultan Abdülaziz paid a visit to Izmir, where, contrary to all precedent, he dined in the houses of some leading Christians. The British consul was to comment: "His Imperial Majesty having visited and dined in Christian houses, [this] is I believe, an event never before heard of as having been done by any former sultan". But because he did not visit the leading Muslims first, the consul reported, "the Mahometan inhabitants feel they have been neglected".[116]

The culmination of the Tanzimat State was the Constitution of 1876, which is seen as the work of Midhat Paşa, one of the giants of the Tanzimat period.[117] For our purposes the most important article is Article 11, which reads:

The religion of the Ottoman State is Islam. Given the preservation of that foundation the practice of all recognized religions in Ottoman dominions is free on the condition that they do not disturb public order and general propriety. The rights granted to various creeds are all under the guarantee of the state.[118]

The Tanzimat State came to an end with the Treaty of Berlin in 1878. This treaty, ending the 1877–78 war with Russia, was a disaster for the Ottoman Empire as it truncated the major part of its Balkan possesions. In eastern Anatolia the provinces of Kars and Ardahan were lost to the Russian Empire. The Sublime Porte lost two-fifths of its entire territory and one-fifth of its population.[119] It can be said that the Ottoman Empire became a majority Muslim empire, possibly for the first time since its foundation.

The jury is still out on the success or failure of the Tanzimat State. In a remarkable essay, Şükrü Hanioğlu observes that the Tanzimat was not an unmitigated failure in terms of responses to the demands of non-Muslims:"[T]heir position improved from a situation at the beginning of

---

[116] Gerasimos Augustinos, *The Greeks of Asia Minor* (London, 1992), p. 197.

[117] Together with Reşid, Ali, Fuad, and Cevdet, Midhat Paşa can be seen as one of the main masterminds behind the Tanzimat State. On him, see İbnülemin Mahmut Kemal İnal, *Son Sadrazamlar* (Istanbul, 1982), vol. 1, pp. 315–415. Mithat was born in Ruscuk (present-day Bulgaria) in 1822. He is famous for his provincial reforms during his tenure of the Danube Vilayet (1863), a pilot project combining the *eyalets* of Vidin, Silistre, and Niş that was intended to be a demonstration of the efficiency of relative de-centralization. In a similar way, his tenure as the Vali of the Vilayet of Bagdad was to serve as a model of modern administration. He served twice as Grand Vizier, in 1872 and 1876. He is seen as the driving force behind the Constitution of 1876. Mithat Paşa eventually fell afoul of Sultan Abdülhamid, who saw him as a threat to his authority, and eventually fell from power. To this day Midhat Paşa is one of the few late Ottoman statesmen looked upon favourably by republican historiography.

[118] *Kanun-u Esasi* 1876. *Düstur* 1. tertip cilt 4.

[119] Stanford J. Shaw and Ezer Kural Shaw, *History of the Ottoman Empire and Modern Turkey* (Cambridge, New York, and Melbourne, 1977), vol. 2, p. 191.

the 19th century where a non-Muslim needed a *ferman* to be able to wear yellow shoes, [to a situation where] after the Reform Edict ... they could become ambassadors and governors". Yet, Hanioğlu adds, the state's failiure to come up with timely solutions led to a radicalization of nationalist separatist movements.[120]

A recent article by Frederick Anscombe takes a view diametrically opposed to the view I have defended here regarding the "proper recognition of the audience" of the Tanzimat. Anscombe declares, "Tanzimat measures, later labelled as westernization, were not designed primarily to appease Christian subjects or foreign powers by promoting Europeanization, let alone secularization. Reform was fundamentally shaped by, and for, Muslims".[121] If this is correct, some Muslims were certainly missing the point, certainly those who saw the Tanzimat as a threat to their dominant position. Then again, Anscombe's position ignores the grey areas where history is made; the Tanzimat was made by "Muslims", certainly, but for whom? And who were these Muslims ? A conservative Islamic jurist like Cevdet Paşa could support the "Auspicious Tanzimat", whereas the man in the street could see it as the beginning of the end. The Şeyhülislam (or the "Chief Mufti", as Anscombe quaintly calls him), Arif Hikmet Efendi, could make the discovery of the murderer of an unknown Christian girl a matter of the "honour of the Sublime State".

I contend that open and unequivocal declarations of guarantees on the part of the highest power in the land, sometimes occasioned by what were after all incidences of minor sectarian conflict or resolvable tax issues, provide interesting clues to the political climate of the Tanzimat State. Yet I also firmly believe that the spirit of the times cannot be explained solely by the bland and ubiquitous catch-all category of "foreign pressure". Even given the fact that the Ottoman Empire was closely bound to France and Britain during the Crimean War, and subseqently through loans to finance a bankrupt treasury and the continuous need for support against Russia, the Ottoman elite, pushed around and bullied as they were, always retained ultimate political agency.

Foreign intervention was a fact, but a close reading of the documents also leads in another direction, one indicating that a sense of the rule of law

---

[120] Şükrü Hanioğlu, "*Osmanlı çöküşü ve günümüz Kürt sorunu*" (The collapse of the Ottoman Empire and the present Kurdish problem), *Zaman*, 22–3 November 2007. In this very thoughtful op-ed piece, Hanioglu gives an excellent thumb-nail sketch of the last century of Ottoman history.

[121] Frederick F. Anscombe, "Islam and the Age of Ottoman Reform", *Past and Present* 211 (2010) 160–89.

as the right and proper thing had taken root among the decision-makers and implementers in Ottoman lands. The stock phrases, "to act according to the requirements of the times" (*icabat-ı asriyyeyye göre hareket*) and "avoiding acts damaging to the trust and security of the reaya" (*insilab-ı emniyet-i reaya)*, became something more like slogans. Statements such as those of Arif Hikmet Efendi are all the more striking as they are not meant for the eyes of any foreign ambassador, but for those of the Grand Vizier alone. Many values and principles, all too often seen as foreign intervention, were in fact homegrown and had been internalised by the ruling elite, if not by the population at large. The Ottoman centre certainly knew that the measures they were implementing were far from popular with the Muslim population, who felt that their position as the dominant element was threatened. This was the reasoning behind the order that apostates were not to be executed but that this was not to to be proclaimed *omni et orbi*. There was mention of "secret instructions" to discourage young children from converting. Another characeristic of the Tanzimat State, compared to earlier periods, was that each case of conversion and/or apostasy, no matter how humble, went to the very top echelons of the state and could come before the Grand Vizier or even the sultan, whereas before they would have been handled locally. In the time frame stretching from the Tanzimat Edict to the Reform Edict, and ending with the declaration of the Constitution of 1876, we witness a critical shifting of the balance in which nothing less than the idea of the rule of law became established forever in Ottoman dominions. In this context the issues of conversion and apostasy became the battleground of the struggle of the Ottoman state to retain its sovereignty and to remain a political player in an arena of world politics that was becoming increasingly inhospitable.

The following chapter will discuss the crisis provoked by the conversion to Islam, subsequent apostasy, and eventual execution of an Armenian Ottoman subject in 1843, and the outbreak of the diplomatic crisis concerning him. The whole issue became a major bone of contention in the public domain. Although the long-accepted punishment for apostasy from Islam was death, this traditional practice now directly contravened the new freedoms apparently guaranteed by the Tanzimat. This "apostacy crisis" was a prime example of the overlap of domestic and foreign policy during the late Ottoman period, as the Porte came under severe pressure from the ambassadors of foreign powers, particularly from Stratford Canning, the overbearing and arrogant British ambassador, who made the issue a cause celèbre and used it to increase his leverage at the Sublime Porte.

2

Conversion as Diplomatic Crisis

Light is the enemy of barbarism. The Turks enlightened, awakened to the principles of Christian civilization would no longer be Turks, and the 'Eastern Question' would be solved. But of all the solutions, that will be the most difficult.

Alexander Rangavis, *Greece: Her Progress and Present Position*[1]

CONVERSION AND APOSTASY AS A DIPLOMATIC ISSUE

In the late nineteenth century perhaps no issue was as politically charged as that of conversion and apostasy. In the geographical area spanning much of what is now the Balkans and the Middle East, on one side stood the "Club of Great Powers", imbued with the ideas of the "White Man's Burden" and the "*mission civilizatrice*", and on the other the Ottoman Empire, the only non-Christian Great Power in the region. There is no doubt that in this confrontation the Ottoman Empire was very much the weaker side. The familiar nineteenth-century theme of "spheres of influence" was being played out over the bodies of non-Muslim subjects of the Ottoman Empire: the Austrians dominated the Balkans; the British protected the Greeks, the Armenians, and the tiny new Protestant community; the Russians claimed a say over anyone from the Caucasus; and the French protected the Catholics in the empire as a whole, and particularly the Maronites of Lebanon.

---

[1] As cited in Gerasimos Augustinos, *The Greeks of Asia Minor: Confession, Community, and Ethnicity in the Nineteenth Century* (Kent, Ohio & London, 1992), p. 197. Alexander Rangavis was the American ambassador to Greece in the 1860s.

The ultimate paragon of the triumphalist attitude of the Western powers was of course someone like Lord Cromer, who was never one to mince his words: "Although there are many highly educated gentlemen who profess the Moslem religion, it has yet to be proved that Islam can assimilate civilization without succumbing in the process".[2] These words are highly symbolic of the apogee of imperialism and colonialism, the time of the "scramble for Africa" and the "opening up" of China and Japan. In all of the empires of the world the dominant powers were Christians, who ruled over millions of non-Christians. Only in the case of the Ottoman state was this power relationship reversed; the Caliph of all Muslims was also the *Padişah* of millions of Christians, something that increasingly came to be seen as an anomalous situation.[3] The Ottoman Empire was seen as an "obsolescent empire ... whose ... days were clearly numbered".[4] Although colonial violence against colonized peoples had come to be an accepted part of imperialism, "Muslim violence, by contrast, was supposedly deliberate, inherent and typical, it reflected an age old fanaticism".[5] This is the attitude that is reflected in the cover illustration for this volume. The deliberately over-the-top depiction of a hapless Christian being forced to bow down over an ostentatiously large copy of the 'Koran' while his wailing women (one of whom wears a prominent cross in her hair, just so we get the point) attempt to tear him away, while mounted *bashi bozouks* mill about in the background, this was a typical Christian depiction of the world of Islam.[6]

In this context it was difficult to imagine why anyone would convert to the religion of a power that was seen as being on its last legs. One of the major actors in this book, Sir Stratford Canning, the British ambassador at the Sublime Porte, had no qualms about stating his position. For Canning, the issue was a matter of civilization; now that Christian Europe was

---

[2] The Earl of Cromer, *Modern Egypt* (London, 1911), p. 584.
[3] Sir G. Campbell MP, "The Races, Religions and Institutions of Turkey", *The Eastern Question Association: Papers on the Eastern Question*, no. 4 (London, 1877), p. 20: "An inferior race, on an inferior religion, inferior in numbers, inferior in intellect, inferior in all economic arts, rules over great provinces ... with the aid of a great army and navy furnished by European money; a Mahomedan police, and a Mahomedan population armed by the government ... who form a garrison to keep down the Christians".
[4] Eric Hobsbawm, *The Age of Empire* (London, 1987), pp. 17, 23.
[5] Ussama Makdisi, *Artillery of Heaven: American Missionaries and the Failed Conversion of the Middle East* (Ithaca and London, 2008), p. 68.
[6] The illustration is from Charles Sumner, *White Slavery in the Barbary States 1853* (Boston, 1853). My thanks to Irvin Cemil Schick for this image.

strong and the Ottoman Empire was weak, Europe was obliged to take a stronger hand in the issue of conversion and apostasy:

The pretension of the Sublime Porte with respect to foreigners adopting the Mahometan religion was not resisted in former times by the leading powers of Christendom. But a mere conjectural inference will hardly suffice to decide the question at once against humanity and against the weighty political considerations which come in aid of that principle. The power of late acquired by Christian Europe may be said to carry with it a duty and a moral responsibility.[7]

In his memoirs Canning was even more candid in his triumphalism:

[T]he despotism of the Koran is evidently yielding to the influences of Christianity, the religion of civilization. ... The Turkish Empire is evidently hastening to its dissolution, and an approach to the civilization of Christendom affords the only chance of keeping it together for any length of time.[8]

THE OPENING SHOTS: THE APOSTASY CRISIS OF 1843

What had provoked the so-called apostasy crisis was the affair of an Istanbul Armenian, Avakim, who had converted to Islam on 11 March 1842 and taken the name of Mehmet. He had then travelled on business to Syria, where he had reverted to Christianity. Arriving back in Istanbul in 1843 under his Armenian persona, he had been recognized and denounced to the authorities as an apostate. His trial had become something of a test of strength between the old guard and the newer, younger, reform-minded cadres led by the foreign minister, Mustafa Reşid Paşa. The old guard won out, and on 23 August 1843 Avakim, otherwise Mehmet, was publicly executed by beheading and his severed head put on public display, all this a mere three years after the announcement of the dawn of a new age heralded by the *Hat-ı Şerif* of Gülhane.[9] The execution had been followed by a posting of placards (*yafta*) in Istanbul stating:

The Armenian shoemaker, Hovagim, son of Yoghia, who last year at the beginning of the month of Mouharrem accepted Islam and was given the name of Mehmet,

[7] Turgut Subaşı, "The Apostasy Question in the Context of Anglo-Ottoman Relations", *Middle Eastern Studies* 38 (2002), 234.

[8] Stanley Lane-Poole, *The Life of the Right Honourable Stratford Canning, Viscount Stratford de Redcliffe, From His Memoirs and Private and Official Papers* (London, 1888), vol. 2, p. 78.

[9] For details of the "*mürted meselesi*" (the Apostasy Affair), as it came to be called, see Selahittin Özçelik, "Osmanlı İç Hukukunda Zorunlu bir Tehir (Mürted Maddesi) (An obligatory postponement in Ottoman domestic law: The Apostasy Matter)", *OTAM* 11 (2000), 347–438.

having denied his faith, and having obstinately refused the offer made to him of becoming Muslim, had the sentence of execution inflicted upon him by *fetva*.[10]

A better opportunity to embarrass the Ottoman government could not have been wished for, and Canning rose to the occasion. His original intention was to have the sultan officially abolish the law decreeing the execution of apostates, but the Foreign Secretary, Lord Aberdeen, backed down and instructed Canning not to push for abolition, but to be content with a promise of non-application. A council of *ulema* was held and regarded the issue as a totally inadmissible intervention in the Ottoman Empire's internal affairs. At this point the Ottomans had to endure the humiliation of the British Ambassador lecturing to them on their own religion.

Canning had a sudden revelation one morning, as he states in his memoirs:

It so happened that on leaving my bed one morning I remembered that some one had given me a French translation of the Koran. Where to find it was the question. My search was amply rewarded, not only by finding the book, but on opening it to fall at once on the passage which made me think that Mohammed in condemning renegades to punishment had in view their suffering in a future state and not their decapitation here.[11]

According to the Austrian *Internuncio*, Sturmer, "everyone, Ottoman and European alike, began to study the Qur'an in order to find in it what each, according to his point of view, wished to find."[12]

The Porte decided that a committee of *ulema* would be appointed to "discuss the matter confidentially taking into account both the demands of the law and its relevance to the delicacy of the times" *(nezaket-i asriye)*.[13] On 3 November 1843, Foreign Minister Rıfat Paşa was to tell Pisani, the Dragoman of the British embassy, that if any case of apostasy were to come up in the future, if it occurred in Istanbul, it would be dealt with at the Porte, and if the case came up in the provinces, it would be dealt with by the

[10] George Young, *Corps de Droit Ottoman*, vol. 2 (Oxford, 1905), p. 11, n. 4. My translation.

[11] Lane-Poole, *The Life of the Right Honourable Stratford Canning*, vol. 2, p. 92. One wonders if His Excellency was familiar with the superstitious practice of letting the Qur'an fall open at random and seeing the page that fell open as an omen.

[12] Subaşı, "The Apostasy Question", p. 13.

[13] As quoted in ibid., p. 31, n. 106. Mesail-i Muhimme Iradeleri MM I 1827. A modern source does in fact confirm that on the issue of capital punishment, "the doctrine was usually formulated in keeping with the social conditions at the time and international relations". See İrfan İnce, "Ridde", *İslam Ansiklopedisi*. p. 91.

local Vali. In either case the death penalty would not be applied, and the affair would not receive any publicity.[14]

During the years leading up to the Reform Edict, there was a rising tide of documentation implying ever-increasing sensitivity to this issue. Sensitivity to outside pressure, as well as to domestic reaction, meant that Istanbul had to walk a tightrope of reiterated orders to the provinces, as well as repeated assurances to the foreign envoys, that it was keeping its house in order and, by clear implication, that it did not need their help.

This was precisely the gist of a conversation between the Ottoman ambassador to London, Ahmed Muhtar Paşa, and Canning, who was on leave in London. In a conversation over dinner at the Ottoman embassy, which the Ottoman ambassador reported on 31 January 1844, the matter of conversion and apostasy came up. Canning brought up the matter of "the recent events where an apostate was executed, this causing very strong feelings among the Powers".[15] Canning then went on at some length about the promises made by the Sublime Porte in this regard. At this point Ahmed Muhtar Paşa replied:

I explained to His Excellency in the calmest manner the religious obligations incumbent on all Muslims in these cases (*bir mecburiyet-i diniyye keyfiyeti*). I also pointed out that the fact that commitments had been made in Istanbul did not mean that such events would not take place in some locality. All we could hope to accomplish would be to try to prevent the occurence of conditions which would bring into force such obligations.[16]

The Ottoman ambassador further pointed out to Canning that "our religious obligations like our nationally established laws are very clear on this matter". He went on, "Like Britain and France, the Sublime State and its subjects are most desirous of being quit of this vexing question".[17] The message behind the diplomatic wording was very clear: do not push us too far in a direction that we intend to take in any case. This was to be the dominant policy stance of the Ottoman government on this issue throughout. Nonetheless, the Ottoman ambassador made a point of telling Canning that there were "religious obligations" to execute apostates that the Porte was doing its best to circumvent. Caught between pressure from the Powers and the sensitivity of their own Muslim population, "The

[14] Subaşı, "The Apostasy Question", p. 16.
[15] BOA HR.MKT 1/53, 10 Muharrem 1260 / 31 January 1844, Muhtar Paşa to the Sublime Porte.
[16] Ibid.
[17] Ibid.

[Ottoman] ministers asked for a period of seven years in which to introduce the idea gradually."[18]

The Ottoman documents are very interesting in this regard. In particular, the memoranda dealing with the proceedings of the various commissions, made up of high-ranking religious and secular officials of the Porte, with a brief to find a solution, abound in the details of how the officials in question agonised over what appeared to be an insoluble problem. The matter was discussed in the High Council of the Tanzimat (*Meclis-i Valayı Tanzimat*), where its members pointed out that their brief was to somehow "confidentially discuss the balancing of *Şer'i* obligations with the delicacy of the times and various other requirements".[19] The commission made it very clear that they fully understood that the foreign powers would not back down on this issue, which meant

that their feelings of friendship and support for the Sublime State may be exchanged with coldness and even enmity ... which will be very dangerous for the [Ottoman lands] many of which are in Europe.[20]

Given that,

the religious difficulties on the one hand and the damage that [this matter] can cause internally [and foreign pressure on the other], means that this is verily a delicate and difficult issue from both angles, in fact we can say that it is a collection of all evils.[21]

It was stated that if an apostate (*mürted*):

were to surface tomorrow there is no way we can enforce the penalty because the Christian states will see this as an insult to themselves, and this could mean that they would confront the Sublime State with all manner of new claims, as is their wont and as we have seen before.[22]

The commission therefore suggested that in cases of apostasy no execution be carried out "without a specific order bearing the Imperial monogram (*tuğra*)". It was also suggested that any apostasy case that emerged from that time on "not be dealt with locally but sent here [to] the Sublime Porte". This was to be "secretly written to all the *Müşir*s of the

---

[18] Subaşı, "The Apostasy Question", p. 7.
[19] BOA, Irade Mesail i Mühimme (IMM), 1828, enclosure 1. Although no date is given, the meetings probably took place just before the Porte's answer to the embassies on 21 March 1844.
[20] Ibid.
[21] Ibid.
[22] Ibid.

provinces".[23] This meeting was evidently the source of the "secret decree" (*irade-i hafiyye*) discussed in the previous chapter. Finally, it was stated that a formal, written, binding declaration to the foreign embassies was to be avoided at all costs, giving them instead "some sort of note".[24]

Shortly before the sultan's declaration, Canning had an audience with him:

Abdu-l-Mejid performed his promise to the letter. He added that he was the first Sultan who had ever made such a concession, and was glad that the lot of receiving it had fallen on me. I replied that I hoped he would allow me to be the first Christian ambassador to kiss a Sultan's hand. 'No! No!' he exclaimed, and at the same time shook me by the hand quite cordially. Thus ended this redoubtable negotiation.[25]

Abdülmecid was probably quite horrified at the idea of a Christian kissing his hand, and it is a measure of Canning's vanity and arrogance that he saw this as a victory.[26] Furthermore, the statement "that he was the first Sultan who had ever made such a concession" was almost certainly uttered in lamentation. It must be recalled that as a young prince Abdülmecid had been exposed to Naqshbandi beliefs and that he had been brought up as a pious youth by his mother, Bezm-i Alem Sultan.[27]

Soon after the audience, on 21 March, the British and French embassies extracted what they thought was a promise from the sultan that he would ban all executions of apostates from Islam in the future.[28]

[23] Ibid. "*Bu tarafa gönderilmeleri hususunun Müşiran bendelerine mahremane yazılması*".
[24] Ibid. "*Şöylece pusula gibi bir varakaya terkim birle mezkur sefaretlere verilmesi*".
[25] Lane-Poole, *The Life of the Right Honourable Stratford Canning*, pp. 96–7. The Dragoman of the British embassy, Pisani, was more realistic: "The Audience set the seal to the whole, and a revolution in Islam was thus peacefully accomplished, though it must be admitted that in later years the Turks endevoured to minimize the concession".
[26] Canning does not seem to be aware of the fact that he was in serious breach of protocol as physical contact with the royal personage was quite out of the question. See Hakan Karateke, *Padişahım Çok Yaşa! Osmanlı Devletinin Son Yüz Yılında Merasimler* ('Long live the sultan!' Ceremonial in the last century of the Ottoman Empire) (Istanbul, 2004), pp. 34–5.
[27] See Butrus Abu Manneh, "The Islamic Roots of the Gülhane Rescript", p. 85.
[28] Baron I. de Testa, *Recueil des traités de la Porte ottomane avec les puissances étrangeres*, t. III (Paris, 1868), p. 226: "Note: De la Sublime Porte aux ambassadeurs de France et de la Grande Bretagne en date du 21 Mars 1844 (20 Safer 1200)." Note that Baron de Testa's calender conversion is wrong. It is also interesting to note that the "Note" specifically mentioned "l'execution d'un Chretien apostat", not a Muslim. My thanks to Edhem Eldem for providing this reference and drawing my attention to the matter of the wording "Chretien apostat".

In fact, for domestic consumption the Porte made it clear that it had merely "postponed" (*tehir*) the execution of apostates, as a *Şeriat* ruling could only be postponed, it could never be changed. As always, a face-saving solution, one that would allow all parties room to manoeuvre, was being sought in order to achieve an objective that was also the objective of the Porte, as seen in the previous chapter.[29] This was what the Ottoman ambassador in London meant when he told Canning that the execution of apostates was "a religious obligation".

Canning was not prepared to grant that manoeuvring space; he proclaimed *omni et urbi* that he had achieved his objectives and that he had procured the actual abolition of the law of apostasy. On the other hand, the Porte felt that the declaration it had made was not officially binding, and that it guaranteed not to abolish the actual law, but merely to prevent executions in the future.[30] The British Foreign Office seemed content for the time being to interpret the Porte's assurance to mean that the sultan's promise covered both the cases of execution of newly converted Muslims and the cases of established Muslims embracing Christianity.[31]

Once the promise was extracted from the sultan, the British embassy made sure that it was circulated to its consular representatives in the provinces. Consul Stevens from Trabzon acknowledged the "circular of the 26th ultimo" on 13 April 1844 informing him that

Your Excellency had received a formal engagement from the Sublime Porte that no Christian shall, in future, be executed or otherwise made to suffer death in Turkey, for having apostatized from Islamism.

The consul also acknowledged the "instructions as to the mode of conduct that I am to follow, in the event of the local authorities showing, at any future period, a disposition to renew the practice."[32]

One of the most shocking aspects of the execution of Avakim was that he had been beheaded wearing Western garb. Avakim's execution in Western dress drew the ire of no less a personage than Prince Metternich, who "expressed his distress over the event". The aspect of Western clothing was taken as a particular insult by the Western press, and the Ottoman

---

[29] Macit Kenanoğlu, *Osmanlı Devleti'inde Fikir ve İnanç Hürriyeti* (Freedom of faith and thought in the Ottoman Empire), unpublished paper, cited with the permission of the author.

[30] Subaşı, "The Apostasy Question", p. 26.

[31] Kenanoğlu, *Osmanlı Devletinde Fikir ve İnanç Hürriyeti*, p. 4.

[32] The National Archives, Public Record Office, Kew (TNA) Foreign Office (hereinafter FO) 195/225, Vice Consul Stevens, Trebizond to Stratford Canning. My thanks to Mehmet Beşikçi for providing the photograph of this document from TNA.

diplomats were instructed to tell their foreign counterparts that the "clothing affair" was not a deliberate provocation but "an oversight" on the part of the Ottoman officials carrying out the execution.[33] According to another source, the body of the hapless Avakim had been dressed in European garb *after* his execution: "The mutilated body was clothed in European costume, and the head carefully covered with a European hat in deliberate and symbolic insult to the European community".[34] Yet it was also this gruesome scene that was to launch the entire debate about the "matter of civilization" (*sivilizasyon meselesi*) that became the central theme around which the foreign ambassadors bent the ears of the Turks.

THE SECOND PHASE: THE REFORM EDICT OF 1856

Even though Canning and his colleagues thought they had procured binding commitments from the Porte, the wording of the actual declaration had deliberately been left vague, as put by a missionary of a later generation: "The wording was, unfortunately, dubious. 'Christian renegade' might denote merely one born a Christian, who had temporarily become a Muhammedan".[35] In 1856 the British and French ambassadors renewed their pressure to have the apostasy law officially and publicly cancelled. At this point the Porte gave a second promise, but resisted appending the promise to the Reform Edict (*Hat-ı Hümayun*) that was pending at the time. The Porte argued that as the matter concerned Islamic law, a general announcement could not be made. It declared that "although a Şeriat ruling may fall into disuse it is not possible to change it".[36] In the event, the Porte ceded on this point, and the following statement was appended to the *Hat-ı Hümayun* that was read on 18 February 1856:

The Sublime Porte renews and confirms the assurances that it had previously given to the Governments of Britain and France regarding the question of the renegades. The Sublime Porte declares in addition that the decision taken at that time will nevertheless be applied to all renegades in general.[37]

---

[33] Özçelik, "Osmanlı İç Hukukunda", pp. 371–2.

[34] H. W. Temperley, *England and the Near East* (London, 1936), p. 225. My thanks to Sinan Kuneralp for this reference.

[35] Julius Richter, *A History of Protestant Missions in the Near East* (Edinburgh and London, 1910), p. 172.

[36] Kenanoğlu, *Osmanlı Devletinde Fikir ve İnanç Hürriyeti*, p. 13.

[37] Young, *Corps de Droit Ottoman*, vol. 2, p. 12. Note that this assurance does not appear in the actual text of the edict. Compare J. C. Hurewitz, *Diplomacy in the Near and Middle East*, vol 1, pp. 149–53.

Although these formulations were a far cry from an open and explicit cancellation of the apostasy clause, it suited all parties at the time to believe that they were. It was simply a matter of allowing the practice to fall into disuse. The Porte could downplay the issue to conservative circles by claiming that it had not actually revoked a *Şeriat* ruling, and the British and French could congratulate themselves on yet another victory for "civilisation".

Finally, in a cabinet meeting in 1857, at the suggestion of no less a personage than the famous jurist and statesman Ahmed Cevdet Paşa, the decision was taken that the punishment for apostasy was to be exile. The Şeyhülislam, Arif Hikmet Efendi, stated that "matters relating to the Şeriat cannot be changed but the punishment can be postponed".[38] This cabinet meeting seems to have been the basis of much of the policy that was discussed in the previous chapter.

The Reform Edict of 1856 was meant to carry out the promises made in the Tanzimat Edict. The Reform Edict is much more detailed and much longer, as well as more specific about religious freedom, stating that

As all forms of religion are free and shall be freely professed in my dominions, no subject of my empire shall be hindered in the exercise of the religion that he professes, nor shall he be in any way annoyed on this account. No one shall be compelled to change their religion.[39]

Another very clear indication that the Sublime State wanted to make it known that it did not need outside interference in matters relating to the religious freedom of its subjects, is the official declaration made in 1851 that the privileges granted to non-Muslim subjects in 1453 by Mehmet the Conqueror, the conqueror of Istanbul, were still in force. It was clearly stated in the declaration that such a confirmation was going to be officially issued as an imperial edict (*Hat-ı Hümayun*) to the Greek and Armenian Patriarchates as well as to the Chief Rabbi and the head of the Protestant community: "The full application of such privileges is a manifestation of the Sublime State's great affection for its subjects, and its determination not to admit any interference or meddling by any other party".[40] It is interesting that the Porte should have hit upon the strategem of using a four-hundred-year-old historical precedent to ward off outside pressure, and indeed the *Hat* of 1856 specifically mentioned Fatih Sultan Mehmed by name: "The powers conceded to the Christian patriarchs and bishops by the Sultan Mahomet II and his successors shall be made to harmonize

---

[38] Kenanoğlu, *Osmanlı Devleti'nde Fikir ve İnanç Hürriyeti*, p. 5.
[39] Hurewitz, *Diplomacy in the Near and Middle East*, vol. 1, p. 151.
[40] BOA HR.MKT 49/95; the only date is 1268 (1851).

with the new position which my generous and beneficient intentions insure to these communities".[41]

It is interesting that the "privileges" granted to the non-Muslim communities by Mehmet II should come up in this context, particularly given that there is now a consensus in the modern literature that these "privileges", which came to be known as the much-cited "millet system", were latter-day accretions that had been retropectively projected into the past as some sort of "foundation myth". It is all the more significant that the Tanzimat State should feel it necessary to re-evoke its own mythology at this time.[42]

Despite all of the Porte's efforts to ward off foreign pressure and to appear to be taking the initiative, the Reform Edict of 1856, unlike the Tanzimat Edict of 1839, was indeed largely the result of foreign pressure. The historical conjuncture has to be recalled at this point. In the year leading up to the Reform Edict (*Hat-ı Hümayun*, 18 February 1856), the Ottoman Empire was fighting the Crimean War against Russia as the ally of Britain and France. The desire to be included in the Concert of Europe that was taking shape after the Treaty of Paris (30 March 1856) ending the Crimean War, which would guarantee Ottoman territorial integrity, must have been instrumental in the concessions the Ottoman side was prepared to make. The contradictions between the edict and the treaty, which usually go unnoticed, have been accurately noted by Caroline Finkel: "The right of the foreign powers to intervene in Ottoman domestic matters was specifically rejected in the Treaty of Paris, but its possibility was implicit in every phrase of the Reform Edict".[43] This factor and the desire to be a member of the club of "civilised powers" (*düvel i medeniye*) certainly pushed the Porte, led by the brilliant twosome, Âli Paşa and Fuad Paşa, to yield perhaps more than was absolutely necessary.[44] Their

---

[41] Hurewitz, *Diplomacy in the Near and Middle East*, vol. 1, p. 150.

[42] The seminal article on the "millet system" is Benjamin Braude, "Foundation Myth of the Millet System", in Benjamin Braude and Bernard Lewis (eds.), *Christians and Jews in the Ottoman Empire: The Functioning of a Plural Society* (New York, 1982), pp. 69–71. The other authors in the two-volume work also debunk the received wisdom of the "privileges". Most of the revisionist authors are of the opinion that the *berats* (privileges) granted to the Greek Patriarch were granted to him personally, not to the church in perpetuity as an institution. In this context, see also Halil İnalcık, "The Status of the Greek Patriarch under the Ottomans", *Turcica*, 21–2 (1991), 411. For a more recent comprehensive critical revision of the millet system, see Macit Kenanoğlu, *Osmanlı Millet Sistemi. Mit ve Gerçek* (The Ottoman millet system: Myth and reality) (Istanbul, 2004).

[43] Finkel, *Osman's Dream*, p. 459.

[44] The rise of Âli and his close associate Fuad Paşa was seen as the eclipse of Reşid Paşa and the arrival of a new Tanzimat cadre. Âli was to serve six times as Grand Vizier until his death in 1871. See İbnülemin Mahmud Kemal İnal, *Son Sadrazamlar* (The last Grand

onetime mentor and later rival, Reşid Paşa, was to bemoan the fact that his successors (for he was no longer in the inner circle when the edict was proclaimed) had given away too much at the Paris conference. Nor was he enamored by the possibility of *"emancipation parfaite"* or *"égalité parfaite"* for non-Muslim subjects. The Ottoman statesman, who is seen as one of the founders of the Tanzimat, was to declare:

> Regarding the content and means of application of the Ferman, it is impossible to deny the requirements of the times and circumstances, nor is it possible to handle our Christian subjects the way we did even twenty years ago, leave alone one hundred. The periodic privileges granted to them by Our August Master and his predecessor sprung from this fact. Nor is it possible to deny that it is necessary to add some suitable measures in the same vein. Yet these things should be done gradually and particularly without the official intervention of foreign states. It is also necessary to accustom the minds of the Muslims and to avoid increasing the privileges of the Christians to a degree that even they could not imagine and thus spoil them. [If this is not done] this will be entirely contrary to and against the six hundred year tradition of the Sublime State and lead to, God forbid, great bloodshed between Muslim and Christian.[45]

In the same memo, Reşid Paşa points out that he was not against reform measures per se, but the fact was that this *ferman* "was unlike other measures that the Sublime State took of it own accord ... and was very damaging to its sovereignty and independence". History was to prove him right.

THE RECOGNITION OF THE PROTESTANT *MILLET* AND THE CRISIS OF 1864

When Stratford Canning talked about "civilisation" he meant essentially Protestant civilisation. The ban on the execution of apostates was intended to clear the ground for the eventual conversion of Muslims to Protestantism. In the event, the success of Protestant missionaries among the Muslims was minimal, and the missionaries were to claim subsequently that they had never intended to "work" among the Muslims, but wanted to concentrate on the Eastern Christians. Yet, as seen in the As'ad Shidyaq affair, there is evidence that they had to make a virtue of necessity. Ussama Makdisi's fascinating study of early American missionary efforts in the Ottoman Empire shows that the early missionaries were completely out of

---

Viziers) (Istanbul, 1982), vol. 1, pp. 4–29. Fuad Paşa served five times as foreign minister; see İbnülemin Kemal İnal, *Son Sadrazamlar*, pp. 149–78.

[45] Ahmed Cevdet Paşa, *Tezakir* (Ankara, 1986), vol. 1, pp. 78–9.

their depth in a Middle Eastern environment, and that their previous experiences among the native Americans had not prepared them in any way for work in a society where they did not hold the whip hand.[46] A book published by a missionary in the mid-twentieth century actually lamented that the main handicap facing missionary work among Muslims was that "the missionary has to strive against Muslim solidarity and it is Islamic 'Brotherhood' which is the greatest barrier for the would-be convert. Enquirers risk ostracism and loneliness".[47]

The Ottoman Protestant *millet* was officially recognized in an imperial decree dated 15 November 1847. In 1850, "British intercession won full official recognition for the Armenian Evangelical Union, and the Protestants were to be a completely separate civil community in the Ottoman Empire".[48]

THE CRISIS OF 1864

Canning's zeal knew no bounds, and he stated in his memoirs that once the apostasy law was abolished, "the main barrier between Turkey and Christendom would be removed", presumably leaving the way clear for the conversion of Muslims to Christianity.[49] The seeds sown by Canning bore their first fruit some twenty years later. Puny fruit though it was, some twelve "Turkish Protestants", they caused a disproportionate amount of noise.[50] Julius Richter, himself a missionary, was to bemoan the "foolish exaggerated reports such as the report that 25,000 or even 40,000 Turks had been converted to Protestantism."[51] The arrival in Istanbul in 1858 of Dr. Gotlieb Karl Phander, who was infamous for his militant anti-Islamic preaching in India, and Dr. Koelle, a German Protestant missionary, set the

---

[46] Ussama Makdisi, *The Artillery of Heaven*, sometime in March 1826. As'Ad Shidyaq, a Maronite Christian from a prominent Lebanese family, announced that he had converted to Protestantism as the result of the influence of the first American evangelists who arrived in Ottoman Lebanon in the beginning of the 1820s. Shidyaq was first cajoled to give up his heresy, then incarcerated, and ultimately tortured on the orders of the Maronite Patriarch, Yusuf Hubaysh. He died in captivity, becoming the first Protestant martyr in Lebanon.

[47] James Thayer Addison, *The Christian Approach to the Moslem* (New York, 1942), p. 300.

[48] Frank Andrews Stone, *Academies for Anatolia*, p. 70: "Protestant Milleti Nizamnamesi" (Regulations of the Protestant millet), *Düstur*, I. Tertib, vol. 1 (İstanbul, 1856), pp. 652-4.

[49] Lane-Poole, *The Life of the Right Honourable Stratford Canning*, p. 95.

[50] *Correspondence Respecting Protestant Missionaries and Converts in Turkey, Presented to both Houses of Parliament by Command of Her Majesty 1865*. House of Commons Parliamentary Papers Online 2005, www.parlipapers.chadwyck.co.uk. My thanks to Sinan Kuneralp for generously sharing this source as hard copy.

[51] Julius Richter, *A History of Protestant Missions in the Near East*, p. 172.

scene for what was to follow. Phander was to start work by "forging the spiritual weapons for the mission in the form of apologetic and polemical tracts [in Turkish]". By 1864 the energetic efforts of Phander and Koelle had indeed produced a handful of Turkish converts.[52] The Turkish converts, or rather their minders, had come up with the harebrained idea of preaching against Islam in public inns, or "*hans*", in Eminönü, the commercial centre of Istanbul. The British chargé d'affaires, Sir H. Bulwer, reported:

> For some time past this sort of public attack on their faith by persons who have deserted from it, has been getting up a strong sentiment of indignation among the Mussulman population of this capital. The renegade Turk is looked upon by them with horror; and his public revilings against the religion he has abjured, and which they profess is considered a public insult.[53]

As a result, the Turkish converts were arrested, the self-styled "prayer houses" were closed down, and the books and papers of the missionaries were seized: "The storm burst suddenly and destructively. Ten or thirteen Protestant Turks in Constantinople were seized without previous warning on 17 July 1864 and thrown into prison. ... Even the missionaries were forcibly driven from their homes".[54] For an experienced "Turkey hand", Bulwer seemed somewhat surprised at this outcome and slow on the uptake. He was certainly mistaken in his assessment of the Ottoman government's attitude: "I do not believe that the Government itself cares about the attempts at conversion from any religious apprehension on the subject; but it is fearful of the public mind".[55] Bulwer went on to report that Turkish Protestant converts had taken to distributing the Turkish Bible openly, pressing it on people in steamships and other public places as well as preaching about the folly of Islam. All this, he said, was causing "a certain effervescence" in public opinion. The minister of police had told him that the "language of the multitude" was as follows:

> Do these people want to pray to God in their own way? Let them do so in their churches. ... But if they want ... to make public war in our own country against our faith, and to encourage other people to join them in this war – then they are abusing our hospitality and protection, and under the mask of friendship, acting as our bitterest foes.[56]

---

[52] Ibid., p. 173.
[53] *Correspondence Respecting Protestant Missionaries and Converts in Turkey*, p. 2. Sir H. Bulwer to Earl Russel, Constantinople, 18 July 1864.
[54] Richter, *A History of Protestant Missions*, p. 174.
[55] *Correspondence Respecting Protestant Missionaries and Converts in Turkey*, p. 2. Sir H. Bulwer to Earl Russel, Constantinople, 18 July 1864.
[56] Ibid.

What Bulwer did not seem to understand was that this was the attitude not just of the faceless "multitude" but of the very men he was dealing with, the Grand Vizier, Âli Paşa, and the foreign minister, Fuad Paşa. What Bulwer was right about was that Âli and Fuad did face a serious conservative opposition that could influence the sultan. Âli and Fuad's argument to Bulwer was, not surprisingly, that the lives of the Turkish converts were in danger and that they should be removed from the capital. Two, in particular, were drawing the ire of the masses because one had been an Islamic cleric (*imam*) and the other an officer in the security forces (*zaptiye*). Bulwer did note, "Fuad and Aali Pashas consider that we have no right to regard these men as Englishmen simply because they have become Protestants: in this I agree".[57]

Indeed, Bulwer was no Canning, and he did not have any particular sympathy for the missionaries; "they consider that religious liberty consists, not in every one being allowed to follow his own religion, but in every one being allowed to attack the religion of his neighbour."[58] Yet the ghost of Canning was evidently in attendance: "Turks should not be punished for becoming Christians, Lord Stratford procured a promise to that effect", wrote Foreign Secretary Lord Russel.[59] A memorandum from the British and Foreign Bible Society also evoked Canning's name. Indeed, the Protestant missionaries "had welcomed the Reform Edict of 1856, as part of their effort to 'enlighten the people', and disseminated knowledge of the *Hat-ı Hümayun* (1856) by publishing and circulating copies of the edict".[60]

The missionaries saw the *Hat-ı Hümayun* of 1856 as the direct result of Canning's "noble efforts".[61] In other words, as far as the missionaries were concerned, the Reform Edict was simply a license to convert Muslims.[62]

How the same document can be interpreted in two diametrically opposite ways comes out very clearly in Âli Paşa's assessment of the situation as reflected in the letter he wrote to the Ottoman ambassador in London, Alexander Musurus. Âli told his ambassador that the missionaries were wilfully misinterpreting the *Hat-ı Hümayun*: "Can it be supposed that

---

[57] House of Commons Parliamentary Papers Online, p. 4.
[58] Ibid., p. 5.
[59] Ibid., Foreign Office, 11 August 1864, Foreign Secretary Earl Russel to H. Bulwer.
[60] Gerasimos Augustinos, *The Greeks of Asia Minor*, p. 77.
[61] House of Commons Parliamentary Papers Online, p. 6.
[62] Richter, *A History of Protestant Missions in the Near East*, p. 173: "This decree seemed to open the way for extensive work among the Mohammedans of Turkey".

whilst condemning religious persecutions, the Sublime Porte has consented to permit offence and insult to any creed whatever? That at the same time she was proclaiming liberty to all non-Mussulman creeds, she had given them arms against Islamism?"[63] Âli had also done his homework on comparative religious liberties: "No European government ... has sanctioned the principle of religious propagandism. In England, in Prussia, in Austria, everywhere propagandism is subjected to the supervision of the authorities."[64] Âli had evidently done serious research on the topic; he argued that "even in England ... one of the most liberal nations ... and the head of civilization" there were laws on the statute books that dated from the time of William III that ordained severe punishments for "speaking, teaching, or denying the truth of the Christian religion and the Divine authority of the Holy Scriptures".[65] Here we observe the very clever synthesis of the "do not push us in a direction we want to take anyway" attitude and a certain cynical pandering to the British self-image. The pandering was all the more cynical as Âli Paşa hated Canning, and was known to have said that he was so vain that "he would not allow the sultan to reign with him. ... Years after Stratford had left Constantinople, Âli still spoke of him with real hatred".[66] Canning had in fact been instrumental in Âli Paşa's dismissal from the Grand Vezirate in 1856.[67]

There the matter rested. The Turkish Protestant Church was a nonstarter. Years later, J. T. Addison, a writer sympathetic to the missionary effort, was to regret the fact that the twelve "Turkish Christians" had been imprisoned: "This sharp reaction was confirmed by the continued hostility of the government, which resented the slightest extension of work beyond the Christian groups. Indeed the Grand Vizier openly declared that, regardless of all *firmans*, conversion from Islam must be made impossible".[68]

---

[63] House of Commons Parliamentary Papers, p. 88. Aali Pasha to Musurus Pasha, the Sublime Porte, 30 November 1864. The instruction of Musurus was to give the letter to Lord Russel.

[64] Ibid., p. 86.

[65] Ibid., p. 87. The Grand Vizier had a firm grounding in comparative theology; "He could discuss theology with ease with bishops, rabbis, and *ulema*". See Fuat Andić and Stephen Andić, *The Last of the Ottoman Grandees: The Life and Political Testament of Âli Paşa* (Istanbul, 1996), p. 31.

[66] Roderic Davison, "Turkish Attitudes Concerning Christian-Muslim Equality in the Nineteenth Century", *American Historical Review* 59 (1954), 844–64.

[67] İbnülemin M. Kemal İnal, *Son Sadrazamlar*, vol. 1 , p. 28.

[68] James Thayer Addison, *The Christian Approach to the Moslem* (New York, 1942), pp. 93–5.

Although, as we have seen, Âli Paşa had declared nothing of the kind, openly or on paper, unfolding events would prove Addison's point.

THE AHMED TEVFIK AFFAIR

After Pfander left Istanbul in 1865, Dr. Koelle was left alone. In the wake of the outcry of the previous year, he changed tactics; rather than out-and-out preaching, he switched to the publication of evangelical propagandist tracts in Turkish. In this effort he engaged the services of Ahmet Tevfik Efendi, a teacher at the Emirgan Rüşdiye school.[69] On 23 September 1879, Ahmet Tevfik and Dr. Koelle were arrested in possession of incriminating documents. These were tracts in Turkish attacking the Muslim faith, designed to weaken the resolve of the believer. The entire affair was to show just how much the political climate had changed with the coming of the more sternly Islamic rule of Sultan Abdülhamid II (r. 1876–1909). The learned judges to whom the case was referred were scathing in their judgement. Ahmet Tevfik should be executed, and even if he were to repent, his repentance was not to be accepted. His crime was greater than simply becoming an apostate himself. He had "actively worked towards the alienation from the faith of his brothers in religion".[70] Of course, Dr. Koelle appealed to the British ambassador, Sir Henry Layard, to have him put pressure on the Porte to free Ahmet Tevfik, return his papers, and to secure the dismissal of Hafız Paşa, the minister of police. The subsequent development of events was to show just how much the political climate had changed since Canning's heyday. Despite pressure from the British, German (for Koelle was a German citizen), and Austrian ambassadors, the Porte stood firm. Abdülhamid II himself granted Layard an audience on 1 January 1880, when he explained that as Caliph of All Muslims, he could not condone the behaviour of Ahmet Tevfik. The Sultan pointed out that Ahmet Tevfik had not been arrested because he had been suspected of apostasy; anyone was free to choose whatever religion they wanted to belong to in Ottoman domains. He had been arrested and condemned precisely because he was a Muslim cleric, and as a Muslim cleric he had been instrumental in the production of literature damaging to Islam. The Caliph of All Muslims then proceeded to produce the pages of the

---

[69] Azmi Özcan, Ş. Tufan Buzpınar, "Church Missionary Society İstanbul'da. Tanzimat, İslahat, Misyonerlik" (The Church Missionary Society in Istanbul: The Tanzimat, reform and missionaries), *İstanbul Araştırmaları* 1 (1997), 63–79.

[70] Ibid., p. 71.

literature seized from Ahmet Tevfik upon which he had underlined the passages he saw as blasphemy (*küfür*).[71] This audience was a far cry indeed from the audience granted to Canning thirty-six years earlier by his father, Abdülmecid I, who had been browbeaten by the arrogant Canning. The entire affair was defused very diplomatically by the sultan, who commuted Ahmet Tevfik's punishment to exile on the island of Chios, agreed to return the papers to Dr. Koelle after he had made the alterations required, but firmly refused to dismiss Hafız Paşa. It was, after all, not worth falling out with the ambassador of the greatest power in the world over the fate of a minor miscreant who would soon be forgotten. And forgotten he was. It appears that he escaped from Chios to London, where "his baptism in 1881 caused a great sensation. . . . But he did not turn out well; in fact he seems to have returned to Islam".[72]

FOREIGN INTERVENTION IN LOCAL
RELIGIOUS POLITICS

Despite the failure of the missionary effort to actively convert Muslims, foreign intervention on religious grounds continued right up to the end of the empire. In the case of a Christian or Jewish convert to Islam who claimed the protection of a foreign power, another level was added to the conversion process described in Chapter 1. The additional dimension was the requirement that the local representative of the foreign power should also be in attendance to witness that the conversion was legitimate.[73]

Many of the conversion cases involved situations where the Ottoman authorities would become embroiled in confrontations with the representative of foreign powers, who would make it their business to "protect" this or that non-Muslim whom they claimed (rightly or wrongly) had been pressured into accepting Islam. This situation was exacerbated by the fact that foreign passports had become very easy to come by. An Austrian procurer of passports boasted,

If a non-Muslim approaches to ask me for citizenship, I can get the passport of the state he chooses, whatever that may be. Lately an Armenian came and asked me for a Wallachian passport. . . . He gave me three hundred *guruş* in return. I can do the same for anybody.[74]

[71] Ibid., p. 75.

[72] Richter, *A History of Protestant Missions in the Near East*, p. 176.

[73] Young, *Corps de Droit Ottoman. Titre XXXI b Changement de Religion*, pp. 9–10.

[74] Kırlı, "Balkan Nationalisms and the Ottoman Empire", p. 254.

On 20 September 1847 the Vali of Damascus reported a case where a local Greek man had converted to Islam, but his wife had refused to accept this and had taken refuge in the house of the Austrian vice consul. Her husband demanded her return as he was going to take her to court to divorce her. The local judge had told the consul that she would be returned after the court case. The consul, "becoming rough and rude", had refused to hand over the woman, imprisoning her on the consulate grounds. The judge had again asked the consul to hand over the woman, but "becoming even more obstinate he refused". The local authorities had then forcibly removed the woman from the consulate. The case was heard, and the woman was divorced from her husband and was about to be returned to the consul when the latter declared that as she had been forcibly removed while under his protection, he would no longer shelter her. Finding herself abandoned by both consul and husband, the woman agreed to become a Muslim and be re-married to her ex-husband. What would be nothing more than an obscure marital tiff makes its way into history because the document bears a marginal note by the Sultan Abdülmecid himself, which reads as follows:

The intervention of these foreign consuls in the provinces in matters that are not part of their duties is injurious to affairs of state. The Reis Efendi should intercede with the ambassadors to get them to order their consuls not to interfere in matters that are beyond treaty obligations.[75]

Yet the archives are full of cases involving the intervention of foreign consuls, some direct, some indirect. In some cases the local consul figures only marginally in local conversion/apostasy cases, and in others he is a central figure. In major centres like Salonica, Bursa, and Adana the consuls would be expected to have quite a bit of clout; in small provincial towns they often wielded disproportionate power.

On 21 October 1847, the Vali of Salonica, Mustafa Paşa, wrote to the Grand Vizier refuting the accusations that Christian girls were being pressured into accepting Islam and were seeking refuge with the foreign consuls.[76] He gave detailed accounts of two cases. The first involved a Bulgarian girl from the *kaza* of Siroz who had eloped with a vineyard-keeper, a certain Hüseyin. Protesting that he had been unjustly accused of

---

[75] BOA Hat-ı Hümayun 20667, 9 Şevval 1263 / 20 September 1847, the Vali of Damascus to the imperial palace. The Reis Efendi was the Reis ul Kuttab or chief scribe, the office that later became the foreign minister.

[76] BOA A/MKT 99/66, 11 Zilkade 1263 / 21 October 1847, the Vali of Selanik, El Seyyid Hafız Mustafa Paşa, to the Grand Vezirate. The girl's name is not given; she is simply referred to as "daughter of Üstuban son of Boçu".

negligence and laxity in this matter, the Vali took pains to point out that he had given strict instructions that they be found, issuing the girl's father a document that would secure him the full co-operation of all the officials in the province. The runaway couple had travelled to Rodosto, another *kaza* in the same *eyalet*, where the girl had converted to Islam of her own free will, and the couple were married. After having lived in Rodosto "for one or two months as husband and wife", they then moved to the *kaza* of Ustruca, where they were arrested by the authorities. There, upon being questioned, and "as the result of having been led astray by certain parties", the woman "gave answers which were not in keeping with her former [conviction in Islam]".[77] The couple were duly sent to Salonica for questioning. There, Hüseyin, who was questioned first, stated that his wife had become Muslim of her own free will and had decided to marry him. He was now "revolted and extremely distraught by her unacceptable behaviour", which led him to "divorce her on the spot". The woman was then put in the house of an official to be brought before the local council the next day. On that day, as she was being taken to the council, a crowd of her relatives descended upon her, and she was spirited off to the dwelling of a certain Babi Abud, a local merchant and an agent of the British consul. Although proper protests were made through the British consul, "it was clear that he [the consul] had a hand in this matter and that such [representations] would be of no use".[78]

The next case reported by Mustafa Paşa was that of Salih Ağa and Litu, the daughter of Yanca, both from the village of Dortuh in the *kaza* of Yenice Vardar. The couple eloped to the neighbouring *kaza* of Sarı Gül, where Litu converted to Islam "of her own free will", and the couple were married. Brought to Salonica, the couple held firm; questioned in the council and entreated by priests and tearful parents, Litu's "conviction in her faith was beyond doubt". At this point, the Vali's report becomes somewhat less than neutral in tone:

Her firmness in her conviction despite all the pressure [was truly commendable]. As she was almost past marriageable age (*biraz geçkince olup*), young and strong, and Salih Ağa was a rich and prominent man in the village, strong and handsome (*yakışıklı ve tuvana*) and it was clear from the circumstances that they had great love and fondness for each other . . .[79]

---

[77] Ibid. It is not stated openly that she became an apostate, but that is the clear implication.
[78] Ibid.
[79] Ibid.

What the Vali was not saying in so many words was, "Leave them alone". He protested that the case had, above all else, been presented by ill-wishers as that of a Muslim man abducting an underage Christian girl, and her parents appealed to the British consul for her return. He entreated his superiors to see the difference between rumour and fact. He did not omit to add that "in keeping with the delicacy of the times and with the rules of proper conduct, I continue to maintain correct relations with the foreign consuls".[80] The documentation on these cases ends here. What is striking, however, is that twenty-nine years later an almost identical incident in the same city would have much more dire consequences, as will be seen later in the "grievous Salonica incident".

Intervention in the fate of converts by foreign consuls could take on dramatic proportions, as shown in the following case. In early 1846, a merchant from Trabzon by the name of Mehmed Ağa arrived in Adana on business, accompanied by "a Georgian concubine (*cariye*) approximately some twenty years of age and a young Abhaz girl of some sixteen years of age".[81] Mehmed Ağa and his companions settled down at an inn. Falling into conversation with other guests, the women were questioned about their ethnic origins:

> The older one admitted that she was of Georgian origin and had voluntarily come to the *kaza* of Acara in Trabzon some six years previously and had then converted to Islam. The other one stated that she was Abhaz by origin and had come some ten years ago and had then converted to Islam. At this point their master hit the older girl without any reason and some perfidious influence was brought to bear by some of the Christians present, leading the girl to cry out and deny that she ever became a Muslim and that she was Georgian.

The Russian deputy consul at Tarsus, a certain William Barker, came to hear of the incident and demanded an investigation, claiming that, as a Georgian, the woman was a Russian subject.[82] The local council was duly convened, and in the presence of Consul Barker the woman once again declared that she had never voluntarily become a Muslim. In these circumstances the council placed her in the custody of one of their members, Hacı

[80] Ibid.
[81] BOA A/MKT 35/45, report of the Administrative Council of Adana (undated). This is based on the context and the date of the instructions sent to the Vali of Adana (11 February 1846); the events mentioned probably occurred in January 1846.
[82] William Barker was an American from a well-established missionary family and was acting as honorary consul for Russia. His missionary background would account for his zealous and overbearing intervention in this case. I owe thanks to Professor Roger Owen of Harvard University for this information.

Sıdkı Efendi, while they awaited instructions from Istanbul. The younger girl insisted that she was a Muslim and was handed back to Mehmed Ağa. At this point dramatic events unfolded:

[The night after the council ruling] at around six in the morning, the Russian Consul broke into the inn with fifteen of his men and forced his way into the merchant's room. He grabbed the Abhaz girl by the collar, and attempted to drag her away shouting all the while 'you are a Georgian' while the girl cried out, 'I am a Muslim *elhamdullilah*'. A crowd gathered to the girl's cries and intervened saying, 'it is against the law to seize a Muslim woman by the collar'. They then threw the Consul and his men out of the inn.[83]

The next day the council met again in the presence of the Russian and British consuls, their dragomans and their staff. At this session Mehmed Ağa produced witnesses from the inn who testified that the Georgian had indeed told them that she had converted of her own free will. He also produced two receipts from the customs authorities in Trabzon, duly certifying that he had paid import duty on the girls, and thus that they were his legal property.[84] The matter did not rest here, however; the Russian embassy in Istanbul intervened, claiming that the women in question were "stolen slaves" and Russian subjects. The embassy further contended that "they had been subjected to force and pain in order to make them convert. One of them had been unable to resist the pressure and had converted while the other remained true to her faith". The Vali of Adana was told by Istanbul that "If subjects of a friendly state express the desire to become Muslim and an Ottoman subject, in order to avoid all future contestation, according to the present treaties, they are to be questioned in front of their consular representatives". If in the course of this questioning it becomes clear that they have indeed been forced to convert, "no pressure of any sort is to be applied, and they are to be sent to Istanbul."[85] The outcome of the case is not clear, but it is unlikely that the women were set free.

The status of concubines *(cariye)* often resulted in diplomatic confrontation in matters of conversion and apostasy. On 27 November 1851, the

---

[83] BOA A/MKT 35/45.

[84] Ibid. Enclosures 3–4, declarations of customs duty, one for each woman, 4 Şevval 1261 / 6 October 1845. Mehmet Ağa may well have been rather disturbed by the religious injunction that forbids a master from having sexual intercourse with a concubine who has become an apostate. See Ömer Nasuhi Bilmen, *Hukuku Islamiyye*, p. 11: "According to Hanefi *fikh* a concubine who becomes apostate is to be imprisoned by her master until she recants. But her master may not approach her [during this time]. Because it is strictly forbidden to have sexual relations with a female apostate".

[85] Ibid., instructions from the Sublime Porte to the Vali of Adana, 14 Safer 1262 / 11 February 1846.

Muhafiz (commander) of the Paşalik of Belgrade wrote to Istanbul about a case involving the alleged abduction of a young Serbian convert girl who had been in the harem of a Bosnian notable, Fazlı Paşa.[86] The summary of the correspondence describes what happened. Sometime in late summer 1850, Fazlı Paşa and his family arrived at the port of Zemun, a port on the Danube in Habsburg territory directly across the river from Belgrade, where they were to board a steamer bound for Istanbul.[87] While they were staying at a local inn the commander of Zemun (*Zomon Cenerali*) sent armed guards to the inn, claiming that the young girl, Mariya, had been taken into Paşa's household against her will and converted by force. Her older brother had reported the matter to the Austrian consul at Belgrade, who in turn had alerted the Austrian authorities in Zemun.[88] There are two diametrically opposed versions of the story. The *Muhafiz* claimed that while the Fazlı Paşa family had been put under armed guard and were being kept under house arrest at the inn, armed men had burst into their rooms, seized the girl, and dragged her screaming to confinement in the town. The reason for this, according to the Austrian side, was that the girl had been questioned and had stated that she had been forced to convert and that she had been given into service of the Fazlı Paşa family against her will. The Austrian authorities stated that slavery was forbidden in Habsburg domains and that according to their law, any slave that set foot in Habsburg dominions and wished to be set free was emancipated. Therefore, Mariya had been taken from Fazlı Paşa's harem, and they had been allowed to leave for Istanbul leaving Mariya behind.[89] The Ottoman side claimed that this was a lie and that Mariya was not a slave but a free

---

[86] BOA HR.SYS 204/17, 2 Safer 1268 / 27 November 1851, the Muhafız of Belgrade to the Sublime Porte. On the legal status of concubines and slavery in general in the Ottoman Empire, see Hakan Erdem, *Slavery in the Ottoman Empire and Its Demise 1800–1909* (London, 1996), especially pp. 102–7: "Measures against the White Slave Trade in the Black Sea".

[87] Zomon, as it was called in the Ottoman documents, was officially known as Semlin in German, Zimony in Hungarian, and Taurunum in Latin. It lies diagonally across from Belgrade and was once a separate port town known as the "last Habsburg border post before the Orient". I owe thanks to Milos Jovanović for these geographical details.

[88] BOA HR.SYS 204/17. The fortress town of Belgrade was part of the rump of what had been Ottoman Serbia until Serbian autonomy in 1878. So there is a somewhat complicated diplomatic structure involved here. As an autonomous state, Serbia had diplomatic representatives in both Ottoman and Habsburg domains. The Austrians kept a consulate in Belgrade which remained officially Ottoman until it was awarded to Serbia by the Treaty of Berlin (1878).

[89] BOA HR.SYS 204/17, 22 Safer 1268 / 17 December 1851, the Ottoman ambassador in Vienna to the Sublime Porte.

person receiving payment for her services. She had converted of her own free will in a *kadı* court and had been given a document (*hüccet*) from the Şeriat court of Bosnia.

The issue continued well into the next year as the Ottoman side continued to press for the girl's release. On 25 August 1852 the Porte received a letter from the Austrian consulate in Belgrade containing the written statements of the commander of Zemun and Milan, son of Ilya, the older brother of Maria.[90] Milan wrote: "[S]ix years ago in the *eyalet* of Bosnia some Muslims captured me and my sister and sent us to Fazlı Paşa who ordered that we be made Muslims." They had refused and had been imprisoned. After one year in prison Maria relented, became a Muslim, and was released. Milan persisted in his refusal and remained in prison for four years. He had been released one year before the date of writing. Milan concluded that "my sister is still a concubine and a slave in the harem [of Fazlı Paşa]."

The commander of Zemun claimed that nobody had forced his way into the harem; two guards armed only with swords had waited at the door but "only to prevent the girl's escape". When Fazlı Paşa had been offered the option of leaving and abandoning the girl, he had taken it and boarded ship. The girl had then been questioned and had confirmed her brother's story. The Austrian official asked, "How can a seven-year-old girl of her own will and desire accept Islam? At such a young age how could she [understand] and negotiate a service contract? She is now eleven years old and even now this is beyond her." The Austrian official then presumed to lecture the Porte on how it should conduct its politics: "If the officials of the Sublime Porte [in Belgrade] write to their superiors giving the facts as they occured they would be doing their country a great service. Maybe these two unfortunate children can be the occasion for the lifting of all oppression from the Christian subjects of the Sultan."[91]

On 19 October 1852 the Ottoman ambassador in Vienna reported that he had once again seen the Austrian foreign minister and requested that the girl be returned. The minister had told him that, since both Milan and his sister were Ottoman subjects, and since there were not actually any legal procedure pending as Milan had only asked for the freedom of his sister and had not taken the matter to any court, "if she managed to cross into Ottoman territory there would be no objection".[92]

---

[90] Ibid., 25 August 1852, the Ottoman Embassy in Vienna to the Sublime Porte, enclosing translation of a letter from the Austrian consul in Belgrade.

[91] Ibid.

[92] Ibid., 5 Muharrem 1269 / 19 October 1852, the Ottoman ambassador in Vienna to the Sublime Porte.

The minister's suggestion was clearly disingenuous as an eleven-year-old girl was hardly likely to take it upon herself to cross into Ottoman territory even if she wanted to. We will probably never know which side was telling the truth, although on balance, the Austrian explanation appears more plausible.

In situations such as this one the Ottomans found themselves squeezed into that uncomfortable position between the frying pan and the fire. On the one hand, they desperately wanted to join the club of "civilized powers"; on the other, they felt that they must maintain their dignity. As in the "concubine case" of Fazlı Paşa, they were not necessarily interested in the fate of some poor and unfortunate eleven-year-old girl. What mattered was that Fazlı Paşa's harem had been violated; armed men had marched in and removed one of his women, and this was a gross insult. On the other hand, to the outside world (in this case, the Austrians) to keep concubines was seen as barbarism.

In an ironic twist of history the Austrians would find themselves in exactly the same situation but in reverse when they acquired control of Bosnia after the Treaty of Berlin of 1878. Robert Donia has shown that this time it was the Bosnian Muslims who would be accusing the Habsburgs of forcibly converting Muslim girls to Catholicism.[93] On 22 August 1890, Uzeifa Delahmatović, a sixteen-year-old Muslim girl working as a servant in the household of Esad Kulović, a Muslim city council member, left his house never to return. It was discovered that she had converted to Catholicism. She was taken to the residence of Archbishop Stadler in Sarajevo, where a hearing was held. In the presence of Kulović and her brother, she declared that "no force had been employed to persuade her to convert" and that she had not been pressured in any way; "she expressed her unequivocal desire to remain a Catholic".[94] Kulović asked the Austrian authorities to do something about the situation, protesting that Stadler and his men had hid Uzeifa from her fellow Muslims. Here the twist becomes even more poignant: "He and other Muslims cited Ottoman practices in which any potential convert was required to consult with the spiritual advisor from each faith before the conversion was officially recognized. They urged the Austrians to follow the Ottoman precedent

---

[93] Robert J. Donia, *Islam under the Double Eagle: The Muslims of Bosnia and Hercegovina 1878–1914* (New York, 1981), p. 55.

[94] On Archbishop Josip Stadler (1843–1918), see Srećko M. Džaja, "Bosnian Historical Reality and Its Reflection in Myth", in Pal Kolsto (ed.), *Myths and Boundaries in South-Eastern Europe*, pp. 106–29, particularly p. 120: "Archbishop Stadler was inclined to proselytize but the Austro-Hungarian administration in Bosnia averted this danger".

in dealing with future conversions".[95] The Austrian Conversion Ordinance of 1891 clearly echoed Ottoman practices. The converting person had to prove that he or she was mentally sound and of the age of discernment. If any of the parties disputed the conversion, the state was to intervene; if force or trickery was suspected, the convert would be moved to a "neutral location" for up to fourteen days. A commission would be established that would decide whether to recognize the conversion "only after hearing from the convert, the appropriate spiritual guardians and other witnesses". Situations very similar to those seen in Ottoman dominions arose: "Strong emotional involvement by all parties often precluded willing acceptance of any government decisions. When the government removed a convert to a 'neutral location' the gendarmes often had to use force to remove an individual from friends and relatives at a time of great emotional crisis". Muslim women converting to Catholicism continued to be a point of confrontation between the Austrians and their new Muslim subjects. Donia mentions some "dozen or more" such cases, which became symbolic events uniting secular and religious Bosnians in their opposition to the Austrians.[96]

Back in the Ottoman domains, the potential converts could find themselves involved in a three-way conflict of sovereignty. Such was the case of a nine-year-old boy, Salomon Bikri, a Jewish subject of Tuscany. On 20 June 1849 the chargé d'affaires of Tuscany in Istanbul complained that the boy, who was in Damascus, had been pressured into accepting Islam and had been spirited off by the inhabitants of that city, who had "claimed that he had an inclination to convert to Islam". The chargé d'affaires for Tuscany was not the only one laying claim to him. The Sardinian consulate also claimed the boy, declaring that because of the recent political changes in Italy, Tuscan subjects who had previously been under Austrian protection were now under the protection of the Kingdom of Naples and Sardinia. The Ottoman authorities were quite unequivocal: "[I]t is highly irregular to seize a child who has not yet converted on the basis of an inclination". In the end, Salomon was handed back to his father, who had become a Sardinian subject.[97]

Even the dead did not escape scrutiny. On 13 September 1852 the governor of Yanya (Ioannina in Epirus, Greece) was ordered to look into

---

[95] Donia, *Islam under the Double Eagle*, p. 56.
[96] Ibid., pp. 59, 114.
[97] BOA A.MKT 210/91, 29 Şaban 1265 / 20 June 1849, the chargé d'affaires for Tuscany, Chevalier Sarafini, to the Sublime Porte.

the death of the servant of a high-ranking Ottoman official. The official had reported that his servant had died soon after converting to Islam. However, the death had occured in somewhat suspicious circumstances, and the Austrian embassy had intervened, claiming that the deceased had been an Austrian subject who had been beaten to death while being pressed to accept Islam. Furthermore, no Austrian official had been present to testify that the conversion was voluntary. It was therefore duly arranged that a team of doctors from the Ottoman and Austrian sides be present as the body was exhumed and an autopsy performed.[98]

A striking case that illustrates very evocatively the problems involving foreign interference comes up on 27 January 1852, in the *sancak* of Lazistan, on the eastern Black Sea coast bordering Russia, where four Georgian boys turned up professing that they had converted to Islam "of their own free will". The Russian consul claimed them as Russian subjects, demanding that his representative verify that their conversion had indeed been voluntary. The *sancak* officials pointed out that the usual procedure in these matters called for the presence of a consular official only if the converts were Russian subjects. If they were Ottoman subjects, they said, procedure simply called for the presence of the local Metropolitan or his representative, the *kocabaşı*. It had also been determined by international agreement that to-and-fro movement of people across the border was to be regulated by passport, but the Georgian children had no passports. Thus, it was implied, the Russian consul could not claim them.[99]

The thread running through the documentation is that the Ottomans felt that the consulates and embassies were constantly looking over their shoulder in matters relating to conversion. Such was the story of Katerina, a Greek woman who was orphaned and left in the care of a certain Talip Ağa in Yanya, who "virtually imprisoned her and applied all manner of threats and promises for her to convert." The British consul in Preveza then became involved, claiming Katerina as a British subject and therefore demanding that a British official be present at the moment of conversion.

---

[98] BOA HR.MKT 49/36, 28 Zilkade 1268 / 13 September 1852, the Ministry of the Interior to the Vali of Yanya.

[99] HR.MKT 42/7, 27 January 1852. In fact, the Ottoman-Russian border was extremely porous. The Ottoman official made reference to an incident in the past when some one hundred people from the town of Arhavi had crossed over to Russia and not returned. On just how porous the borders in the region were, see Thomas M. Barret, "Lines of Uncertainty: The Frontiers of the Northern Caucasus", in Jane Burbank and David Ransel (eds.), *Imperial Russia* (Ann Arbor, Mich., 1998), pp. 48–173.

The Ottoman government instructed the governor of Yanya to ascertain whether Katerina had converted voluntarily and whether she was in fact a British subject. It was clearly stated that no consular representative was needed if she was not.[100]

The critical sticking point in most of the cases was the age of the potential convert. Such was the case of the Greek girl Vasilaki, a resident of a modest quarter in Istanbul, who claimed that she was an Austrian subject. Vasilaki, the daughter of a deceased stonemason and Austrian subject, Istefanaki, had decided to convert and marry Kadri, a Muslim Ottoman subject, also a stonemason. She had been sent by Kadri to the Directorate of Religious Sects (*Mezahip Müdüriyeti*) for her conversion formalities. On 3 July 1911 the Austrian embassy claimed that her mother had lodged a complaint that she was being kept there against her will and that she was underage. The Austrian consulate demanded that an Austrian interpreter be present at the proceedings. The minimum legal age of conversion for girls at the time was fifteen; Vasilaki was claiming to be twenty-one. The Ottoman authorities pointed out that "as the Austrian law even permits conversions at fourteen years of age, they should have nothing to say on this matter".[101] It appears that the Ottomans had done their research as the minimum age of conversion in the Habsburg domains at the time was indeed fourteen.[102] As in the case of the Bosnian Muslims mentioned earlier, who some years previously had advised the Austrians to take a leaf out of the Ottoman book regarding matters of conversion, here too it seems that the Ottomans were well informed about legal statutes on the "other side".

The question of the age of majority is also at issue in the case of Vasilya, a Greek girl and citizen who eloped with her Muslim lover in the Vilayet of Aydın. It was reported on 2 December 1911 that she had been taken into the custody of the police while her official procedure was pending. A crowd of Greeks had protested to the French consul in Aydın, who protected Greek interests. Although the Vilayet of Aydın reported that she was over

---

[100] BOA HR.MKT 47/81, 26 Sevval 1268 / 13 August 1852, the Sublime Porte to the Vali of Yanina.

[101] BOA DH.ID 116/22, 20 Haziran 1327 / 3 July 1911, the Ministry of Justice and Religious Sects to the Foreign Ministry. It is unclear why the parties in question did not produce birth or baptism certificates.

[102] My thanks to Professor Peter Urbanitsch from the University of Vienna for this information. E-mail from Prof. Urbanitsch dated 10 November 2008: "In 1868 this age-limit was lowered to 14 (Law No. 49 of 25 May 1868 on interdenominational relations, Article 4), and it referred not only to Christian denominations, but to Jews as well."

the legal age of fifteen, the French consul claimed that she could not be considered an adult until she was twenty-one.[103]

Although the French were self-consciously secular at home, they did not flinch from using religion – that is, Catholicism – as a tool of leverage in the Ottoman Empire. Their particular protegées were the Maronites of Lebanon, who provide our next case. On 14 January 1895 the Vali of Beirut wrote that two young Maronite girls who were employed as servants in Tripoli had applied to become Muslims. The girls were sisters named Sa'adi and Mes'ude, the daughters of one Cerbis Fazıl. The older of the two had been duly converted according to the formal procedure, but just as the procedure was about to be repeated for the younger girl, the Maronite Patriarch had intervened, claiming that the girls were underage.[104] The church registers of the girls' village, Tenvirin, had been consulted, and the Maronite Patriarch was claiming that according to the registers, both girls were underage. The affair had come before the local council as tension was mounting between the Muslims and the Patriarchate. The Vali of Beirut also noted that "the affair is sure to draw the attention of the French Consulate", suggesting that in order to avoid the "wagging of tongues" the girls should be removed to Istanbul.[105]

The next day the Mutasarrıf of Lebanon, Naum Paşa, wrote that the Maronite Patriarch was increasing his pressure on the issue and that it was necessary to "let this issue pass over without taking on the colour of a crisis leading to the involvement of foreigners".[106] Yet this was exactly what was happening. The Patriarchate claimed that the girls were twelve and ten years old, respectively, and therefore underage. Yet the elder, Sa'ida, had presented a petition to the authorities stating that she had not been pressured in any way but was accepting Islam of her own free will. The administrative council of Tripoli had questioned her and found that "she

---

[103] BOA DH ID. 11/52, 29 Tesrin-I Sani 1327 / 2 December 1911, cipher telegramme from the Vilayet of Aydin to the Ministry of the Interior.

[104] BOA A.MTZ.CL 2/97, 1 Kanun-u Sani 1311 / 14 January 1895, the Vali of Beirut, Nasuhi Paşa, to the *Mutasarrıf* of Lebanon. My thanks to Engin Akarlı for this reference. The *Mutasarrıf* was the Ottoman governor general for the Lebanon. He had to be chosen from among the Christian officials of the empire. The *Mutasarrifate* regime had been established in 1861 as a compromise between foreign pressure for the protection of Christians in the Lebanon and Ottoman sovereignty in the province. On the subject of the Mutasarrifate, see Engin Akarlı, *The Long Peace: Ottoman Lebanon 1861–1920* (Berkeley and London, 1993). See also Kamal Salibi, *The House of Many Mansions: The History of Lebanon Reconsidered* (Los Angeles, 1988).

[105] BOA A.MTZ.CL 2/97.

[106] Ibid., 2 Kanun-u Sani 1311 / 15 January 1895, the Mutasarrif of Lebanon, Naum Paşa, to the Sublime Porte.

appeared to be some seventeen or eighteen years of age". Her conversion had duly been carried out, and the Ministry of Justice and Religious Sects had been informed. Ten days later the matter had indeed reached the dimensions feared. Naum Paşa was told that the girls were "squeezed in between the Patriarchate, the Muslim population, and the French Consulate". He was duly instructed to send the girls to Istanbul.[107] On 6 February the Vali of Beirut reported that the girls had been embarked on the ship *Taif*, accompanied by an official, and sent to Istanbul, where they would be put in the care of the Ministry of Police.[108] The girls arrived safely in Istanbul, and one year later we find them "put up as guests in the home of a police officer".[109] One year after that, the Ministry of Police is instructed to "to find suitable husbands for them and marry them off". The girls evidently had their own plans and made it known that "they were not interested in marriage" but wanted to be given into the care of one Shaikh Abu Mohammad Tabha of Tripoli, with whom they planned to go on the *haj*.[110]

This curious little episode bears important clues regarding the relationship of the convert to the state, and about the sheer power of foreign intervention. In a sense, Sa'adi and Mes'ude as converts are taken into the foster care of the state. They are sent to the capital and put up as guests. The "foster parent" – in this case, the Sublime Porte – attempts to arrange marriages for them. All this because there is only a hint of foreign intervention; nowhere in the documents do we actually find a protest from the French consulate or others.

This case also invites comparison to that of As'ad Shidyaq, a Maronite who had been converted to Protestantism by American missionaries early in the century. In that case, Isaac Bird, one of the missionaries, had bemoaned the fact that there was not enough "English and American influence" in the Ottoman Empire enabling them to protect him.[111]

Of course, conversion and apostasy were also about money. Traditionally, new converts received a symbollic sum of money, the *kisve bahası*, which was meant to launch them into their new lives as

---

[107] BOA A.MTZ.CL 2/97, 26 January 1895, Naum Paşa to the Sublime Porte.
[108] Ibid., 24 Kanun-u Sani 1311 / 6 February 1895, the Vali of Beirut, Nasuhi Paşa, to the Sublime Porte.
[109] Ibid., 11 Mart 1312 / 24 March 1896, the minister of police to the Sublime Porte.
[110] Ibid., 14 Şevval 1313 / 29 March 1896, the Sublime Porte to the Ministry of Police; 17 Zilkade 1313, the Sublime Porte to the Vilayet of Beirut.
[111] Makdisi, *The Artillery of Heaven*, p. 147.

Muslims.[112] As the nineteenth century rolled on, however, more effective measures were considered. A memorandum dated 28 July 1889 prepared by the Director of Sects (*Mezahib Müdürü*), Ziver Bey, discussed various options. Ziver Bey began by saying that

> It is well known that the Embassies and the Patriarchates place great difficulties in the way of anyone who wants to convert [to Islam] sometimes focusing on a particular case and making a big fuss. The matter of conversion also draws the attention of many Muslim subjects.[113]

It was also well known that no matter how firm the resolve of a potential convert may have been, if they were poor, the promise of money from the Christians was something that they found difficult to resist. Ziver Bey went on to broach an even more delicate topic:

> What is even worse is that cases of apostasy have begun occuring among new converts who find themselves poor and destitute after their conversions. This is a matter touching upon the honour of Islam that is upheld as the greatest of requirements by the Sublime State and is causing much sadness and despair.

Ziver Bey then discussed several options. One was the formation of a sort of community coffer whereby people would contribute money for the upkeep of new Muslims. However, Ziver Bey was not too sanguine about this option, commenting; "Muslim folk are not used to such organized matters". What was even more of a problem was that "it would be very difficult to keep such a [coffer] secret and this would bring down the disasters of the wrath of Christian bigots, so terrifying in our present times".[114] The next option was the creation of a fund in the official treasury for the support of needy converts, but this option was also not without danger as "it would show up in the state budget and could not be kept secret". Ziver Bey finally concluded that the only viable option was the charity of the sultan, "which the August Person has never witheld in the matter of the defence of the honour of Islam".[115]

Several things are remarkable about this document. First and foremost, the Ottomans felt they were on the defensive on their own home ground. To feel that they had to keep secret what was, after all, a perfectly legitimate exercise such as a community coffer, for fear of "Christian bigots", is

---

[112] Anton Minkof, *Conversion to Islam in the Balkans: Kisve Bahası Petitions and Ottoman Social Life 1670–1730* (Leiden, 2004).

[113] BOA Yildiz Esas Evraki (YEE) 35/27, 15 Temmuz 1305 / 28 July 1889, the director of sects, Ziver Bey, to the ministry of justice and religious sects.

[114] Ibid.

[115] Ibid.

the clearest indication that they felt cornered on their own turf. In much the same way, to feel that the budget would be scrutinized by hostile eyes and that any expenditure for the support of needy converts had to be kept off the books is a further manifestation of extreme insecurity. In fact, the offer of sultanic charity was indeed accepted, and the needy converts did receive "a little something", albeit on a highly irregular basis.[116]

THE "GRIEVOUS SALONICA AFFAIR"

In early May 1876 a young Bulgarian girl in a village near Salonica decided to convert to Islam. Little did she know that she was about to make history. By the end of that week a major diplomatic crisis had broken out, and two foreign consuls, the French and the German, had been killed by a rioting mob. Given the sacrosanct position of foreign consuls in Ottoman territory, this was a scandal of unprecedented proportions. The incident was all the more serious because it occurred not in some remote Anatolian town but in the empire's second-largest city.

The girl was Stephana, daughter of the late Delyo Goya, from the village of Avrathisar. Apparently she converted in order to elope with her Muslim lover.[117] However, it seems that "both the girl and her mother had a notorious reputation that went beyond the boundaries of the village."[118] Whatever Stephana's morals, we have definite information that she boarded a train bound for Salonica on that fateful day, 7 May 1876, with the intention of going to the *Konak* of the Paşa to have her formal conversion procedure carried out, and to briefly take her place in history. As Gradeva and Kuneralp point out, there are many missing pieces in this tale. Did Stephana elope, or was she abducted by order of Emin Efendi, a powerful local notable who had his eye on her? Given the fact that it was highly unlikely that a peasant girl would have been able to organize a train journey to appear before the local administrative court on her own, Gradeva and Kuneralp come up with the following working hypothesis:

[116] See, the discussion on the language of officialdom in the Conclusion. The term used in such matters is "*bir mikdar şey*" as it was considered rude to mention the word "money" in such a context.

[117] Rossitsa Gradeva and Sinan Kuneralp, *On Love, Religion, and Politics: Salonica (1876) and Ruse (1910).* Unpublished paper cited with the specific permission of the authors. I wish to thank both authors for sharing this fascinating piece with me.

[118] Ibid., p. 3. Roderic Davison, one of the few historians to take note of the incident, also noted that it concerned "a Bulgarian girl of dubious morals". See R. Davison, "Turkish Attitudes Concerning Christian-Muslim Equality in the Nineteenth Century", *American Historical Review* 59 (1954), 844–64.

"that she was manipulated and things went off the course which the planners set".[119] She was accompanied by "two black women and the *imam* of the village".[120] Unknown to Stephana, her mother had boarded the same train but was sitting in a different carriage. It was upon the train's arrival at the station of Salonica that the "grievous Salonica affair" (*Selanik vak'a-i müellimesi*), as the Turks called it, began in earnest.

As they descended from the train, Stephana's mother appealed to the Christians at the station that her daughter was being taken off to be converted by force. At this point, Yanko Abott, the German consul, "publicly tore off the *yaşmak* (veil) that Stephana was wearing, knowing most certainly that such a gesture of provocation would incense watching Muslims"[121] Stephana's mother again appealed to the Greeks on the platform that her daughter was being taken off to be forcibly converted to Islam. Some Greeks then seized her from the police and spirited her off to an unknown destination in the carriage of the American consul, Hadji Lazaros. The fact that the Muslims believed a foreign consul to be involved was to have dire consequences.

The following morning a group of Muslims called on the Vali, Mehmet Refet Paşa, demanding that the girl be brought to the *Konak* for the formal procedure of conversion. Meanwhile, a crowd that was about to become a mob was gathering outside. The American consul was away, and his brother, who was acting for him, claimed that he did not know where the girl was, which was a lie, as he knew that she was being kept in the house of another Greek notable.[122] The crowd, its numbers had swollen by the arrival of some five hundred armed Albanians, now became a mob and threatened to storm the American consulate.[123] The Vali told the

---

[119] Gradeva and Kuneralp, *On Love, Religion and Politics*, p. 4.

[120] Ibid., n. 16. The source cited by the authors here is the account of Pericles Hadji Lazaro, a Bulgarian notable of Salonica and the consul of the United States, in (Andonis Vakalopoulos, A. *Ta dramatika gegonota tis Thessalonikis kata to Maio 1876 ke i epidrasis tous sto Anatoliko zitima – Makedonika*, t.2 (Thessaloniki, 1953), pp. 193–262.

[121] Gradeva and Kunerlap, *On Love, Religion and Politics*, pp. 4, 7. The authors point out that the actual national identity of the consuls was a slippery concept: "The event drew attention to the in-bred, endogamous consular world in provincial Ottoman towns. Henry Abbot, the murdered German consul was a Greek speaking Levantine who had become a British subject only in 1872, Jules Moulin, the murdered French Consul had married his sister. The US consul, Perikles Hadji-Lazaro, was a Bulgarian of Russian nationality, whose brother in law was the physician of the Russian Embassy in Istanbul and an uncle of the Russian consular agent in Larissa".

[122] Mark Mazower, *Salonica: City of Ghosts* (London, 2004), p. 172.

[123] Ibid.

deputation that "this was an affair for the authorities and that they should disperse", promising the delivery of the girl.[124] The mob then repaired to the nearby mosque, the Saatli Cami (the Clocktower Mosque). At this point the French and German consuls appeared on the scene. Although Mazower maintains that the "French and German consuls happened by ill luck to walk by the mosque", the Ottoman documentation contradicts this and shows that the consuls deliberately came to the mosque.[125] Salim Bey, the chief of police, saw them approaching the mosque in the company of Captain Hasan Efendi; "he called out to him, scolding him, saying 'why do you bring the consuls here at a time like this?'" Evidently the consuls had asked the Ottoman officer to accompany them to the mosque.[126]

The character of Jules Moulin, the French consul, played a fatal role in the story. Gradeva and Kuneralp characterize him as a "Gallic Firebrand" who "tended to behave more like a colonial administrator than a consular agent". Moulin, together with the German consul, Yanko Abbot, turned up at the mosque and proceeded to revile the already very angry and dangerous mob; "it was Moulin's impetuousness and hot-headedness that cost him his own life and that of the German consul".[127] Hearing that the consuls were then taken hostage by the mob, the Vali immediately went to the mosque and was shut up in the same room as the consuls, with only a handful of police guarding them. He tried to reason with the mob, but they told him, "[W]e will kill you all, we want the girl".[128] According to the Ottoman memorandum:

[The members of the mob] climbed up through the metal bars outside, and came up the stairs, breaking off the iron bars of the windows and, overpowering the few police officers, they burst into the room. The consuls were killed by blows from iron bars and pieces of chairs, the Vali also received a blow to the head and was briefly knocked senseless.[129]

After recovering and finding that the consuls had been murdered, Refet Paşa ordered Salim Bey to "guard the bodies" as he returned to the *Konak*. By this time the girl had been produced, and hearing that she had been released and had arrived at the *Konak*, the mob dispersed, firing shots in

---

[124] BOA HR.SYS 16/293, 7 August 1876, memorandum on the grievous Salonica incident (*Selanik Vak`a–i müellimesi*). My thanks to Sinan Kuneralp for bringing this file to my attention.

[125] Mazower, *Salonica*, p. 172.

[126] BOA HR/SYS 16/293.

[127] Gradeva and Kuneralp, *On Love, Religion and Politics*, p. 6.

[128] BOA HR.SYS 16/293.

[129] See Plate 3 and Plate 8.

celebration.[130] Meanwhile, what were the security forces of the second-largest city of the empire doing while their governor was being beaten about the head by an angry mob? Even the polite official language of the Ottoman document cannot hide their sheer incompetence. Salim Bey explained the delay in his bringing troops to scene as a result of "not having written orders". The captain of the Ottoman corvette, the *İclaliye*, did land a party of marines but, for reasons that are unclear, marched them to the garrison barracks and not to the mosque. When he did get to the garrison where he met Ata Bey, the corporal of cavalry, they "had quite a long conversation about how all the consuls of the city should protest the improper behaviour of the American consul" rather than rushing soldiers to the scene.[131] The chief of police, Salim Bey, Corporal of Cavalry Ata Bey, and the captain of the *İclaliye* were all found guilty by the court-martial of various degrees of "slackness and negligence of duty". Salim Bey and Ata Bey were sentenced to being stripped of their rank; to being expelled from the police force and the army, respectively; and to serve sentences of ten and five years, respectively, of "fortress imprisonment". Riza Bey got off relatively lightly with forty-five days' imprisonment and suspension from the navy for one year.[132]

The consequences of the event for the Ottoman state were dire. Although the sultan immediately sent his ADC to the French and German embassies to present his condolences, and a commission of enquiry did arrive forthwith at Salonica, what was at issue was the prestige of the Great Powers. This was symbolized by the warships from various countries that anchored off Salonica and trained their guns on the citadel. The ultimate insult of the French naval squadron not firing the customary salute to the citadel was avoided at the last moment.[133] As aptly put by Mazower: "The symbolic power of the 1876 murders lay precisely in the fact that the victims were consuls, members of perhaps the most privileged political class in Salonica".[134] An imperial commission of enquiry, headed by Vahakn Efendi, an eminent member of the Istanbul Armenian

[130] BOA HR.SYS 16/293, memorandum based on the proceedings of the court-martial of the police chief (*Alay Beyi*), Salim Bey, Corporal of Cavalry Ata Bey, and the captain of the ship *İclaliye*, Riza Bey. Presided over by *Ferik* Necip Paşa.

[131] Ibid.

[132] Ibid.

[133] TNA, FO 195/1107, 14 May 1876, British Consul Blunt to Sir Henry Elliot. Blunt commented on the unwillingness of the French squadron to salute the citadel: "The etiquette question was most inappropriate and I may say improper". Blunt enclosed a list of the warships in the port. Of the total of fourteen ships, only six were Ottoman.

[134] Mazower, *Salonica*, p. 176.

community, and a high-ranking bureaucrat, arrived and soon earned the respect of the foreign community, even if it had to tread lightly to avoid antagonizing the Muslim population.[135] Thirty-five arrests were made; the accused were tried, and six were hung publicly, with the boats from the warships of the foreign powers standing offshore to bear witness. The French ambassador at the Sublime Porte, De Bourgoing, even asked for capital punishment for Refet Paşa, but Paşa was simply demoted. Meanwhile, Abdülhamid II had acceded to the Ottoman throne on 24 August. His coronation gift was to try to find the FF 900,000 compensation that the Ottoman state was forced to pay as compensation to the families of the two consuls.[136]

The basic, and obvious, question is the following: how did the conversion to Islam of a young peasant girl precipitate a major diplomatic crisis? The question is all the more relevant when we bear in mind that in the cases mentioned earlier, also occurring in the Vilayet of Salonica and also involving the conversion of young Christians and meddling consuls, nothing remotely similar happened.[137] The answer must lie in the historical context. The events coincided with the outbreak of the Bulgarian crisis, which was to lead to Gladstone's famous pamphlet "The Bulgarian Horrors".[138] Tension was high, and rumour abounded:

The Bulgarian insurrection actually broke out just three days before the killing of the consuls in Salonica; rumours of the rising had reached the city, together with reports of outrages on Muslim villagers and of plans to drive them from their homes.[139]

---

[135] FO 195/1107, 11 May, Blunt to Elliot: "I believe that the Commission are acting cautiously with regard to the arrests." It is significant that the Porte should send an Armenian official to head the commission. No doubt this was not accidental, as a high-ranking Christian official would make a good impression on foreign public opinion. Vahakn Efendi (Hovhannes Vahanyan) was a prominent jurist, had served as under-secretary of justice, and had been part of the commission that had drafted the Constitution of 1876. He had also worked with Cevdet Paşa in the Ministry of Justice. See Vartan Artinian, *Osmanlı Devleti'nde Ermeni Anayasası'nin Doğuşu 1839–1863* (The birth of the Armenian constitution in the Ottoman Empire) (Istanbul, 2004), pp. 78, 84, 93, 118. My thanks to Aylin Beşiryan for this information.

[136] Gradeva and Kuneralp, *On Love, Religion and Politics*, p. 7. As the Ottoman treasury was bankrupt it was unable to raise the sum, and Sultan Abdülhamid had to borrow the money from his personal Greek banker, Zarifi.

[137] See above, pp. 85–87.

[138] Magnus, *Gladstone*, p. 242; W. E. Gladstone, *The Bulgarian Horrors and the Question of the East* (London, 1876).

[139] Mazower, *Salonica*, p. 178.

As always in such situations, rumour and word of mouth played a large role in the escalation of the event, with Christians and Muslims feeding off each other. On 16 May the British consul, Blunt, wrote to the vice consul in Kavala that he was pleased to hear that the rumour to the effect that the Muslims of Kavala were planning a "general massacre of the Christians" was unfounded.[140] On 20 May the vice consul in Janina was to report:

At Janina also the authorities took a very sad view of the affair but the mass of the musselmen [sic] in that place did not share the same feeling but on the contrary seemed to think that it served the consuls right for interfering in other peoples' business.[141]

The discrepancy between the feelings of Ottoman officialdom and those of the population at large has to be explained. For senior officialdom, the Salonica affair was indeed "grievous", as it seemed to confirm the worst stereotypes that they were trying desperately to distance themselves from. For the masses of humble folk, however, the issue was seen as a threat to what they held most dear – their honour.[142] To a great extent the feeling of insecurity and wounded honour had to do with the role of women. Women were seen as the repository of a community's honour, and it was not such a huge leap for the honour of the community to become the honour of the nation. For the Christians this was a perfect example of what Irvin Schick has termed "the mobiliz[ing] of centuries old gender and sexual stereotypes in the service of nationalist policies".[143] And this was even more true for Muslims, accustomed as they were to seeing themselves as the ruling element and fearing an imminent Bulgarian insurrection descending upon Salonica. In the immediate wake of the murders, in the atmosphere of general panic, there were very real doubts as to the loyalty of the troops, most of whom, it was feared, sympathized with the mob: "The Salonica Batallion in particular is comprised chiefly of peasants from the adjoining villages who all more or less have friends and business connections with the Mahometan population in this town".[144] What would today be called

[140] FO 195/1107, 16 May 1876, Consul Blunt to Vice Consul Gawelkiewicz in Kavala.
[141] FO 195/1107, 20 May 1876, Vice Consul Blakeney to Consul Blunt.
[142] BOA HR/SYS 16/293. The file includes a list by profession of the arrested and condemned men. They included porters, slaughterhouse workers, menial men at arms (*kavas*), ice salesmen, carpenters, and a barber. It is highly likely that many of the actual culprits were not arrested. As always in cases like this, it was more important for justice to be seen to be done.
[143] Irvin Cemil Schick, "Christian Maidens, Turkish Ravishers", in *Women in the Ottoman Balkans*, p. 295
[144] FO 195/1107, 11 May 1876, Consul Blunt to Sir Henry Elliot.

public opinion was a very real consideration in the planning of the funeral of the consuls. Although the French and some of the other foreign representatives wanted something resembling an occupation, with large numbers of troops landing from the ships in the harbour, Blunt counseled moderation: "[A]ny unnecessary foreign military display at funerals may be dangerous in present critical state of affairs and should be avoided if possible".[145] In the event, the funeral was very carefully stage-managed, with the cortege being led by a company of Ottoman infantry followed by the Vali, Eşref Paşa, and the imperial commissioner, Vahakn Efendi, with the representatives of the foreign community following behind.[146]

Indeed, the various parties were right to worry about Muslim public opinion. The gristly spectacle of the public hangings, in particular, had created a great deal of resentment well beyond the walls of Salonica. On 11 August the Foreign Ministry sent a circular telegramme to the Ottoman embassies in London, Paris, and Berlin. The ambassadors were instructed to make representations at their respective posts to the authorities there, telling them not to insist on further executions: "You are of course aware of the terrible effect that the first six executions had on the population of Salonica and what an echo they created in the whole empire". The ambassadors were instructed to point out that "only time could now calm sentiments" and that new executions would only cause unnecessary provocation. They were to argue that the commutation of the sentences to hard labour for life "would have a much more salutary effect on the public mind . . . then the spectacle of an implacable justice that they do not even see the aim of."[147]

Two of the three officers who were convicted, Salim Bey and Rıza Bey, were exiled to the island of Rhodes. Evidently rumours circulated that they had been received as heroes on the island and were getting preferential treatment in prison. The Mutasarrıf of Rhodes denied this and stated that he had been on the ship that had brought the convicts to Rhodes; "the reason why the notables, officials and population of this place were there on the quay was to meet me merely out of respect for my rank". He

---

[145] FO 195/1107, 10 May 1876, Consul Blunt to Sir Henry Elliot.

[146] FO 195/1107, 20 May 1876, Consul Blunt to Sir Henry Elliot: "Every one admired the energy and goodwill with which the Governor General and the Imperial Commissioner comported themselves to keep order throughout the town and to render every possible honour to the funerals".

[147] BOA HR.SYS 16/293, 11 August 1876, the foreign minister, Safvet Paşa, to imperial embassies in London, Paris and Berlin. The document states that at the time of writing ten men had been executed.

disclaimed the rumour that the population had given the prisoners a heros' welcome. He also denied that Salim Bey had been given private quarters. Rıza Bey was free to walk around the fortress, he said, as he had been given a lighter sentence.[148] As is often the case, what the Ottoman official denied is most likely to be what in fact happened; it is highly likely that the crowd that had turned out to meet the ship was there to do honour to the convicted officers. The Salonica affair had become a cause celèbre and no doubt many thought Salim Bey and Rıza Bey had been sacrificed to foreign pressure.

A remarkable assessment of the background for the Salonica affair was written by the dragoman of the Vilayet, Dimitraki Efendi:

The quite justifiable wish of the Imperial Government to make use of the patriotism of the Muslims to rid itself of its internal enemies and to stifle the Bulgarian revolution, had somewhat over excited the masses in the Vilayet and a marked coldness between Christians and Muslims had been the consequence.[149]

CONVERSION AND APOSTASY IN TURBULENT RUMELI

Well after the "grievous Salonica affair", the Ottoman Balkan provinces – or Rumeli, as the Turks called the region – continued to be a flashpoint of religious and national tensions. A special inspectorate for the Vilayets of Rumeli (*Rumeli Vilayatı Müfettiş-i Umumiliği*) was created in 1903 and headed by one of the empire's most distinguished statesmen, Hüseyin Hilmi Paşa, with the task of carrying out the census in Ottoman Macedonia.[150] In this tense milieu, and against the general backdrop of the Macedonian Crisis, conversion and apostasy cases can be seen as a microcosm of broader national tensions.[151]

On 9 January 1903 the Vilayet of Yanya reported that two converts, a boy and a girl named Vasil and Katrina, had caused a commotion in the *kaza* of Losna. Although they were both over fifteen, and therefore above the minimum legal age for conversion, and although their conversions

[148] BOA HR.SYS 16/293, 1 Kanun-u Evvel 1292 / 14 December 1876, the Mutasarrif of Rhodes to the Sublime Porte.
[149] Ibid., 25 October 1876, report by the dragoman of the Vilayet of Selanik, Dimitraki Yenidunia, to His Excellency Safvet Paşa, foreign minister.
[150] Ipek Yosmaoğlu, "Counting Bodies, Shaping Souls: The 1903 Census and National Identity in Ottoman Macedonia", *IJMES* 38 (2006), 55–77.
[151] On the background to the "Eastern Rumelian Crisis", see F. A. K. Yasamee, *Ottoman Diplomacy: Abdülhamid II and the Great Powers 1878–1888* (Istanbul, 1996), pp. 153–78.

had been carried out in the *kaza* council according to the proper procedure, in the presence of the delegate of the Greek Metropolitan, as soon as
they came out of the government building the delegate had proceeded to
cause a commotion. He had "claimed that the conversions were forced
and had provoked the Christians, of whom there were many, being
market day, saying 'there is no government' [these children have been
forced]".[152] The crowd had surged against the security forces, but an
incident had been averted. The Mutasarrıf of Berat (in present-day
Albania) had reported that the delegate was probably acting at the behest
of the Greek consul at Berat, who had encouraged him to stage a
provocation.[153]

A remarkable aspect of this affair was that the Greek consul at Berat had
made no official *démarche*. The Ottoman authorities knew about his
intentions because, as a subsequent cipher telegramme from Yanya stated,
"we have had access to the correspondence between them". To put it
plainly, they had intercepted the telegrammes sent by a member of the
diplomatic corps.[154] The Vali of Yanya did, however, have the presence of
mind to declare, "Although we should utterly reject the intervention of the
Consul in matters beyond his authority, this much commotion cannot be
without cause and we should closely look into the matter to see if anything
untoward has come to pass".[155]

A few days later another telegramme from the Greek consul was intercepted, claiming that the Christian girl had changed her mind about
converting and had been replaced by an impostor, a Muslim girl who
had been presented to the commission of inquiry in her stead. The Porte
evidently took these claims very seriously, and on 21 January the Vali of
Yanya was ordered to intensify his investigations, because

although what the Consul claims is highly unlikely, his claims cannot be entirely
without foundation, even the rumour of such events, leave alone their actual

---

[152] BOA DH.MKT 829/60, 27 Kanun-u Evvel 1319 / 9 January 1903, the Vilayet of Yanya to
the Ministry of the Interior. This voluminous file contains some fifty folios of correspondence relating to the investigations carried out by Hüseyin Hilmi Paşa, inspector of Rumeli.

[153] Ibid. The Vilayet had ordered that a commission of inquiry consisting of one Muslim and
one non-Muslim member be sent.

[154] Ibid.

[155] Ibid. Enclosing a telegramme from the Greek consul of Berat to the Greek consul at
Monastir: "*Consulat de Grece Monastir. Fille et jeune homme mineure sont detenus aux
zapita de Leoussian autorite locale refuse de les remettre a Metropole et cherche les
convertir emotion generale. Veuillez prevenir Excellence Hilmi Pacha. Counsul Berat
Svoronos*".

occurrence, is not to be tolerated. We must not give our enemies the slightest excuse to attack us.[156]

Meanwhile, tension between the Muslim and Christian communities was mounting. According to the Vali of Yanya, the intrigues of the consul and the delegate of the Metropolitan were the result of "national feeling (*hissiyat-ı milliye*)".[157]

A few comments are in order here. First, the Porte clearly sensed that something suspicious was indeed going on, hence the order to "secretly investigate further". Second, in noting the intervention of the Metropolitan delegate based on "national feelings" (*hissiyat-i milliye saikasiyla*"), the Porte was well aware that the issue was far broader than the conversion of two adolescents. The way in which the conversions of obscure figures could become considerations in high politics is observable in the suggestion of the Vilayet of Yanya that no further measures be taken given that "this would only further enflame Greek public opinion that is presently in a great state of excitement over the Bulgarian issue".[158] The conversion of two obscure adolescents had thus become an international crisis involving the Porte, the kingdom of Greece, and the local Ottoman Greek (*Rum*) community.

One year later the matter still had not been settled. Osman Fevzi Paşa was to write on 29 March 1904 that Vasil and Katrina, now called Ismail and Hamide, had been living in the house of a certain Bayram from Losna. However, they had been "threatened by the Christians and have now escaped". Vasil had taken refuge in the Greek consulate in Berat, while Katrina had sought sanctuary with the local Metropolitan. It was the intention of both to commit apostasy.[159] The Vali referred to a previous correspondence with the Ministry of Justice, where "it was made clear that in the case of those who chose to commit apostasy the procedure is to remove them to another location". He also pointed out that as both the boy and the girl were Ottoman subjects, it was highly irregular for the Greek consul and the Metropolitan to give them refuge.[160]

---

[156] Ibid., 8 Kanun-u Sani 1319 / 21 January 1903, the Sublime Porte, Ministry of the Interior, to the Vilayet of Yanya.

[157] Ibid., 12 Kanun-u Sani 1319 / 25 January 1903, the Vali of Yanya to the Sublime Porte.

[158] Ibid., 1 February 1903, the Sublime Porte to the Vilayet of Yanya. The words used here are "*Yunan efkâr-ı umumiyesi*", meaning citizens of Greece rather than Ottoman Greeks (*Rum*).

[159] Ibid., 16 Mart 1320 / 29 March 1904. Cipher telegramme from the Vilayet of Yanya to the Sublime Porte. The names Vasil and Katrina suggest that the converts in question may have been of Slavic origin.

[160] Ibid.

The concern was, as always, foreign meddling in their religious affairs:

[It] is extremely necessary that no ground or excuse be given for censure on the part of foreigners and that they be prevented from carrying their interference as far as our religious affairs.[161]

The case of Vasil and Katrina evidently came across the desk of no less a personage than the Grand Vizier, Ferit Paşa, who wrote to the Ministry of the Interior, telling them that he had made the necessary *démarches* with the Greek embassy in Istanbul and the Patriarchate. The embassy had agreed to instruct the consul at Berat to hand Vasil over to the Ottoman authorities. Ferit Paşa made it very clear that when the pair were handed back, as confirmed apostates, "they should be removed from their locality and sent to a suitable place to avoid causing the excitement of the Muslim population".[162]

The file that these documents come from also contains a detailed report by the inspectorate for the Vilayets of Rumeli detailing some fifteen cases of abducted girls and forced conversions occurring in the year 1903.[163] In the majority of the cases the abducted girls were returned to their families and the culprits given prison sentences. However, in cases where the girls had been forced into Islam but had subsequently married Muslim men, the authorities were reticent about pursuing the matter. In these cases the formula always went as follows: "[A]fter conversion and marriage it is no longer in the public interest, nor is it wise to carry out further investigations. The complainants are to be given suitable answers and the matter closed".[164] Evidently the authorities were reluctant to transgress the sanctity of the household as this would raise more hackles with the Muslim population.

CONCLUSION

In examining the rather opaque documentary story of Ottoman conversion policy and ideological control in the late Ottoman era, the interesting thing is precisely what the documents do *not* tell us. The constant repetition of orders "not to do something" is a fairly clear indication that the undesirable act was in fact being committed. Forced conversion, although

---

[161] Ibid.
[162] Ibid., 23 May 1322 / 5 June 1904, Grand Vizier Ferit Paşa to the Ministry of the Interior, Sublime Porte Secretariat No. 913.
[163] Ibid., report by the Inspectorate of Vilayets of Rumeli.
[164] Ibid.

repeatedly banned by the centre, was in fact taking place. The impression derived from the documentary evidence is one of worry verging on panic among the Ottoman elite; set upon by ambassadors, consuls, missionaries, and sundry other meddlers, they were finding it increasingly hard to retain their ultimate sovereignty. The fact that the *Hat-ı Humayun* of 1856 was seen, quite rightly, as a foreign imposition by no less a personage than Reşid Paşa himself, and his warning that it would raise the expectations of the *reaya* to unsustainable levels is worth remembering in this context. In the increasingly cramped space between foreign pressure, the religious sensitivities of their own subjects, and (last but by no means least) their own sincere conviction that a fundamental revamping of the state ideology was vital, the Ottoman élite desperately strove to remain masters in their own home.

The eloquent example of Ziver Bey, who emphasized that even something as straightforward as the setting up of a community coffer for needy converts had to be kept secret from "foreign bigots", speaks volumes about this feeling of being restricted in their own domain. On the other hand, in the mindset of the diplomats and missionaries, the sheer effrontery of a Christian envoy preaching about the Qur'an to the Caliph of Islam, or the gall of missionaries provoking recent Turkish converts to publicly denounce Mohammed as a false prophet in the capital city of the Caliphate, did not seem abnormal to most people in the West, so firmly convinced were they of the superiority of their "civilisation". To say that missionaries going around the capital city publicly insulting the dominant official religion were causing "a certain effervescence" was the height of conceit.

By the second half of the century the wielders of the "artillery of heaven", unlike the earlier American missionaries operating in Ottoman Lebanon in the 1820s, no longer felt the need to "placat[e] Ottoman rulers by avoiding Muslims" and focusing on Eastern Christians.[165]

An imperial order dated 1 August 1897 clearly reflects the concerns of the centre as it provides for the constitution of a mixed commission whose specific brief was

to prevent the spread of the influence of foreigners and to ensure that each remains in his own confession, and to prevent the conversion of His Imperial Majesty's subjects to Protestantism as well as other foreign creeds.

[165] Makdisi, *The Artillery of Heaven*, p. 100.

The commission was to be made up of three Muslim officials (one each from the Şeyhulislam's office, the Ministry of Education, and the Ministry of the Interior), two Armenians, and one Greek Orthodox.[166]

The cases discussed here also illustrate that conversion and apostasy cases had become symbolically loaded issues as they overlapped with nationalist agendas on the part of former subject peoples, such as the Greeks, as well as those of peoples beginning to agitate for autonomy or independence, such as the Serbs and Bulgarians. In the 1903 census in Macedonia some villagers had actually wanted to be registered as belonging to the Serbian denomination (*Sırb mezhebi*) but had been told that this was out of the question because "Serbness is not a denomination but a nationality (*Sırblık bir mezheb olmayub milliyet bulunduğuna*)".[167] As in the case of the Salonica affair, the people involved became symbols of national honour: the contested girl symbolizing the honour of the Christians and Muslims, and the Ottoman officials, who were perceived as having become scapegoats for the ire of the foreigners, becoming heroes defending the national honour of the Ottomans.

In the event, the number of Muslim conversions to Christianity remained minimal, but this was not something that could have been taken for granted at the time. As far as the missionaries were concerned, the Ottoman state gave as good as it got. The memorandum prepared by the sultan for Ahmed Şakir Paşa reflected this state of mind: "Although the Sublime State cannot force anyone to accept Islam, we can never tolerate the conversion of Muslims to Christianity."[168]

On the other hand, the official declaration by the highest authorities in the land that each Ottoman subject was free to practice whatever religion he or she chose, together with the spreading belief that the death penalty was no longer the punishment for apostates, was to have some unforeseen results. Right across the empire there emerged, men and women who had been officially Muslims, but who now declared that they had been secretly Christian all along and wanted to be recognized as such.

---

[166] BOA, Irade Hususi 123, 3 Rebiyülahir 1315 / 1 August 1897, Yıldız Palace Imperial Secretariat No. 3659.

[167] Yosmaoğlu, "Counting Bodies", p. 65.

[168] BOA. YEE A-24/X/24/132, 28 Kanun-u Evvel 1314 / 11 January 1898, decoded cipher telegramme from Yıldız Palace to Ahmet Şakir Paşa.

3

"Crypto-Christianity"

'I have held the said Gasparo to be a Marrano. And we hold Marranos to be those who, like ships, sail with two rudders'.

Venetian Rabbi Chain Saruc's testimony before the Inquisitional Tribunal of Venice (1580)[1]

'Turkish stupidity, or rather perhaps Turkish indifference to what lay beneath the surface so long as appearances were more or less kept up ... Thus arose the bodies of the so-called Crypto-Christians'.

R. M. Dawkins, "The Crypto-Christians of Turkey"[2]

CRYPTO-CHRISTIANS AND THE REFORM EDICT OF 1856

Simultaneously with the events described in the last two chapters, across a broad geographic region ranging from Albania to the Pontus on the Black Sea coast, people emerged, taking the official declaration of religious freedom at its word, to announce that in their hearts they had never been Muslims and had secretly adhered to their former (Christian) faith. As the historical and political conjuncture changed from the relatively liberal Tanzimat State to the much more authoritarian conservative rule of the Hamidian State, crypto-Christianity came to be seen as even more of an aberration.

Anthony Bryer, in his seminal study of crypto-Christianity, was to observe that after the Crimean War, when the British and French became

---

[1] Anthony Molho, "Jews and Marranos Before the Law: Five Mediterranean Stories", *GRAMMA* 6 (1998), 13–30.
[2] R. M. Dawkins, "The Crypto-Christians of Turkey", *Byzantion* 8 (1933), 247–75.

the self-appointed guarantors of the Christian populations of the empire, "What the Allies had not bargained for was the number of supposed Christians, supposedly registered as Muslims, who now emerged out of the woodwork to declare themselves under British and French – and Russian – protection".[3] The people who emerged as secret Christians were spread over the entire Ottoman Empire and were known by a number of names, such as "*meso-meso, paramesoi,* and *dipistia* in Greek; in Serbia *droverstsvo;* in Cyprus *patsalosi* (piebalds), *apostolikoi* (wild carobs) or *linovamvakoi* (linen-cottons); in Albania *laramanoi* (motleys)". Bryer was to note some of their most typical common characteristics:

'Nineteenth-century accounts of the crypto-Christians after they had emerged have the air of well worn anecdote, but are consistent. They had held double names, Christian and Muslim (where Mehmet and Ali were avoided). They were baptized and kept fasts, but underwent *sünnet* (circumcision) and had two marriages, with a Christian *koumbaros* and a Muslim master of ceremonies. Their daughters did not marry out and Muslim brides brought in were secretly baptized. They went to the mosque in Ramadan; sometimes they were buried in a Muslim cemetery even – but with simultaneous Christian service. . . . Elsewhere the crypto-Christians had a cant language [and used it] in front of real Muslims they referred to swine as their "parents-in-law".[4]

One of the definitive factors in the religious strategy of Ottoman crypto-Christians was military service. Although after the Tanzimat reforms it had become accepted in principle that all Ottoman subjects would perform military service, in practice the process was delayed. The main reason was the obvious reluctance on the part of the non-Muslim population, who did their best to avoid military service. Another very important factor in this delay was the reluctance of the Muslim officialdom to accept such a measure. Yet the principle remained the rule even if it was not applied. The first service to admit Christians was the navy, which readmitted Ottoman Greeks in 1845 after they had been purged during the Greek War of Independence. In 1850 it was decided that non-Muslims would be admitted to the Military Academy. In 1856 it was decided to postpone the conscription of non-Muslims, and it was determined that they would pay a "military donation" (*bedel-i askeri*), in effect an exemption tax. Effective conscription in all the services was actually implemented in 1910. [5]

---

[3] Anthony Bryer, "The Crypto-Christians of the Pontos and Consul William Gifford Palgrave of Trebizond", *Deltio Kentrou Mikrasiatikon Spoudon*, Bulletin of the Centre for Asia Minor Studies, Athens (*DELTIO*) 4 (1983), 15.

[4] Ibid., pp. 16, 21.

[5] On the issue of military service, see Eric-Jan Zurcher, "The Ottoman Conscription System in Theory and Practice", *International Review of Social History* 43 (1998), 439–40. For a

The phenomenon of crypto-Christianity and the official reaction to it was also overdetermined by the realities of international power politics discussed in the previous two chapters. Of the two major cases to be examined here, the Kromilides were to openly declare their Christianity in the relatively more tolerant context of the Tanzimat State, whereas the Stavriote declaration coincided with the more self-consciously Islamic regime of the Hamidian period.

Another factor relating to crypto-Christianity was of course geography. Most crypto-Christian communities were to be found in the mountains or other remote areas, where the established orthodoxies were not able to penetrate or penetrated only superficially. As the great Fernand Braudel declared, "In the mountains then, civilization is never stable"; hill peoples resisted or yielded only superficially to established religion and had to be constantly conquered anew.[6]

A fascinating recent study by Yorgos Tzedopoulos makes the connection between this "coming out" process all over the empire and the "Tanzimat reforms ... which granted religious freedom and made conversion possible, at least theoretically for Muslims."[7] This placed the Ottoman administration in a serious quandary. On the one hand, it had indeed promised religious freedom to its subjects; on the other hand, there seems to have been a genuine fear that apostasy from Islam would become so widespread as to threaten the state itself.[8] The term "apostasy" is used deliberately here, for as far as the Ottomans were concerned, the people in question were becoming apostates from Islam, which only recently had been a crime punishable by death. As seen earlier, the Sultan had officially banned the execution of apostates, yet the social stigma, albeit reduced, was still very powerful among the population at large.[9] Indeed, apostasy and crypto-Christianity were seen almost as a contagious disease that had to be kept

more detailed study, see Ufuk Gülsoy, *Osmanlı Gayrımüslimlerinin Askerlik Serüveni* (The military service adventures of the Ottoman non-Muslims) (Istanbul, 2000).

[6] Fernand Braudel, *The Mediterranean and the Mediterranean World in the Age of Philip II* (London, 1972), vol. 1, pp. 34–5.

[7] Yorgos Tzedopoulos, "Public Secrets: Crypto-Christianity in the Pontos", *DELTIO* 16 (2009), 165.

[8] Their worries were not without grounds. The Protestant missionaries believed that crypto-Christianity was a good way of evangelizing among Muslims: "It is the conviction of a large number of workers among Moslems that the ultimate hope of bringing Christ to the Moslems is to be attained by the development of groups of followers of Jesus who are active in making Him known to others while remaining loyally a part of the social and political groups to which they belong in Islam." See, James Thayer Addison, *The Christian Approach to the Muslim* (New York, 1942), p. 305.

[9] See Chapter 1 in this volume.

in check. Even before the Reform Edict openly declared religious freedom, there had been a spate of apostasy in Rumeli. On 11 March 1844, the Müşir of Rumeli, Mehmed Reşid Paşa, reported that in Noveberde in the *sancak* of Niş, three Christians who had some time earlier converted to Islam had reverted to Christianity. The Paşa made sure to stress that "apostates of this nature are numerous in those parts and the matter may infect others".[10]

This did indeed seem to be happening, in the new atmosphere of promised religious freedom, as one group after another came forward and declared that they had always been Christian. Antonina Zhelyazkova has noted that some Albanian Catholics had adopted Islam only in order to avoid paying the *cizye* (poll tax). They secretly continued to observe their old customs, and in remote areas the local priests allowed them to take part in services. Men took communion in secret and married Christian women, "declaring that they did not want the name of Christ to leave their homes for good".[11] These people now declared that they wanted to worship openly as Christians. Similar practices were seen among the formerly Orthodox of Ispat, Berat, Skopje, and Montenegro.

Stavro Skendi also records the curious case of the Shparataks, from the region of Shpat northeast of Berat and near Elbasan, who seemed to actually "shop around" for religious faith depending on which was more advantageous at the time. The Shparataks were Albanian crypto-Christians who had two names, a public Muslim one and a private Orthodox Christian one. As far as the Ottomans were concerned, they were Muslim, and in 1832 the Ottoman government ordered them to arms. At this point they decided to cast off the cover of Islam and declared that they were Christians. For reasons that are unclear, Skendi seems unsure of his source, which declares that because of "good administration" the authorities tolerated the situation. "Was it because the Ottoman government, tired of the 1821 Greek Revolution, wanted to prevent Albanian revolts or was it because it was on the road to the reforms of 1839?"[12] The Shparataks came under pressure again in 1846, when the

---

[10] BOA Irade Dahiliye 4627, 19 Safer 1260 / 11 March 1844, Müşir of Rumeli Mehmed Reşid Paşa to the *Serasker* (commander-in-chief). Nonetheless, the measure taken was no worse than their imprisonment.

[11] Antonina Zhelyazkova, "Islamization in the Balkans as an Historiographical Problem: The Southeast European Perspective", in Fikret Adanır and Suraiya Faroghi (eds.), *The Ottomans and the Balkans: A Discussion of Historiography* (Leiden, 2002), pp. 244–5.

[12] Stavro Skendi, "Crypto Christianity in the Balkan Area under the Ottomans", *Slavic Review* 26 (1967), 227–46; see Natalie Clayer, *Religion et Nation chez les Albanais XIX–XX e Siècles* (Istanbul, 2002).

law of conscription was applied in Albania and the Ottoman authorities demanded that the Albanian provinces provide their quota of recruits. Again they protested that they were Christians. The residents of Eşbat (as the Ottomans called the region) appear once again in 1889, when a series of reports stated that they numbered some 4,000 souls, 1,600 of whom professed Islam in public but practiced Christianity in private. The reports stated that "this was well known by the Ottoman administration". They had always performed military service. The worry as expressed in the reports was that this new trend to profess Christianity openly in public could spread to the other villages in the area. What is interesting here is that, as will be seen later in the cases of the Kromlides and the Istavri, what had been common knowledge in the pre-Tanzimat period and had not constituted a problem, became a political problem in the Hamidian era: "It appears that to leave the state of Crypto-Christianity and to declare publicly Christian faith was perceived by the Ottoman administration as an act of political disloyalty ... with the growth of non-Muslim nationalisms."[13]

The matter came up again in 1897, when the governor of Elbasan asked them to make up their minds – to serve in the army if they were Muslims, or to pay taxes if they were Christians. At this point the Shpataraks decided to declare that they would become Uniates enjoying the protection of Austria-Hungary. The Shparataks then became a bone of contention between the Porte, who wanted to keep them as loyal Muslim subjects; Austria, which somewhat reluctantly gave them support; and Russia, which did not want to lose an Orthodox Balkan population.[14]

A Bulgarian source indicates that in at least one case a Christian population was punished for "coming out". Several villagers in Skopska Crna Gora who had been crypto-Christians "trusted the *Hat-ı Şerif* and came out into the open as Christians". Despite declarations of religious freedom, the villagers were exiled to Anatolia. As a result of the intervention of the ambassadors of the Great Powers the exile was lifted, and they were allowed to return. During their exile and return they were subjected to ill-treatment, and half of them perished. All this happened in the 1840s, "[at] the time that Mustafa Reşid Paşa was solemnly affirming that the empire was on the road to Europeanization and modernization. One had

---

[13] Akşin Somel, "The Problem of Crypto-Christians in Albania during the Hamidian Period", in his *South East Europe in History: The Past, the Present and the Problems of Balkanology* (Ankara, 1999) pp 117–24.

[14] Skendi, "Crypto Christianity in the Balkan Area under the Ottomans", p. 241 and n. 67.

to admit nonetheless that a certain measure of 'progress' had taken place, at least all these people were not massacred on the spot for having rejected Islam."[15]

Particularly important groups of crypto-Christians were the Hemşinli, who were Armenians from the Pontos who inhabited the coast and the mountain fastness in the north-east Black Sea region.[16] The Hemşinli had been forced to convert in the late seventeenth and early eighteenth centuries; some had continued to worship Apostolic Christianity secretly. These people were known as the *kes-kes* (Armenian for "half-and-half"). They spoke Armenian and until the late nineteenth century secretly celebrated the Transfiguration of Christ (*Vartavar*) and baptized their children with holy water (*miwron*). After the Reform Edict of 1856, some Hemşinli living in the Karadere region east of Trabzon attempted to revert to their old faith.[17] They broached their intention to their local *ağa*, Suiçmezoğlu, who assented and told them to make a list of the families who wanted to return to Christianity. When three officials from Istanbul came to Sürmene, the matter was put before them. At this point the *mollahs* from Of, a neighbouring region inhabited by Laz, famous for their Muslim zeal, intervened and stated that if the Hemşinli were allowed to revert, so should they, as they had been converted from Greek Orthodoxy. The ploy worked, as the officials, fearing the scandal of the prospect of the famous "*hocas* from Of" (*Oflu Hoca*) becoming apostates, hurriedly left the area promising to return, but never did. Both the Greeks and the Muslims claimed the Oflis, the first as early martyrs, the latter as a legendary mass conversion. What Michael Meeker observes regarding the Oflis is valid for crypto faiths in general at this historical conjuncture: "These older traditions acquired a new colouring with the advance of a nationalist outlook and expectation during the second half of the nineteenth century".[18]

---

[15] A. Velkov, E. Radusev, E. Siljanova, M. Kalicin, and A. Radusev, *Sources Ottomanes sur le Processus d'Islamisation aux Balkans (XIV–XIX siècles). Traduction des documents* (Sofia, 1990), pp. 33–4. My translation, with thanks to Maria Todorova for checking the bibliographical details.

[16] Claire Mouradian, "Aperçus sur l'Islamization des Arméniens dans l'Empire Ottoman: le cas des Hamchentsi/Hemşinli". Paper presented at the conference Conversion to Islam in the Mediterranean World, Rome, 4–6 September 1997. Cited with permission of the author.

[17] Hovann H. Simonian, "Hemshin from Islamicization to the End of the Nineteenth Century", in Hovann Simonian (ed.), *The Hemshin: History, Society and Identity in the Highlands of Northeast Turkey* (London, 2007), pp. 52–99.

[18] The image of the "Hoca from Of" (*Oflu Hoca*) has become a Turkish stereotype for zealous, even bigoted, Islamic faith. The region is even today reputed to produce Islamic clerics; as the saying goes, "Of (only?) produces *Hocas*" (*Of 'dan hoca çıkar*). Anthony

Nonetheless, some Hemşinli families did revert to Christianity in 1858. Another wave of apostasy is recorded by the British Consul Palgrave in 1869. This involved a group of converted Armenians living in the Yomra district, closer to Trabzon. Palgrave told his superior, Ambassador Henry Elliot, that the intended apostates had given him a petition claiming that if they were successful, some 2,000 families would emulate them. Palgrave also stated that their only aim was to avoid military service. Their plans did not work because, together with the families who had become apostates in the late 1850s, they were put in the category of *tanassur* (convert to Christianity) and told that the acceptance of their new status as Christians did not excuse them from military service.[19]

Simonian makes the following telling point: "In the conservative milieu of the Pontos, religious and secular authorities did not share the liberal ideas coming from Istanbul. Not only did they not display any zeal in implementing the new reforms, but often they did their best to obstruct them".[20] The observation of the intrepid traveler Edith Durham regarding the Albanians can be said of crypto-Christians in general: "The ground fact is this. The North Albanian tribesman is an Albanian first. He has never absorbed the higher teaching of either Christianity or Islam. ... Christ and Mohammed are to him two super natural 'magic dickies', each able, if propitiated, to work wonders."[21] Evidently a considerable number of people hitherto considered Muslim now chose to declare that they had been something else all along. Or, in another manner of speaking, they wanted to opt for a very different "magic dickie".

Bryer also noted their zeal. See Anthony Bryer, "Nineteenth Century Monuments in the City and Vilayet of Trebizond: Architectural and Historical Notes", *Archeion Pontou* 29 (1968–69), particularly pp. 109–10, n. 3: "The Oflis are among the curiosities of Lazistan. They were supposedly Greeks who were said to have converted to Islam. ... Whatever the truth of this oft-quoted story, the Oflis combine a fanatical devotion to Islam with the retention of the Pontic Greek dialect". On the overlap of religion and nationalism in the case of the Oflis, see Michael E. Meeker, "Greeks Who Are Muslims: Counter Nationalism in Nineteenth Century Trabzon", in David Shankland (ed.), *Archeology, Anthropology and Heritage in the Balkans and Anatolia: The Life and Times of F. W. Hasluck, 1978–1920* (Istanbul, 2004), p. 309:

[19] Simonian, "Hemshin", p. 76. As will be seen later, this was the same category that was applied to the neighbouring Kromlides in precisely the same period. It seems to have been a general pre-emptive policy.

[20] Ibid., p. 77.

[21] M. Edith Durham, *High Albania* (London, 1909), p. 313.

TWO SPECTACULAR CASES OF CRYPTO-CHRISTIANITY:
THE KROMLIDES OF THE PONTOS AND THE STAVRIOTES
OF AKDAĞ MADEN

One of the most interesting instances of revelation of crypto-Christianity occurred in the eastern Pontus, in the region of Kromni, a mountainous area between Trabzon and Gümüşhane (Argyroupoli). The Kromlides were Greek-speaking Muslims who in 1857 declared their Christian identity and claimed the right to be recognized as Orthodox.[22]

Yorgos Andreadis claims that the Kromlides community had intended to declare their Christianity in the immediate wake of the declaration of the Gülhane Edict of 1839, but had been advised by the Metropolitans of Trabzon and Chaldea not to be in too much of a hurry as it was unclear whether the rights granted to Christians extended to the crypto-Christians: "It had not been said anywhere that Muslims could abandon their religion and take another". The debate between the Kromlides and the Metropolitans lasted five years; "the Metropolitans knew about the fate of the Armenians who had declared themselves. The state had imprisoned them". In 1843, while an Armenian apostate was in the process of being tried in the court of Trabzon, the Metropolitans counseled prudence and told the Kromlides' leader, Molla Süleyman, to await the outcome of the trial. The Armenian was convicted of apostasy and executed. This was too much for the octogenarian community leader, Molla Süleyman, who collapsed on hearing the news.[23]

The Kromlides (Kurumlu in Turkish) were a silver-mining community inhabiting fifteen villages that had converted to Islam sometime in the mid-seventeenth century.[24] Andreadis claims that for centuries the Kromni had practiced Islam in public and Christianity in private, usually in secret chapels hidden under big houses (*konak*). The Krumi, as he calls them,

---

[22] Tzedopoulos, "Public Secrets", p. 169.

[23] Yorgo Andreadis, *Gizli Din Taşıyanlar* (Those with a secret religion) (Istanbul, 1999), pp. 66–7. Originally published as *Oi Klostoi* (Thessaloniki, 1995). The author is a descendant of a Kromlides family, and the book is based partly on the oral history accounts of his grandmother, Sophia Yazıcıoğlu/Grammatikopoulos, who was the granddaughter of Molla Süleyman, the community leader at the time of the declaration of the Kromlides. This is a very useful book, although there are no sources indicated, and the layout is somewhat amateurish. Andreadis gives population figures of 6,000–10,000 in Kromni and 60,000 in Argyroupoli. It is interesting that Andreadis should mention Armenians, who were probably the Hemşinli. It is also natural that the Metropolitans would have news of the tribulations of another Christian community in the same region.

[24] Ibid., p. 14. Andreadis states that the Kromlides must have converted around 1650.

were by no means a marginal community; in fact, they were the notables and élite of the region. The "overt Christians" were supported by the crypto-Christians in their dealings with Ottoman officials, who were not too intrusive as the miners were seen as a somewhat privileged community who supplied an essential service and in return were exempted from military service. The Muslim religious leaders, the *mollas*, were also the Orthodox priests. Baptisms and other Orthodox observances were carried out secretly, and outwardly, Andreadis claims, the Kromlides were indistinguishable from Muslims. Andreadis also paints a picture of life among the Kromlides as one of continuous subterfuge and fear of disclosure to their Muslim neighbours.[25]

Yorgos Tzedopoulos paints a very different, and more historicized, picture. First of all, he points out that it would be impossible for such a community to remain clandestine for such a long time. Tzedopoulos rightly criticizes the crypto-Christianity narrative that is imbedded in the discourse of Greek nationalism, which is a diachronic interpretation of secret faith under the public mask of Islam and a heroic return to the "true faith". Thus the Greek nationalist "equated crypto-Christianity with crypto-Greekness".[26] Another important issue is the whole question of secrecy. Just how secret were the beliefs of the Kromlides? Here Tzedopoulos follows Luise White:

'[Secrets] change and are negotiated and renegotiated regularly. Secrets and secrecy are social acts, constantly aware of audiences and publics. . . . When we realize how poorly secrets are kept, how selective and managed tellings 'leak' information to a wide variety of audiences, it seems clear that secrets ironically are ways of making information known.'[27]

Tzedopoulos' point is that "nobody was really surprised when some 17,000 Kromlides declared their Christianity in 1857."[28] This observation was also made by the British consul in Trabzon, Alex Stevens, who upon hearing about the declaration of the Kromlides remarked upon "the extreme indifference with which all Mahomedans talk of the intended

[25] Ibid., pp. 24, 25, 33–5. Particularly striking is his claim that the Kromlides did their best not to marry their marriageable daughters to "Turks", but did not object to taking brides from the Turks. The young Muslim bride was not allowed access to her husband until she had been baptized and initiated into the ways of the Kromlides by her mother-in-law and other female relatives.

[26] Tzedopoulos, "Public Secrets", p. 168.

[27] Luise White, "Telling More: Lies, Secrets, and History", *History and Theory* 39 (2000), 22, as cited in Tzedopoulos, "Public Secrets".

[28] Tzedopoulos, "Public Secrets", p. 169.

change: – from time immemorial a suspicion has been attached to the inhabitants of the district of Kooroom, that they are neither Mussulmans nor Christians".[29]

In some of the regions where the Kromlides lived, they made up, together with "real" Christians, the majority of the population. According to the "census" carried out by the acting British Vice Consul Stevens, the Santa district was the only area in the Pontic range "with no Muslim residents". Bryer puzzles over the issue: "I fail to understand the necessity for secret Christianity in an area which had no Muslims, and tentatively suggest that the crypto-Christians of Santa may have once been Muslims who, because of the overwhelming majority of Christians who surrounded them, were in the process of becoming Christian."[30] So crypto-faiths could be a two-way conduit; one automatically assumes that any conversion had to be from the weaker (usually Christian) to the stronger (usually Muslim) side.

Why did the Kromlides undertake such a move? Naturally, Greek nationalist historiography portrays this episode as a sort of neo-martyrdom wherein the religious impulse was paramount. There is an alternative explanation. The silver mines of Gümüşhane and Kromni had become uneconomic by 1857, and the state had decided to close them down. This meant that the Kromlides would be liable to conscription like all other Muslims: "After the failing of the mines [of Kromni] the *kryfoi* of Kromni, seeing no more profit in being Muslim, wishing also to avoid military service, and putting much hope on the Hatt-i Humayun that affirmed freedom of religion, dared cast aside the mask of Islam and presented themselves to the world as Christians."[31]

Indeed, in the beginning the entire affair was treated as something of a joke: "At first the Turks made fun of the event. The saying 'the High Street has turned to mud. The Kromlides have turned to *gavurs* (infidels)' spread throughout Trabzon."[32] Humour, however, was soon to give way to concern, particularly when the Kromlides sent a delegation to Istanbul to present their case to the ambassadors of the Great Powers. The text of the

[29] Byer, "The Crypto-Christians of the Pontos", p. 35.
[30] Bryer, "Nineteenth Century Monuments", p. 112.
[31] Tzedopoulos, "Public Secrets", p. 176, citing A. Parcharidis, *History of Kromni* (Trebizonde, 1911), p. 49.
[32] Yorgos Andreadis, *Gizli Din Taşıyanlar* , p. 76: "*Uzun sokak çamur oldu. Kromlidesler gavur oldu*".

petition shows that they were very much in tune with the power politics of the time:

'We depute these gentlemen [the Kromlides` representatives] by our firm and common decision to effect by the way they deem appropriate the disclosure of our up to the present hidden from the Ottomans Christian Orthodox religion. Hence we plead their Excellencies the Ambassadors of the Imperial Powers of England, France, Austria, Russia and Greece ... to lead them [the representatives] into doing what is necessary for our religion and freedom'.[33]

This move could not have made them popular at the Porte, which was extremely sensitive about what it called the "wagging of tongues" and "loose talk", as we have already seen many times. The Kromlides had indeed opened a can of worms.

The Porte did not take long to retaliate. It could not refuse outright to recognize the claims of the Kromlides as it had just made public declarations of religious freedom. But, as the saying went, "the Ottoman knows many tricks" (*Osmanlıda oyun çok*). The trick in this case was to create a special category for the reborn Christian Kromlides, the "*tenassur-u rum*" (literally "Christianized Orthodox", actually meaning "converts to Christianity"). It is worth noting at this point that although the Kromlides were, officially speaking, mere apostates (*mürted*), the state was creating a discrete category whereby it could punish them without incurring the wrath of the Powers or contravening the newly declared freedom of religion. The Kromlides, while hoping to get the best of both worlds, ended up getting the worst. "Thus the Kromlides were obliged to serve in the army as former Muslims *and* be recorded under both their Muslim and Christian names. In this way the Ottoman state ascribed officially to the Kromlides the double identity they had given up in favour of Christianity."[34] To the diabolically clever move of the state was added the cruelty of the local Muslims, who forbade their erstwhile co-religionists from paying homage to their dead in Muslim cemeteries. The logic was that as Christians they had no claims over the mortal remains of Muslims.[35]

For generations the Kromlides had tried to shake off their *tenassur* identity. One way of doing this was through the manipulation of official documents. Children born into *tenassur* families were ascribed to Christian families, or the names and identities of deceased Christians

---

[33] Tzedopoulos, "Public Secrets", p. 177.
[34] Ibid., p. 180.
[35] Andreadis, *Gizli Din Taşıyanlar*, pp. 70–1.

would be substituted for *tenassur* names. The aim in both cases was to reduce the number of *tenassur* to a minimum.[36] Ottoman archival sources indicate, however, that at the very least the practice of double-naming continued.

On 19 February 1903 the Population Registry Bureau (*Sicil-i Nüfus Idare-i Umumiyesi*) reported a curious case that had come before it. Two non-Muslims from Trabzon had applied to the Vilayet authorities to register a change of address. Their names appeared as follows: "Baki son of Osman Konstantin son of Mustafa Yani, and (the second person) son of Baki, Yani Osman Kostantin."[37] When the Vilayet of Trabzon was asked "why Muslim names were accompanied by Christian names", it replied, "In the *nahiyes* of Yumra and Maçka attached to Trabzon and in Trabzon itself and in the *kaza* of Dorul attached to the *sancak* of Gümüşhane, approximately some seventy-five years ago, some of the population in the villages who had been Orthodox converted to Islam and later committed apostasy (*irtidad etmiş*)". The Vilayet went on to say that "The names that they took at the time of their apostasy were recorded in the 'old registers' (*defter-i atik*) in red ink, when the registers were renewed in the recent census of 1299 (1881–1882) the said names were copied [into the new registers *defter-i cedid*] exactly". In the subsequent correspondence between the province and the Porte "regarding this matter of Christianization and apostasy (*keyfiyet-i tanassur ve irtidad*)", it was reported that the people in question had been registering their children under Greek names but that they had "been regularly obliged to perform military service".[38] Although the order of events mentioned in the document, Orthodoxy–Islam–Orthodoxy, does not reflect the Kromlides' story, the fact that the approximate date fits, and the fact that the geography (Dorul is almost certainly Torul) is exactly the same, make it highly likely that the people in question were *tannasur-u rum* Kromlides. The fact that the document specified that they had been "obliged" to perform

---

[36] Tzedopoulos, "Public Secrets", p. 181, n. 64. Tzedopoulos is quite rightly suspicious of his sources here because such manipulation "would require the forbearance of local authorities".

[37] BOA DH.MKT 656/25, 21 Zilkade 1320 / 19 February 1903, Population Registry Bureau to the Sublime Porte: "*Baki oğlu Osman Kostantin veled-I Mustafa Yani ve Baki oğlu Yani Osman Kostantin*". They were evidently father and son.

[38] Ibid. The census referred to here is the census that was carried out between 1882 and 1885. In 1903 it became compulsory to have an Ottoman identity card, called the *nüfus tezkeresi*, which had to be produced for all official transactions, including the sale and purchase of property. This compulsion may have been the reason why these people surfaced in the first place. On this issue, see Chapter 4 in this volume.

military service also points in this direction. What probably happened was that when the old register was copied into the new one, the red ink was disregarded and the names were copied in black, thus erasing all trace of the apostasy. It is also possible that some collusion or bribery may have occurred here.[39]

The same document also mentions a similar case involving people from the *kaza* of Giresun, also on the Black Sea coast. These latter were said to be "originally Orthodox (*Rum*) who had converted and submitted to conscription for many years who now declare that they want to go back to their old religion". The Porte harbored no illusions about them: "It is quite clear that their deviation into apostasy (*girive-i irtidada sapmalari*) is purely for the purpose of avoiding military service. This should not be allowed on any account as such perfidious claims of Christianity will be materially and morally extremely injurious. . . . Wherever such people are encountered they should be immediately conscripted". The Porte also declared that "a person cannot have two names, wherever such a claim is made [if the person is officially Muslim] they should not be listened to and their identity papers corrected, bearing only the Muslim names."[40]

Yet, as in so many other instances where the official orders and the reality on the ground did not match, the practice of double-naming evidently persisted. A few months later the Porte was to issue almost exactly the same order with an interesting addendum: "The existence of such people [bearing double names] on their identity papers is harmful not just in their own locality, but elsewhere. When such people travel here and there they will be a bad influence on people in other localities and this will cause much wagging of tongues".[41]

Evidently what we are facing here is a typical case of double naming where a person was Osman or Constantine depending on who was asking. The phenomenon was quite common in Anatolia and the Balkans. As noted by Mark Mazower: "The uses of secrecy also lay behind the custom of double naming, in which Suleiman turns out to be known as

---

[39] I would like to thank Cem Behar for the point about the re-copying of the registers. Although the date of conversion/apostasy mentioned in the document is approximate – "some seventy-five years ago" – it would date their conversion to around 1828, which would be about right as the date of conversions after the failure of the silver mines. See Bryer, "The Crypto-Christians of the Pontos", p. 32: "By 1829 the famous declining silver mines of Argyropolis were in their last gasp". The officials in question may have been speaking on the basis of imprecise local lore.

[40] BOA DH.MKT 656/25. The Porte referred to an order sent to the Vilayet of Trabzon to that effect, dated 11 Temmuz 1301 / 24 July 1895. Evidently the problem had a history.

[41] Ibid., Ministry of the Interior to the Sublime Porte, 12 Safer 1321 / 10 May 1903.

Constantine, Hussein as Giorgi. A double name allowed one to dodge between inconvenient categories, also serving to keep a man's real name hidden. ... [M]ultiple names were a weapon of the weak against the strong."[42] The descendants of the Kromlides seem to have turned the tables on the state by converting an originally discriminatory category into an ambiguous identity that could be made to work for them.

THE STORY OF THE STAVRIOTE/ISTAVRI

When the mines of Kromni stopped working, many of the miners sought work elsewhere in the empire and abroad. One such group was the Stavriote, who immigrated to the region of Akdağ Madeni near Yozgat in the Vilayet of Ankara in central Anatolia. The Stavriote had not taken part in the action of 1857. William Hasluck recorded their existence as "crypto Christians proper, belonging to the Greek rite and Greek by speech, [who] existed till recent years in the neighbourhood of Trebizond: they were known generally as the 'Stavriotae' from Stavra in the ecclesiastical district of Gümüşhane. They are said at one time to have numbered 20,000 in the Vilayets of Sivas, Angora, and Trebizond, now all have returned to open profession of their faith".[43]

The Stavriotes officially requested to be recognized as Christians on the basis of the Constitution of 1876, which confirmed religious freedom. Unfortunately for them, their "emergence" as Christians was badly timed. The relatively tolerant atmosphere of the late Tanzimat State had ceded to the much more strictly Muslim *etatisme* of Abdülhamid II (r. 1876–1909).[44]

After the upheavals of the Armenian massacres in the 1890s, a leading military figure, *Müşir* Şakir Paşa, was appointed general inspector for Eastern Anatolia. Şakir Paşa came across the Stavriotes during his travels and referred to them as the "people of two cults" (*iki ayin icra eder ahali*), and, as such, they were highly anomalous in the Ottoman system. In earlier, more tolerant periods they had been ignored, but now, in a period of crisis, they became the focus of the unwelcome attention of the state.[45]

---

[42] Mazower, *The Balkans*, pp. 63–5. The concept of "weapons of the weak" owes its origin to James C. Scott, *Weapons of the Weak: Everyday Forms of Peasant Resistance* (New Haven, Conn., 1985).

[43] William Hasluck, *Christianity and Islam under the Sultans*, vol. 2, pp. 469–70.

[44] On Muslim *etatisme*, see Selim Deringil, *The Well-Protected Domains* (London, 1998), Chapter 2.

[45] BOA YEE A/24-X/24/132, the inspector of Eastern Anatolia, Şakir Paşa, to the Vilayet of Ankara, 11 Ağustos 1313 / 23 August 1897.

They had presented a fake registry of births, deaths, and marriages, greatly downplaying the number of births. Şakir Paşa felt that all this was very dangerous as "such an example can cause confusion in the minds of other simple Muslims", meaning, perhaps, that they might be tempted to come up with a similar story. Yet the inspector general of Anatolia recommended nothing worse than the temporary exile of the community leaders and the reprimanding of the Patriarch of Trabzon. He added that "reliable *imams* should be sent to their villages, they should be severely adjoined to send their children to school and give them Muslim names."[46] The fear that apostasy might be contagious was behind Şakir Paşa's order to the Vilayet of Trabzon to investigate whether more Muslims were about to renege on their religion. On 3 May 1899 the Vali of Trabzon reported that "he had carried out secret investigations in Durul and Kurum which revealed that there was no such talk or inclination among the Muslim population".[47]

Another interesting aspect of the suspicion surrounding the Istavri leaders was that they had somehow been linked to the Armenian troubles. When the Vali of Ankara reported that the Istavri leader, Kobcu Oğlu Ibrahim Efendi, should be removed from his post on the Administrative Council, the reason given was "his closeness to those people calling themselves Istavris and his encouragement of the Armenians in their perfidious activities".[48] Even if it were untrue, this latter accusation would be sure to discredit any official.

The region continued to come up in dispatches. On 8 December 1900 the Vali of Trabzon reported that he had never ceased his vigilant observations of the *nahiyes* of Maçka and the *kaza* of Durul. Interestingly, however, the governor makes no mention of crypto-Christianity, merely stating that "some seventy or eighty years ago some of the Muslims of these parts, falling prey to the deceptions of priests became Christian." This had come to the attention of the authorities during the census of 1853: "Because Christians do not give soldiers and as these people had converted to Christianity, at the time it was felt that if they were exempted this would set a bad example. Therefore they were registered in the population registers as *mutenassır* and they are liable for military service". The Vali

---

[46] Ibid.
[47] BOA YEE A-24/X/24/132, 23 Zilhicce 1316 / 3 May 1899, the Vali of Trabzon, Mehmed Kadri, to Şakir Paşa.
[48] BOA DH.MKT 494/18, Enclosure 21, 24 Teşrin-i Sani 1310 / 7 November 1894, the Vali of Ankara, Memduh, to Mutasarrıf of Yozgad. This is a very interesting (and very large) file running to some hundred folios on the Istavri question. On the "Armenian troubles", see Chapter 5 in this volume.

declared that "because close attention was given to the matter no further Christianization has occurred". However, he pointed out that in said villages of the *mutenassır*, "there are no places of worship but the churches and no schools but those of the Christians". Because of this "abandoned state" of the Muslim population of the region "a time may come when these too will turn Christian". The only solution was to provide schools in these areas as well as small mosques (*mescid*).[49]

There is a very interesting, albeit sporadic, paper trail relating to the Stavriote/Istavri in the Ottoman archives. On 3 January 1901 the Istavri presented a petition to the Ministry of the Interior. It is worth quoting this document *in extenso* as it sheds considerable light on this elusive question:

'Your servants are from the Istavri people from the town of Ak Dağ Madeni attached to the *sancak* of Yozgad. Our fathers and forefathers were all Muslims but somehow (*her nasılsa*) to avoid military service, for some time hence, we have now become outwardly (*zahiren*) Muslim but inwardly Orthodox (*batınen Rumuz*). Our leaders [from the Kobcu Oğlu clan] Kobcu Oğulları Mustafa and Şakir and Mahmud and Kara Mustafa son of Hüseyin who have always duped us are now pressuring us to turn Christian. Since the year two hundred and ninety-six [1879–80] they have prevented us, numbering some two hundred families, from openly registering our births in the population registers. We are being shamed before our neighbours who call us, 'those of two religions' and our Muslim sentiments are being ruined. Meanwhile we are being pressured by the government to register our births but we fear our leaders who can easily destroy us.'[50]

The petitioners duly requested that their leaders be removed from the area, whereupon they would gladly register their births. The Istavri in question did not seem unduly troubled about reconciling their open admission of being inwardly Christian and outwardly Muslim with sensitivity to their "Muslim sentiments" (*hissiyatı İslamiye*). They also seem to think that being "inwardly" Christian was enough to get them out of military service. Some nine months later the *Mutasarrıf* of Yozgad ordered an investigation. What brought the matter to the attention of the authorities was the rumour that a priest named Kyrilos had been collecting money from the Istavri population under the guise of collecting money for a school and was then

---

[49] BOA Y.MTV 209/89, 25 Teşrin-i Sani 1316 / 8 December 1900, the Vali of Trabzon, el Seyyid Mehmed Kadri, to Yıldız Palace Imperial Secretariat.

[50] BOA DH.MKT 494/18, Enclosure 24, 18 Kanun-u Sani 1317 / 31 January 1901, petition from Istavri residents of Ak Dağ Maden to the Ministry of the Interior. The population registers being referred to here are the "current registers" (*vukuat defterleri*), which would record, on a daily basis, the births, deaths, marriages, and migrations. On this point, see Cem Behar, "Sources pour la démographie historique de l'Empire Ottoman. Les *tahrirs* (dénombrements) de 1885 et 1907", *Population* 1–2 (1998), 161–78.

sending the money to Greece. Kyrilos was also reportedly encouraging some of the Muslim population to convert to Christianity. Two officials were sent and carried out a detailed inquest in the town of Akdağ Maden. The following are excerpts from the interviews they conducted.[51]

The first person interviewed was the teacher (*hoca*) of the *rüşdiye* (secondary school), Hacı Tevfik Efendi, who had informed on Kyrillos.

"Hoca Efendi! Do you know the priest Kyrilos the Orthodox priest of your *kaza*? Where is this Kyrilos from?"

"I came to Maden twenty years ago. I have known him ever since. I have always known him as someone from here. I do not know where he is really from."

"Do you know Kobcu Oğlu Mustafa and Şakir Efendi, Derviş Vecir Ali and the Chief of the Municipality Ibrahim and the Director of the Tobacco Rejie Rıza Efendi? Do you frequent them? What is their religion? What sort of men are they?"

"For a time I taught Kobcu Oğlu Mustafa and Şakir Efendi as well as Derviş Vecir Ali. Ever since I have been here I have seen them as Muslims. Later they committed apostasy. The man called Pir (Derviş) Ali also committed apostasy. They now go . . . to the church. They have now become Christians.[52] Although the Kobcu Oğlu brothers and Derviş and Pir Ali became apostates their apostasy was not recognized by the Ministry of Justice and Religious Sects. Hence they are still known as Muslims and are called by Muslim names."

"Are the daughters of these men, Kobcu Oğlu Mustafa and Şakir and Pir Ali, always married off to Christians? By what names are their children called? Do you have any information on that?"[53]

"Yes, they marry their daughters to Christians. They also take brides from Christians. Their newly-born children are given Christian names."

The next person interviewed was Ibrahim Oğlu Mustafa Efendi (Kobcu Oğlu) from the Istavri community.[54]

"What is your name? How old are you? What is your profession? Are you married? What is your nationality?"

"My name is Mustafa Efendi son of Ibrahim. I am a shopkeeper. I am fifty-two years old. I am married. I am a subject of the Sublime State."

"Do you have another name particular to the Istavri?"

"Yes I do. It is Nikola."

"When did you join this Istavri community?"

---

[51] BOA DH.MKT 494/18, Enclosure 27, 12 Eylul 1317 / 25 September 1901, detailed Report of an investigation carried out by an official from the *Defter-i Hakani* of Yozgad (signature illegible) and the commissar of police, Mecid Sabit. I have quoted this particular file *in extenso* because it is one of the very rare cases where the Ottoman archives actually give a voice (literally, in this case) to the people involved.

[52] Ibid., p. 1.

[53] Ibid., p. 2.

[54] Ibid., p. 3. Date of interview 13 Eylul 1317 / 26 September 1901.

"The name Istavri is the name of a village. I am actually from the Orthodox community (*Rum*). My father Ilya came here from Gümüşhane. I was born here."

"As you say you are from the Orthodox community, and that your name is Nikola, why do you also have a Muslim name?"[55]

[No answer was given to the last question]

"What are the names of your children?"

"We have always been Orthodox (*aba an ced Rum cemaatindeniz*). Everyone knows. We are registered in the church. At some date we began to be conscripted and that was when we came to be called by Muslim names. We still give soldiers. For the last fifty-eight years when children are born they are given Christian names and our religious rites are carried out in the church. Our births, deaths and marriages are recorded in the church register. The people called the Istavri here number one hundred and fifty families. They all have two names."[56]

"At some date you became Muslims and took up Islamic ways and practices. You passed for Muslims for quite a long time and went to [Muslim] schools and *medreses* where you learned from Muslim books. Then you committed apostasy and joined the Orthodox community. All of this is recorded in the official registers."

"We have always been Christians but we still go to Muslim schools to learn how to read and write. If we had ever [really] become Muslims, there are all these Muslims here, we would have taken brides from them and given brides to them. Ask [anyone] if such a thing ever came to pass?"

"To whom are your daughters married?"

"One is married to Lazar the jeweler, the other to Mihal the blacksmith. Another is married to someone from our clan (*mezhebimizden*), Ismail son of Salih, an Istavri who has the Christian name of Konstantin son of Panayot."

The next person to be interviewed was Yusuf Ağa Zade Nuri Ağa, who had also informed on Kyrilos.[57]

"Do you know of anyone from the Muslim community or any converts who later turned Christian and apostate (*tenassur ve irtidad etmiş*)?"

"There are those who are called the Istavri who number some one hundred and fifty families who used to call themselves Muslims. They used to take brides from Muslims. They were constantly with the Muslims. They used to come to the mosque. Now these people go to the church. They give and take brides from Christians. They are known by Muslim and Christian names. Apart from them, none of the Muslims has become a Christian. All this is known to the government".

The commission of enquiry then wrote a long summary report. It declared that Kyrilos was in fact from the island of Corfu and had "through devious

---

[55] Ibid., p. 4.
[56] Ibid. This would place the date as 1853, which more or less approximates the date of the Kromlides' declaration of 1857.
[57] Ibid., p. 5, 14 Eylul 1317 / 27 September 1901, Yusuf Ağa, Zade Nuri Ağa, merchant, thirty-eight years old, from the Ashali neighbourhood in Maden.

means" acquired Ottoman nationality. He had been collecting money under false pretences and sending the money to Greece. He had also "caused some four hundred people in two hundred and fifty households, who had always been Muslims, to Christianize and become apostates".

Kyrilos had also been responsible for marrying the daughters of these Muslims, Kobcu Oğlu Mustafa, Şakir, and Derviş, to Christians. He had also taken the daughter of Pir Hasan for his own wife. The Commission concluded:

'Those people whom he encouraged to Christianize and become apostates were actually [originally] Orthodox, who, quite some time ago, took on Islamic names, studied in Islamic educational institutions, attended the mosque, and for years, fulfilled the obligations of Islam. But they avoided taking brides from those who had always been Muslims or giving brides to them, marrying only within their own group; thus abstaining from forming true material and moral ties [with the Muslims]. After the war of "ninety-four" [H.1294/C.E. 1878–79] they started to go to the mosque sometimes and to sometimes go to the church, following the rites of both religions. In their community they would be called by their old [Christian] names and among the Muslims they would be called by their Muslim names. These are the people called the Istavri.'[58]

An earlier, more detailed report by the Kaymakam of Akdağ Maden stated unequivocally that the main aim of the Istavri was to avoid military service. There were 581 Istavri in Akdağ Maden itself and in the surrounding villages. They had been known as Muslims until the census of 1882, when they had declared that they were Christians. The official instructions were to ignore their claims and to keep treating them as Muslims.[59] Yet, the Kaymakam reported, "the Istavri were most determined and united. They openly worshipped in the Christian manner despite all warnings. They have taken to openly using their Christian names and it is feared that in time their Islamic identity will be entirely lost." Kryrilos and the Istavri were in fact so powerful that "they have come to believe that the dismissal or rotation of any state official is the result of their deceitful machinations".[60]

Kyrilos proved to be a tough nut to crack. His reputation evidently preceded him, even in the upper reaches of the Ottoman bureaucracy. On 8

---

[58] Ibid., p. 6. The reference to "the war of '94" is evidently a mistaken reference to the war of 1877–78, which came to be called the "war of '93" (H 1293).

[59] Ibid., Enclosure 38, 5 Şubat 1318 / 18 February 1902, the Kaymakam of Maden to the Mutasarrıf of Yozgad.

[60] Ibid.

March the Vali of Ankara was to report that Kyrilos had "imported seditious literature from Athens and was using this to confuse the minds of the local population."[61] In addition to the commission of enquiry mentioned earlier, the Mutasarrıf of Yozgad sent an agent to investigate Kyrilos's activities secretly and report on what was going on in the Istavri community. He duly reported back that although their original informant had reneged on his information and was now claiming that Kyrilos was in fact not marrying off Muslim girls to Christians, his secret investigation had shown that this was in fact the case.[62] Apparently some of Kyrilos's tactics amounted to open blackmail. A petition from the Christians of the village of Güllük claimed: "Just as we were praying in our church for the long life of our Sultan he entered the church, took the Bible from our priest and forced us all outside. He then closed the church." The petitioners claimed that he said he would refuse to let them use the church until they gave him the money he demanded, which was between 100 and 500 *kuruş* per household.[63]

On 3 November 1902 the Mutasarrıf of Yozgad reported that he had invited Kyrilos to his office, where the latter had "used threatening language and carried on in a manner unsuitable for a government office". Kyrilos was also falsely claiming to be the representative of the Patriarch of Gümüşhane. The Mutasarrıf concluded that "this Kyrilos is a most evil and harmful man" (*şerir ve muzir bir adam olup*).[64]

A few weeks later it was reported that Kyrilos had "secretly wed to his son Demistocles, the daughter of Kobcu Oğlu Mustafa Efendi". This was said to be most untoward as "the *Şeriat* forbids the marriage of a Muslim to a foreigner". Kyrilos had been warned but had completely ignored all warnings.[65]

---

[61] Ibid., Enclosure 39, 23 Subat 1318 / 8 March 1902, the Vali of Ankara, Mehmed Memduh Paşa, to the Ministry of the Interior.

[62] Ibid., Enclosure 15, 12 March 1318 / 25 March 1902, Mehmet Ta'ali, special agent sent to investigate this matter, to the Mutasarrıf of Yozgad. It is quite possible that the original informant had been threatened by Kyrilos.

[63] Ibid., Enclosure 22, 25 Mart 1318 / 7 April 1902, the petition signed by the headman (*muhtar*) sent to the Mutasarrıf of Yozgad.

[64] Ibid., Enclosure 6, 21 Teşrin-i Evvel 1317 / 3 November 1901, the Mutasarrıf of Yozgad Rükneddin to the Sublime Porte.

[65] Ibid., Enclosure 12, 8 Teşrin-i Sani 1317 / 21 November 1901, the Kaymakam of Maden to the Mutasarrıf of Yozgad. Kobcu Oğlus's daughter, an official Muslim, would indeed be debarred by the Şeriat from marrying a non-Muslim. The reference to "foreigner" here evidently means Christian.

Kyrilos seemed indomitable. When the Kaymakam of Maden protested the marriage of the daughter of Kobcu Oğlu Ibrahim to a certain Yanko, and the marriage of the daughter of Kobcu Oğlu Şakir to a certain Fides, Kyrilos coolly replied that "İbrahim and Şakir have been worshipping openly and faultlessly in the Christian way for generations. The Sublime Porte is fully in cognizance of their status as Istavris".[66]

In fact, Kyrilos also seemed to be set on converting "real" Muslims to Christianity. On 28 April 1902 the headman (muhtar) of the village of Koyunlu reported that a young man named Sofracıoğlu Ömer had fallen in love with a Greek girl from Maden. The girl had converted to Islam, and the couple had then spent a few days in Koyunlu. Ömer had decided to take employment in his wife's Christian neighbourhood and had then been taken into the army. When he returned, "he and his wife had both been tricked by Kyrilos Efendi and had both become apostates from Islam and had become Christian".[67]

The Kaymakam of Maden was to write another long report on the same day. He confirmed that in fact Kyrilos had converted Ömer to Christianity; it was specified that Ömer was not an Istavri, and that he had gone missing for the previous days; "clearly he has been hidden away as a result of the said priest's machinations". The official made a clear distinction between the "Istavri tribe" (kabile-i mezkur) and other Muslims: "[t]hose who do not belong to the said tribe [who reside] in other villages". Kyrilos was also active among them. The Kaymakam stressed that "unless the said priest, together with his henchmen Kobcu Oğlu Mustafa, Şakir and Ibrahim Efendi are removed from here, we can expect much more difficulty in the future. This is the only way we can stop this Christianization and apostasy (tanassur ve irtidad)". He also confirmed that Kyrilos had been collecting money for "the Greek seditious committee called the Etniki Eteria".[68] A Greek source based on Greek and Russian diplomatic documents also makes frequent reference to Kyrilos.[69] In a communication dated 8 April 1899, the Russian embassy mentioned "the priest whose removal had been requested by the Porte, is named Kyrilos, he is the

---

[66] Ibid., Enclosure 22, signed as "Deputy of the Greek Patriarchate Kyrilos".

[67] Ibid., Enclosure 22, 15 Nisan 1318 / 28 April 1902, the Muhtar of Koyunlu, Mehmed, to the Kaymakam of Maden.

[68] Ibid., Enclosure 25, 15 Nisan 1318 / 28 April 1902, the Kaymakam of Ak Dağ Maden to the Mutasarrıf of Yozgad.

[69] Konstantinos Fotiadis, Piges tis istorias tou kryptochristianikou provlimatos (History of the Crypto Christian Question) (Thessaloniki, 1997). My thanks to Yorgos Tzedopoulos for this reference and the translations.

delegate of the archbishop".[70] It appears that Kyrilos was in regular contact with the Russians. On 9 April the Russian embassy in Istanbul wrote that the Kaymakam of Akdağ Maden had put two of its wealthiest inhabitants in chains and sent them to Ankara. The two men, named as Nikolaos Kioptsidis and Chatzi-Isaak Kiopstidis, had been jailed and then exiled; the former was none other than Mustafa Kobçu Oğlu and the latter Mahmud Kobçu Oğlu.[71]

The most detailed account of Sofracıoğlu Ömer's apostasy is to be found in the record of a long series of interviews.[72] The story that emerges is very interesting in its details. It appears that at the age of twelve or thirteen Ömer, who had been orphaned at a tender age, was given as a servant to the "Greek" family of one Eftim Aniki, where he worked for one year.[73] He then served in the family of another "Greek", Çopur Nikola, the uncle of Eftim, for another four years. While he was in Nikola's household he met and fell in love with a Greek girl, Peti (or Peni, she is referred to by both names), daughter of Deli Yani, who was either a relative or close friend of Çopur Nikola. He then took the girl to his home village of Koyunlu where he told his family that he intended to convert her to Islam and marry her. However, while they were staying with the Sofracıoğlu family, it became evident that neither he nor his intended prayed at prayer time and that (although it was the month of Ramazan) they did not fast. It was also curious that the girl's family did not pursue her in any way. It was thus discovered that Ömer had in fact already converted to Christianity. This had occurred in 1890 when he was taken to the Metropolitanate in Kayseri, where he was baptized and the couple were married. All of the five people interviewed agreed that Kyrilos was the moving force. In fact, Ömer and his wife soon went back to the Christian neighbourhood, where they were seen going to church. The Sofracıoğlu family then decided that the one way to cure the boy was to send him to the army. So they did, and Ömer served in the Hicaz for two years. Meanwhile, while Ömer was in the army, his wife had given

---

[70] Ibid., p. 130. The "archbishop" mentioned here is the Metropolitan of Chaldia Gümüşhane, who had under his jurisdiction all the mining communities founded by the Pontic miners.

[71] Ibid., p. 133. This is the same Mustafa Kopçu Oğlu questioned earlier.

[72] BOA DH.MKT 494/18, Enclosure 28. Beginning with the interview of Sofraci Oğlu Ismail Durmuş, older brother of Ömer, 23 Nisan 1318 / 6 May 1902. Report and depositions of interviews signed by Hacı Arif Efendi, official in charge of the investigation.

[73] Although the references in the documents are always to "Greeks", it is highly likely that these families were in fact Istavri families who had declared their Christianity.

birth to a girl who died soon afterwards and was buried as a Christian. When he returned, the Muslim family immediately placed him under observation in their home and forbade him from going to his wife; they also arranged for some *ulema* to come and preach to him. All of this was to no avail, however, and Ömer escaped to join his wife. He had then gone missing. His brother Ismail had informed the Kaymakam and the military authorities about the circumstances of the apostasy and Ömer's disappearance.[74]

The following are excerpts from some of the interviews relating to this story. The first person to be interviewed was Ömer's older brother, İsmail.

İsmail was asked about his family and the circumstances of his brother's apostasy.

"We were three brothers. One of my brothers died doing his military service in Yemen. The other, because he was an orphan was given as a servant to the Christians in the Istanbulluoğlu neighbourhood in Akdağ Maden. This is the Ömer who somehow became an apostate."

"How old is this Ömer now and where is he? Who did he serve in the Istanbulluoğlu neighbourhood? How old was he when he began his service? How many years did he serve them? Why did he convert?"

"My brother Ömer must have been twelve or thirteen when he became a servant in the household of Eftim Aniki from Karahisar, he was to receive a hundred *kuruş* every six months. Then he served for four years in the household of Çopur Nikola the uncle of Eftim. While he was there he established an interest in the girl Peni, who was a relative or friend of Nikola and was the daughter of Kozlis Oğlu Deli Yani. In the year 1312 [1898] he brought this girl to the house of our uncle Ali saying I am going to make this girl a Muslim and I am going to marry her. But because this was the time of the Armenian troubles we did not immediately proceed with her conversion. However, we noticed that neither of them prayed, and though it was the month of Ramazan, nor did they fast. When I asked Ömer about this he said that he had preferred Christianity, that they had given him a lot of money and he had become an apostate to marry this girl. He then encouraged me and my family to become Christian. I of course refused very sternly and encouraged and threatened him, telling him to go back on his apostasy. When I found out that he would never come back to Islam, I arranged for him to be taken into the army."

"Do you know what name they gave your brother? Did he tell you?"

"Yes he did. His name was Yani. As he told me they sprinkled water on him and did whatever they do for baptism."

"Who did this?"

"All those who gave my brother money to convert. But it was Eftim Efendi who encouraged him and the priest, who was then the schoolteacher, and is now the delegate of the Metropolitan, Kyrilos, who arranged it."

[74] BOA DH.MKT 494/18, Enclosure 28.

The above is a short excerpt from testimony spanning several folio pages. There are several important aspects to be considered in the passage. It should be noted that the term "somehow" (*her nasılsa*) occurs here. Ömer is mentioned as having "somehow" converted. This was a term used regularly in official Ottoman parlance when the scribe wanted to make a reference to an event that was somehow embarrassing, yet had to be mentioned. The other interesting point is the reference to the "Armenian troubles" as the reason for the delay in the conversion of the girl. This is very likely a reference to the official discouragement of the conversion of Christians during the Armenian massacres of the 1890s. Ismail's statement that Ömer turned up at his uncle's house in 1312 (1898) would place the date at about the right time. Moreover, perhaps the most striking thing in Ismail's testimony is the claim that Ömer attempted to proselytize him and his family.[75]

The interview of one Mustafa Ağa is particularly interesting as it casts light on how the Istavri were seen in the area.

"Do you know Sofracıoğlu Ömer from your village? Is this Ömer from Muslim ancestry or is he an Istavri from Maden who practice two rites?"

"Yes, I know him. There is nothing suspicious in Ömer's family or lineage. They are a *yörük* family who have always been Muslims. In fact our village (Koyunlu) is older than Maden and we suspect no one. Ömer committed apostasy."[76]

Another resident of the village of Koyunlu, Mehmed Kethuda, was also asked about the religious inclinations of the Sofracıoğlu family.

"Are there any Christians in your village?"

"Our village has always been entirely Muslim. It is in fact older than the *kaza* of Maden."

"In your village live Sofracıoğlus Durmuş and Ömer. Do you know them? Are they Muslims? Or are they Istavri who practice two rites?"

"Yes, I know them. They are *yörüks*, the sons of Ismail Çavuş, and have always been Muslims. We have no Istavris in our village."

"How do you know that Eftim Efendi and the priest Kyrilos were responsible for Ömer's apostasy?"

"This boy grew up in Eftim Efendi's household almost as his child. We were greatly anxious about his apostasy [and] they encouraged it and are still encouraging it. Many people in our village know this."[77]

[75] Ibid., and see Chapter 5 in this volume.
[76] Ibid., the testimony of Ibiş Kahya Oğlu Mustafa Ağa from the village of Koyunlu, 23 Nisan 1318 / 6 May 1902. The *yörük* were originally nomadic peoples of Anatolia.
[77] Ibid., the testimony of Mehmed Kethuda, son of Mustafa Kahya, 23 Nisan 1318 / 6 May 1902.

It emerges from the above that the Istavri were always suspect and were distinguished from "true" Muslims. Although Mehmed Kethuda stated that everyone knew that Eftim and his entourage encouraged Ömer, and although there is no mention of whether they were Istavris, as they are referred to as Greeks or Christians, it seems highly likely that they were Istavris who had declared their Christianity. On 1 May 1902 the Vilayet of Ankara decided that Ömer had to be found and "secretly sent somewhere far away so that he can serve as an object lesson to others".[78]

Apparently object lessons were indeed needed, because soon after the Sofracıoğlu Ömer affair a very similar case occurred. The Mutasarrıf of Yozgad reported that a certain Velil, the son of Molla Osman, had been placed, like Ömer, in service in the household of a Greek family in Maden. After he had been with them for some seven or eight years, it began to be put about that he too had been "tricked by the [Greek] community" into converting. The Mutasarrıf reported that these cases of the misleading of Muslim boys were the result of "evil machinations" on the part of the Greeks. He made sure to stress that "these are sensitive issues and all investigations must be carried out secretly and with the utmost care."[79] On 19 May 1902 the Vali of Ankara reiterated that "these evil machinations" had to be stopped at all costs.[80]

Whatever the aims of the Istavri community may have been in declaring their Christianity, they certainly included avoiding military service. The Vilayet of Ankara reported that the total number of soldiers mobilized from Ak Dağ Maden since 1879 was thirty-nine. Of these, only four had actually been put into uniform, and four others had paid the bedel. The remaining thirty-one conscripts were "absent because they circulate here and there with their Christian names", thereby making it difficult to trace them as Istavri liable for military service. Moreover, the fact that since 1877 the Istavri had refused to register their births, deaths, and marriages in the Muslim registers meant that a large portion of their population was unaccounted for, making it impossible to trace who was liable for service.[81]

---

[78] Ibid., Enclosure 20, 18 Nisan 1318 / 1 May 1902, the Vilayet of Ankara to the Ministry of the Interior.

[79] Ibid., Enclosure 30, 29 Nisan 1318 / 11 May 1902, the Mutasarrıf of Yozgad to the Vali of Ankara.

[80] Ibid., Enclosure 31, 12 Mayıs 1318 / 25 May 1902, the Vali of Ankara, Mehmed Memduh Paşa, to the Ministry of the Interior.

[81] Ibid., Enclosure 32, 12 Mayıs 1318 / 25 May 1902, the Vilayet of Ankara to the Ministry of the Interior.

The Istavri were actually recognized as Greek by the Greek Orthodox Patriarchate in Istanbul. On 13 June 1902 the Greek Patriarch wrote to the Ministry of Justice and Religious Sects: "[These people] who were inwardly Christian, because of the requirements of the times appeared as Muslims for a period, have been recognized as Christians since the Auspicious Tanzimat. Since then, like all the other Christians they have been openly worshipping according to their faith." The Patriarch protested that they were being forced by the local authorities to send their children to Muslim schools and register themselves in the population registers as Muslims.[82]

One of the main reasons the Istavri leaders seemed to be unassailable was the fact that they were extremely rich and used their wealth to buy political influence. On 11 December 1902 a report dealing with this aspect of their power stated: "The said persons who are holders of great fortunes, use this money to secretly work towards encouraging Muslims to become apostates. They work towards this aim all the time, and have established such a diabolical tribe (*iblisane bir kavmiyet*) that one is shocked."[83] The report mentioned by name a Kavasoğlu Ibrahim and his brother-in-law Hüsnü:

'[B]oth of whom are shown to be Muslims and the other apostates put all of their fortunes at their disposal and aid them secretly to make sure that they always hold government offices. ... If these apostates remain where they are and if Ibrahim and Hüsnü Efendi continue to hold government offices, God beware, they will poison all the Muslims in Maden through some means, either with money or with women. In fact Ibrahim Efendi, during the late Armenian troubles stirred up the Armenians.'

The report then gave a long account of how Ibrahim Efendi was removed from government positions by the order of the various Valis of Ankara but, "through the protection of Kobcu Oğlu Mustafa who has millions at his disposal, was reinstated to his position on the local court". The writer of the report was unequivocal about the connection between money and power, repeating that Kobcu Oğlu controlled "millions of lira":

[82] Ibid., Enclosure 33, 31 Mayıs 1318 / 13 June 1902, the Patriarch of the *Rum* Millet to the Ministry of Justice and Religious Sects. The Patriarch in question was Joachim III (1901–12), who was one of the most important Patriarchs of the modern period. See www.patriarchate.org/patriarchate/former-patriarchs/joachim-iii-2nd-time.

[83] Ibid., Enclosure 36, 28 Teşrin-i Sani 1318 / 11 December 1902, the investigating official, Mehmet Arif, to the Sublime Porte.

Through the use of this fortune and their political influence the apostates in our area will never be registered in the population registers and our brothers here will lose all peace of mind. . . . Please may God will that these apostates be chastised and that any means possible be used to put down this secret committee and avert the danger.[84]

These are very strong words. We note again the ultimate accusation, "having encouraged the Armenians", which was sure to catch the attention of the upper echelons of the state, possibly reaching the sultan himself. Furthermore, the Istavri are classified as "apostates" (*mürtedler*) who have become a "clan" or "secret committee", an accusation very likely to provoke the fears of a notoriously suspicious sultan. Another salient point is the mention of "poisoning through women", clearly a reference to the apostate lads being married off to "Greek" girls. Nonetheless, it seems clear that the Kobcu Oğlu clan did indeed have political clout, because soon after their imprisonment in Ankara in April 1899 Kyrilos was informed by the Russian embassy that "After an order by the Minister of the Interior, Mahmud and Mustafa Kiouptsidis from Akdağ have been freed and sent home".[85]

It seems that the Istavri question was still on the agenda one year after Mehmed Arif Efendi's report. On 18 November 1903, the Ministry of the Interior composed a memorandum summarizing the situation. In addition to Kryrilos, who had arranged for the marriage of the daughter of the Istavri Kobcu Mustafa to his son Demistocles, the Istavris Şakir and Hüseyin Efendis had married their daughters to one Nikola from Talas and one Madrike, son of the priest Panayot. The memorandum also pointed out that the poorer Istavri were being forcibly prevented from registering their births, deaths, and marriages in the Muslim registers. It was still feared that "unless the priest Kyrilos and his henchmen among the Istavri are removed, it is possible that the Istavri population who appear as Muslims in the registers will all become apostates." Naturally the state took a very bureaucratic and pragmatic approach. The memo pointed out that if the Istavri were left in their present condition, they were in a state of limbo:

'[A]s the said people cannot be made to register as Muslims the state loses military man power. As they are also not registered openly as Christians the state treasury loses income from the *bedel-i askeri*.'[86]

---

[84] Ibid. Mehmed Arif was evidently out of his depth in money matters as "millions of lira" at that time would amount to a sizeable portion of the state budget.

[85] Fotiadis, *Piges tis istorias*, pp. 136, 140, documents from the Russian embassy in Istanbul.

[86] BOA DH.MKT 494/18, 5 Tesrin-I Sani 1319 / 18 November 1903. So it seemed that the Istavri were really, in the words of Bryer, "getting the best of both worlds". See Bryer, "The Crypto-Christians of the Pontos", p. 21.

The year 1905 saw a concerted effort to solve the Istavri problem. The Vilayet of Ankara was ordered in no uncertain terms to register the Istavri as Muslims. The minister of the interior, Mahmud Memduh Paşa, together with Şakir Paşa made this into something of a pet project. The protestations of the Patriarchate and the foreign embassies were of no avail. In several instances the Mutasarrıf of Yozgad and the Vilayet of Ankara actually declared that they had granted freedom of religion. This proved, however, to be a subterfuge designed to force more Istavri into the open. The priest Kyrilos Caratzas and several Istavri leaders were marched to Ankara, where they died in prison.[87]

Both the Istavri and the Kromlides were actually recognized as Christians in 1910 after the Young Turk Revolution. As the Young Turks actually enforced military service obligations for Muslims and non-Muslims alike, there was no longer any advantage in claiming non-Muslim status. "In 1910 the Kromlides and the Stavriotes were permitted to register solely with their Christian names."[88] This meant that they would be forcibly deported during the population exchange between Greece and Turkey in 1923–24.

There is, however, an ironic sequel. Just before they were deported, the Kromlides pleaded with the officials in the exchange commission that they were Muslims: "Please save us, we are actually Muslims they cried". Their pleas were ignored.[89]

What should we make of these rather puzzling documents? It is fairly clear that we are in the domain of what Yorgos Tzedopoulos calls "public secrets", or what Louise White refers to as "secrets as a way of making things known". One of the people interviewed by the commission, Nuri Ağa, actually said that the condition of the Istavri was "known to the government". The fact that at some point the Istavri "sometimes went to the mosque and sometimes to the church" certainly puts a new light on the question of "crypto" religion. At some stage in their history, probably around the mid-1850s, there was nothing "crypto" about the Istavri. The priest Kyrilos said as much when he claimed that the "state was fully in cognizance of the status of the Istavri". It also appears that they were left pretty much to their own devices. The state seems to have forgotten about them after Şakir Paşa, and they come up again only because the "perfidious

[87] Deringil, *The Well-Protected Domains*, p. 81. See also R. Janin, "Musulmans Malgre Eux, Les Stavriotes", *Echos D'Orient* 15 (1912), 495–505.
[88] Tzedopoulos, "Public Secrets", p. 184.
[89] Robert Enhegger, "Evangelidos Misailidis ve Türkçe Konuşan dindaşları" (Evangelidos Misailidis and his Turcophone co-religionists), *Tarih ve Toplum* 9 (1988), 177, n. 2.

priest" Kyrilos is reported to be collecting money for Greece. The gist of the summaries in the reports just quoted is that it is almost normal for the Istavri to "Christianize and become apostate" because they had been Christian in the first place – because, in a manner of speaking, they had never been "real" Muslims. The Kaymakam of Akdağ Maden did indeed distinguish between the Istavri "tribe" and other Muslims. Similarly, the people interviewed in the case of the apostate Ömer/Yani made it clear that they did not consider Istavris true Muslims. The very questions the interviewer asked also implied that there was a clear prejudice and that Istavris were somehow suspect.

Another interesting clue is the passing mention of the apostasy of the Istavri "not being recognized" officially by the Ministry of Justice and Religious Sects; the implication is that apostasy was now a legal category recognized by the state, as in the case of the Kromlides, who became *tanassur-u rum*. Indeed, the term *"tanassur ve irtidad"* – literally, "to Christianize and apostatize" – seems to set them apart from straightforward apostates, who are called simply *"mürted"*.

Apart from allegedly collecting money for a foreign power, Kyrilos's cardinal crime was that he had performed the marriage ceremonies of women who were still officially Muslim to Christian men (indeed, marrying one himself). In their petition the Istavri "people" claimed to be Muslim while admitting that they were "inwardly" Christian. Yet they seemed to think that their outward conformity to Islam was the persona they preferred, and moreover, all the more striking, they did not seem to perceive any contradiction in this state of affairs. Although the petition, claiming genuine adherence to Islam, and the interview of Kobcu Oğlu, where he categorically stated that they had always been Christians, seem at first glance to be diametrically opposed, a careful reading reveals that Kobcu Oğlu refers to his Istavri son-in-law as "from our confession, an İstavri" (*mezhebimizden*) whose Muslim and Christian names he cites in one breath. This seems to imply that the internal/external dichotomy as expressed in the petition was not a dichotomy at all. Is it totally unreasonable to speculate that the Istavri/Kromlides actually sincerely believed in *both* their religions?

Yorgos Andreadis recounts how the main source of his book, his grandmother Afrodite, always said that she wanted to be totally washed after her death, "as was the Muslim funerary custom".[90] Furthermore, all the Greek names that the family took that Andreadis mentions are direct translations

---

[90] Andreadis, *Gizli Din Taşıyanlar*, p. 43.

of Turkish names; Yazıcıoğlu becomes Grammatikopoulos, Başoğlu becomes Kephalides, Melekendon becomes Angelopoulos, and Cevahir becomes Adamantia. Even as he tries to show how the Kromlides were genuine secret Christians, Andreadis makes a telling comment: "In Kromni there were no secret priests but Muslim *mollas* showed people the way. In the days of ignorance and darkness ... these *molla* priests kept Kromni loyal to Christ".[91]

There are, however, some very important loose ends in all these stories. Why would wealthy "Greeks" want to convert poor Muslim boys to Christianity and marry them to their daughters? How did Ömer expect to convert a Christian girl to Islam when he was himself already a Christian? One also has to bear in mind that all the testimonies referred to here were written by official scribes who framed the questions and answers to suit their agenda or brief. The answer may lie within the family structures of the Kromlides/Istavri. The family structure of the Pontic area south of Trabzon was organized in patrimonial clans.[92] This meant that families exchanged women for reproduction, and there were strict rules of exogamy forbidding marriage between cousins. Olga Sapkidi's sources mention prohibition of marriage stretching all the way to the seventh-degree relatives.[93] Men were usually not exchanged and, even after marriage, remained in the households of their fathers. An exception was made only when there was no son in the family to continue the blood-line. In this case a groom who would live with his wife's family would be taken: "then the groom became a '*sogambros*' and he had to take the surname of his wife, which is the surname of the household whose reproduction and continuation he was called [upon] to secure". The arrangement would require the agreement of the household of the groom, "which meant he had to insure with his choice a higher social position or prestige".[94] It is highly possible that Ömer/Yani was a "*sogambros*". He had already been in the families of Eftim and Çopur Nikola for some years as a trusted servant, and Deli Yani was either their relative or a close friend. He and Peti may

---

[91] Ibid., pp. 79, 80, 82.

[92] Olga Sapkidi, "Family Structure in the Pontos", *Encyclopedia of the Hellenic World*, vol. 1: Asia Minor (http://asiaminor.ehw.gr/forms/fLemma.aspx?lemmaid=7481&contlang=58). I owe thanks to Yorgos Tzedopoulos and Eleni Gara for this reference and the insights that they were kind enough to share with me on the story of Ömer/Yani, which inform my analysis here.

[93] Sapkidi, "Family Structure in the Pontos".

[94] Ibid. The word "*sogambros*" means "internal groom" and is reflected exactly by the term "*içgüveysi*" in Turkish, which means exactly the same thing.

actually have loved each other. We can likewise speculate that Deli Yani did not have a son and that he had prohibitively close blood ties with the Christians in the area. It is also worth noting that Deli Yani did not seek a groom from the more established Muslim families in the area but rather from a Yörük family, who were probably considerably poorer and of lower status, who would be prepared to assent to such an arrangement.[95] One of the respondents in the inquest mentioned that "these boys are orphans". It is also possible that Ömer's family did indeed assent, and that would account for Peti's "embracing Islam" at the behest of Ömer/ Yani. This could have been a face-saving arrangement whereby for Ömer's family it was a marriage between Muslims, and for Peti's family a marriage between Christians. Certainly, when things became complicated and the authorities became involved, Ömer's brother would declare that "he had scolded Ömer" and that he had arranged for him to be conscripted into the army. Moreover, the fact that Ömer and his wife went back to his wife's family and that both were seen attending church strongly implies that Ömer/Yani was living the life of a good *"sogambros"*. Although all of this is speculation, except for the position of the *"sogambros"*, it remains possible that for Deli Yani family was more important than religion. It is therefore also possible that the case of the "conversion" of the boy Velil was a similar *"sogambros"* story. It is also worth noting that Ömer was from a Yörük family, and as Tzedopoulos points out, some of the original Kromlides were actually Christianized and Hellenized Turkmen.[96]

CASES OF DOUBLE IDENTITY

On 20 July 1913 the Vilayet of Sivas reported a very puzzling inheritance dispute in the *kaza* of Tokad. The case involved a certain Ali Mümtaz, who

[95] The *Yörüks* were reknowned for their heterodoxy and syncretism. See Hasluck, *Christianity and Islam under the Sultans*, particularly p. 130: "It is generally reported of Yuruks that circumcision is not usually practiced among them".

[96] Tzedopoulos, "Public Secrets", pp. 174–5: "Some of the nineteenth century Kromlides were reportedly not descendants of converts to Islam but Muslims (often of Turkmen origin) who had been linguistically Grecisized and practiced a syncretistic form of Christianity." Fotiadis's Russian source also mentions another possible *"sogambros"* in the family of Yusuf/Iosif Kahvecioğlu. Iosif does not have a son, so he marries his daughter Sultana to a Muslim, a certain Savvas/Derviş. See Fotiadis, *Piges tis histories*, p. 140, the Russian embassy in Istanbul enclosing a "List of the Christians of the mine of Akdağ of the diocese of Chaldia who are not recognized as such by the Imperial Government but are regarded as Ottomans [Muslims]." What follows is a list of 150 families with the members of each one, their Christian and Muslim names, and their places of residence. *Piges tis histories*, p. 141. My thanks to Yorgos Tzedopoulos for providing and translating the reference.

had died intestate, leaving considerable wealth and apparently having no
heirs. The curious thing was that Ali Mümtaz was buried in the Armenian
cemetery by Armenian priests. Soon after the funeral a certain Karabet
Asfaryan materialized, claiming that the deceased had been in fact Bogos
Asfaryan, his older brother. When an investigation was carried out, it
turned out that Bogos had converted to Islam in 1896 and had been an
official Muslim until his death in 1909. Bogos Asfaryan/Ali Mümtaz had
thus led a double life for thirteen years.[97] As the amount of wealth
(probably in the form of real estate) was considerable, the authorities
had to take a close look at the matter. In its records, the Ministry of
Justice and Religious Sects found that Bogos had indeed legitimately converted and that his conversion had been recorded at the ministry. What the
ministry claimed had happened was that Bogos had been registered as an
Armenian in the old population registers (*defter-i atik*), but his new
Muslim identity had not been registered in the new registers. He had
therefore fallen into the category of "unregistered population" (*nüfus-u
mektume*). After his conversion he had "never been seen fulfilling his
religious obligations and he acquired property both as Ali Mümtaz and
Bogos Asfaryan".[98] Moreover, the deceased had never had his identity
papers corrected. The ministry officials were certainly not pleased, either
with the deceased or with their underlings in Tokad:

'[H]e did not sever his relations with his previous community and did not seriously embrace Islam, nor did he take any measures against any claims on his
wealth by the Armenian community in the event of his death, all of this points in
the direction of his [eventual] apostasy. . . . The fact that he was known as Muslim
there and that he bought property in his Muslim name, yet the fact that the
authorities allowed his body to be buried by Armenian priests cannot be called
proper procedure.'

Therefore, the Ministry concluded, "if a legitimate heir comes forth, in
order to avoid complications between the two communities as to his
[Ali/Bogos] true faith", any property acquired as Bogos Asfaryan should

---

[97] BOA. DH. ID 116/70, 7 Temmuz 1329 / 20 July 1913, the Vilayet of Sivas to the Ministry
of the Interior, Secretariat of the Vilayet of Sivas, No. 21814. The date of the conversion
fits the date of the Armenian massacres in the 1890s, when many Armenians converted in
order to save their lives. See Chapter 5 in this volume.

[98] Ibid., 18 Ağustos 1329 / 31 August 1913, the Ministry of Justice and Religious Sects to the
Vilayet of Sivas, response to a query from the Vilayet of Sivas regarding the property of the
late Ali Mumtaz, who died heirless in Tokad, appearing as a Muslim, signed by Deputy
Minister Ali.

be given to the heirs, and any property acquired as Ali Mümtaz should be left to the state treasury (*mirî*).[99]

It appears that Bogos fashioned himself as a Muslim vis-à-vis the state and as an Armenian vis-à-vis the Armenian community. Another aspect of the affair is that as Tokad was a small place, this deception could not have been carried out without the full knowledge of both communities and the authorities.

A similar case came up in the dispatches from Diyarbakır on 17 April 1910. A man calling himself "the convert Ali Riza" had presented himself at the government offices and declared that he wanted to revert to his original faith; he was Armenian and was called Kevork. Upon investigation it was discovered that Kevork had indeed converted twenty-two years previously and that his conversion had been approved locally and with the Ministry of Justice and Religious Sects. It now became apparent that Ali Riza/Kevork had been a local businessman who had gone bankrupt and converted "in order to solve his difficulties", presumably meaning that he thought that conversion would wipe out his debts. When it failed to do so, he had decided to return to his old faith. He was "frequently applying to the government offices to have his apostasy recognized".[100] When the Vali asked Istanbul what his line of conduct should be, he was told, "although it is natural that you should apply the law ... In matters such as these the governors are advised to act in accordance with local conditions and to avoid anything likely to give rise to conflict among the population".[101] Although it is not indicated anywhere in the document that Ali Rıza/Kevork led a double life, it is highly likely that everyone in Diyarbakır knew his origins.

Another case of double identity was reported on 29 May 1912 from the *sancak* of Amasya. It involved an Armenian woman named Lusiya Kazazyan, who had converted to Islam on 15 October 1905 but now wanted to return to her former faith. Her formal conversion procedure had been carried out, and she had taken the name Ayşe Sıdıka. The Ministry of Justice and Religious Sects had duly registered her conversion and had approved of her being issued new identity papers. Yet it appears that the matter was not quite so straightforward. Lusiya/Ayşe had also been involved in local politics as a dedicated supporter of the

---

[99] Ibid.

[100] BOA DH.MUI. 86–12, 4 Nisan 1326 / 17 April 1910, cipher telegramme from the Vilayet of Diyarbekir, signed by Vali Galip.

[101] Ibid., 6 Nisan 1326 / 19 April 1910, cipher telegramme from the Ministry of the Interior to the Vilayet of Diyarbakir.

Committee of Union and Progress and was also reputed to be of somewhat loose morals, making her a target for the conservative opposition.

The Mutasarrıf Nureddin Bey was to write to his superiors in Istanbul:

'According to precedent and previous practice in such cases where [the Christian] person has converted to Islam but has later become apostate, the person must produce a certificate from their Patriarchate testifying that they were hitherto unregistered in the census registers. In this case, making absolutely no mention of the apostasy (*keyfiyet-i irtidaddan kattiyetle bahs edilmiyerek*), they are registered as new entries in the population registers as done for other hitherto unregistered persons and are given an Ottoman identity certificate'.[102]

As seen in the earlier case of Bogos Asfaryan, the category of "unregistered population" was a very useful way of solving the problem as the person did not officially exist until he or she had been registered and issued identity papers. Nureddin Bey further recommended that in order to pre-empt any undue provocation of the population "who may get excited", Kazazyan should be temporarily removed to another place.[103] It seems that the matter did not end there. Some five months later Nureddin Bey's successor as Mutasarrıf, Ahmed Macid Bey, would write to his superiors that

'We should remember that the Great Powers have been pressuring the Sublime State to include the freedom of apostasy formally in treaties and that it has always rejected this, saying that the Islamic religion would not allow it. ... This place [Amasya] is very conservative and deeply religious and cannot be compared to other locations where the ideas of freedom have taken root. ... Although the violence of the *Şeriat* ruling for those who commit apostasy is well known, and although we cannot interfere in matters of conscience, it is still disturbing that the rejection of the greatest of revealed religions should be reduced to a mere administrative matter.'[104]

The solution proposed by the Ministry of Justice and Religious Sects is significant here. To officially allow a convert to Islam to register as "unregistered population" and to make no mention of a previously held faith in the newly issued identity papers shows that the state colluded to an important extent in the self-fashioning of the convert. Naturally the state's attitude was prompted by the desire to avoid complications, popular reaction, etc. But in instances like that of Lusiya Kazazyan and Bogos Asfaryan, it allowed people to "legally disappear" and be born again,

[102] BOA DH.ID 116/72, 19 Kanun- u Sani 1328 / 31 January 1912, the Mutasarrıf of Amasya, Nureddin Bey, to the Ministry of the Interior.
[103] Ibid.
[104] Ibid. BOA DH.ID 116/72, 16 Mayis 1328 / 29 May 1912, the Mutasarrıf of Amasya, Ahmet Macid, to the Ministry of the Interior.

very often in another locality, with a new identity. The case of Bogos/Ali is all the more striking as the "convert" in question was allowed to legally disappear (and to acquire property as a Muslim) yet remained in full view of the community. Although Ahmed Macid did not approve, he was quite right: the matter of apostasy from Islam *was* being reduced to a mere administrative measure.

A similar case involving double naming was reported from the Vilayet of Erzincan on 30 December 1901. An Armenian by the name of Keşişoğlu Krikor had converted in 1887 and taken the name Hidayet. He had later apostatized and again started using his old name. It was determined that "it is unsuitable that he go here and there sometimes appearing as an Armenian and at other times as a Muslim". It was determined that he should be exiled to Rhodes, as he was also "suspected of perfidious activities".[105]

One of the most spectacular cases of double identity that I have encountered is the case of the Armenian Bishop Harutyun of Sis. On 28 November 1886, the sultan's private secretary, Süreyya Paşa, reported that "The Archbishop of Sis Artin Efendi has recently converted to Islam and taken the name of Mehmet Emin Efendi".[106] The person converting was none other than Harutyun Achabayan, one of the most senior clerics in the Catholicosate of Cilicia.[107] This is a very interesting case because it enables us to undertake a contrapuntal reading of the Ottoman and Armenian sources.

First, the story as it appears in the Ottoman documentation. The initial emergence of Artin/Harutyun/Emin Efendi in the above document is followed by a considerable paper trail. On 4 July 1888 it was reported that Emin Efendi had sent a telegramme to the Porte, requesting that his monthly stipend be augmented by five hundred *kuruş*, as "he was ailing in body and had many dependents" . He also requested permission to move himself and his family, who consisted of eight souls, to Istanbul and was awaiting the sultan's permission to do so. He also pleaded poverty and

---

[105] BOA DH.MKT 1906/15, 17 Kanun-u Evvel 1317 / 30 December 1901, the Secretariat of the Ministry of the Interior.

[106] BOA DH.İD 866/81, 1 Rebiyülevvel 1303 / 28 November 1886, the imperial private secretary, Süreyya Paşa. Sis is present-day Kozan in the province of Adana.

[107] I am indebted to Kevork Bardakjian for the information on Bishop Harutyun. Bardakjian very generously traced him in the Armenian sources and translated them, and states that "This man was consecrated bishop at the age of twenty by Giragos II; and he ordained 60 priests and consecrated one Catholicos". E-mail communication dated 24 November 2006.

requested funds for the move. He was accordingly awarded 2,000 *kuruş*, and the Vilayet of Adana was reminded that he had already been given 5,000 *kuruş* as an "imperial favour".[108]

By 17 July we see that Mehmet Emin Efendi had departed from Adana having received his travel expenses.[109] Upon arrival in Istanbul, "because of his special position" it was arranged that he be settled in a house specially rented for him, and that it be ensured that his salary "be paid regularly without falling into arrears". In return for all this royal favour, Emin Efendi was expected to earn his keep. He was to do this by working for the Press Office, "because he reads and writes good Armenian".[110] Apart from the tragic irony of an Armenian bishop being set to work translating Armenian newspapers, there is another possible dimension; no doubt some of the literature that came his way would have consisted of politically sensitive material in Armenian that the Palace and the Porte would want to keep tabs on. It is worth pointing out that Mehmed Emin Efendi was certainly getting special treatment. At a time when it was quite normal for state officials' salaries to fall into arrears, it was ordered specifically that he be paid regularly.[111] Yet, despite specific instructions, it appears that his salary did fall into arrears; by November he was writing that he "was in a state of great need". The Ministry of the Interior was duly instructed again that his accumulated salary should be paid and that his salary should not fall into arrears.[112] No less a personage than the Grand Vizier himself, Kamil Paşa, acknowledged the order and instructed the Ministry of Finance to make regular payments "on the basis of the transfer of the salary that Mehmed Emin Efendi had been receiving in Kozan". This reference is all the more interesting as it shows that well before his transfer

---

[108] BOA DH. MKT 1506/68, 24 Şevval 1305 / 4 July 1888, the Sublime Porte to the Vilayet of Adana. These were considerable sums of money. At the time an average government official would receive something around 1,700 *kuruş* a month. On salary levels of Ottoman officials, see K. Boratav, G. Ökçün, and Ş. Pamuk, "Ottoman Wages and the World Economy", *Review* 8 (1985), 379–406; and P. Dumont and F. Georgeon, "Un bourgeois d'Istanbul au debut du XXeme siècle", *Turcica* 17 (1985), 127–88. My thanks to Cem Behar for this information and these references.

[109] BOA DH.MKT 1526/60, 20 Zilkade 1305 / 17 July 1888, the Sublime Porte reporting on correspondence received from Adana.

[110] BOA DH.MKT 1531/104, 29 Zilkade 1305 / 7 August 1888, the Minister of the Interior to the Sublime Porte.

[111] On the matter of official salaries falling into arrears, see Carter Findley, *Ottoman Civil Officialdom* (Princeton, NJ, 1989), pp. 293–332.

[112] BOA Irade Dahiliye 86541, 27 Safer 1306 / 2 November 1888, Yıldız Palace Imperial Secretariat, Imperial Secretary Süreyya Paşa.

to Istanbul, Mehmed Emin had been on the state payroll.[113] By January 1889 we find Emin Efendi installed in a house rented for him in the Cerrah Paşa district, with a monthly rent of 120 *kuruş*.[114]

When put against the Armenian sources, it appears that the case as reflected in the Ottoman documentation is merely one facet of a long and tragic tale. After the death in 1866 of his mentor the Catholicos of Cilicia, Giragos II, Bishop Harutyun Achabayan had been involved in the secret consecration of Bishop Nigoghos as Catholicos. This consecration was opposed by the Armenian Patriarchate of Istanbul, who replaced him in 1871 with Bishop Mgrdich Kefsizian. Catholicos Kefsizian persecuted those bishops who had secretly consecrated Nigoghos, particularly Bishop Harutyun, and "so intensified his persecution that Harutyun Episkopos became a *dajig* (Muslim) taking the name of Emin [Efendi] but he did not leave Sis".[115]

As to the circumstances of Bishop Harutyun's conversion, the Armenian source provides the following details. When Bishop Harutyun was the prelate of Antioch he met a woman named Miriam, who told him that she wanted to be divorced from her husband, who was impotent. The bishop dissolved the marriage and married Miriam to his assistant as a "nominal spouse". Miriam then became pregnant: "Bishop Harutyun found himself between two swords, the persecution of the Catholicos Mgrditch on the one hand, and the pregnancy of Miriam on the other. He solved the problem by converting to Islam, and harboured a grudge against Mgrditch."[116] Although he supposedly became Emin Efendi, he remained Christian at heart. He had three children (two girls and a boy), and he baptized all three himself. "As a Muslim İskender was recruited [into the army and] having completed his service, returned to Sis. They arrested him and subjected him to torture [to force him] to deny his faith; he did not."[117]

There is an interesting epilogue to İskender's story in the Ottoman paper trail. On 4 September 1902, no less an authority than the Ottoman Council of Ministers discussed the matter of İskender. It had been put before the

---

[113] BOA DH.MKT 1581/84, 29 Safer 1306 / 4 November 1888, the Grand Vizier, Kamil Paşa, to the Ministry of the Interior.

[114] BOA DH.MKT 1570/115, Selh-i Rebiyülahir 1306 / 2 January 1889.

[115] Papgen Guleserian (Papgen A. Atoragits Gatoghigos Medzi Dan Gilio), *Badmutyun Gatoghigosats Giligio (1441-en minchev mer orere)*, 2nd ed. (Antilias, Lebanon, 1990), column 690.

[116] Ibid.

[117] Guleseiran, *Badmutyun*, translation by Kevork Bardakjian.

council that "Iskender, the son of the late Emin Efendi, and his daughters insist that they are Christians". It had been established that

'İskender, although known in his locality as a Muslim, in his primary examination, had denied his faith and insisted that he was an Armenian and had married an Armenian. ... This is clearly the result of his wish to avoid military service. ... It should be made clear to the Vilayet of Adana that the statements of those who commit apostasy are not to be taken into account, and that they are to be conscripted forthwith into the army'.[118]

According to the Armenian sources, it appears that for a long time after his conversion Harutyun/Emin Efendi led a double life:

'A pseudo-Muslim Emin Efendi, as an Achabahyan, served the altar of the *Ach* [i.e., the Reliquary containing the relics of St-Gregory the Illuminator's right hand] which the *Achabans* [i.e., custodians of the Reliquary] had not removed after the Ach had been moved to the Monastery, during the reign of Catholicos Teodoros. ... They had assigned a special room for the Ach, and had erected an altar in the image of Lusavorich [i.e., St. Gregory the Illuminator] and an ever-burning lamp. Emin Efendi personally attended the altar and the ever burning lamp, and prayed there alone. ... Bishop Giragos Pekmezian, once reviled this pseudo-Muslim spitting on him and telling him 'you destroyed your future for a woman, otherwise you were a man worthy of becoming catholicos'. Those who knew him have characterized this former bishop as an opportunist and a hypocrite.'[119]

How does a man who could have been ordained as one of the most high-ranking clerics in the Armenian Apostolic Church end up translating newspapers for the sultan, who became the bane of Ottoman Armenians?[120] What tentative conclusions can we draw from a comparative reading of the Ottoman and Armenian sources? Although the precise date of Harutyun's conversion is unclear, it occurred after 1871, when Bishop Mgrdich Kefsizian became official Catholicos and started persecuting him. It also appears that he met Miriam after this date. In any event, after his conversion he remained in Sis, as the Armenian source indicates. As the Ottoman documents state that the salary he was to receive in Istanbul was the "transferred salary he drew from the Kozan Public

---

[118] BOA MV (Meclis-i, Vükela) 104/72, 30 Cemaziyelevvel 1320 / 4 September 1902, the deliberations of the Council of Ministers regarding İskender, son of the late Emin Efendi. There is a discrepancy between the Armenian and Ottoman accounts. The Armenian source indicates that İskender declared that he was a Christian *after* his return from the army, yet we learn that Emin Efendi is in fact dead by 1902.

[119] Guleseiran, *Badmutyun*, translation by Kevork Bardakjian.

[120] There are four hierarchical Sees in the Armenian Apostolic Church: the Catholicosate of Etchmiadzin, Cilicia (Sis), Jerusalem, and Istanbul. See Hratch Tchilingirian, *The Armenian Apostolic Orthodox Church* (www.sain.org).

Coffer", Harutyun/Emin was apparently receiving an Ottoman salary the whole time he was tending the eternal flame of Saint Gregory the Illuminator as a "pseudo-Muslim".[121] The Armenian source states that he personally baptized his children, yet his son was called İskender, indicating that he had a Muslim public identity and was conscripted into the army as a result. Who were the eight members of family that Mehmed Emin Efendi brought with him to Istanbul? We can only surmise that the group included Emin and Miriam, the servant who was the nominal "husband", and maybe İskender and his spouse along with one of the daughters and her husband, as well as his second (unmarried?) daughter.

In conclusion, what can we say about this story, which abounds in loose ends and unanswered questions? Sis in the 1870s was a small place, and the scandal surrounding Harutyun's "conversion" must have been the perfect example of a "public secret". Harutyun lived in his native Sis for at least ten years as a "pseudo-Muslim". What made him decide to leave and go to the capital? One can only guess. Maybe he had had enough of being "spat upon" and pushed around by his native Armenian community. On the other hand, that same community did not ban him from serving at the altar of one of the holiest relics of their faith. Thus one can argue that Bishop Harutyun was a "double crypto" or a "public crypto", because he was receiving a salary from the Ottoman government and was thus considered a convert, while as far as the Armenian community was concerned he was still an Armenian and a "pseudo-Muslim".

The Ottoman state was never "ethnicity blind" when it came to appointment to important official positions. At the time that they were apparently tolerating Bishop Harutyun's double persona, a contemporary, the Armenian Metropolitan (*marhasa*) of Erzurum, Artin Zahabedyan Efendi, became a candidate for the Istanbul Armenian Patriarchate. His candidacy was discussed in the Council of Ministers on 23 March 1885. The matter before them was "the rumour that this man had once been a Muslim and had at some time committed apostasy [and had become a Christian]". The Ministers pointed out that "although the private life of this man cannot be held against him", it was still necessary to investigate the matter and to determine whether "the spread of these rumours would have any political consequences on his appointment to such a position". During the course of their deliberations, the Minister of Pious Foundations, Kâmil Paşa, declared that "these were baseless rumours

---

[121] BOA İrade Dahiliye 86541, 27 Safer 1306 / 2 November 1888, "*Kozan Mal Sandukuna muhavvel bulunan beş yüz guruş maaşının buraya nakli*".

put about by ill wishers" who wanted to discredit Artin Efendi. He declared that the candidate possessed all the qualifications necessary for the appointment.[122]

The question is, in whose eyes were these rumour-mongers seeking to discredit Artin Efendi? It is highly likely that if he indeed turned out to be an apostate from Islam, despite the polite fiction about his private life not being held against him, he would not be acceptable to Ottoman official-dom. Nor would he be acceptable to the Armenian Church hierarchy, particularly the senior Katogigos of Echimiadzin, if he turned out to be a converted *dajig* (Muslim). It seems the rumours had no effect, and Zahabedyan was actually ordained as Patriarch.[123]

Double identity could also appear in the guise of a confrontation between subjects and the state over tax and/or military service obligations. On 12 June 1850 the Eyalet of Urfa reported that two men named Hacu and Asib, who had been arrested for robbery, had converted to Islam eighteen years previously and had now reverted to Christianity. It had been determined that "because their conversion had been forced it was not valid". The Eyalet of Urfa had been asked to look into the matter and determine where these two men had lived since their conversion and to determine whether "they had paid their *cizye* secretly or openly as *reaya*". Upon investigation of the *cizye* registers at Urfa, it transpired that "both Hacu and Asib had taken their *cizye* receipts for the years 1849 and 1850." The two men were summoned before the local administrative court, where they were invited to return to Islam, "but proved stubborn in their apos-tasy".[124] The key term here is having "paid their *cizye* secretly or openly". The only reason a person who was ostensibly a Muslim would pay *cizye* secretly would be to enable him to claim at some subsequent date that he had always been a "*cizye* payer" (*cizyegüzar*) and therefore a non-Muslim. On the other hand, if he paid *cizye* openly, he was obviously a *reaya*. What seems to be happening here is that the men in question were taking out a form of re-insurance. Possibly, when confronted by the tax collector they would claim Muslim status, or, inversely, when confronted by the conscription officer they would produce their *cizye* receipts as proof of their status as *zimmis*.

[122] BOA MV 2/28, 10 Mart 1301 / 23 March 1885.

[123] He served from 1885 to 1888 as Harutyun I Vahabedyan. See Vartan Artinian, *Osmanlı Devleti'nde Ermeni Anayasası'nın Doğuşu 1839–1863* (Istanbul, 2004), p. 141. My thanks to Aylin Besiryan for this reference and the comment about Etchmiadzin.

[124] BOA A.MKT.UM 18/39, Gurre-i Şaban 1266 / 12 June 1850, the Muhafiz of Urfa, Esseyid Hasan Mümtaz, to the Sublime Porte.

All of these cases have interesting similarities. The people in question who have either led double lives or have appeared in one identity or another at different times seem to have done so over a long time span: Bogos is Ali for thirteen years; Lusiya is Ayşe for seven years; Krikor is Hidayet for four years; Hacu and Asib had been Muslims for eighteen years; and Bishop Harutyun is Emin Efendi for nearly ten years. As in the earlier cases of the Kromlides and Stavriote, it is more than likely that their identities were "public secrets". In fact, the reason they came to the attention of the authorities at all was not their religious affiliation, but other factors. Bogos was rich and had a contested inheritance; Lusiya seems to have been involved in one way or another in the local politics of Tokad; Krikor is suspected of perfidious activities; Hacu and Asib had been pursued because they were accused of robbery. Thus, until challenged in some way by circumstances arising from events that did not necessarily have to do with their religious identity, their double identities had not been disclosed.

CONCLUSION

Both the Kromlides in 1857 and the Istavri in 1879 took the Tanzimat State at its word. The Kromlides trusted the *Hat-ı Humayun* of 1856 and the Istavri the Constitution of 1876. Both turned out to be wrong. Nonetheless, the Porte was also caught in a quandary. It had made binding and public declarations of religious freedom in front of foreign witnesses. It had also made promises to its subjects, both Muslim and *reaya*. Now it seemed to be faced with the danger that the crypto phenomenon would infect a much larger segment of the population and that the declaration of religious freedom would lead to much more complicated consequences than it had foreseen. The two cases discussed here, though involving very similar communities, occurred in very different historical conjunctures. The Kromlides were hoping to ride on the crest of reforms that seemed to be expanding. The Istavri, on the other hand, made their move just as Abdülhamid II was about to abrogate the Constitution and to close down the Parliament at the beginning of a regime that would put its emphasis on Islamic unity.

The whole issue of crypto-religion and its relationship to state power raises some interesting questions. Particularly in cases such as the Kromlides, where the secret was a public secret, the question seems to revolve around a process that one might call "bluff and counter-bluff". When the Kromlides or the Istavri "came out", they were in a sense bluffing the state by confronting it with its own promises and commitments. What they had not bargained for, however, particularly in the case of the Kromlides, was the state seeing their bluff and coming up with the diabolically clever counter-bluff of the *"tenassur-u rum"*. After all, the "secret" of double faith "had always been known to the state", as one of the people interviewed declared. So, to return to the theme of polite fiction, what was being torn asunder here was the veil of polite fiction that the Kromlides or the Istavri were Muslims.

As to crypto-faith and syncretism in general, a few comments are in order here. Crypto-faiths were evidently not static systems of belief, nor were they a one-way street. The direction of conversion was not always Christianity to Islam, but could also be Islam to Christianity by way of syncretism, as seen in the case of the Turkmen and Alevi in the hinterland of Trabzon and Gümüşhane.[125] It is important at this point to distinguish between syncretism and crypto-Christianity. Crypto-Christianity (or any crypto-faith, for that matter), is a set of beliefs that one practices consciously, knowing the possibly dire consequences if one is discovered. Syncretism suggests a set of beliefs and practices that seem to be acquired ad hoc or are remnants of previously held beliefs that have filtered into the "new" faith. Clearly, the border between crypto-Christianity and syncretism is porous, and one may, and often does, blend into the other. Hasluck has admirably delineated the paths that such influence and counter-influence could follow. A Muslim or Christian sanctuary could become "ambiguous" through the circulation of the legend that the saint worshipped by Muslims had secretly converted to Christianity or vice versa, or that a Muslim saint's sanctuary was shared by a Christian.[126] The great attraction of the Sumela monestary for Muslims is a good example. Anthony Bryer also gives a detailed account of the funeral of a highly respected Orthodox archbishop of Trabzon who was honoured by Muslims, who closed their shops and followed the funeral cortege.[127] In time such a figure could become a saint for both religions.

Crypto-Christianity has also provided suitable material for quasi-racist stereotyping. R. M. Dawkins seemed to envision a sort of "hierarchy of crypto-ism". At the bottom are the adherents of a "mystical syncretism" brought about by "dervish influence". This shades into the "great class of indifferents", of which Dawkins gives the Albanians as the most current

---

[125] Tzedopoulos, "Public Secrets", pp. 174–5.
[126] Hasluck, *Christianity and Islam under the Sultans*, p. 570.
[127] Bryer, "Nineteenth Century Monuments in the City and Vilayet of Trebizond", p. 105.

example. Next are the "imperfectly converted", who seek moral but mostly material help "from whatever holy man and holy place ... may be at hand". At the apex of the hierarchy are the "genuine Crypto-Christians: who *ex animo* believe in Christianity and hate Islam."[128] Dawkins gives flesh and blood to his categories. At the bottom are the *linobambaki* of Cyprus, who had "not much [that was] heroic about [them]" and were always "rather a joke to their fellow Christians". They were nothing like the Kourmoulides of Crete, who were in a state of constant insurrection, and consequently "nowhere else was the struggle against the Turk so continuous or so heroic". His highest praise is for the "Stavriotai of the Pontos ... the most important of all. If the Linobambakoi represent the comedy of the Crypto-Christian way of life, the Stavriotai represent its tragedy".[129] Clearly Dawkins's sliding scale of "heroism" functioned in proportion to his own and his subject's "hatred" of the "Turks" and Islam.

Naturally no religious community is going to welcome the conversion of any of its members to another faith; the official nationalist grand narratives of conversion seem to favour forced conversion over voluntary. Then, after all, there is someone else to blame, the aggressor, the "Turk" whom it was impossible to resist; therefore, as a tragic and inevitable result of pressure, some of the community took this road in order to survive.[130] This narrative is not actually wrong; very often that is what happened; it is just that the forced conversion narrative was always more attractive for nationalist discourses. It is also convenient to believe in members of the crypto-Christian community "hating Islam" for hundreds of years, although it is difficult to conceive how one can actively hate a faith one has practiced for so many generations. When he was questioned, the Istavri notable Mustafa Kobçu Oğlu quite openly stated that "they had always been Christians" but had posed as Muslims in order to send their children to Muslim schools so that they could learn to read and write. Why would someone voluntarily send their children to the school of the "hated faith"? He also referred to the Istavri as *"mezhebimiz"*, "our faith". It may just be possible that some cyrpto-Christians actually believed in *both* the faiths they professed.

Crypto-Christianity as it played out in the late Ottoman Empire also provides interesting glimpses into the different perceptions of the self, that

---

[128] Dawkins, "The Crypto-Christians of Turkey", p. 273.

[129] Ibid., p. 274.

[130] Stavro Skendi, *Balkan Cultural Studies* (New York, 1980), p. 160: "The crypto-Christians [in the Balkans] it is believed, emerged in periods of outbursts of anti-Christian fanaticism".

of the individual often clashing with the identity the state power wanted to assign to its subjects. We saw how the process of registration of identity proved to be a very slippery business as the people who were supposed to be registered and controlled proved able to deliberately fall between the cracks. That was the story of the "double-namers". In the days before photo-IDs, men could successfully avoid conscription by circulating under Christian names. It was actually quite easy to "disappear" and become invisible to state authorities. A timely greased palm could make sure that the red ink in the old population register, marking you as a convert with your previous Christian name as well as your new Muslim name, was copied into the new register in good black ink, thus enabling what was supposedly impossible that is, that Yani was at the same time also Ahmet. On the other hand, the system could be used in one's favour by actually seeking registration as "unregistered population" and asking on that basis to be issued new identity papers, which would conveniently omit any mention of past conversion or apostasy.

Another aspect of conversion narratives like that of Bishop Harutyun is that they are a vivid illustration of Ottoman weakness. In vivid contrast to the "symbolic victories" and the public flouting of the conversion of distinguished figures such as the Orthodox priest, Mehmed of Athens, who converted in front of Ahmed I (1603–17), or the Hungarian İbrahim Müteferrika, who became famous for founding the first Ottoman printing press in the eighteenth century, Bishop Harutyun is treated almost as an embarrassment and is hidden away in an obscure post translating newspapers.[131]

Crypto-Christianity also serves to illustrate the way in which the rise of nationalism articulated with and acted upon the processes of conversion and apostasy during this turbulent period. A phenomenon that had been either deliberately ignored or unknown now acquired explosive properties. In a political conjuncture where grey areas and polite fictions were no longer tolerated, the souls and bodies of the crypto-Christians became contested territory between rival nationalisms, the Great Powers, and the Sublime Porte. The ups and downs of the nationalist narrative in Greece relating to the Kromlides, who went from heroic secret resisters to elements defiled by Turkishness and Islam, so convincingly illustrated by Tzedopoulos, is very much a case in point.[132] Maurus Reinkowski also points out that many of the crypto-Christian peoples of the Balkans and

---

[131] Krstic, "Illuminated by the Light of Islam", pp. 54, 59, 61.
[132] Tzedopoulos, "Public Secrets", pp. 188–90.

the Middle East emerged as a result of the rise of nationalism and European intervention: "[T]he emerging nation states of the 19th and early 20th century demanded unambiguous confessions of loyalty. And indeed, Europeans, when describing crypto-religious groups in purely confessional terms, talked very much along the lines of nationalist argument."[133]

The mass apostasy that the Ottomans feared and that the missionaries and their supporters wanted did not happen. Either the crypto movements remained hidden, or their effects were contained. Moreover, at precisely the time when the Ottomans feared that many might be about to leave their ranks, history gave them a new resource, the career converts of the failed "Springtime of the Peoples".

---

[133] Maurus Reinkowski, "Hidden Believers, Hidden Apostates: The Phenomenon of Crypto-Jews and Crypto-Christians in the Middle East", in Dennis Washburn and Kevin A. Rheinhart (eds.), *Converting Cultures: Religion, Ideology and Transformations of Modernity* (Leiden and Boston, 2007), pp. 409–33.

4

Career Converts, Migrant Souls, and Ottoman Citizenship

"For you know, Aubrey, do you not, that Bonaparte turned Turk?"

"I heard of it Sir, of course; but no one has ever asserted that he recoiled from swine's flesh or a bottle of wine. I put it down to one those foolish things a man says when he wishes to be elected to Parliament, such as 'give me your votes and I undertake to do away with the National Debt in eighteen months'. I do not believe, he is any more a Mussulman than I am. You have to be circumcised to be a Turk."

"For my own part I have no knowledge of the gentleman's soul, or heart or private parts."

Conversation between Commodore Jack Aubrey and
Lord Keith, Supreme Commander of the Fleet, Royal Navy, in the novel
The Hundred Days by Patrick O'Brian

WHAT DID IT MEAN TO "BECOME AN OTTOMAN" IN THE NINETEENTH CENTURY?

The whole issue of crypto-Christianity posed critical challenges to the Tanzimat State as it seemed to be the thin end of the wedge that could become the undoing of the project. The process of the "coming out" of the crypto-Christians overlapped with the "coming in" of new people. After the "springtime of the peoples" in 1848, Europe was to face the most serious challenge to the imperial system since the French Revolution. The fallout of the failed revolutions in Hungary and Poland were the thousands of refugees who sought asylum in Ottoman domains. Like the crypto-Christians who openly declared their "true" faith, the influx of a large number of foreigners, many of whom at least nominally converted to Islam, caused a further transformation in the politics of conversion. This issue was to be coupled with the idea of formal citizenship after the formulation of the Ottoman Citizenship Law of 1869. After the promulgation of this law, Ottoman citizenship was to be officially decoupled from religion as conversion to Islam would no longer be a sufficient condition for Ottoman citizenship, and it became the rule that each case be considered on its merits. Nonetheless, in practice Islam was to remain the primary focus of Ottoman identity and to become even more so during the Hamidian period. Yet it was in 1885, during the Hamidian period, that the practice of obligatory identity papers was instituted for all Ottoman citizens regardless of religion.

The most important transformation in the politics of conversion was that the late Ottoman Empire seemed to develop what might be called a "hierarchy of conversion".[1] This was a sort of sliding scale of conversions whereby the status that the state accorded the convert was based on criteria like usefulness or nuisance potential, ranging from the high-ranking qualified military experts, which would put them at the top of the hierarchy; to the tolerable but not necessarily desirable conversions of middling elements such as railway technicians, policemen, etc., to the downright undesirables such as the European rif-raff who converted to escape crimes, unhappy love affairs, or debts.

According to Ottoman tradition based on the Islamic law of subjecthood, conversion to Islam on Ottoman soil made the convert automatically a subject of the Sultan/Caliph. As put in a major recent study by Macit Kenanoğlu:

'Although Islamic jurists in the classical period did not use the term *citizenship*, (*vatandaşlık*) the concept of citizenship was known to Islamic law. According to Islamic law, those belonging to the Islamic state that has established sovereignty over the *Dar ul Islam* become the *ehlü dari'l Islam*, that is to say the people, the subjects of the Islamic state ... Because Islam subsumes faith and citizenship.'[2]

Yet many if not most of the neophyte Muslims remained nominal converts; their conversions amounted to little more than a polite fiction. Nonetheless, the term "career convert" as I use it here is not intended to imply that all of these men were insincere in their pledge of service to their new sovereign – far from it, as seen in the case of the commander-in-chief

---

[1] I am indebted to Ussama Makdisi for this concept of the "hierarchy of conversions".
[2] Macit Kenanoğlu, *Osmanlı Millet Sistemi*, p. 13. The italics are in the original. On this see also Ömer Nasuhi Bilmen, *Hukuk-u Islamiyye*, Chapter 3, "Dar-ül Harp-Dar ül Islam".

of the Ottoman forces in the Crimean War, Ömer Paşa Latas, a Croat by origin.[3]

So what did it mean to "become an Ottoman" in the nineteenth century? One of the interesting aspects of the relationship of the Hungarian converts to their new country was that they always referred to the Ottoman sultan as the "Sultan of the Turks".[4] They also addressed the Ottoman officials as "Turks", and were somewhat confounded to find out that many of them were not Turkish at all, but were Ottoman to the core, as in the case of Ömer Paşa Latas himself, who was living proof that a successful career convert could achieve the highest honours. As commander-in-chief (*Serdar-ı Ekrem*) of the Ottoman forces during the Crimean War, Ömer Paşa was awarded the Grand Cordon the Military Order of the Bath in 1855, one of the highest decorations bestowed by the British crown.[5] He must have served as a role model for many of the neo-Ottoman Hungarians. Another curious twist to the way in which the Hungarians related to their new society was that because they saw the Ottoman Empire almost as a Turkish nation-state, and because they were imbued with the ideals of Romantic Revival nationalism, they had very little sympathy for insubordination on the part of the subject peoples of the empire; hence their willingness to volunteer to suppress the Bosnian rising. In fact, what had brought down the Hungarian Revolution was to

---

[3] Ömer Paşa Latas (1806–71) was born Mihailo Latas in Serbian Kraina Janja Gora, the municipality of Plaski in present-day Croatia. Educated at military school, he joined the frontier regiment. Latas fled to Bosnia in 1823 to escape charges of embezzlement. There he converted to Islam while he was serving as a tutor to the children of a Turkish merchant. When the family moved to Istanbul, he came with them. He was appointed lecturer at the Turkish military academy and moved up through the ranks. His highest rank was to be commander of the Ottoman Army in the Crimean War. An Ottoman biographical ency-clopedia has the following short entry on Ömer Paşa: "Originally one of the German Slavs. Studied mathematics in his native land. Came to the Ottoman lands and entered the entourage of Senikli İbrahim Paşa and became a Muslim. Reached the highest ranks in the Ottoman army, Commander in Chief of Ottoman Forces during the Crimean War, twice the Muşir of Rumelia." *Sicil- i Osmani* (Istanbul, 1983), vol. 4, pp. 1322–3.

[4] Kemal Karpat, "Kossuth in Turkey: The Impact of the Hungarian Refugees in the Ottoman Empire 1849–1851", *Hungarian Heritage Review* 23 (March 1990), 23.

[5] Cevdet Paşa, *Tezakir. Tezkire*, no.7, "Bakiyye-i Vekâyi-i sene 1271", p. 52. Cevdet mis-takenly states that Ömer Paşa was granted the Garter, "*dizbağı nişam*". See *The Times* of 3 September 1855: "The Investiture of Omar Pasha with the Grand Order of the Bath was performed with much ceremony on the 11th [August] at the official residence of the English Ambassador at Pera." My thanks to Edhem Eldem for this clarification and this reference. Ömer Paşa had also served in Lebanon against the Druze in 1843, and he is referred to in the Arabic literature as *al-nimsawi*, or the Austrian. My thanks to Ussama Makdisi for this information.

a great extent the Hungarian nationalists' inability to come to terms with their own minorities, the Croats, Serbs, and Romanians. What was taking place was that the romantic Hungarian nationalists, even as neophyte Muslims, were bringing their own migrant bourgeois central European notions of liberal Romantic Revival nationalism into a late Ottoman Islamic context.[6] Such men would have no sympathy for insurgent Bosnian Beys or Arabs or Druzes, whom they were likely to see as seditious elements or savage rebels. Now owing allegiance as Muslim (nominal or not) subjects of the Muslim sultan, whom they saw as the "Sultan of Turkey", they adjusted to their new roles remarkably quickly. The chapter that follows traces the transformations in the politics of conversion as they emerge in cases ranging from illustrious Hungarian officers to Bulgarian brigands turned into Muslim policemen, and how this related to the changes in the concept of Ottoman citizenship.

CAREER CONVERSIONS OR MIGRANT SOULS: THE HUNGARIAN REFUGEES OF 1849[7]

During the Hungarian uprising of 1956, on 23 October, the Hungarian demonstrators facing Soviet troops in Budapest rallied around the statue of General Joseph Bem, one of the heroes of the Hungarian Revolution of 1848. Situated on the Bem Rackpart on the banks of the Danube, the statue depicts Bem in a heroic pose, one arm in a sling, the other pointing into the distance. The aim of the demonstrators who made Bem the focal point of their rally was to celebrate him in his persona as an anti-Russian fighter. Bem, who was Polish, had been a leader of the 1830 uprising in Poland against the Russians, and had later come to Hungary to take a leading role in the Revolution of 1848. Today he is still one of the heroes in the pantheon of post-Soviet Hungary. Hardly any of the demonstrators of 1956 would have known that Joseph Bem, heroic commander of the

---

[6] On the Hungarian intolerance for any idea of autonomy for any of the other peoples of the Habsburg Empire, see Keith Hitchins, *The Rumanian National Movement in Transylvania 1780–1849* (Cambridge, Mass., 1969), p. 183; Robert W. Seton Watson, "The Era of Reform in Hungary", *Slavonic and East European Review* 21, part 2 (1943), 166; Gelu Neamtu and Ioan Bolovan, *The Revolution of 1848–1849 in Transylvania* (Cluj Napoca, 2004), p. 35.

[7] I owe thanks to Kahraman Sakul for his help in compiling the material for this section.

honvéd forces, died as Murad Paşa, a circumcised Muslim and an Ottoman officer.[8]

The nineteenth century ushered in a new kind of "renegade", the romantic who adopted a "pet cause" as his own and was even prepared to die for it, the ultimate example of which is of course Lord Byron. But the rising tide of Romantic nationalism did not always run against the Ottoman Empire. After the "Springtime of the Peoples" from the 1830s to the 1850s, many Poles, Hungarians, Italians, and others, fleeing Austrian and/or Russian enemies, took refuge in Ottoman domains. This placed the Ottoman élite in something of a quandary. The Ottoman Empire was every bit as legitimist a monarchy as Habsburg Austria and Romanov Russia. The Ottomans could not be expected to love nationalist separatists and had as much to lose by their activities as Austria and Russia, if not more, because they were weaker. Yet it was this very weakness that made it tempting to welcome the newcomers as most of them were trained military men with specialist skills. One Turkish historian has actually referred to them as a "providential hail of trained *cadres*".[9] But the idea of "the enemy of my enemy is my friend" as a modus operandi could, and did, get them embroiled in severe diplomatic crises, as both Austria and Russia demanded that the "insurgents", as they saw them, be handed over to be tried for treason. This was made all the more complicated by the fact that the Sublime Porte had treaties of extradition with both Austria and Russia dealing with the reciprocal return of fugitives.[10] On the other hand, one of the main aims of the Ottoman state after the Tanzimat reforms of the 1840s was to appear as a member of the "civilized powers", and what better way to do so than to extend its magnanimous protection to romantic fugitives who happened to be universally popular in the two more powerful states that they needed to court, that is, Britain

---

[8] I would like to thank my friend and colleague Andras Kovacs from the Central European University, Budapest, for bringing Bem to my attention. On the symbolic significance of the statue during the demonstrations of 1956, see Gabor Bona, *The Hungarian Revolution and War of Independence of 1848–49* (New York, 1999), p. 483. The *honvéd* were the Hungarian national army.

[9] İlber Ortaylı, *İmparatorluğun en Uzun Yüzyılı*, pp. 29, 30.

[10] The treaties in question were the Austrian-Ottoman Peace of Belgrade of 1739, whereby diplomatic representatives of Austria were granted jurisdiction over Austrian subjects in Ottoman territory, and the Treaty of Küçük Kaynarca of 1774, which granted Russian authorities similar powers.. The critical article is Article 2, which states that all prisoners taking refuge in either empire would be sent back: "With the exception however of those who, in the Empire of Russia, shall have entered the Christian religion, and in the Ottoman Empire the Mahometan religion." See J. C. Hurewitz, *Diplomacy in the Near and Middle East*, vol. 1, pp. 47–51, 55.

and France? This is not to say that there was not a genuine feeling of sympathy for the fugitives, and there were illustrous precedents.[11] The famous conservative jurist Ahmet Cevdet Paşa cited a *sura* from the Qur'an justifying Grand Vizier Reşid Paşa in his determination not to hand the Hungarians over to their enemies:

'The Hungarians were forced to take refuge in the Ottoman lands. The Austrians and the Russians demanded their return. Many people in high places were afraid of provoking the wrath of these two neighboring Great Powers. . . . Reşid Paşa, in keeping with the ruling in the Qur'an ('if one of the infidels (*mushrikin*) asks you for refuge you offer him refuge') persisted in his resolve to protect and shelter the fugitives thus earning the admiration and great honour of the Europeans and Americans for the nation of Islam.'[12]

Soon after the defeats of the Hungarian forces in the summer of 1849, Hungarian, Polish, and Italian forces began to flood into Ottoman territory seeking asylum, many of them accompanied by their families. Bem led a spectacularly successful campaign against the Austrian forces until they had to ask for Russian support. On 6 July 1849 Bem's *honvéd* forces were conclusively defeated by the Russians under General Lüders, and some 1,120 Hungarians crossed the Danube and sought refuge with Ottoman forces in the garrison border town of Vidin. Among them were General Bem, Count Batthany, and thirty-six officers. Thus began one of the most delicate operations of diplomatic tightrope-walking that the Ottoman Empire was to experience in the nineteenth century. Under severe pressure from Austria and Russia to hand over the "rebels", the Ottomans sought to find a way to save the asylum seekers and yet avoid the combined wrath of Austria and Russia.

By late summer the list of refugees seeking asylum in Ottoman territory was beginning to look like a "who's who" of the Hungarian revolution as Bem was soon joined by General Mor Perczel, General Lazar Mesaros, General György Kmetty, the Polish General Dembinski, as well as ex–Foreign

---

[11] A prominent Hungarian revolutionary of the eighteenth century, Ferenć Rakoczi, had also been given asylum in Ottoman territory. After making a brief bid for Hungarian independence from the Habsburgs in 1711, Rakoczi had ended up in exile in the small town of Tekirdağ (Rodosto) on the shores of the Marmara Sea, where he died in April 1735. The house he lived in is still a museum. On him see Agnes Varkongy, "Rakoczi's War of Independence and the Peasantry", in Janos M. Bak and Bela Kiraly (eds.), *From Hunyadi to Rakoczi: War and Society in Late Medieval and Early Modern Hungary* (New York, 1982), p. 385.

[12] Ahmet Cevdet Paşa, *Tezakir* (Ankara, 1986), vol. 1, p. 12. The *sura* is *Al-Tawba* 9:6: "*Wa in ahadun minal-mushrikîn istijaraka fa 'ajirhu.*" My thanks to Alexis Wick for his help with the transliteration.

Minister Count Kazmer Batthyany and Prime Minister Bertalan Szemere, "A few government commissioners and officials completed the émigré's civilian population."[13] On 22 August the crisis reached its peak when the leader of the Hungarian revolutionaries, Layos Kossuth, himself sought refuge in Ottoman dominions travelling on a forged British passport under the name of "Bloomfield".[14] By October the remnants of the Hungarian army piled up on the Ottoman border together with civilian dependents and camp followers numbered some 3,700. The major portion of these returned as part of a "repatriation mission" arranged by imperial authorities on October 21. Nonetheless, "Hungarian emigrant communities – taking into account the constant fluctuation of their population – amounted to anywhere between 1,200 and 1,500 during the 1850s. ... The émigrés' community initially centred itself within the Ottoman Empire".[15] Some Turkish sources have claimed that in the first days, faced with the reluctance of the Ottomans to let them in, the refugees actually *threatened* to turn Muslim on the spot.[16] On 26 August the Ottoman envoy, Fuad Bey, who had been sent out to Bucharest with the specific brief of looking into this matter, reported, "If they are pressured the least bit more, the lot of them will become Muslim. Although this is a good thing, it is highly likely to complicate matters as it will not be possible to refuse them."[17]

Those refugees who made it clear that they had no intention of even flirting with Islam were still to be given refuge as a personal favour of the sultan. However, the converts "received preferential treatment from the very start".[18]

At this point General Bem together with 256 of his followers announced that he had converted to Islam and had taken the name Murad Paşa. He was received with great pomp and ceremony by Ferik Halim Paşa, the

---

[13] Gabor Bona, *The Hungarian Revolution and War of Independence*, pp. 440–1. Bona gives the total figure of émigrés at around 500, most of whom were *honvéd* officers and soldiers: "there were also about twenty commissioned field officers (colonels, lieutenant-colonels, and majors), 120 junior officers ... and 260 non-commissioned officers and private soldiers".

[14] It seems Kossuth contacted Ömer Paşa, commander of the Ottoman armies in Wallachia, before he presented himself at the border. See Denes A. Janossy, *Great Britain and Kossuth* (Budapest, 1937), p. 32.

[15] Bona, *The Hungarian Revolution*, p. 441.

[16] Abdullah Saydam, *Osmanlıların Siyasi İlticalara Bakışı ya da 1849 Macar Leh Mültecileri Meselesi* (The Ottoman attitude to political asylum or the Hungarian and Polish refugees of 1849), offprint from *Belleten* 66 (1997), 339–85.

[17] BOA DUIT 75–1/11, lef. 3. As quoted in Abdullah Saydam, "Müslüman olan Macar-Leh Mültecileri Meselesi" (The affair of the Hungarian and Polish refugees' conversion to Islam), *Toplumsal Tarih* 4 (1995), 34–53.

[18] Karpat, "Kossuth in Turkey", pp. 18–23.

commander of the Ottoman forces at Vidin. This development caused the rumour to spread in European capitals, encouraged by Austrian and Russian agents, that the Ottomans were forcing the refugees to convert. In fact, one particularly fantastic rumour was to the effect that Kossuth himself had converted. The rumours were ugly, to the point that they claimed that the "Turks" were molesting the women and children of the refugees. This caused Kossuth to write a letter to Lord Palmerston complaining about pressure being put on him and his followers to convert to Islam; the letter got out to the press, causing much distress at the Sublime Porte. Although the nature of this pressure remains unclear, it seemed real enough to Kossuth and his friends: "Only his conversion to Islam, together with that of his fellow-refugees could save them from extradition in case of the Porte being unable to avoid the united Russo-Austrian demands. This was the advice that some of the ministers forwarded to Kossuth."[19] He would later disclaim the letter and write a public declaration to the Ottoman grand Vizier, Mustafa Reşid Paşa, as well as respectfully thanking sultan Abdülmecid I for his protection and hospitality. He admitted that the letter to Lord Palmerston had been written in a moment of despair, "when it seemed that we had no choice but that between renunciation or extradition".[20]

Although the Ottoman authorities were justified in denying accusations of forcible conversion, the wording of the instructions sent to the governor of Vidin imply that conversion *was* implied as an option to save the skins of the refugees: "If things take a turn for the worse, according to our treaties with Russia, Muslim refugees cannot be turned back. It is a matter of lightly implying (*hafifce hikaye*) that there may be a similar way to protect them [the Hungarians] if this causes them some comfort (*teselliyat*)."[21]

The key terms in this document are "lightly implying" and "comfort". Any historian familiar with the subtleties of Ottoman chancery language will get the message here. The Hungarians and Poles were being told in plain language: "We cannot offer you asylum publicly as we have explicit treaty obligations with Russia and Austria, but we may be able to save you".[22] In actual fact the governor of Vidin wrote to the Porte

---

[19] Janossy, *Great Britain and Kossuth*, pp. 36–7.
[20] For the full text of the letter, see BOA DUIT 75–2/6.
[21] BOA Dosya Usulu Tasnif (DUIT), no. 75–1/30, lef. 1. As quoted in Saydam, *Osmanlıların*, p. 352.
[22] Charles d'Eszlary claims that some 3,500 Hungarian and other troops had been turned over to the Austrians and that this had a determining effect on the others in their decision to convert. See Charles d'Eszlary, "l'emigration Hongroise de Louis Kossuth en Turquie entre 1849– 1850", *VI Türk Tarihi Kongresi* (Ankara 1967), pp. 430–50.

guaranteeing that no pressure had been applied. What had happened was that some Hungarian and Polish refugees, communicating through interpreters, had insisted that they wanted to become Muslims; they had "been told the consequences of such a step, such as never being able to return to their homelands, but they had insisted".[23] At this point it is highly likely that they had been made aware of the exclusion clauses in the treaties:

'There was only one legal way out of the dilemna and the Turks tried it. If the exiles were to convert to Islam, none of the treaties would apply to them. Turkish generals harangued the refugees, promising them high ranks in the Ottoman army. Generals Bem and Guyon and a few other Poles and Hungarians decided to undergo the rather formal ceremony of conversion. Kossuth himsef would not hear of conversion and in a bitter letter to 'Murad Pasha' (Bem) he denounced those who had given in to the Turks.'[24]

At this point, on 18 September 1849, two letters were received at the camp in Vidin. Both were adressed to Kossuth; one was from the ambassador of the Habsbug Empire in Istanbul, Count Andrassy, himself a Hungarian, the other from the ambassador of the Polish government in exile, Count Czaykowski. The letters stated that only conversion would assure that the refugees were not handed back, and "the letters also stated that after a time they would be allowed to go back to their own religion and go to whatever country they wanted, or, if they so wished, they could stay and take up positions in the Ottoman army".[25]

The position of the refugees must be considered here. They had been sequestered in a garrison town that could scarcely support itself, let alone a new population of several thousand desperate men and their families. For some two or more months they expected daily to be handed over to their enemies to face, almost certainly, execution. Rumours must have been rife and morale low. Although the official position of the state regarding conversion was very subtle, this did not prevent "a number of zealots [from] attempting to persuade them to accept Islam by reminding them that they might otherwise be surrendered to the Austrians and Russians."[26]

---

[23] DUIT, no. 75–1/41, lef. 5, letter from the governor of Vidin dated 21 October 1849, as quoted in Saydam, *Osmanlıların*, p. 352, n. 42.

[24] Istvan Deak, *The Lawful Revolution: Louis Kossuth and the Hungarians, 1848–1849* (New York, 1978), p. 340.

[25] Bayram Nazir, *Osmanlıya Sığınanlar. Macar ve Polonyalı Mülteciler* (Those who took refuge with the Ottomans: The Hungarian and Polish refugees) (Istanbul, 2006), p. 82.

[26] Karpat, "Kossuth in Turkey", p. 22.

Some of their comrades had already converted and were telling them that it was not so bad; others were putting pressure on them to convert.[27] Meanwhile, the Porte was frantically seeking a solution that would satisfy all parties. At this point France and Britain made it clear that they supported the Ottoman Empire in its reluctance to give up the refugees. British support went so far as to send a squadron of the Royal Navy, which took up station just outside the Dardanelles.[28] There was also the mounting feeling in Istanbul that it would be very damaging to the international prestige of the sultan if he were ever to hand over to their executioners men who had put themselves at his mercy.[29]

On 18 February 1850, Lajos Kossuth and his party, numbering fifty-seven people, embarked on the Ottoman ship the *Tair-i Bahri* bound for Gemlik on the western Anatolian coast. On 31 March 1850 the refugees had reached Kütahya, the small town where they would be interned until their release in August 1851. The group included illustrious names like Count Casimir Batthyany, General Mesaros, General Perczel, Adolphe Gyurman, and Alexandre d'Asboth. After his release, Kossuth arrived in Southampton on 28 October 1851, where he made a speech thanking the Ottoman state for its hospitality.[30]

The story of the "Muslim Hungarians" remains more curious. The latest Turkish source states that the group of Muslim Hungarians who left Vidin on 1 November 1849 numbered 241.[31] It had been decided to send Bem (Murad Paşa) and his party of fifteen separately to Aleppo, where they would be interned until things quietened down; they would

---

[27] One of the great fears of the Ottoman authorities was actually that fighting would break out between the converts and their erstwhile co-religionists. By 26 September the governor of Vidin wrote to Istanbul that the total number of refugees had reached some 6,000 souls. The Ottoman government undertook to feed, clothe, and shelter them. Saydam provides a table showing the numbers of raincoats, underwear, boots, socks, and so forth that were provided. See *Osmanlıların*, p. 355.

[28] Ibid., p. 370.

[29] The overwhelming majority of the refugees were Hungarians, together with a "considerable number" of Poles and 400 Italians. See ibid., p. 355.

[30] Ibid., p. 384. There is considerable material in Turkish on various aspects of Kossuth's internment. See, for example, Abdullah Saydam, "Kütahya'a Mülteci bir Cumhurbaşkanı: Louis Kossuth" (A refugee head of state in Kütahya: Louis Kossuth), *Tarih ve Toplum* 28 (1997), 5–14; Bayram Nazir, "Lajos Kossuth'u Kütahya'dan kaçırma girişimleri" (Attempts to abduct Lajos Kossuth from Kütahya), *Tarih ve Toplum* 36 (2001), 15–19.

[31] Nazır, *Osmanlıya Sığınanlar*, p. 119. See also Karpat,"Kossuth in Turkey", p. 22: "A list of the Hungarian and Polish refugees who were given military appointments in the Ottoman army shows that 193 were assigned to various units in Rumeli, while twenty-one were sent to Istanbul. Thus the number of officers converted to Islam was well over 200".

then be employed in active service. Bem kept petitioning for active service in Ottoman armies in Rumelia, where he would have a chance to fight the Russians. The Porte, on the other hand, thought this unduly provocative at this time and felt that he should be stationed in the Arab provinces. Accordingly, Bem and nineteen of his followers, all of whom had taken Muslim names, arrived in Aleppo in the early spring of 1850. The group included Major General Kmetty (Ismail Paşa), Major General Stein (Ferhad Paşa), Zarzecsky (Osman Bey), Woronieczky (Yusuf Bey), Grimm (Mustafa Bey), Baroti (Osman Bey), Toult (İbrahim Bey), Fiala (Ömer Bey), Hollan (İskender Bey), Nemegyei (Ömer Bey), Albert (Selim Bey), Orosdy (Ömer Bey), and Schinberk (Tahir Bey); each was given a salary according to his rank.[32]

A certain mystery surrounds the life story of Murad Paşa. Although he was Polish, his illustrious role in the Hungarian Revolution identified him with the Hungarians (*Macar*) as far as the Ottomans were concerned. He was never referred to as Polish (*Lehli*).[33] There is never any doubt about the sincerity of his conversion in the Turkish literature on the subject: "Murad Paşa's sole aim after his conversion to Islam was to be of service to his new country and to his sovereign Abdülmecid whom he esteemed highly. He hated Russia with a passion".[34] Indeed, what seems to have convinced him to convert was the statement made by his hosts that those who converted would fight against Russia in the Ottoman army.[35]

Bayram Nazir claims that,

'[N]o special ceremony was carried out for those who converted. Those who were to accept Islam kneeled before the Müftü in the mosque and repeated the *şehadet*. They also stated that they were converting of their own free will and desire. ... Ceremonies such as circumcision and the cutting of the hair were postponed.'[36]

Bem is the only one among the senior Hungarian refugees who appears in the sources as having been circumcised at Vidin. A contemporary source gives a very detailed account of his circumcision, and, as it is the only such

[32] Nazir, *Osmanlıya Sığınanlar*, pp. 369–71.
[33] See, for example, Bayram Nazir, "Macar özgürlük savaşçısı Osmanlı Murad Paşa'sı, Jozef Bem'in Ölumu üzerine bir tekzip yazisi" (A declaration of denial regarding the death of Josef Bem, Hungarian freedom fighter and the Murad Paşa of the Ottomans), *Toplumsal Tarih* 12 (1999), 32–4. The *Encyclopedia Britannica* refers to Bem as "also called Murad Pasha" and mentions that "as governor of Aleppo, where at the risk of his life, he saved the Christian population from being massacred".
[34] Nazir, *Osmanlıya Sığınanlar*, p. 32. Although some sources claim that Ben (Murad) was appointed Vali (governor) of Aleppo, this is unlikely.
[35] Ibid., p. 85.   [36] Ibid., p. 86.

account, it is worth quoting in some length. It describes Bem's first days at Vidin:

General Bem had been wounded in seven or eight places and was under the care of special surgeons and doctors. One day he came to the mosque where Muslims were praying. He entered the mosque and said that he wanted to be honoured with Islam. He was introduced into the faith according to the proper custom. However, he then asked the *imam* of one of the military units "what do I have to do to fully become a Muslim?".The *imam* advised him to become circumcised. General Bem immediately called for his local aid and told him that he wanted to be circumcised. The matter soon reached the ears of the Müftü of Vidin and other officials. Because his wounds had still not healed, he was cautioned that to add yet another wound would cause a loss of blood which could cause him to lose his life, and he was advised to delay his circumcision until his wounds had completely healed. Because he was adamant, having no other choice, the army surgeon was summoned and he was circumcised.[37]

Bem was treated with great respect by his Ottoman hosts, who no doubt knew that he was a brilliant soldier who had commanded an army of 30,000 men and 110 guns and had almost won. On the other hand, the *honvéd* General was "under no illusion about his fate if he fell into Russian hands".[38] Nor could the Hungarians have harbored any illusions about what would happen to them if they fell into Austrian hands. Austrian vengeance had been brutal. From 1848 to 1850 some 150 people had been executed, and a total of 1,200 were imprisoned in fortresses. All the leaders of the revolution who had escaped were tried in absentia. They were sentenced to death and hung in effigy, "their names symbolically nailed to the gallows".[39] A quiet life as a Muslim certainly seemed the lesser evil. Not that this was an easy decision; one of the exiles, Gábor Egressy, agonised over it in his diary. He refers to the "diabolical" alternative of having to choose between the "terrible logic of retaliation" and denying "the homeland, the nation, the family and memory", becoming exiled both physically and spiritually.[40]

---

[37] Mehmed Tevfik, *Cok Yasa! Csok Jasa! Yadigâr-ı Asrı Abdülhamid Han* (Long Live! Memento of the century of Abdülhamid Han) (Istanbul, 1294), pp. 9–10. This is a volume written as the account of an official visit by an Ottoman delegation to Hungary in 1878. They were invited by the Hungarians as a gesture of thanks for the granting of asylum in 1848. My thanks to Professor Geza David of Budapest Elte University for this reference.

[38] Ian Roberts, *Nicholas I and the Russian Intervention in Hungary* (London, 1991), pp. 211, 213. The Russians gave the Ottomans a list of some 1,000 Poles whom they wanted returned.

[39] Bona, *The Hungarian Revolution and War of Independence*, p. 436.

[40] Gábor, *Törökörszági Naplo 1849–1850*. My thanks to Lilla Balazs for this reference. www.terebess.hu/keletkultinfo/index.html.

Other Hungarian followers of Bem are also variously described as "out of exigency becoming Mohammedans", as in the case of John Fiala.[41] Similarly, Albert Anzelm was "forced by circumstances to become Mohammedan", together with Julian Kune. All of these men ended up in America. It is highly unlikely that they remained Muslims.[42]

After his appointment to Aleppo with the rank of *Ferik* (the highest rank in the Ottoman Army at the time, corresponding to Army Commander), with a top salary of 7,500 *kuruş*, Bem plied the Porte with many projects that he envisioned as uplifting and progressive, such as that of building a gunpowder works in Aleppo. He died on 10 December 1850, in Syria fighting the Druze, and was buried with full military honours.[43] The state paid all his debts and decided to erect an ornamental headstone. His belongings were taken to Europe by Ismail Paşa (General Kmetty). In 1929 his remains were taken to Poland via Istanbul and Budapest; "his coffin was wreathed in Polish and Turkish flags as it left Sirkeci station." The remains were placed in a mausoleum in Tarnov, his hometown in Poland.[44] Another heroic figure of the Hungarian struggle, General György Kmetty, also converted to Islam together with Bem, and served with him in Aleppo as Ismail Paşa. After Bem's death he went to London. When the Crimean War broke out he returned to the Ottoman Empire and fought with distinction in the defence of Kars, a key fortress in eastern Anatolia. In 1856 he was promoted to the rank of *Ferik* and decorated by the sultan. He then went back to London, where he died in retirement on 25 April 1869. He received a pension from the Ottoman state until the day he died. He was buried in Kentsal Green cemetery in London. His gravestone was donated by the Ottoman embassy, and a resumé of his life and career were inscribed in Turkish, Hungarian, English, and Latin.[45] The inscription on the headstone reads as follows: "George Kmetty (İsmail Paşa) 1813–1869. Lieutenant-General of the Ottomans. Defender of Kars.

---

[41] Edmund Vasvary, *Lincoln's Hungarian Heroes: The Participation of Hungarians in the Civil War 1861–1865* (Washington, DC, 1939), p. 52.

[42] Ibid., pp. 43, 63, 64.

[43] It was rumoured in Europe that he had been poisoned by the Ottomans. In response to this rumour, the Ottoman chargé d'affaires in Brussels, Eugene de Kerckhove, published a denial in the *L'Independence Belge*. See Bayram Nazir, "Jozef Bem'in Ölümü Üzerine bir Tekzip Yazısı" (An article of denial regarding Jozef Bem's death), *Tarih ve Toplum* 23 (1988), 23–34.

[44] Nazir, *Osmanlı'ya Sığınanlar*, pp. 376–7. See also www.manofpoland.net.

[45] Edit Tashnadi, "18–19 Yüzyılda Osmanlı'da Macar Mültecileri" (Hungarian refugees in the Ottoman Empire in the eighteenth and nineteenth centuries), *Tarih ve Toplum* 36, no. 215 (November 2001), 71–5.

Chief of the forces in Syria. In whom Hungary mourns a brave commander in her National War 1848–49. Erected by the command of the Sultan".[46]

The Ottoman government was bestowing the highest honours on an apostate. Clearly there is a contradiction here. Or is there? It may very well be the case that all along the Ottomans knew that the "conversions" of these people were symbolic and treated them as a polite fiction. How sincere were their conversions? This is an issue hardly touched upon in the Turkish literature, where the conversions are taken at face value.[47] It seems legitimate to speculate that for many of the "converts" this may have been the case. The list is too long to elaborate on here, but a few more cases may be mentioned, such as Jozsef Kollmann, who fought in the Crimean War under the name of Fevzi Paşa, and Sandor Farkas, who taught for many years in the Ottoman Military Academy as Macar Osman Paşa (Osman Paşa the Hungarian) and who was the father of Nigar Hanim (Binti Osman), renkowned as Turkey's first woman poet.[48]

There are many similar life stories, such as that of another "Hungarian", Count Richard Guyon, in fact a British subject, who initially distinguished himself by fighting brilliantly during the Hungarian Revolution. In the Ottoman Empire, after arriving in Vidin with Bem, he converted to Islam and took the name of Hürşid Paşa. Guyon/Hürşid Paşa is a very good example of an ambiguous "conversion". Originally sent to Damascus together with Bem, Guyon was recalled to Istanbul just before Bem's death. There is some doubt about whether he actually converted, and at least one source specifically states, "He was greatly importuned to embrace Mohammedanism with all the allurements of high honour and military command. . . . He resolutely declined conversion, but accepted the duties of an anomalous office".[49] During the Kars campaign in northeastern Anatolia in 1854, Guyon was largely responsible for setting up the

---

[46] James Stuart Curl, *Kentsal Green Cemetary: The Origins and Development of the General Cemetery of All Souls, Kentsal Green London 1824–2001* (London, 2003), p. 259. My thanks to Tom Garnett of University College, London for this reference. See Plate 2.

[47] For instance, Saydam, in his otherwise admirably documented study, refers to "*Mirliva* (Major-General) Kamti" (Kmetty) as "one of the refugees who had converted to Islam". See *Osmanlıların*, p. 377.

[48] Many Hungarian refugees also remained in the Ottoman Empire and took up humble trades like carpenter, coachman and leatherworker. See the table on p. 19 of Saydam. *Osmanlilarin*. Comp. BOA A.MKT.NZD 11/89, 27 Ramazan 1266 / 6 August 1850, Ahmet Efendi and Veli Ağa, two Hungarian converts who were employed in municipal building services in Istanbul.

[49] The *Daily News* of 14 May 1855 reported that "he is literally adored by the troops". See www.batteryb.com/Crimean_War /biographies/genguyon.htm.

logistics of the defence of the key fortress town against the Russians. He was so popular with the ordinary Ottoman soldiers that they supposedly shouted "We want Hürşid Pasha!" (*Hürşid Paşayı İsteriz!*), demanding that he be put in overall command. He was not, and was blamed for the eventual rout of the Ottoman army at the battle of Kürekdere. He died in Istanbul in 1855, unemployed. His gravestone in the British military cemetery in Haydarpaşa bears the following inscription in Hungarian: "Turkish Paşa, Son of France, Born in England, Hungarian Nationalist".[50]

The Hungarian converts became something of a legend in the domains of the sultan. The intrepid Arminius Vambery was to note: "We then lived in the era of Hungarian refugees. Some hundreds of my countrymen made believe that they had been converted to Islam. A popular belief had got abroad that the whole Magyar people would acknowledge Mohammed as their prophet, and whenever a Mohammedan came across a *Madjarli* the fire of the missionary was blazing in his heart".[51]

In many ways Arminus Vambery is the ultimate career "convert". The quotation marks around the word "convert" are deliberate here. Although Vambery professed Judaism, Islam, and Calvinist Protestantism at different stages in his life, he claimed to be a freethinker and never to have believed in any of them. He was to be an impoverished Jewish tutor, an Istanbul *Efendi*, a wandering *haji* and dervish, a leading Hungarian orientalist, a secret (double) agent, and a guest of Queen Victoria at Windsor, all in one lifetime. He was born in 1831 or 1832 as Haim Wamberger into an orthodox Jewish family in the village of Duna Szerdahely in Hungary (now Dunjaska Streda in the Czech Republic), situated on an island in the Danube.[52] In the book that made his fame, *Travels in Central Asia*, he makes no mention anywhere of his Jewish origins.[53] In his autobiography, written and published after he had "arrived" as an established international figure, he is much less coy about his Jewish origins, mentioning them as a "problematic blessing".[54]

---

[50] Tashnadi, "18–19 yüzyılda Macar Mültecileri", p. 75. "*Török Fö.Tabornok. Frankhon ivadéka. Angolhon szülöttje. Magyarhon Vitézze*" (see Plate 1).

[51] Arminius Vambery, *Arminius Vambery: His Life and Adventures by Himself* (London, 1883), p. 13.

[52] Lory Alder and Richard Dalby, *The Dervish of Windsor Castle* (London, 1979), pp. 16–17. His date of birth is not clear. Jews in Habsburg Hungary were not required to register their births. He later "chose" 19 March 1832.

[53] Arminus Vambery, *Travels in Central Asia: A Journey from Teheran across the Turcoman Desert on the Eastern Shore of the Caspian to Khiva, Bokhara and Samarkand. Performed in the year 1863* (London, 1864).

[54] Arminius Vambery, *The Life and Adventures of Arminius Vambery by Himself* (London, 1883), vii: "I was born in Hungary in 1832 in the small town of Duna Szerdahely".

Vambery also moved in Hungarian émigré circles in Istanbul in the early 1850s. In a biography of the great Hungarian traveller, there is a photograph of Vambery sitting at a table with Daniel Szilanyi, identified only as a "former officer of the Hungarian Army of Liberty". Both are in Turkish dress, wearing a fez, and Szilanyi is smoking a water pipe.[55] Further on in his travels, in Diadin, Persia, Vambery ran across General Kolmann, now Fevzi Paşa, one of the first Hungarian émigrés with whom Vambery had become acquainted in Istanbul.[56] When Vambery first arrived in Istanbul in 1857 as a young man of twenty-five, the city was full of Hungarian refugees, many of whom no doubt have fallen through the cracks of history. One of Vambery's main sponsors in the Ottoman capital was in fact Ismail Paşa/ General Kmetty, who got him his first job as a tutor in the home of Hüseyin Daim Paşa. Kmetty was also to help him when he turned up in London in 1864 upon his return from Central Asia. By this time Ismail Paşa/Kmetty was living in London as a popular member of the London social set.[57]

Whether or not Vambery was right in his claim that his countrymen "made believe that they converted" (and he would know something about "make believe"), the Ottoman archival records provide ample evidence that at least some were genuine enough. A register spanning the years H. 1265–68 (1849–53) records the conversion of 35 Hungarians out of a total of 340 conversions listed. At over 10 percent of the total number of converts listed in the register, the Hungarians are the single largest group of Christian converts apart from Ottoman Greeks and Armenians.[58]

A typical entry in the register reads as follows:

> One has presented himself here who was originally of the Hungarian *millet* (*an asl macarlu*), he was offered the faith [he converted], given the name Ahmed Tevfik and was sent to the official hospital (*bimarhane*) for his circumcision.[59]

This particular register actually records the conversion of two Hungarians on the same day; although they are separate entries, the wording is virtually identical:

---

[55] Alder and Dalby, *The Dervish of Windsor Castle*. The photograph appears on p. 48. No information is given on Daniel Szilanyi.

[56] Ibid., p. 69.

[57] Ibid., pp. 243–4.

[58] BOA Bab-ı Âli Evrak Odası (BEO) A-592 Sadaret Nezaret ve Devair 634. My thanks to Dilek Akyalçın-Kaya for this reference.

[59] Ibid., 20 Muharrem 1267 / 25 November 1850. The original names of the converts are not mentioned.

"One who has presented himself here sent by the Foreign Ministry who was originally of the Hungarian *millet* was offered the religion and given the name Mehmed was sent to the official hospital for his circumcision."[60]

In most of the cases of Hungarian converts the record states that they were sent by the Foreign Ministry, presumably because of their status as political asylum seekers. There is one entry of a Hungarian conversion *en famille*:

Mehmed Tevfik who was originally a Hungarian subject, his wife Ayşe Sıdıka, his elder daughter Fatma al Zehra and his other daughter Hadice and his other daughter Emine, all sent by the Foreign Ministry were given their names and all five members of the family were honoured with the glory of Islam. They have been sent to the *Muşir* Paşa of the Ministry of police to be shown a place.[61]

Another entry deals with a father and son:

Mahmud and his son Mehmed who were originally Hungarian subjects have been honoured with the glory of Islam have had the religion presented to them and have been sent to the Chief of Staff (*Babı Seraskeri*) for their circumcisions. Because they were sent from His Highness Ömer Paşa Commander of the Army of Rumeli they have been sent back to him. (Marginal note: because this was according to an Imperial order there is no petition).[62]

These two seem to be a particularly well connected father and son, because the Ömer Paşa in question was Ömer Paşa Latas himself. On 14 April 1850 a group of 200 newly converted Hungarians were attached to the force that was being mustered at Şumnu to quell the uprising in Bosnia: "As they were leaving the city the *müftü* sacrificed a sheep to them and lifting up his hands, said 'I pray for your victory'. After intonations of 'amen' the newly converted refugees set off with their newly found brothers in religion for Bosnia".[63] The greatest irony was that the Bosnian Beys

---

[60] Ibid., 6 Ramazan 1267 / 5 July 1851. The procedure for the other Hungarian is exactly the same except that he was named Ahmed. Also dated 6 Ramazan 1267.

[61] Ibid., 29 Şevval 1265 / 17 September 1849. "To be shown a place" presumably meant a dwelling place.

[62] Ibid., 23 Muharrem 1266 / 9 December 1849. This last note was presumably because the convert would make his application to convert by a petition, so Mahmud and Mehmed, by being presented directly by the sultan, were being given preferential treatment. It would be fascinating to know just who these people were; unfortunately, the register does not provide their original Hungarian names.

[63] Nazir, *Osmanlıya Sığınanlar*, pp. 186–7.

whom they were being sent to put down had been Muslims since the fifteenth century.[64]

POLISH REFUGEES AND CONVERTS

In the first days after the military *débacle* of August 1849, Polish refugees actually outnumbered Hungarians.[65] Leading names among them converted to Islam, such as Szarcinsky (Osman Bey), Tabatinsky (Ali Bey), and Count Kossielski (Sefer Paşa), all of whom took up military duties in the Ottoman Empire. This development was severely criticized by Austria and Russia, who accused Ömer Paşa of forcing these men to convert.[66] Ahmet Vefik Bey (later Paşa) was sent as the sultan's special emissary to Vidin, where he was to tell the refugees:

I give you my word of honour that you will not find more noble and magnanimous protection anywhere as that extended to you by my Master Sultan Abdülmecid. If any of you want to stay with us they will be given a military or civilian position in keeping with his present rank or station, without needing to change his religion.[67]

Although the Ottoman authorities repeatedly denied such accusations of forced conversion, there does seem to be the possibility (as in the case of the Hungarians mentioned earlier) that conversion was at least suggested as an option: "Although the Ottoman authorities vehemently denied such accusations, it is clear that as a result [of conversion] they were able to become Ottoman subjects and guarantee their safety from the danger of being returned'.[68] Ortaylı goes so far as to claim that "these Polish officers became the vanguard of Ottoman modernisation during the century of the Tanzimat".[69]

---

[64] Ömer Paşa Latas's intervention in Bosnia broke the resistance of a local elite of notables who fought against the Tanzimat reforms which damaged their privileged position. The historian and Nobel laureate Ivo Andrić wrote a novel about Ömer Paşa Latas, emphasizing "The cruelty and historical hatred of converts towards their former nationals." See Boyan Aleksov, "Serbian Historians on Religious Conversions", p. 169.

[65] See the table given by Saydam, where he gives the figure of 833 Poles versus 53 Hungarians for the date of 28 August 1849. Saydam, *Osmanlıların*, p. 350.

[66] İlber Ortaylı, "Osmanlı İmparatorluğu'nda Askeri Reformlar ve Polonyalı Mülteci Subaylar"(Military reforms in the Ottoman Empire and the Polish refugee officers), in İlber Ortaylı, *Osmanlı İmparatorluğu'da İktisadi ve Sosyal Değişim. Makaleler* (Economic and social change in the Ottoman Empire: Articles) (Ankara, 2000), pp. 185–91.

[67] Ibid., p. 189.   [68] Ibid.

[69] Ibid.

One illustrious example is Count Constantine Borzecki (Mustafa Celaleddin Paşa). The son of a minor Polish aristocrat, Borzecki had come to Istanbul in the autumn of 1849 and had converted to Islam. According to the memoirs of his son Enver, "He at first accepted Islam for its practical aspects but later became a true Muslim".[70] We learn also from his son that he did not frequent European circles in Istanbul, preferring the company of Polish converts like himself: "These people, who had severed their ties with their own civilization, but who were not really accepted by conservative Muslim circles, only felt at home among their own kind".[71] Nonetheless, Mustafa Celaleddin Paşa fought valiantly in the Crimean War and died from wounds suffered during the fighting with the Montenegrin rebels in 1876. Interestingly enough, Mustafa Celaleddin Paşa's renown in the Ottoman Empire and present-day Turkey is not for his military exploits but for his pioneering work in Turcology. His book *Les Turcs Anciens et Modernes* is generally recognized as the first work to systematically analyse the origin of the Turkic peoples. The great Turkish poet Nazım Hikmet was his great-grandson.[72]

Another migrant soul was Count Michael Izador Czaykowski. He was a Polish patriot who fled to Istanbul in the 1830s; he first worked as the director of the *Agence d'Orient*, a news wire service based in Pera. He later converted to Islam and took the name Sadık Paşa. He also renamed his two sons, Adam and Ladislas, Enver and Muzaffer, though they and their mother remained Roman Catholics. Czaykowski's life project became the effort to secure Ottoman backing for Polish military action against Russia in the Caucasus. From 1844 to 1848 he constantly sought the Porte's backing for a military force made up of Polish refugees and Polish deserters from the Russian ranks. The Porte's response was lukewarm, although he did get some backing; even during the height of the tension in 1849 the Porte repeatedly postponed his plans. The Crimean War seemed to provide a golden opportunity for Sadık Paşa's plans. He was made commander of the so-called Sultan's Cossack Regiment, which was first intended to fight in the European theatre but

---

[70] Jerzy S. Latka, "Polonya, Mültecileri ve Yeni Fikirler" (Polish refugees and new ideas), *Tarih ve Toplum* 10 (July 1991), 23–37.

[71] Ibid.

[72] Mustafa Celaleddin Paşa, *Les Turcs Anciens et Modernes* (Istanbul, 1869). The basic premise of the text was the theory of "Turco-Aryanism", which claimed that the Turks were an Aryan race and hence that the European prejudice against them was ill-founded.

was later assigned to the Caucasus front. The Sultan's Cossacks were never deployed.[73]

In 1914, just on the eve of the war that would end the Ottoman Empire, the Young Turk government appointed a new ambassador to Washington. Before he left to take up his post, the new ambassador paid a courtesy call on his counterpart, Henry Morgenthau, the American ambassador in Istanbul. He was introduced as Alfred Budanski, "a Christian Ottoman of Polish origin". Just before he left, Budanski paid another call on Morgenthau and surprised him by saying, "My name is no longer Alfred Budanski. Yesterday I became a Muslim and my name is now Ahmed Rüstem Paşa".[74] There are some interesting discrepancies in the information given by Heath Lowry in the article just cited. Far from having converted "yesterday", Alfred was the son of Bilinski (first name unknown), a Polish refugee who had sought refuge in the Ottoman Empire in 1854, converted to Islam, and taken the name Sadeddin Nihat Paşa. Sometime in the early 1880s Alfred Bilinski converted to Islam and took the name Ahmed Rüstem. Having entered the Ottoman diplomatic service, he served in various posts, the last one being as ambassador to Washington in 1914. He clashed with the American press over the treatment of the Armenians in the Ottoman Empire, publishing articles claiming that the treatment meted out to the Armenians in the Ottoman Empire was far better than the treatment of the American blacks or the Philipinos. He wrote a very strongly worded letter to President Woodrow Wilson, for which he was asked to apologize. Ahmed Rüstem Bey refused and, resigning his post, returned to Istanbul; from there he crossed over to Anatolia to join the nationalists around Mustafa Kemal.[75]

After the war, on 22 September 1919, at Sivas in central Anatolia, Mustafa Kemal received the American delegation led by General C. Harbord. In the entourage that welcomed the American delegation was the *ex*-ambassador, now calling again himself "Alfred Rüstem Bey".[76] Alfred Rüstem's career, therefore, was to span both the Ottoman and Republican periods.

---

[73] Stefaniya Skochen, "Polonya Kuzey Kafkasya İlişkileri" (Polish relations with the Caucasus), *Tarih ve Toplum* 29 (June 1998), 55–7.

[74] Heath Lowry, "The Ottoman Renaissance: The Conqueror's Dream", *Cornucopia* 34 (2004), 28–9.

[75] Şenol Kantarcı, *Ahmed Rüstem Bey* (Istanbul, 2009).

[76] Mehmed Ali Kışlalı, "Atatürk, Ermenistan, ABD" (Ataturk. Armenia and the USA), *Radikal*, 18 March 2005.

OPPORTUNISTS AND "HUMBLE PIE" CONVERSIONS

Below the social standing of the illustrious career converts, one finds hundreds of cases of men and women of more modest backgrounds for whom conversion to Islam and taking refuge in the Ottoman Empire was almost a cheaper alternative to immigration to America. Some were unscrupulous adventurers and others simply losers. These people were very carefully watched by the Ottoman authorities, and one gets the feeling that they were not all that welcome.

"It is undesirable that such people of unknown reputation and identity accumulate in Istanbul"; so wrote the minister of police, Saffet Paşa, on 1 June 1902 regarding a certain "Abdelhak". Abdelhak was "a Pole who had been a French subject" and who had converted to Islam in the Ottoman North African province of Tripoli (*Trablusgarp*). The minister made it clear that "the normal practice in such cases is that such people are not sent to Istanbul but to other vilayets". In keeping with this practice, Abdelhak had been sent to Konya, where he had been kept under surveillance. It was ordered that he be found some employment; he had accordingly been employed as a policeman. Now he declared that he was unhappy; "as he did not speak Turkish he now wanted to leave this place". It was also suspected that he might "take refuge in the Russian Consulate" as this consulate protected French subjects in Konya. The minister made it very clear that "because of the great number of people of this ilk for whom it is very difficult to find money ... It is extremely undesirable for them to be set free in Istanbul without making sure of the sincerity of their conversions and ascertaining that they are of good repute".[77] A week later, some further details surfaced about Abdelhak. The Ministry of Interior wrote that he had been in the French navy when he converted in North Africa and had been sent to Istanbul by the Ottoman authorities; from there he had been sent to Konya, where he had been enrolled as a policeman. It is also interesting that the Ministry of Interior stated that "by converting he does not lose his original citizenship". Clearly Abdelhak was in a very different category compared to the more illustrious converts mentioned earlier, who had been granted Ottoman citizenship.[78]

---

[77] BOA DH.MKT 523/32, 23 Safer 1320 / 1 June 1902, the Ministry of Police no. 298, the minister, Saffet Paşa, to the Ministry of the Interior.
[78] Ibid., 26 Mayis 1318 / 8 June 1902, the Ministry of the Interior Secretariat to the Ministry of Police (*tebdil-i mezheb etmekle tabiyet-i aslisini zayi etmiyeceği*).

It appears that the police force was a sort of dumping ground for converts of uncertain provenance and doubtful loyalty. This is not surprising as it was the least prestigious of the services. One such case is that of "the Bulgarian brigand (*komitacı*) Ustoyanov (Stoyanof)", who surrendered to the authorities in Salonica. Here we have a perfect case of a poacher turned game keeper, as Stoyanof moves up through the ranks of the Ottoman police force, ending up as Mehmed Sadık Efendi, a chief constable (*Serkomiser*) in the police force of Istanbul.[79] On 27 January 1906 he appears in the official record as "Mehmed Sadık Efendi who had been a Bulgarian brigand but has surrendered and converted". He had also sent two letters to Ottoman military commanders in the area informing on his former comrades. The attitude of the authorities was initially sceptical, but it seems that Mehmet Sadık soon convinced them of his loyalty. On 12 June the Vali of Salonica wrote that Mehmet Sadık, "from whose loyal service we have benefited", had been summoned by imperial order to Istanbul, where he had been given seven gold *liras* and sent back. He had now "completely spent this money and was destitute". The Vali also pointed out that "because of the danger in these parts from the Bulgarian committees it is unsafe to keep him here"; he duly recommended that Mehmed Sadık be sent elsewhere with a suitable salary.[80]

A few months later Mehmet Sadık was seriously wounded while fighting his erstwhile comrades, but was said to have "distinguished himself and was instrumental in the capture of a band (*çete*) of some thirty brigands together with their leaders". He had also proven himself in the "cutting down and questioning of Bulgarian brigands as well as the capture of rifles and bombs". Not surprisingly, "the perfidious elements" in the area were "looking for an opportunity to kill him".[81] Some three months later Mehmet Sadık's star seemed to be on the rise. The Ministry of

---

[79] BOA ZB (Zaptiye Nezareti) 451/59, 14 Kanun-u Sani 1322 / 27 January 1906, the minister of police to the Vilayet of Selanik. A *komitacı (komitadji* in Bulgarian) is a brigand or a freedom fighter depending on which side of the political spectrum you are on. The word is of Slavic origin.

[80] BOA Y.MTV 299/1, 30 Mayis 1323 / 12 June 1907, the Vali of Selanik, Mehmed Rauf Paşa, to the Imperial Palace Secretariat. It must be born in mind that these were the years when the struggle between the Internal Macedonian Revolutionary Organization (IMRO) and the Ottoman forces was at its peak. It is unclear which particular group of "Bulgarian brigands" Stoyanof had belonged to. On the "Macedonian Question", see Mark Mazower, *The Balkans*, pp. 4, 93, 94.

[81] BOA. Y.MTV 301/113, 16 Agustos 1323 / 29 August 1907, the General Military Inspection Committee (*Umum Teftiş-i Askeri Komisyonu*). Çete is derived from the Bulgarian *cheta*, meaning "armed band".

Police ordered that he be sent to Istanbul from Salonica, where he had "given loyal service". An imperial *irade* had been issued appointing him chief constable (*Serkomiser*) with a salary of 1,000 *kuruş*.[82]

These somewhat suspect conversions occur throughout the period of this study. On 24 March 1852 the Vilayet of Erzurum reported that a French doctor by the name of Monsieur Merlot had converted and taken the name of Murad Efendi, and had been a "guest in the house of the Vali" pending an investigation into his circumstances. The Vali pointed out that "as he is destitute he wishes to set up a medical practice". Upon investigation the Porte wrote to the Vali to the effect that Merlot/Murad had "outstanding gambling debts of seven thousand five hundred *kuruş*" owing to a French citizen and that the French embassy was interceding in favour of his creditor. It was therefore determined that Merlot/Murad could indeed practice medicine in Erzurum but that "his accumulated salaries are to be added up"; after the said sum was deducted and handed over to the French consul in Erzurum, he could keep the balance.[83] Evidently M. Merlot had tried to convert to escape his gambling debts, but his stratagem failed.

Negotiation seems to have been the key word in another case of career conversion, that of Halil Said Shihab, the Maronite *müdir* of the district of Dayr al Qamar in the Shuf mountains of Lebanon. Halil Said appeared in Istanbul on the eighth of November 1898, stating that he had converted to Islam and that he wanted a government post.[84] A descendent of an illustrious figure of the Maronite Shihabs, Amir Bashir Shihab, Halil declared that he had moved to Istanbul with all of his family. He also declared that as he had been receiving a salary of 1,900 *kuruş* as *müdir*, he now desired a salary of "at least four thousand *kuruş* in order to keep up a comparable lifestyle" in Istanbul. He also stated in his petition that he wanted a position in the Council of State (*Şurayı Devlet*) or Board of Taxation (*Cemiyet-i Rüsumiye*). He was duly given an audience with the minister

---

[82] BOA ZB 610/9, 19 Eylül 1323 / 2 October 1907, the Ministry of Police to the Vilayet of Selanik; Irade Hususi 89, Yıldız Palace Imperial Secretariat no. 3678, 28 Receb 1325 / 6 September 1907, signed by the imperial private secretary, Tahsin Paşa. Imperial Order decreeing that Mehmet Sadık Efendi be employed in Istanbul as chief constable (*Serkomiser*).

[83] BOA HR.MKT.54/86, 2 Cemaziyelevvel 1268 / 24 March 1852, the Vilayet of Erzurum to the Sublime Porte; 6 Rebiyulahir 1269 / 17 January 1853, the Sublime Porte to the Vilayet of Erzurum.

[84] BOA İ.RSM (İrade Rüsumat) 9.1316-N-6, 26 Teşrin-i Sani 1314 / 8 November 1898, petition presented by Mir Halil Sa'id Shihab to the Office of the Grand Vizier. My thanks to Malek Sharif for this reference.

of interior and awarded a salary of 3,000 *kuruş*, and an *irade* was issued for his "appointment to a position in keeping with his condition".[85]

It remains unclear what the Ottoman state had to gain from the conversion of Halil Said Shihab, except perhaps the prestige of the scion of such an illustrious family becoming a Muslim. On the other hand, it is equally unclear what Halil Said had to gain by this act, except perhaps a comfortable sinecure in Istanbul with a good (negotiated) salary.[86]

Another case emanating from Lebanon was that of Muhlis Es'ad. Originally a Maronite Christian, he had converted to Islam some years previously while he had been director of the post and telegraph office in the *kaza* of Shuf. Muhlis Es'ad presented a petition stating that after his conversion he had travelled widely in the Christian villages and "encouraged many people to come to Islam". He claimed that he had done this at great personal expense. The self-designated missionary strongly implied that he would like an "imperial favour, an invitation to Istanbul and possibly a decoration" for his trouble.[87]

Conversion to Islam was often seen as providing opportunities for people who were marginal eccentrics in their own country. One such person was Muhammed Muhtar Bey, appearing in the despatches as "the [converted] twenty-seven-year-old son of Monsieur Vatin, retired General from the Belgian army". Muhammed Muhtar had become the chief reporter of the Belgian newspaper *Opinion*, in which he had taken to publishing long articles extolling the virtues of Islam and supporting the Ottoman Empire. He had been forwarding these to his friend in Istanbul,

---

[85] Ibid., the minister of the interior, Memduh Paşa, to the Grand Vizier's Office, 2 Şaban 1316 / 16 December 1898; memorandum of Grand Vizier Rıfat Paşa, 25 Şaban 1316; announcement of *irade* by Sultan's private secretary, Tahsin Paşa, 1 Ramazan 1316. It seems that fluid religious allegiances were well precedented in the Shihab clan. See Engin Akarlı, *The Long Peace: Ottoman Lebanon 1861–1920* (Berkeley and Los Angeles, 1993), pp. 13–16, 21: "For over a hundred years after [the battle of] Ain Dara [1711] the Shihabs remained the paramount clan of the old 'Druze Mountain' without a serious internal or external challenge". Originally Sunni Muslims, a branch of the Shihab family converted to Maronite Christianity. Amir Bashir Shihab became Amir of Lebanon in 1788. "The *amir*, who practiced Sunni Islam in public and Christianity in private, allowed a Maronite priest to take charge of his spiritual life." On the other hand, Kamal Salibi unequivocally states, "Bashir was born a Maronite and died a Maronite. ... But he made no show of the Christian faith he formally professed." See Kamal Salibi, *A House of Many Mansions: The History of Lebanon Reconsidered* (London, 1988), p. 109.

[86] It should be remembered that the sums in question here are considerable amounts. See Chapter 3, n. 116, in this volume.

[87] BOA Y.PRK. UM 29/26, 17 Kanun-u Sani 1309 / 30 January 1893, the Vilayet of Beirut to the Imperial ADC, Derviş Paşa,

Abdullah Hasib Bey, the inspector of foreign schools.[88] Hasib Bey treated the letters with caution, saying that he had merely kept up a casual correspondence with Muhammed Muhtar, yet he admired the fact that "he was sincerely attached to the Sublime State and the August Personage of the Caliph of Islam". He said his correspondent was to be commended for single-handedly defending Islam in a Christian country and publishing articles favourable to the Ottoman state. Hasib Bey also enclosed a translated summary and commentary by the editor of *Opinion* of the article by Muhammed Muhtar. In the article Muhammed Muhtar stated, in sum, that Islam was to be the salvation of black Africa and it should be encouraged to spread in the Belgian Congo. The "black population" of the Congo should be "not politically but spiritually united with the Ottoman Caliphate". Indeed, Islam had been much more successful in sub-Saharan Africa because "Islam is a very simple religion suitable for the simple minds and intelligence of the blacks". Islam should more aggressively oppose the activities of Christian missionaries. Indeed, Islam had been so successful in Africa that "We now see composition and debating competitions among the Touareg and geometry being taught in the Sudan". All this was due to the work of Islamic missionaries, and the Ottoman state should be even more involved in spreading Islam in Africa. Claims such as these, stretching the limits of credibility (composition competitions among the Tuareg?), were not uncommon among converts of dubious provenance. No doubt Muhammed Muhtar was expecting some form of royal favour, either some money or a decoration.[89]

Another, and rather sad, marginal case was that of Ahmed Hamdi Efendi, the son of the Russian General Nikolayef Dorovich Ivanof, who had converted to Islam in 1892. After his conversion he had been studying in Istanbul, but had been sent back to St. Petersburg at the insistence of his father. He had then run away and come back to Istanbul, and was then sent to Konya, where, "after completing his necessary term of service", he had been appointed to Izmir to serve in the police. After someone informed on him for some alleged illegal activity, he was sent back to Konya, from whence he had come back to Istanbul. He had presented a petition stating that "[because] he was destitute and did not want to be handed back to his father whom he hated, and because he spoke six languages, he was asking

---

[88] BOA Y.PRK .MF 2/10, 14 Kanun-u Evvel 1306 / 27 December 1890, letter to an unknown recipient from Abdullah Hasib, the inspector of foreign schools.

[89] Ibid. Enclosed translation of an article in *l'Opinion*.

to be appointed to a position of police commissar third class". His request was refused.[90]

These marginal cases were always considered suspect and kept under police surveillance. Such was the case of a certain Mehmed Said, who had been a French doctor by the name of Petri Gaston Diyumi. After converting, Mehmed Said had gone to Egypt, where he had become involved in the clandestine activities of the *Hizb-u Watani* (Nationalist Party) and had been exiled by the British. He had married and settled in Nablus in Ottoman Palestine. The authorities reported that there was nothing suspicious about his behaviour.[91]

Another such case was a German who had become Mehmed Sadık Efendi, a cavalry officer who had been assigned to the Sixth Army in Iraq "because of his suspicious behaviour". He now wanted to resign from his post. Permission was granted, but it was specified that "he be kept under surveillance everywhere he goes".[92]

CONVERSION AND CITIZENSHIP

As the Ottoman state found itself surrounded by former subject peoples who now had states of their own, the "nationality" of Greek, Bulgarian, and Serbian ex-subjects became a problem. As seen in the case of the Hungarian and Polish refugees around mid-century, the rule had been applied in such a way that if a person converted to Islam in Ottoman territory, he or she was automatically considered an Ottoman subject. Yet this was to have unwanted consequences as time went by. As the century drew to a close and the twentieth century began, Ottoman lands became a refuge for various shades of suspicious characters. This made the Ottoman authorities suspicious of "converts" who might be converting with ulterior motives, such as espionage or commercial penetration. Also, these converts were often escaping from the consequences of a crime such as murder, embezzlement, theft, or desertion from military service. As a result, a

---

[90] BOA ZB, 334/9, 18 Mayis 1325 / 31 May 1909, the Ministry of the Interior to the Ministry of Police, no. 328.

[91] BOA DH.MKT 1373/97, 22 Muharrem 1304 / 11 October 1886, memorandum of the Ministry of the Interior. The name of the person is difficult to decipher as the Ottoman scribes wrote down the foreign names as they heard them, and it may well be an incorrect spelling. Unless the name is very obvious, like Yani or Maria, the spelling in the Ottoman document has been used.

[92] BOA Y.MTV 60/78, 11 Mart 1308 / 24 March 1894, the Office of the Chief of Staff, Serasker Rıza Paşa.

number of restraints and interdicts were brought into play. The Ottoman Citizenship Law of 1869 (*Osmanlı Tabiyet Kanunamesi*), which had a direct bearing on the issues of conversion and apostasy, was an interesting document. It was very inclusive on the matter of who might be of benefit to the state, but equally exclusive when it came to the question of whom the state would be obliged to protect and provide for. Partly based on the Napoleonic *Code Civile*, it has been hailed as "[the advent of] secular principles because the primary differentiating criterion in a person's citizenship status was no longer whether they were Muslim or Christian but whether or not they were Ottoman."[93] The law instituted the category of "foreigner" (*ecnebi*), which included all foreign nationals regardless of religion; it also formalized the concept of "Ottoman".[94]

Another important consideration was to be the status of Muslims who were not subjects of the Ottoman Empire. As more and more Muslims came under the rule of Christian empires, by the end of the century there were far more Muslims who were subjects of the British Raj or under Dutch, French, or Russian rule. These were to be subsumed under the title of "foreign Muslims" (*ecnebi müslüman*). This measure was actually deemed necessary because it was feared that the Muslim subjects of foreign powers could act as potential fifth columns and infiltrate the holy land of Hicaz. [95]

Yet religion continued to be a factor in affairs of citizenship. In many of the cases appearing in the archival record relating to previously subject peoples, we see this yoking together of religion and citizenship. One such case was reported from the Vilayet of Kosovo on 14 January 1894. It involved a certain Milan Raković, who had fled from Serbia, where he was wanted for theft and murder. Raković had been arrested by the Ottoman military authorities and was now being kept in Senice. The Serbian embassy had demanded that he be handed back. Claiming that he was sure to hang if handed back, Radović had converted and

---

[93] Gülnihal Bozkurt, *Batı Hukuku'nun Türkiye'de benimsenmesi* (The adoption of Western law in Turkey) (Ankara, 1989), p. 23.

[94] Düstûr 1 Tertip 1 1289 (1872), 16–18. The parts of the law that are particularly germaine to our topic here are article 3, which allowed a "foreigner" (*ecnebi*) to apply for Ottoman citizenship after five years' residence in the Ottoman Empire; article 4, which states that the Ottoman state can waive this condition for those foreigners whom it considers "exceptional cases" and to whom it sees fit to grant Ottoman citizenship; and article 9: "Any person living in Ottoman domains is considered an Ottoman subject and is treated as an Ottoman subject. If he is of foreign nationality he must prove his nationality according to accepted procedures".

[95] Deringil, *The Well Protected Domains*, Chapter 2.

taken the name Mehmed.[96] When the Serbian embassy insisted on his return, they were told that in the year 1891 a certain Ali Bin Ibrahim from Drama had deserted from the Ottoman army and had crossed over to the Serbian side. When the Ottoman authorities asked for his return, they had been told that he had become a Christian and therefore could not be handed back. As this created a precedent, Milan/Mehmed would not be returned. One year later the matter was still not resolved as the Serbian embassy was claiming that the treaty stipulations applied only to ordinary criminals and not to political crimes. As Racović was a deserter, this was a political crime. They did not recall any case involving an Ali bin Ibrahim.[97] It is important to note here that the extradition treaty with Serbia must have included a clause whereby if the escapees converted to Christianity or Islam, respectively, they could not be extradited. It will be recalled that it was such treaty clauses that had saved the Hungarian asylum seekers in 1849.

The Ottoman Council of Ministers debated a similar case on 13 June 1901. A Russian soldier named Comzu from the Sixth Cossack Regiment at Oltu, being pursued for theft, had crossed the border, taken refuge in the Vilayet of Erzurum, and converted to Islam. The Russian authorities were now negotiating his return in exchange for an Ottoman soldier by the name of Ömer, who had deserted and was being held by the Russians at Oltu. The ministers agreed that the treaty stipulations were very clear regarding the exemption from extradition of those who had converted to the religion of the other side. However, there was no indication that Ömer had converted to Christianity. The ministers duly concluded that Ömer could be extradited from Russia. Comzu, by contrast, even if his conversion was due to fear, had converted and was thereby exempt from extradition.[98]

The Sixth Cossacks seemed to take quite an interest in Islam. On 6 June 1903 it was reported that three of its members had crossed over to the Ottoman side and declared that they had converted. The Ottoman Foreign Ministry had instructed its ambassador in St. Petersburg to inform the Russian government about the event. The minister did specify, however, that these neo-Muslim Cossacks were not to be trusted "as they may have

---

[96] BOA DH.MKT 71/14, 1 Kanun-u Sani 1310 / 14 January 1894, the Vali of Kosovo, Haci Mehmed Hafız, to the Ministry of the Interior, Secretariat of the Vilayet of Kosovo, no. 373.

[97] Ibid., 8 Safer 1313 / 31 July 1895, the foreign minister, Tevfik Paşa, to the Ministry of the Interior.

[98] BOA MV 102/52, 25 Safer 1319 / 13 June 1901, the minutes of the meeting of the Council of Ministers. Oltu, today a sub-district of Erzurum, had been in the Russian-occupied part of Anatolia since the war of 1877–78. See Map 2.

converted in order to act as spies", and he advised that they be stationed in localities far from the border.[99]

The Russo-Ottoman border seems to have been quite an active place at the turn of the century as regards matters of conversion and apostasy. On 26 May 1907 the Ministry of Police reported that "Ahmed Tevfik Efendi and Hasan Raşid Efendi, originally Russian subjects who recently came to Istanbul and were honoured with the glory of Islam", had been detained by the Russian consulate in Istanbul. The two young men, who had been registered as students in Istanbul after their conversion, had been given Ottoman passports and had gone to the consulate to procure visas to visit their homes in their native town of Kazan. The consul had refused to recognize their conversion, confiscated their passports, and jailed them in the consulate prison. After the protests of the Porte, they were released.[100]

On 21 June 1894 the Vilayet of Yanya reported that a certain Yani, son of Andon Kasilupanoplu, and his wife had arrived there "as refugees wanting asylum and to convert to Islam". The Greek consul in Yanya and his dragoman together with two armed *kavass* (consulate orderlies) had forced their way into the inn where the couple were staying and "attempted to drag his wife off to the Consulate". The police had intervened, and the Vali had been notified. When the Greek consul was confronted about the matter he claimed that the persons in question were parading under false identity and were wanted in Athens for stealing 44,000 franks. Both the couple and their rooms were searched, and nothing was found.[101] The couple may well have wanted to convert in order to escape pursuit.

The Ministry of Police records at the beginning of the twentieth century abound with cases of suspect conversions. On 5 March 1905 it was reported that a certain Andon Diragić had deserted from the Hungarian army and converted to Islam, offering his services to the Ottoman army. He had been assigned to the police in the Vilayet of Ankara.[102]

---

[99] BOA A.MKT.MHM 732/7, 24 Mayis 1319 / 6 June 1903, the minister of foreign affairs, Tevfik Paşa, to the Sublime Porte.

[100] BOA DH.MKT 1170/84, 13 Rebiyulahir 1325 / 26 May 1907, the minister of police to the Ministry of the Interior.

[101] BOA DH.MKT 257/29, 17 Zilhicce 1311 / 21 June 1894, the Vilayet of Yanya Secretariat No. 79 to the Ministry of the Interior, signed by Vali El Hac Zeki.

[102] BOA ZB 338/61, 20 Subat 1321 / 5 March 1905, the Ministry of Police to the Foreign Ministry. Some six months later it was reported that he had been moved to Edirne under police escort. ZB 379/84, 16 Kanun-u Evvel 1321 / 29 December 1905.

Hungary continued to provide more than its fair share of converts. On 15 March 1906 the Ministry of Police reported that a student "who had arrived last year to study in Istanbul" had converted and taken the name Fuad Eminüddin. It was stipulated that he be "secretly kept under surveillance".[103] Eminüddin was actually Jorj Misaros Leon, a member of the Association Asiatique of Budapest, who had arrived with a letter of recommendation from Arminius Vambery himself and had converted to Islam on 3 December 1905. The Ottoman embassy in Vienna was asked to investigate his background.[104]

The Ottoman police were certainly kept busy with the surveillance of suspect converts.[105] Such was the case of a Russian, Manuel Nayilev, who arrived in Taşluca in Ottoman Kossovo having crossed over from Bosnia at the end of 1909. Nayilev claimed that he had converted to Islam in Bulgaria some two years previously, and that he now wanted his conversion to be recognized officially and to become an Ottoman citizen. The authorities in Kossovo had passed him on to the governor of Salonica, where he was being detained for questioning. Nayilev appears to be something of a mystery man, as it was rumoured that he had a shady past and was suspected of having previously committed a crime in Salonica. The governor therefore postponed the conversion procedure pending an extensive investigation, and Nayilev was sent to Istanbul under escort.[106] Upon being questioned, Nayilev said that he was forty-four years old, had been employed in his native town of Virhofka as a shop assistant, and had for some ten years " been thinking of converting to Islam". He had travelled from Russia to Port Said; he had acquired a passport from the Russian consulate there and had turned up in Taşluca via Bosnia. All he wanted was to become a Muslim and an Ottoman citizen. When the investigations in Salonica and Scutari did not turn up evidence of any criminal past, Nayilev was duly released from custody,

---

[103] BOA ZB 379/6, 2 Mart 1322 / 15 March 1906, the Ministry of Police, memorandum. A few months later the police reported that Eminuddin had been joined by another Hungarian student, Zoltan Mandos. The "watchers" had reported that the two seemed exclusively interested in their studies. ZB 379/67, 6 Ağustoe 1322 / 29 August 1906.

[104] BOA ZB 338/72, 2 Mart 1322 / 15 March 1906, the Ministry of Police to the Foreign Ministry.

[105] In the archival funds of the Ministry of Police, BOA *Zaptiye* (ZB), and the Ministry of Interior General Security, BOA *Dahiliye Emniyet-i Umumiye* (DH.EUM), there are literally hundreds of cases very like the samples cited here.

[106] BOA DH.EUM. THR. 25/4, 19 Kanun-u Evvel 1325 / 31 December 1909, the governor of Selanik to the Istanbul Directorate of Police.

and his request for formal conversion was referred to the Ministry of Justice and Religious Sects.[107]

People who converted for no ostensible reason became the object of extreme scrutiny and suspicion. It was sometimes even required that they prove that they were not insane. Such was the case of the Greek subject Kaliyaris, who turns up in the police record in 1910. Kaliyaris was sent to the official hospital (*bimarhane*) "where he was watched day and night" by "experts on mental disorder to see if he displayed any physical or mental signs of mental illness".[108]

Another such person who converted for no apparent reason was a German by the name of Josef Ishmael, who claimed to have converted and to have taken the name Yusuf Reşid. Yusuf now requested that he be "exceptionally" (*istisnaen*) granted Ottoman citizenship. The police investigation report noted that "no undesirable behaviour [on his part] had so far been noticed", but it did not omit to point out that although Yusuf's conversion had been duly registered at the Ministry of Justice, he continued to use his German name professionally. The police also reported that he had recently moved to another neighbourhood and gave his precise address.[109]

CITIZENSHIP DEFINED AND DELINEATED

As the nineteenth century ended, the Porte began to consider the relationship of citizenship and religion on a comparative basis and sought to find out what the practice was in other states. On 3 March 1888, the Ottoman ambassador in Rome, Photiades Paşa, was asked to enquire whether Italian subjects lost their citizenship if they converted to Islam. Photiades replied that they did not.[110]

As the flotsam and jetsam of a Europe in turmoil continued to turn up in increasing numbers over the last years of the nineteenth and the first decade of the twentieth century, the Ottoman authorities decided to curtail access

---

[107] Ibid., 6 Kanun-u Sani 1325 / 19 January 1910, deposition of the Directorate of Police, signed "Manuel", enclosing the final report from the Directorate of Police to the Ministry of Justice and Religious Sects.

[108] BOA DH.EUM.THR 38/53, 14 June 1326 / 27 June 1910, the Ministry of Police to the Ministry of the Interior.

[109] BOA DH.ID 61-1/63, 17 Kanun-u Sani 1330 / 30 January 1914, Istanbul General Directorate of Police, no. 12394, to the Ministry of the Interior.

[110] BOA HR/MTV 568/36, 3 March 1888, the foreign minister, Said Paşa, to the Ottoman ambassador to Italy, Photiadis Paşa. My thanks to Sinan Kuneralp for this reference.

to Ottoman citizenship. On 19 March 1912 the Council of State (*Şurayı Devlet*) prepared a memorandum dealing with the issue of citizenship. It had been determined that in order to apply for Ottoman citizenship, foreign subjects did not have to apply for permission from their own country. The Council of State referred to a regulation it had promulgated on 18 January 1894 to the effect that even those foreigners not fulfilling the requirements of the Citizenship Law could become Muslims and apply to the Ministry of Interior in Istanbul or to the local authorities in the provinces, whereupon they would be issued Ottoman identification papers certifying that they were Muslims, but they would not be considered full Ottoman citizens. Now the Ottoman government had gone one step further and explicitly declared that conversion to Islam did not automatically entitle the convert to Ottoman citizenship. It had been decided that each case should be considered on its merits and decided upon according to the Nationality Law. The reason for this decision was very clearly stated:

'It has come to our attention that some foreigners who have committed crimes in foreign countries seek asylum in Ottoman domains in order to escape punishment and convert to Islam in order to acquire Ottoman citizenship. They then claim Ottoman protection and this causes complications and difficulties for the Sublime State. Therefore it has been decided that from now on conversion will not be a sufficient condition for the granting of Ottoman nationality (*ihtidanın tebdil i tabiyete sebeb i münferid ad olunmaması*).'[111]

One year later this was confirmed by an imperial decree.[112]

One of the key issues that come up very often in matters of citizenship is the issue of the property of those who give up or lose their Ottoman citizenship. A memorandum of the Council of State dated 28 December 1881 presented a detailed discussion concerning two types of cases: those who gave up their Ottoman citizenship voluntarily and with the approval of the state, and those who gave up their citizenship without official approval. The second version proved to be a particularly thorny issue. The Council of State brought together experts from the Legal Advisors Bureau of the Sublime Porte and religious authorities (*ulema*), experts on Islamic property law.[113] The gist of the discussion is extremely interesting as it reflects a clash between normative/positivist, nationalist legal

[111] BOA DH.HMŞ 13/48, 10 Rebiyülahir 1331 / 19 March 1912, the Sublime Porte Legal Advisors' Bureau, the memorandum of the Council of State (*Şurayi Devlet-i Tanzimat*).
[112] Irade Dahiliye (DH.ID) 116/60, 17 Mart 1329 / 26 March 1913, draft circular from the Ministry of the Interior.
[113] BOA Y.A RES 19/24, 25 Muharrem 1299 / 28 December 1881, memorandum of the Council of State.

standards and Şeriat rulings. According to the Ottoman Citizenship Law
regarding those who had left Ottoman citizenship without official approval, their act was not recognized, and they continued to be considered
Ottoman citizens. However, if the state chose to do so, it could annul their
citizenship and forbid their entry into Ottoman domains. Moreover, their
property could not be made over to their children or parents whether they
were foreign citizens or Ottoman citizens; it would be considered deserted
property (*mahlul*), in effect being confiscated. It was here that an interesting divergence occurred between the secular and religious experts.
According to the latter, as the person whose citizenship was annulled
was considered dead (*fevt eylemiş*), income from the property they
owned (*akaratı memluke*), according to the Şeriat, was liable to inheritance
by their heirs, who were Ottoman subjects. One of the highest ranking
ulema, holding the rank of *Sadır-ı* Rumeli, Seyf el Din Efendi, was invited
to give his views. The worthy *alim* declared that although the confiscation
of any state land (*arazi-i amiriye*) held by one who had lost citizenship was
admissible, income from private property was inheritable, and according
to the Şeriat could not be confiscated.[114] In the subsequent discussion the
secular wing of the council carried the day, openly declaring that the
measure was intended as "some sort of punishment for those who changed
citizenship [without leave]" and that the measure was designed to "prevent
the changing of citizenship"; thus the property of those who left Ottoman
citizenship without leave "was to come under political confiscation even if
there were heirs".[115]

Some nine years later the same issues were still being debated in the
highest reaches of the Ottoman establishment. A minute from the Ottoman
Cabinet dated 4 June 1890 recorded that among the issues discussed were
the following: "What happens to the property of a woman who is an
Ottoman citizen but marries a foreigner? Is the property of someone who
has left Ottoman citizenship with official leave inheritable by his heirs? Is the
property of one who dies as an Ottoman citizen inheritable by heirs who are
foreigners?" All of these matters were referred to the Council of State.[116]

It is highly likely that the issue of citizenship, its acquisition, and its loss
were closely linked to the changes in the international political conjuncture.
Particularly after the outbreak of the Armenian crisis of the mid-1890s, the

---

[114] Ibid. The *Sadr-ı Rumeli* was the highest-ranking judge after the Şeyhülislam. *Kadi*s
holding this rank usually went on to become Şeyhülislam. My thanks to Cem Behar for
this information.
[115] Ibid. "*tebdil-i tabiyet edenler hakkında bir nev mecazat olmak lazım geleceği*".
[116] BOA MV 10/44, 22 Mayis 1306 / 4 June 1890.

matter of foreign protection of Ottoman subjects became a critical issue. On 29 January 1894 a memorandum from the Yıldız Palace clearly pointed out: "It is not permissible for anyone to leave Ottoman citizenship without obtaining an Imperial *Irade* permitting them to do so". This was also to be announced in the press. The memorandum openly stated, "[T]he misunderstandings on this issue which have been particularly exploited by the Armenians [should be cleared up]".[117]

The issue of an official identity became increasingly salient as the century neared its end. Particularly in matters of official appointments to senior ecclesiastical positions, the requirement of Ottoman citizenship became paramount. On 13 July 1895 the Council of Ministers discussed the appointment of one Gerasimos (Yerasimos) Efendi as the Greek Orthodox Patriarch for Antioch. There was some hesitation as to the appropriateness of his appointment because "he had been born in Greece and his father still lives in Greece". Upon investigation, the council was informed that though this was indeed the case, "the candidate had been living in the diocese of the Patriarchate of Jerusalem since he was seven or eight years old". He had indeed risen to the rank of Metropolitan and had also served in Istanbul as the deputy for the Jerusalem Patriarchate. It was concluded that "even if his father is a Greek citizen, he [Gerasimos] is a loyal Ottoman citizen and his grandfather was an Ottoman citizen, therefore there is no objection to his appointment as Patriarch of Antioch".[118]

It is important to note that until the second half of the nineteenth century there was no systematic registration of births, deaths, marriages, or migration. The first nineteenth-century census was completed in 1831 and was rather haphazard and disorganized. The first Regulation for Population Registration (*Sicil-i Nüfus Nizamnamesi*) was formulated in 1878. This led to the first compilation of permanent population registers, the *sicil-i nüfus* , which come up very frequently in the chapters of this book. As put by Cem Behar: "For the first time in the secular pluralist history of the Ottoman censuses , the individual was taken as the unit of calculation, irrespective of gender, age, profession or fortune. The modernisation of the structure of the Ottoman state, which had begun timidly

---

[117] BOA Irade Hususi 56, 21 Receb 1311 / 29 January 1894, Yıldız Palace Imperial Secretariat, signed by Imperial Secretary Süreyya Paşa. On the Armenian crisis, see Chapter 5.

[118] BOA MV 4/27, 30 Haziran 1301 / 13 July 1895. The same condition applies today; according to the Lausanne Treaty of 1923, the Greek Orthodox Patriarch in Istanbul has to be a Turkish citizen.

in the 1840s with the reforms of the Tanzimat were thus concretized in the domain of statistics".[119]

For the first time, these statistics included women. Moreover, another first for the 1885 census was the institution of the "identity card" (*Nüfus Tezkeresi*), which became an obligatory document for all official trans- actions such as buying and selling and the application for an internal passport. The application of the regulation making the identity card obli- gatory remained sporadic until 1903, when a new, firmer regulation was instituted. Another striking thing about the 1885 census is that it listed the Ottoman population according to "nation" (*millet*) for the first time. The categories were "Muslims (without any other ethnic specification), Greek Orthodox, Armenian, Bulgar, Catholic, Jewish, Protestant, Latin, Monophysite, Gypsy non-Muslims, Foreigners and 'others'".[120]

By the turn of the century it had become established that anyone apply- ing for an official government position was required to present a valid Ottoman identity certificate. But the requirement was one thing, the reality on the ground quite another. On 5 July 1903 the Ministry of the Interior was still bemoaning the fact that not only did some people who applied for government positions still not have a valid identification certificate, some had not even been registered in the population registers.[121]

Official identity was still largely determined by religion, yet it seems as though religious identity was not as immutable as it had once been. On 28 October 1893 the Population Registration Bureau reported that a certain Aleksi from Yanina, who had converted to Islam on 16 July 1887 and taken the name Hüseyin, now wanted to go back to his old name and religion and be issued identity papers in his old name. The Population Registration Bureau added that there was also "an Armenian" (no name was given) who was in the same position.[122] Clearly, by 1893 changing religious identity had become nearly a commonplace.

On 6 May 1894 the Ministry of the Interior noted that in the Vilayet of Syria, "[some] Greek Orthodox are converting to Catholicism, then after a

---

[119] Cem Behar, "Sources pour la demographie historique de l'Empire Ottoman. Les *tahrirs* (dénombrements) de 1885 et 1907", *Population* 1–2 (1998), 161–78. My translation.

[120] Cem Behar, "Qui Compte? Recensements et statistiques demographiques dans l'Empire ottoman, du XVIe au XXe siècle", *Histoire & Mesure* 13.5 (1998), 135–46.

[121] BOA ZB 18/107, 9 Rebiyulahir 1321 / 5 July 1903, the Ministry of the Interior Secretariat, signed by the minister of the interior, Mehmed Memduh Paşa.

[122] BOA Y.PRK.AZJ (Yildiz Perakende Arzuhal ve Jurnaller) 27/84, 15 Teşrin-i Evvel 1309 / 28 October 1893. The Population Registration Bureau also stated that they had made no move to fulfill the desires of the applicants.

time converting to Protestantism and later converting back to Orthodoxy." The ministry noted that this was causing confusion in the population registers and reminded the Vilayet that all non-Muslims who converted had to have their identity papers checked yearly.[123] It is interesting that the only thing the state took issue with was the fact that this shopping around in religions was causing confusion in the records.

The revision of the Population Registration Law was discussed at length during the debates of the Second Parliament (1909–14). One of the key issues was, "[W]hat should be the content of the new Ottoman identity certificates?" Deputy Hamparsum Boyaciyan suggested that a category entitled "nationality" (*milliyet*) should appear on the document because, given the fact that religion could be changed owing to the freedom of religion guaranteed by the constitution, "we would be building on a more solid foundation [if we include nationality]".[124] Another debate raged over what to do about foundling children who had been discovered with no indication as to their ethnicity. The Muslim deputies had demanded that such a child automatically be registered as a Muslim. This was objected to by the Christian deputies. The deputy for Salonica, Artas Yorgaki, asked: "What are we going to do if such a child is found in a village where there are no Muslims? How can we call the child a Muslim? It is most likely to be one belonging to people of the village."[125]

CONCLUSION

The story of the career conversions of the migrant souls remain full of questions, many of which will never be answered. As to why they took refuge in Ottoman lands, it would be simplistic to contend, as one Turkish

---

[123] BOA DH.HMŞ 17/41, 29 Şevval 1311 / 6 May 1894, the Sublime Porte, Ministry of the Interior. Of course it must be remembered that Syria and Lebanon were areas where religious identity was very porous. See Makdisi, *The Artillery of Heaven*, p. 80.

[124] Fevzi Demir, "Osmanlı Kimliği Üzerine Osmanlı'nın Son Tartışması: Osmanlı'da Hüviyet Cüzdanı nasıl olmalı?" (The last discussion on Ottoman identity by the Ottomans: What should the Ottoman identity card look like?) *Kebikec* 10 (2000), 245–51. Hamparsum Boyaciyan had been a legendary figure of the Armenian Revolutionary Federation during the Armenian crisis of the 1890s. Therefore, when he mentioned "nationality" he definitely meant nationality as in "nationalism". See Chapter 5 in this volume.

[125] Ibid. In the end, the entry on "nationality" was not included. The Population Registry Law was passed on 27 August 1914 and, although it underwent important changes, remained in force until the new law, No. 1587 of 5 June 1972, was passed.

author does, that "[they came] because this country was of a different culture and had remained completely outside European currents of thought".[126] If anything, those who came and stayed, apart from practical considerations such as physical survival, did so because, by and large, the parameters of the world they saw in Istanbul or elsewhere in the Ottoman Empire were not all that different from the places they had left behind.

A constructive comparison can be made here with Linda Colley's seventeenth- and eighteenth-century captives who found themselves to some degree helpless vis-à-vis their Indian, North African, or native American captors.[127] The nineteenth-century career convert was different in several respects. First, he was usually free to move back and forth between his old world and his adopted country, unless, like the Hungarians just discussed, there were political or other circumstances hindering his return. Kmetty/İsmail Paşa moved back and forth between his Ottoman and Hungarian persona; Ladislas Czaykowski/Sadık Paşa went back to Poland to work for Polish independence. Vambery was a veritable chameleon who donned his character of "Reşid Efendi" whenever he came to Istanbul. It must be recalled also that the Ottoman officials sent to Vidin to smooth over the "crossing" actually told the prospective converts that they could go back to their original religion if they wished once the danger was over.

Second, unlike the captives of Tipu Sultan of Mysore in the 1780s, or the English sailors captured by the Barbary corsairs, the nineteenth-century convert, even if he converted to Islam, was not actually forced to convert. Third, he "crossed over" at a historical conjuncture when the power relationship was reversed; here it was the host society and polity that was in a position of weakness compared to the world he came from. Yet there are also important similarities with earlier periods, the most notable being that men of humble or middling social origins could rise to positions of power that would have been unattainable to them in their land of origin. Moreover, once having "gone over", both the renegades of the earlier periods and the nineteenth-century career converts in the Ottoman Empire could become thoroughly acculturated in their new surroundings.

The commander-in-chief of the Ottoman army during the Crimean War was Ömer Lütfi Paşa, a converted Croat from a modest background. General Bem was immediately made a *Ferik* (army commander) upon

---

[126] Taner Timur, "Karl Marx ve Johann Bangya, nam I diger Miralay Mehmet Bey" (Karl Marx and Johann Bangya, otherwise known as Lieutenant Mehmet Bey), *Tarih ve Toplum*, no. 35 (November 1986), 14–15.

[127] Linda Colley, "Going Native, Telling Tales: Captivity, Collaboration and Empire", *Past and Present*, no. 168 (August 2000), 170–93.

converting. All his companions who came with him received ranks that were either comparable or superior to the ranks they had held as Christians. At a more humble level, the ex-brigand Stoyanof/Sadık received a very respectable salary and held a good rank as chief inspector of police (*Ser Komiser*). There was little difference for a Hungarian or a Polish professional soldier between, say, taking up service for the Ottoman sultan or for the Union army during the American Civil War.[128] In the case of a Pole, service in the Ottoman ranks had the added attraction of furnishing the opportunity to strike a blow against the hated enemy, Russia.

For the Ottoman Empire, this "providential hail of qualified cadres" could only have been welcome. Yet we have seen that there was a definite hierarchy of conversions, lower-class converts being much less welcome. We have seen that many of the refugees became attached to their new homeland, but they seem also to have remained a distinct cast whose stigma of "foreigner" or "infidel" never really vanished. The refugee, even if he was a convert, even if he rose to the rank of Paşa, would always be "*gavur* (infidel) so and so Paşa" in private conversation. Ömer Paşa was referred to in the Arabic literature as *al-nimsawi*, or the Austrian, when he fought against the Druze in Mount Lebanon in 1843.[129] So can we speak of a class of nineteenth-century *devşirme*, a sort of latter-day Janissary? What was the difference between an Ottoman high official who had been taken into the Ottoman elite through the child levy during the earlier period and the migrant soul of the nineteenth century? It is quite clear that the way in which the Ottoman elite viewed non-Muslim origins had greatly changed by the nineteenth century. One of the most illustrious figures of the Tanzimat era, İbrahim Edhem Paşa, who actually rose to the rank of Grand Vizier, made a rather lame effort to hide his origins as a converted Greek slave, and his son, Halil Edhem Paşa, put about the fake story that his father had Circassian Muslim origins. Why did he feel obliged to do so? According to Edhem Eldem: "It is possible that the fact that Edhem Paşa was an exceptional case, an anomaly in an age where

---

[128] Of the 4,000 or so Hungarians in the United States in 1860, "About 800 of them served in the Union Army of whom 80 to 100 were officers". See Eugen Pivany, "Hungarian American Historical Connections", a treatise read (in part) on the occasion of assuming his seat as the foreign member of the Hungarian Academy of Sciences, Budapest. Translated from the Hungarian, 4 October 1926, published in 1927, pp. 57, 58. My thanks to Zolt Banheggy for this reference. See also Vasvary, *Lincoln's Hungarian Heroes.*

[129] Personal communication from Ussama Makdisi.

modernity, modern identity and citizenship [had become the norm] made him an anachronistic exception".[130]

How did these people see the land that they had adopted and the people that had suddenly become their co-religionists and co-citizens? Obviously, each case must be considered separately as the migrant souls were extremely internally differentiated, ranging from bona fide aristocrats to humble peasants and technicians. The other open question is, how far can one "adopt" an identity?

A Polish convert, Isa Saharin (Pruski), who had been attacked in the press for his frank criticism of the Ottoman Empire, was to reply in an equally frank manner:

Poland is my Mother and Turkey is my Stepmother. Until my Mother is resurrected my aim is to work for the good of my adopted country. Because of this, as a Muslim, I have the right to state my views on anything that I choose. It is my right to praise the good and criticise the bad things that I see here. It is my purpose to always wish the best for this country and work towards overcoming all the difficulties.[131]

Some chose to reconcile their two identities, as in the case of Mustafa Celaleddin Paşa, who, with his theory of "Turco-Aryanism", sought to show that his adopted country and native culture were actually not alien.[132] In cases such as that of Sadık Paşa, it is highly unlikely that they became practising Muslims given the fact that their families remained Christian. Some became thoroughly Ottoman, or even Turkish, to the point of becoming militant Turkish nationalists, such as Alfred Rüstem. Such was also the case of Hasan Enver Celaleddin Paşa, who was to continue the work of his father and write articles based on his father's notes, which would actually be inspirational for latter-day proponents of ideological Turkism (*Türkçülük*).[133] In a sense, Enver Celaleddin was echoing his father's words: "[Therefore] there is no racial connection between the Turks and the Chinese. The Turks are a member of the

---

[130] Edhem Eldem, "İbrahim Edhem Paşa Rum Muydu?" (Was İbrahim Edhem Paşa a Greek?), *Toplumsal Tarih* 16 (October 2010), 2–12. Edhem Paşa was one of the thousands of residents of the island of Chios enslaved after the punitive raid of Ottoman forces (1821) during the Greek War of Independence.

[131] Latka, "Polonya Mültecileri", p. 53.

[132] Ibid., p. 54. Latka points out that for two years he attended a seminary where he would have been exposed to the standard Catholic image of "The Turk" as a great danger to Christian civilization.

[133] "Türkçülüğün Tarihinden Hasan Enver Celaleddin Paşa nın Edebiyat ı Umumiyye Mecmuası Yazıları", *Tarih ve Toplum* 2 (January 1984), 15, 18.

white races like the Europeans. Moreover, the Turkish race is one of the oldest of the white races."[134]

Perhaps the most difficult question is the question of the *sincerity* of the conversions of the migrant souls. Murad Paşa (Bem) was circumcised. For others, such as Ismail Paşa (Kmetty), an Islamic persona was a character mantle that was assumed as a matter of convenience. Still others, such as the brigand-turned-policeman Stoyanof, used Islam and Ottoman citizenship as a means of furthering opportunist careers as adventurers operating in the interstices of Turco-European cultural *millieux*.

The fact that the modern Turkish sources used here do not in any way bring up the matter of the sincerity of the conversions is indicative of a certain frame of mind. If even modern published sources take the Islam of the convert at face value and simply assume that there was nothing unusual about the fact that Ismail Paşa should revert to being Kmetty in London, and then resume his identity as Ismail Paşa when he returned to Turkey, this is also indicative. None of the modern Turkish sources dealing with the Hungarian or Polish converts that I have seen mention even the possibility that the conversions may have been nominal. The modern sources have the same mindset as their subject matter; as far as they are concerned, it was enough for "so and so Paşa" to go through the motions of being a Muslim.[135]

The relationship between citizenship and religion in the twilight of the Ottoman Empire followed the ups and downs of political conjuncture. The Hungarian and Polish refugees were saved by the yoking together of the ancient practice of conversion that made one automatically a subject of the sultan /Caliph, and the specific bilateral treaties whereby conversion absolved them from the extradition clause. As the century wore on, the Tanzimat State felt the need to regulate citizenship on a basis that would have an equivalent in international law; hence it passed the Citizenship Law of 1869. Yet conversion to Islam still facilitated (even if it did not ensure) Ottoman citizenship, causing many dubious characters to take refuge in Ottoman domains. Similarly, the category of "foreign Muslims" also indicated that Islam was no longer a sufficient condition for citizenship. Finally, just as the Ottoman Empire was about to plunge

---

[134] Enver Celalettin Paşa, "Türklerin Aslı" (On the Origins of the Turks), *Edebiyat-ı Umumiye Mecmuası*, no. 31 (2 June 1917). As reproduced in *Tarih ve Toplum* 7, no.1 (January 1984).

[135] Nazir, *Osmanlı'ya Sığınanlar*, pp. 81–7. In this latest major work on the issue the author does not in any way adress the sincerity of the conversion.

into the war that was to be its end, it actually formally broke the connection between religion and citizenship.

However, none of the conversions mentioned here, even those occurring under highly dubious auspices, were rejected. The Şeriat ruling, which was always interpreted as meaning that anyone who declared that he or she wanted to embrace Islam was entitled to be initiated into the faith, seems to have been the operative principle in all of the cases mentioned. Even someone so obviously dubious such as the Belgian propagandist for Ottoman missionary activities in the Belgian Congo was still treated as more than a quack journalist; the prodigal son of the Russian general was not dismissed outright; and the Cossacks who had suddenly become enamored of Islam were admitted. Others like them, whose provenance and loyalty were dubious at best, were made Ottoman policemen. There is no mention of the outright rejection of any of the conversions discussed in this chapter, even if they were patently bogus. This is in stark contrast to the treatment of the Armenian converts in the next chapter, where desperate people resorted to desperate measures to have their conversions accepted.

5

Conversion as Survival

Mass Conversions of Armenians in Anatolia, 1895–1897

Asia Minor is indeed the trunk of Turkey, the real Turkey.

Leon Trotsky[1]

The British Ambassador [Sir Philip Curie] was a very nasty man. He had an audience with me once, at the time of the Armenian crisis. He crossed his legs and began to yell at the top of his voice, saying you do such and such things to the Christians. I was so angry that I said to myself, now I shall get at your throat and kill you, but what can I do, I am in a responsible, official position (*memurum*). My Ottoman nerves were so infuriated that I was barely able to control myself. Tears came to my eyes after the Ambassador left; I cried ...

Abdülhamid II to his doctor, Atıf Hüseyin[2]

THE END OF THE TANZIMAT STATE

The Tanzimat State ended with the reign of Sultan Abdülhamid II (r. 1876–1909). Apart from the obvious factor of separatist nationalism,

A previous version of this chapter was published as an article in *Comparative Studies in Society and History* 51 (April 2009), 344–71, "'The Armenian Question Is Finally Closed': Mass Conversions of Armenians during the Hamidian Massacres of 1895–1897". Although the Armenian genocide of 1915 is still a very politically vibrant issue, and a great deal of literature continues to be devoted to it, the massacres of the 1890s have received surprisingly little attention. I have deliberately excluded the conversions that occurred in 1915 as I intend to write a monograph dedicated specifically to that issue.

[1] Leon Trotsky, *The War Correspondence of Leon Trotsky: The Balkan Wars 1912–13* (New York, 1993), p. 240.

[2] Engin Deniz Akarlı, *The Problem of External Pressures, Power Struggles, and Budgetary Deficits in Ottoman Politics under Abdulhamid II (1876–1909)*, unpublished Ph.D. dissertation, Princeton University (1976), p. 52. Akarlı is citing the unpublished personal diaries of Atıf Hüseyin, the sultan's private doctor.

it foundered on strong vested interests on the part of Muslims and non-Muslims alike who did not want to change the status quo, popular resistance to more direct and efficient rule, and on the failure to integrate the peripheral elements into its project.[3]

Unlike the Tanzimat State that had still sought to include the non-Muslim population in its project, even as it balked at the prospect of the emergence masses of crypto-Christians, and even as it accepted the nominal conversions of various classes of Christian asylum seekers – some of them very dubious characters – the mass conversion of Armenians during the massacres of the 1890s was to reflect a fundamental change in the Ottoman politics of conversion. The Armenians who converted to save their lives were not accepted as real Muslims; the sultan and his bureaucracy feared that they could serve as a potential fifth column, or that they would complain to the representatives of the foreign powers that they had been converted by force.

Although many of the reforms relating to infrastructure, education, and the modernisation of the bureaucracy begun during the Tanzimat State were to continue, the basic nature of the Hamidian era was to be very different. This was no longer a period when the state made promises to its subjects, Muslim and *reaya* alike. After the loss of the bulk of the Christian population in the Balkans, the Hamidian regime fell back on what it saw as the only reliable elements, the Muslims.[4] Parliament was abrogated, the Constitution suspended, and Mithat Paşa exiled and later executed.[5] After the disastrous war with Russia in 1877–78, leading to the loss of the greater part of the most valuable remaining Ottoman lands in the Balkans, the sultan and his entourage feared that Anatolia, the last stronghold, would go the same way. The Armenian population of the Ottoman Empire was the last of the Christian communities to make a bid for autonomy.[6] After the establishment of the Armenian revolutionary

[3] On popular resistance, see Ahmet Uzun, *Tanzimat ve Sosyal Direnişler*. On the centre and periphery issue, see Şerif Mardin, "Center-Periphery Relations: A Key to Turkish Politics?", *Daedalus* 39 (1972), 169–90.

[4] Stephen Duguid, "The Politics of Unity: Hamidian Policy in Eastern Anatolia", *Middle Eastern Studies* 9 (1973), 130–55.

[5] Ibrahim Hakkı Uzunçarşılı, *Midhat Paşa ve Taif Mahkumları* (Midhat Pasa and the convicts of Taif) (Ankara, 1985). There is considerable controversy over the question of Midhat Paşa's incarceration in the prison of Taif and the manner of his death. Although it is fairly certain that he was murdered on the orders of the sultan, no official *fetva* was issued by the Şeyhülislam, and to this day no trace has been found of an official order to have him executed.

[6] The literature on the Armenian Question is vast. A sample of some of the most recent important works on the Armenian Question are: Taner Akçam, *A Shameful Act: The Armenian Genocide and the Question of Turkish Responsibility* (New York, 2006);

organizations, the Dashnaktsuthiun and the Hunchakian, in the closing years of the nineteenth century, the "revolutionary committees", as they came to be known, deliberately sought to emulate the Balkan model of activism. The Greek, Montenegrin, Serbian, and Bulgarian *komitaji* were adopted as role models. Revolutionary agitation was to lead to foreign intervention and the eventual creation of an autonomous or independent Armenia.[7] Vahakn Dadrian is perfectly correct when he states that "the Armenian Question had become an extension of the Eastern Question, the Turco-Armenian conflict functioned as an integral part of that crucible, i.e. as a test case for the preservation of the empire."[8] An Ottoman document emanating directly from Yıldız Palace at this time clearly drew the parallel: "However, the Armenian affair is not like the Bulgarian or the Serbian affairs, because it has arisen in Anatolia which is the crucible of Ottoman might".[9] The possible emergence of an Armenian state in eastern Anatolia had to be prevented at all costs. An Ottoman document published soon after Abdülhamid's deposition openly asked: "Did they [the Dashnak] intend to take the same road as the Bulgarians, that is to say, use Russian support to achieve unity and then turn on the Russians?"[10]

Arminius Vambery, whom we met in the previous chapter, recounts that in the course of one of his audiences with Abdülhamid, the latter told him:

By taking away Rumelia and Greece, Europe has cut off the feet of the Turkish State body. The loss of Bulgaria, Serbia and Egypt has deprived us of our hands, and now by means of this Armenian agitation they want to get at our most vital parts and tear out our entrails – this would be the beginning of total annihilation, and this we must fight against with all the strength we possess.[11]

Raymond Kevorkian, *Le Genocide des Armeniens* (Paris, 2006); and Fuat Dündar, *Modern Türkiye'nin Şifresi* (The code of modern Turkey) (Istanbul, 2008).

[7] See Louise Nalbandian, *The Armenian Revolutionary Movement: The Development of Armenian Political Parties through the Nineteenth Century* (Berkeley, Los Angeles, and London, 1975), p. 94.

[8] Vahakn Dadrian, *The History of the Armenian Genocide: Ethnic Conflict from the Balkans to Anatolia to the Caucasus* (Providence, RI and Oxford, 1995), p. 185.

[9] BOA Y.PRK. BŞK 32/94, Yıldız Palace Imperial Secretariat, 1585, 20 Safer 1311 / 2 September 1893.

[10] Osman Nuri, *Abdülhamid-i Sani ve Devr-i Saltanatı.* (Abdulhamid the Second and his reign) (Istanbul, 1327/1909), p. 863.

[11] Lory Alder and Richard Dalby, *The Dervish of Windsor Castle*, p. 359. Arminius Vambery prided himself on the fact that he had the sultan's confidence and was the only foreigner who could get an audience at short notice. He appeared before the sultan in his persona of a Hungarian convert, Reşid Efendi.

This fear lent a deeper dimension to the Hamidian policy regarding Anatolia, which has been described as the "politics of unity".[12] The Islamic population had to be wooed to the side of what came to be considered "official Islam". This was a defensive policy that emphasised the sultan first and foremost in his capacity as an Islamic ruler, the Caliph of All Muslims (*Halife-i Müslimin*), but also as a legitimate autocrat like his contemporaries, the kaiser and the tsar.[13]

Although Marc Baer compares Mehmed IV (r. 1648–87) and Abdülhamid and draws the conclusion that both "encouraged a revival of piety" and attempted to establish direct links with the people, and that Abdülhamid's "revival of piety also occurred during a period of crisis and was also linked to conversion", the comparison is somewhat forced, to say the least. Mehmed IV was a ruler who commanded an empire that was still one of the greatest in the world, whereas Abdülhamid ruled a state that was fighting for its very survival. Nor did Mehmed IV have to contend with the question of nationalism.[14]

The Armenian Question, as it came to be called, became a theatre of conflict between the Great Powers, particularly Britain and Russia, with Germany and France playing a secondary role. Britain, led by the Liberal giant Gladstone, took a close interest in the fate of the Ottoman Armenians, who were seen as "Christians in peril".[15] The Armenian massacres actually brought Gladstone out of retirement and enraged him to the point that he declared that Turkey "deserved to be wiped off the map".[16] One of the major influences on the fate of the Ottoman Armenians was the thorny question of "Armenian Reform" in the six vilayets, which became a sticking point between the sultan, his government, and the Powers, particularly the British.[17] The "six provinces" (*vilayatı sitte*) of Sıvas, Erzurum, Mamüretülaziz, Diyarbakir, Bitlis, and Van, where the great majority of the Ottoman Armenians lived, provide the geographical setting for this chapter. The Armenian revolutionary organizations, the

---

[12] Duguid, "The Politics of Unity".

[13] Selim Deringil, *The Well-Protected Domains*, Chapter 2.

[14] Marc Baer, *Honored by the Glory of Islam*, pp. 250–1.

[15] Donald Bloxham, *The Great Game of Genocide: Imperialism, Nationalism, and the Destruction of the Ottoman Armenians* (Oxford, 2005).

[16] Philip Magnus, *Gladstone: A Biography* (London, 1963), p. 430.

[17] Armenian reforms had been officially included in the Treaty of Berlin (1878) under Article 61. See J. C. Hurewitz, *Diplomacy in the Near and Middle East* (1956), vol. 1, p. 190: "The Sublime Porte undertakes to carry out, without further delay, the improvements and reforms demanded by local requirements in the provinces inhabited by the Armenians, and to guarantee their security against the Circassians and the Kurds" (see also Map 2).

MAP 2. The Six Vilayets (*Vilayat-ı Sitte*), the primary geography of the Armenian massacres. (Map courtesy of Ömer Emre)

Dashnak and the Hunchak, had been working hard to enliven nationalist consciousness among the largely peasant population of these regions, with uneven success. Yet the Ottoman state, in the shape of Sultan Abdülhamid, his bureaucracy, and the Turkish/Kurdish élites in the six vilayets, came to see the "Armenian committees" as a very real threat to their dominant position. The Armenian Question became Abdülhamid's primary bête noire as he "came to fear the Armenians and became firmly convinced that all Armenians were under the control of the committees".[18] Broadly speaking, this was the political and social context in which the widespread massacres, mass conversions, and in some cases re-conversions, of the Armenian population in the region occurred.[19] Many Armenians converted to Islam in order to escape death; some later converted back to their former faith, some did not.

The Ottomans saw the reform issue as unacceptable interference in their internal affairs. The Sublime Porte also feared that this was a first step in

[18] Osman Nuri, *Abdülhamid-i Sani*, p. 823.
[19] On the Armenian revolutionary organizations the seminal works are still Louise Nalbandian, *The Armenian Revolutionary Movement*, and Anahide Terminassian, *Nationalism and Socialism in the Armenian Revolutionary Movement* (Cambridge, MA, 1984).

securing autonomy and perhaps even eventual independence for the Armenian vilayets. Russia, very often at odds with its own Armenian population in the Caucasus and, since the war of 1877, occupying the regions of Kars and Ardahan, adjacent to the Armenian-populated vilayets of eastern Anatolia, was a major player in the region, and in this sense the Armenian Question also overlapped with the Great Game in Asia.[20] Germany became the closest ally of the Ottoman Empire during the reign of Abdülhamid, but played a relatively minor part in the Armenian Question at this time.[21] France had an interest in the Armenian Question because it could not afford to leave the scene to Britain. One of the major sources used in this chapter, and set against Ottoman archival material, is the correspondence of the French consul, Gustave Meyrier, who was an eyewitness in Diyarbakır during the massacres.[22]

Another critical issue that provides the background for the massacres and conversions was the rise of Turkish/Ottoman nationalism. Although it would be somewhat premature to talk about Turkish nationalism as it was understood after the Young Turk Revolution of 1908, there were nonetheless stirrings in that direction among Ottoman ruling circles beginning in the late nineteenth century. In the memoirs of Hüseyin Nazım Paşa, the minister of police during the turbulent 1890s, the tenor of the writing verges on racism. After the Zeytun uprising in 1895, Nazım Paşa is informed that among the documents captured from the Zeytun rebels there is the correspondence of a certain "Little Hasan" (Küçük Hasan), who is mentioned as a Turkish official working for the Armenians and providing them with vital information:

I was particularly distraught to the point of becoming ill by the thought that a Turk should become the tool of the committees who were thirsting for Turkish blood. However, after a thorough investigation, we learned that the said person was actually an Armenian convert, and by posing as a Turk son of a Turk, had used

---

[20] Ron Grigor Suny, *Looking Toward Ararat: Armenia in Modern History* (Bloomington, 1993). This is by far the best source to date on the fate of the Russian Armenians in imperial Russia. On the history of modern-day Soviet Armenia, see Claire Mouradian, *L'Arménie* (Paris, 1995).

[21] Margaret Lavinia Anderson, "Down in Turkey Far Away: Human Rights, the Armenian Massacres, and Orientalism in Wilhelmine Germany", *The Journal of Modern History* 79 (2007), 80–111. This fascinating article explains how the Zionist leader Theodor Herzl actually considered propagandizing for Abdülhamid in return for concessions in Palestine.

[22] Gustave Meyrier, *Les Massacres de Diarbekir. Correspondance diplomatique du Vice-Consul de France*, presentée et annotée par Claire Mouradian et Michel Durand-Meyrier (Paris, 2000).

the committee for his personal gain. In this way, in keeping with his nature, he killed two birds with one stone by aiding his people and filling his purse.[23]

As will be seen later in the issue of official reluctance or unwillingness to crack down on the perpetrators of the massacres, there was a very real notion of "us" and "them" – the former being the Muslims, that is, Turks, Kurds, and others; the latter being the Armenians. This attitude would later become prominent in the leadership of the Young Turks. Ahmed Rıza "jotted the following in his private notebook, 'Christians acquired privileges when they rebelled [and] they desired to rebel when they acquired privileges'".[24]

In almost all the cases of mass conversion cited here the explanation given by Ottoman officials was that the Armenians were converting because "they feared the Kurds". The "Kurds" referred to are mostly the nomadic population of eastern Anatolia that had shared that geography with the Armenians for centuries. Although the Armenian peasant population had always been subject to oppression at the hands of the Kurdish *ağas* or *şeyhs* (tribal chieftains or headmen), what has been described as a "benign symbiosis" had nonetheless existed.[25] Or, as Christopher Walker has elegantly phrased it, "Armenians and Kurds got on with one another tolerably, but not particularly well".[26] Yet some Armenians characterized their relationship with the nomadic Kurds as being that of "brothers of earth and water".[27] What then set the two peoples, Kurds and Armenians, against each other?[28] Several factors disrupted this precarious equilibrium. First, the effects of the centralizing reforms of the mid-nineteenth century began to be felt in the "six provinces" only in the 1870s.[29] Since the reforms, the Armenians of Anatolia had suffered from two main ills: double taxation and the depredations of the Kurdish tribes. Even after they had paid their taxes to the state, the

[23] Hüseyin Nazım Paşa, *Hatıralarım. Ermeni Olaylarının İçyüzü* (My memoirs: The inside story of the Armenian incidents) (Istanbul, 2003, first published in 1924), pp. 258–9.

[24] Şükrü Hanioğlu, *Preparation for a Revolution: The Young Turks 1902–1908* (Oxford, 2001), p. 40.

[25] Suny, *Looking Toward Ararat*, p. 101.

[26] Christopher Walker, *Armenia: The Survival of a Nation* (Chatham, Kent, 1991), p. 137. Walker's is still the most detailed study on the 1890s massacres.

[27] Jelle Verheij, "Les frères de terrre et d'eau: Sur le role des Kurdes dans les massacres arméniens de 1894–1896", *Les Cahiers de l'autre Islam* 5 (1999), 225–76.

[28] Nalbandian, *The Armenian Revolutionary Movement*, p. 7. Nalbandian notes that on some occasions, like the 1862 risings in Van and Zeytun, Armenian and Kurdish peasants had fought together against their oppressors.

[29] Janet Klein, *Power in the Periphery: The Hamidiye Light Cavalry and the Struggle over Ottoman Kurdistan*, Ph.D. dissertation, Princeton University (2002), p. 116.

Kurdish *şeyhs* of the area would demand further payment.[30] The power of the big Kurdish lords, the *mir*, who controlled vast territories, was broken by policies of centralization in the second half of the century. By the 1880s the power of the last great warlord of the region, Bedirhan Bey, had been eliminated, and intra-tribal feuding recommenced.[31] When these regional warlords lost their weight, a power vacuum in the region was filled by "tribes which had hitherto been kept in check by the *mirs*."[32] It was from these tribes that the Hamidiye Light Cavalry was to be recruited in the early 1890s. This cavalry was made up of lower-level tribes organized into Cossack-style irregular cavalry units by Abdülhamid II and his entourage. Ottoman cavalry officers were actually sent to the military academy in Petrograd to learn "Cossack-style drill" (*kazak usulü talim*).[33] The official primary aim of these units was to quell what the state saw as "the perfidious and subversive activities of the Armenian brigands".[34] The sultan's policy was to kill two birds with one stone – to intimidate the Armenian population, and to secure the loyalty of the Kurds. In a manner of speaking, the Armenians were the bait for Kurdish obedience and loyalty: "By thus providing paid employment of high prestige and a virtual license to raid, the Sultan hoped to install in the Kurds a strong loyalty to him personally."[35] It was these units that would feature prominently in the massacres and mass conversions of 1895–97 organized and led by Zeki Paşa, who was later to become infamous as the author of the Sasun massacre.[36]

MOUNTING TENSION AND MUTUAL DEMONIZATION AMONG MUSLIMS AND ARMENIANS

A close reading of the sources, archival and secondary, sheds light on the gradual, and then rapid, increase in the tension between the Armenians and Muslims of the Ottoman Empire, leading up to the massacres of

---

[30] Dadrian, *The History of the Armenian Genocide*, p. 114.
[31] Van Bruinessen, *Agha Shaikh and State: The Social and Political Structures of Kurdistan* (London, 1992), pp. 181–2: "The denser the administrative network of the state became, the smaller and simpler the tribes".
[32] Klein, *Power in the Periphery*, p. 118.
[33] Selim Deringil, "Ottoman to Turk: Minority-Majority Relations in the Late Ottoman Empire", in Dru Gladney (ed.), *Making Majorities: Constituting the Nation in Japan, China, Korea, Malaysia, Fiji, Turkey and the US* (Stanford, CA, 1998), pp. 217–26.
[34] Ibid., p. 220.
[35] van Bruinessen, *Agha, Shaikh and State*, p. 186.
[36] Deringil, *Ottoman to Turk*, pp. 222, 223. On Zeki Paşa and the Hamidiye regiments, see Bruinessen, *Agha, Shaikh and State*, p. 187; and Klein, *Power in the Periphery*, p. 162.

1894–96 that provided the backdrop to many cases of mass conversion. Little by little, any improvement in the conditions of the Christians in the empire, assured by the Tanzimat State, was whittled away. Already in 1878, an Armenian priest, Bogos Natanyan, was to record the appalling condition of the Armenians in Palu, who suffered from the depredations of the Kurds: "O dear God, did you create the Armenians so that they become bait for these savages? ... If the Ottoman state wants to assure the peace and security of its subjects, it should banish these upstart Beys from this area and forbid them from taking official positions".[37] The Hamidian regime instituted a tax collection system whereby some of the Hamidiye regiments continued to act as tax farmers (*mültezim*) propagating the regime of double taxation. The practice of using the police force to collect taxes, which the previous reign had attempted to replace with a more rational tax collection system using civilian collectors, continued alongside the tax farming system whereby the Armenian population was subjected to oppression and violence from the Hamidiye tribes, who were now joined by the official security forces.[38]

Missionaries like Edwin Munsell Bliss reported "systematic insults to the faith of Christians" inflicted by officials, "something that would have been impossible in previous reigns".[39] It is ironic that perhaps one of the most astute observations on the whole Armenian Question should be made by an Ottoman prince who spent almost his entire life under house arrest. Salahaddin Efendi, the son of the deposed Sultan Murad V, would pen the following lines in his diary:

A few Armenians lose their minds and falling under the influence of that inevitable product of modern progress and civilization [nationalism], become enamored with the idea of independence. This small group meets with a violent reaction. ... That small group has increased and their increasing numbers has increased their power

---

[37] Arsen Yarman, *Palu, Harput, Çarsancak, Çemişkezek, Çapakçur, Erzincan ve Civar Bölgeler. Raporlar* (Palu, Harput, Çapakçur, Erzincan and neighboring areas: Reports). (Istanbul, 2010), translated from Armenian by Arsen Yarman and Sirvart Malhasyan, vol. 2, pp. 114–15. Bogos Natanyan was the official envoy of the Armenian Patriarchate who was sent on an inspection mission to eastern Anatolia in 1878.

[38] Nadir Özbek, "Anadolu Islahatı, 'Ermeni Sorunu' ve vergi tahsildarlığı 1895–1908" (Anatolian reform, the 'Armenian Question' and the system of tax collection), *Tarih ve Toplum*, no. 9 (Winter 2009), 1–19.

[39] Rev. Edwin Munsell Bliss, *Turkey and the Armenian Atrocities: A Reign of Terror: From Tartar Huts to Constantinople Palaces* (Philadelphia, 1896), p. 351. As can be gathered from the title, Bliss was no Turcophile. Yet the accounts given in the book of the lead-up to the massacres and their execution, after allowances for gross prejudice, are still important as many are based on eye-witness accounts, and Bliss did criticize some European newspapers for exaggerating and publishing "reports of the most thrilling type". See p. 346.

and daring. This daring is met with blood and many, the innocent as well as the guilty are killed. ... It is a great pity for both races! ... I hope this does not poison the Ottomans.[40]

Unfortunately, poison them it did, and some of the Ottomans, Muslim and Christian, came to see each other as actual or potential enemies. A very important and tragic aspect of the crisis was that at least some of the Ottoman ruling élite began to see the Armenians in racist terms, as seen in the following quotation:

As was shown by the recent demonstration [the 1890 demonstration in Istanbul] with the purpose of creating an independent Armenian state, the Armenians are like ticks (parasites, *kene*) sucking the blood of the Sublime State and occupying its attention. It is well known that ever since the aforementioned people, or maybe one should say, traitorous, people have taken refuge in the Sublime State, they have caused great material and moral damage. Although the Christians and Jews have always kept their names and never attempted to change them, the Armenians, whose very nature is penetrated by ingratitude [have followed a different course]. They have changed their names from Karabet, Kirkor or Bedros to Sıdkı, Nail, Sezai or Sırrı or other Muslim names purely with the perfidious desire to pollute future generations of Muslims with Armenian blood. [When these Armenians with Muslim names] are sent to the vilayets with official duties, they marry local Muslim girls whose families, deceived by the Muslim names, give their daughters to them. When this Armenian official is relieved of his duties after fathering a few children [he returns to Istanbul] abandoning his Muslim wife and children never to mention their names again.[41]

---

[40] Edhem Eldem, "26 Ağustos 1896 'Banka Vakası' ve 1896 'Ermeni Olayları'" (26 August 1896 'Ottoman Bank Incident' and the 'Events of 1896'), *Tarih ve Toplum* 5 (2007), 113–46. On 26 August 1896 a group of some twenty Dashnak militants raided the Ottoman Bank in Istanbul and held some of the staff for ransom, declaring that they would blow up the bank if their demands were not met. Prince Salahaddin's diaries span the entire period of his incarceration and are part of the personal archive of Edhem Eldem. Prince Salahaddin Efendi (1861–1915) was kept under house arrest during the entire reign of Abdülhamid II. Although he penned the section above in September 1896, soon after the Armenian attack on the Ottoman Bank, it seems that he was well informed on the Armenian issue in general. For a first-hand account of the Ottoman Bank raid, written by the leader of the Dashnak band that carried it out, see Armen Garo, *Bank Ottoman* (Detroit, 1990).

[41] BOA Y.PRK.Ş 3/55; memorandum by Esseyid Mehmed Hulusi, member of the Ottoman Senate (*Meclis-i Ayan*), 9 Kanun-u Evvel 1306 / 22 December 1890. My thanks to Noemi Levy for this reference. Although the racist and paranoic nature of this statement is obvious, there are some interesting ambivalences and contradictions in the document. Mehmed Hulusi does not tell us if the so-called Armenian impostors actually converted to Islam. Nor does he clarify under what circumstances the children were brought up. A child born to a Muslim father is automatically considered a Muslim. My thanks to Christoph Neumann for helping me decipher the signature seal.

This aspect of "sexual/matrimonial intrigue" seems to be a recurring motif. On 2 November 1893, the commander of the Ottoman Fourth Army, Zeki Paşa, reported that a certain Osman Yakup had been "maliciously beguiled" by the Armenians into converting to Christianity.[42] He had been lured away from Islam by the promise of marriage to a pretty Armenian girl from the village of Pur, in the vilayet of Bitlis. During the interrogation of said Osman he had revealed that he was in fact a deserter from the twenty-third cavalry brigade in Muş:

After his desertion he came to Bitlis where he was approached by some Armenians who appealed to his lower nature by proposing that, if he converted to the Armenian faith, they would give him forty *liras* and marry him to an Armenian girl. Then he was taken to the village of Pur, where he saw the girl, in whom he developed a most vivid interest (*alaka-i şedide*). Thereupon he accepted their offer, was taken to the nearby church with the girl, where he converted to Christianity according to the Armenian rites, was married to the girl, and took the name of Mıgırdıç.

At this point the matter had come to the attention of the military authorities, who went to Pur, there finding him in the company of his wife, and arrested him. During his interrogation he testified to the following:

He confessed that he had been converted to Christianity according to the Armenian faith. The Armenians then told him that he would in appearance remain a Muslim and continue to serve in the Ottoman army. He was then taken to the Armenian Catholicos in Van, together with his wife, and his apostasy was also recorded there. Osman also testified that there were some twenty others like him, all deserters from the army. He had been told that they too had been converted "through money and other means" and placed in military units in Istanbul.[43]

What can be drawn from this document? It is highly unlikely that a simple cavalryman could make up the complicated and convoluted story he told. Furthermore, the great ease with which Osman converted to the Apostolic Armenian faith seems to be a transposition into the Christian setting of the simplicity of conversion to Islam. The most striking thing about this case is

---

[42] BOA Y.MTV 86/72, 20 Teşrin-i Evvel 1309 / 2 November 1893, cipher telegramme fom Zeki Paşa, the commander of the Fourth Army in Erzincan, to General Staff.

[43] Ibid., imperial order (*Irade*) dated 1 Zilkade 1311. It appears that "turning" people from the other side was a practice used by both camps. On 6 March 1892 the governor of Bitlis, Tahsin Paşa, reported that a young Armenian from the district of Kığı had converted to Islam and declared that he was ready to provide information on the activities of Armenian revolutionaries. The document states that he is to be used, although he is not to be trusted. See BOA Y.MTV 75/132, 23 Şubat 1308 / 6 March 1892.

that it did not happen. A report from the Ministry of the Police dated 2 May 1894 clearly stated that:

When questioned in a very thorough manner here the above mentioned could not repeat the statement he made in Bitlis and gave several [different] versions of it. He later changed his language entirely and told a different story stating that as he was a deserter, hoping for clemency and reward, and under the pressure and direction of the police officials, he had made the above confession [to the officials in Bitlis]. It transpires from the above that the prisoner is simply an ordinary deserter who tried to save himself through lies and deceit.[44]

We may therefore surmise that somebody concocted this scenario with a view to convincing the sultan that a serious plot was afoot among the Armenians. Nor were Abdulhamid's officials above making up stories that they thought would curry favour with their master. It must also be borne in mind that Zeki Paşa was the sultan's brother-in-law and, as such, might have allowed himself even more levity as far as the truth was concerned, as the story does seem to be particularly concocted to provoke the sultan's legendary paranoia.[45]

On the Armenian side we have some evidence that demonisation of the "Turks" had become almost a folkloric aspect of everyday life:

I remembered that whenever a Turk passed by our house, my mother would say, 'there's a dog walking by'. We would run over and ask, "Mother where is the dog?' and my mother would answer: 'That Turk is a dog'. This is the way they would teach us that the Turk meant a dog.[46]

In a similar vein:

"We called the Turkish cemeteries 'Gor'. We didn't call them cemeteries".

---

[44] BOA. Y.MTV 97/76, 25 Şevval 1311 / 2 May 1894, report from the minister of police, Nazım Bey.

[45] Abdülhamit Kırmızı, *Abdülhamid'in Valileri. Osmanlı Vilayet İdaresi, 1895–1908* (Abdülhamid's governors: Provincial administration in the Hamidian state) (Istanbul, 2007), pp. 105–9. See, in particular, the section entitled "Fooling the Sultan", where Kırmızı actually cites many examples of governors and imperial ADCs distorting the correspondence or telling downright lies. One particular official actually openly stated, "[L]et them inform on me as much as they like, I have a great capital at my fingertips and that is lies. I lie, distort and deny as I wish ..." (p. 106).

[46] Armenian Research Centre (henceforth ARC), Dearborn, Michigan, GEN 29, interview with Mrs. Dickranoohi Nedourian. However, one must bear in mind that these oral accounts are recorded in the archives of the ARC long after the events, and most of the interviews involve people who were actually born in the early 1900s. Thus their focus is 1915, not the 1890s. Nonetheless, as with the subject interviewed here, their testimony is important because it sometimes provides insight into how family lore saw the "Turks". I owe thanks to Prof. Dennis Papazian for allowing me to have access to these archives.

"What does the word 'Gor' mean?"

"I don't know, but maybe it was a word of ridicule. It was believed that the bodies turned into dogs at night and followed you if you happened to be near a 'Gor'. And if something prevented that dog from returning to the grave, then a dead Turk would be lying there the next morning."[47]

Evidently the canine metaphor cut across the religious divide. On 2 May 1895 it was reported from Arapgir, in the vilayet of Mamuretülaziz (present day Elazığ), that "The carcass of a dog has been thrown through the window of the Armenian church. . . . The dog's head has been thrown into the Protestant prayer house. Both bore a wooden placard in the shape of a cross, bearing a threatening message in very vulgar Turkish". The event threatened to become a full-blown incident "as a few hundred Armenians gathered and started shouting and demonstrating and the Muslim population was calmed by a military show of force."[48] The Ottoman government hastened to declare that this affair was "a provocation staged by Armenian subversives seeking to sow seeds of perfidy between Muslim and Christian". The Ottoman embassies in European capitals were instructed to publish articles to that effect in the local press.[49] Both the Berlin and London embassies of the Porte published articles declaring unequivocally that "the vigorous measures of the Ottoman officials prevented a serious outbreak and it has become evident that the acts were committed by Armenian subversives".[50] There is a very real aspect of blaming the victims in this affair. The Armenian Patriarchate was warned by the government to "prevent such acts not in keeping with the nature of being an obedient and loyal subject". Accordingly, both the Armenian Patriarchate and the Protestant community issued written statements supporting the government position.[51] On the other hand, the act itself – a dog's carcass thrown into both Armenian Apostolic and the Protestant places of worship – the somewhat choreographed presentation, placards in the shape of a cross, and a message in "vulgar Turkish", all seem a bit too "pat", leading the strong suspicion that it may indeed have been a provocation on the part of one side or the other.

[47] ARC, GEN 29, interview with Mr. Antranig Shamigian. The interviewee was born in Keghi (Kığı) in 1898.
[48] BOA Y.A HUS 326/75, Grand Vizier Cevad Paşa to the Imperial Receiver's Office, no. 4300, 19 Nisan 1312 / 2 May 1895.
[49] BOA Y.A HUS 327/110, 17 Zilkade 1312 / 13 May 1895, the foreign minister, Mehmed Said Paşa, to the Grand Vizier, Foreign Ministry Chancery no. 897, enclosing a translation of article published in the Berlin press.
[50] BOA Y.A HUS. 327/125, 4 May 1895, Ottoman embassy in London to the Sublime Porte.
[51] BOA Y.A HUS 326/75, 327/110.

A case that smells even more like provocation occurred, again, at Arapgir. About one month before the case just described it was reported that the Catholic bishop and the Protestant community leader had complained that "a piece of wood in the shape of a cross had been nailed to the door of the Catholic church". To the "cross" a piece of paper was attached bearing the legend in Turkish: "People of America, the Armenian Catholics and Protestants have gone bezerk. If they want to live in peace they should come to the one true religion otherwise they will become targets". The placard also bore "writing in English, French and German". The local *kaymakam* was ordered to find and punish the culprits with all possible haste.[52]

Provocative placards (*yafta*) seem to have been quite the rage of the time. It was reported from the vilayet of Trabzon that placards in Turkish had appeared on the walls of mosques in the town of Samsun on a Friday, presumably for people to see after the Friday prayers. One of these placards was duly removed and sent to Istanbul. For once, we have a copy in the file, and it is worth quoting *in extenso*:

O people! Those of you who are Muslims you must be fearful for the honour of your families. Because our wives and daughters are frequenting the shops of the infidels (*kafirler*) and in these shops they expose their faces and hands. They indulge in shameful acts with the infidels to an extent never even done with their husbands. ... even the daughters of men whom we otherwise know as men of honour carry on in an unmentionable manner with the sons of the shopkeepers. ... The honour of Islam demands that we defend it against our enemies and not to surrender it in this fashion. ... If anyone removes this placard, which is unofficial, he will suffer the wrath of Allah![53]

It was later found that the placards had been the work of one Mehmed Efendi, who had been apprehended and questioned. He had been summoned to Trabzon, where "it became clear that he did not intend to create a disturbance or excite the populace". He was dismissed with no worse than a scolding and told to stay in Trabzon, where he had relatives.[54]

Although in this case Mehmed Efendi seems to have been something of a crank, and no serious consequences ensued, the case is indicative of the times. The open reference to Christians as "enemies of the faith" and the

---

[52] BOA Y.A HUS 325/98 11 Nisan 1311 / 24 April 1895, Grand Vizier Cevad Paşa, Imperial Receivers' Office no. 4175.

[53] BOA Y.A HUS 327/22, 6 Zilkade 1312 / 29 April 1895, the Vali of Trabzon, El-Seyyid Mehmed Kadri, to the Ministry of the Interior, the Vilayet of Trabzon, no. 64, enclosing one of the placards.

[54] Ibid.

open call to the male population on the most sensitive issue, women's honour – this could have ended up very ugly. Very soon after this, it did. The first of the Armenian massacres was in fact to occur in Trabzon on 13 September 1895. A potentially much more serious case was reported from Yozgad in central Anatolia, where graffiti had appeared on the inside of the lavatory door of the main mosque. The graffiti read, "Turks open your eyes! Be prepared for the beginning of next month!". The Mutasarrıf of Yozgad had duly removed the writing, but he had not failed to report the case to his superior, the Vali of Ankara. The Vali wrote a long report on the incident. Why would a piece of graffiti on a lavatory wall attract so much attention? The Vali pointed out that such graffiti often appeared "on walls of inns, or carved on large trees, or in public toilets and this was a common practice in Anatolia." The next part of the report grew more serious:

However, given the delicacy of the times [this can be serious]. At present there are eighteen Armenians being detained in prison in Yozgad. As these prisoners are leading figures in the Armenian community here, this [the writing of graffiti] may be an act of their friends or relatives designed to excite the minds of their followers. As long as these people are detained it is to be expected that they will carry out such demonstrations and that this will renew the hatred and anger of the Muslims.[55]

The Vali recommended, therefore, that the detained Armenians be brought to court as soon as possible so that the affair could be brought to an end.[56] That a piece of graffiti on a lavatory wall should be deemed important enough to report to the Grand Vizier is indicative of the state of tension in Yozgad. Another factor has to be taken into consideration at this point, and that is the significance of rumour. In all the cases just cited – the dog, the placards, the graffiti – whoever the perpetrator was, was counting on the effect of rumour. Rumour that the "Armenians are taking over" or, conversely, that "the Muslims intend to massacre all the Armenians" fuelled the anxiety of both sides.[57]

[55] BOA Y.A HUS 329/47, 11 Mayıs 1311 / 24 May 1895, the Vali of Ankara, Mehmed Memduh Paşa, to the Office of the Grand Vizier. Presumably the lavatory was outside the main building of the mosque and was open to the public.
[56] Ibid.
[57] Peter Lienhardt, "The Interpretation of Rumour", in J. M. H. Beattie and R. G. Lienhardt (eds.), *Studies in Social Anthropology: Essays in Memory of E. E. Evans-Pritchard* (Oxford, 1975), pp. 110–37. "The tendency of human beings to prefer blaming their misfortunes on other people, against whom they can react, rather than on accident is scarcely to be doubted" (p. 118).

Reports continued to come in bringing into sharp focus the increasing tension on both sides. From Kekerli, a village in the vilayet of Bitlis, it was reported that a group of Armenians had interfered with the call to prayer (*ezan*). Apparently eleven Armenians had been involved and had fled when the gendarmes arrived; "seven Muslims and three Armenians witnessed the act". It was claimed that "the village headman (*muhtar*), a certain Sarkis, and ten members of the village's elders council had been involved." Sarkis had apparently confessed. Once again, the blame was put squarely at the door of the Armenians: "The aim of the Armenians was to provoke the Kurdish tribes in the area and create an incident that would postpone the collection of their taxes".[58]

The issue was discussed at the highest level with a view to its possible implications for world public opinion. The considerations were the following: Should the Kekerli incident be published in the press or not? What would be the pros and cons? On the one hand, it was thought, it was a case that was favourable to the Muslim side, presumably because it made the Armenians look bad as they had interfered with the Muslims' freedom to worship. On the other hand, to report on the Kekerli affair "and to forbid reporting on cases like the Tokad and Erzurum incidents, where the dead were mostly Armenians, would leave the Sublime State open to accusations of bias and distortion". In the end a decision was taken to censor all three cases.[59]

This discussion shows that even in the most trivial of incidents, the Ottomans felt that the world was looking over their shoulder. Furthermore, the fact that Kekerli had an Armenian headman implies that it was a mainly Armenian village.

There is also evidence that shows that there was an official attempt to distance the two communities from each other. A circular directive in 1893 ordered that no Muslim children should be sent to Armenian schools. The vilayet of Ankara duly reported: "There are no Muslim children in the Armenian schools in the vilayet proper. We have issued the appropriate order to the districts to show the utmost vigilance in the matter of preventing Muslim children attending Armenian schools."[60] The vilayet of Adana also

[58] BOA. Y.A HUS 323/16, 14 Mart 1311 / 27 March 1895, telegramme from the Vilayet of Bitlis; Y.A HUS 325/97, 28 Şevval 1312 / 24 April 1895, the Grand Vizier and imperial ADC, Cevad Paşa, Imperial Receivers' Office, no. 4174.
[59] BOA Y.A HUS 323/62, 22 Mart 1311 / 4 Nisan 1895, the Grand Vizier and imperial ADC, Cevad Paşa, to the Receivers Office of the Sublime Porte, no. 3809.
[60] BOA Y.MTV 86/99, 27 Teşrin-I Evvel 1309 / 9 November 1893, cipher telegramme, the governor of Ankara to Yıldız Palace.

confirmed that "according to our investigations there are no Muslim children, boys or girls, in the Armenian schools in the vilayet, nor will they be allowed to attend such schools in the future."[61] The vilayet of Aydın was to report, "[I]n the centre of the vilayet and in its dependencies the Armenian population is only 1600, according to my investigations, neither in Izmir nor in the dependencies are there any Muslim children in Armenian schools."[62] It is also significant that these cipher telegrammes were sent to Yıldız Palace and not to the Ministry of Education, indicating that the sultan took a personal interest in the matter. Strict censorship became even stricter as "the word *Armenia* was struck out of every book".[63]

The mounting tension between Christians and Muslims in Anatolia has been remarked upon by recent research in Turkey. Oktay Özel, who has studied the inter-sectarian relations in the Black Sea region, comments:

> The propaganda of the Armenian revolutionary organizations and their military activities further heightened the tension between the Muslim and Christian populations, which broke out into open conflict. These conflicts were to be reflected at the local level with raids, counter raids and murders between houses and villages. ... The tendency of the Anatolian Muslim population towards violence directed at Armenians increased under the influence or Abdülhamid's policies[64]

Özel points out that in the regions stretching from the central Black Sea and Sıvas to Erzurum, the population on both sides (Christian and Muslim) became drawn into a cycle of violence, either directly or through the activities of "brigands".

THE HAMIDIAN MASSACRES AND THE MASS CONVERSIONS OF ARMENIANS

It was against this background that the series of events that have gone down in history as the "Armenian massacres" occurred. One vilayet after another experienced the same pattern: inflammatory speeches by mullahs

---

[61] BOA. Y.MTV 84/44, 6 Teşrin-i Sani 1309 / 19 November 1893, cipher telegramme, the governor of Adana to Yıldız Palace.

[62] BOA Y.MTV 87/53, 7 Teşrin-i Sani 1309 / 20 November 1893, cipher telegramme, the governor of Aydın to Yıldız Palace.

[63] Bliss, *Turkey and the Armenian Atrocities*, p. 349.

[64] Oktay Özel, "Muhacirler, yerliler ve gayrımüslimler. Osmanlı'nın son devrinde Orta Karadeniz'de toplumsal uyumun sınırları üzerine bazı gözlemler" (Immigrants, locals and non-Muslims: Some observations on social harmony in the central Black Sea in the last days of the Ottomans), *Tarih ve Toplum* 5 (2007), 93–112.

at Friday prayers, attacks on Armenian shops and property, and retaliation in self-defence on the part of Armenians, followed by widespread, and
apparently organized, slaughter, rape, and the abduction of women.[65]

Particularly after the Sason massacre (18 August to 10 September 1894),
the 1895–96 Zeytun uprising, and the massacres that occurred in 1895–96
in various localities, there is no doubt that the majority of the Ottoman
Armenians in Anatolia lived in a state of terror.[66] Even in the documents
published by the modern Turkish state on the basis of the official papers of
Hüseyin Nazım Paşa, the chief of police, the discrepancies in the number of
the dead on both sides is a giveaway.[67] In the "troubles" at Trabzon on 13
September 1895, the Muslim dead numbered 11, whereas the Armenians
lost 182.[68] In Erzurum on 23 October, the ratio was five Muslim dead to
fifty Armenians. Similarly, in Bitlis on 26 October, the toll was 38 Muslim
dead and 135 wounded, 132 Armenian dead and 40 wounded.[69] It is worth
pointing out that in almost all the cases there were far more Armenian dead
than wounded, suggesting a very unequal struggle. In Diyarbakır on 10
October, the Police Commissariat reported 70 Muslim dead and 80
wounded against more than 300 Armenian dead and 100 wounded.[70] In
Bayburt on 4 November, against 8 dead and 11 wounded on the Muslim
side, the Armenians lost 170 dead with 35 wounded.[71]

---

[65] I do not intend to retell the grisly story of the massacres here. My aim is simply to give a
background to the conversions that occurred at this time. There are relatively few comprehensive accounts of what happened, the most comprehensive still being that of
Christopher Walker, *Armenia: The Survival of a Nation*; see particularly pp. 121–173.
The official Turkish narrative states that it was the Armenian committees who were
responsible for widespread "uprisings" during this time. A vast apologetic literature exists
on the topic, and the "Armenian perfidy" genre continues to be the dominant discourse
among mainstream Turkish historians. For a representative sample of the apologist
literature, see İsmet Binark, *Ermenilerin Türklere yaptıkları Mezalim ve Soykırım'ın
Arşiv Belgeleri* (Archival documents on the cruelty and genocide perpetrated by
Armenians against Turks) (Ankara, 2001). For a recent example, see *Osmanlı
Belgelerinde Ermeni İsyanları 1878–1909* (Armenian uprisings according to Ottoman
Documents (Ankara, 2008, 4 vols.), an official publication of the Turkish State Archives).
[66] Dadrian, *The History of the Armenian Genocide*, pp. 113–31.
[67] The sheer discrepancy in the number of Muslim and Armenian dead is something that even
official documents carefully chosen to make the modern Turkish case, namely, that what
happened was legitimate self-defence against Armenian "terrorism", could not hide. In
this, I follow the method used by Edhem Eldem in his "26 Ağustos 1896 'Banka Vakası' ve
1896 'Ermeni Olayları'".
[68] Hüseyin Nazım Paşa, *Ermeni Olayları Tarihi* (The history of the Armenian events)
(Istanbul, 1998), vol. 1, p. 94.
[69] Ibid., pp. 98–99.
[70] Ibid., p. 102.
[71] Ibid., p. 103.

Diyarbakır, the scene of one of the worst massacres on 2–5 November 1895, features largely in the documents on conversion. On 2 November the French consul, Gustave Meyrier, was to telegramme his ambassador, Paul Cambon, "The city is engulfed in fire and blood. Save us".[72] On 10 November 1895, the Vali, Enis Paşa, reported: "In some areas entire villages of Armenians have been converting and this is causing the *kaza* authorities to ask for instructions. As these conversions are not very convincing I humbly ask for instructions."[73]

The governor was referred to an *irade* dated 1 Teşrin-i Sani 1311 (14 November 1895) that established the official position:

[According to the *irade*] in order to avoid the misrepresentation of the conversion of the Armenians, if they apply again when order is restored, then their conversions can be processed according to the proper procedure. Until then the matter should be passed over with wise measures.[74]

This formula of "wise measures" is repeated throughout the documentation and in the context is clearly a euphemism for "palliative" or "temporary". The official position appears to have been the following. If the mass conversion of the Armenians was accepted, this would appear to the outside world as an official policy of mass forced conversion. Furthermore, the inter-communal tension created by the recent "disturbances" (*iğtişaşat*) had still not abated: "You are to bear in mind that to cause offence to one section of the population at a time when we are trying to win the hearts of the population will lead to untold complications".[75] Presumably the "section of the population" that was being spared was the Muslims, who would be offended by what they would perceive as insincere conversions.

In the wake of the general atmosphere of massacre and insecurity that reigned in Anatolia during this period, case after case of mass conversion was reported from the vilayets. On 5 November 1895 the vilayet of Erzurum reported that in the previous week three villages, Hınzırı, Korikul, and Humlar in the kaza of Tercan, had expressed a desire to "convert to Islam of their own free will". However, the

[72] Meyrier, *Les Massacres de Diarbekir*, p. 85 (my translation).
[73] BOA A.MKT.MHM 636/25, 29 Teşrin-i Evvel 1311 / 10 November 1895, the governor of Diyarbakir, Enis Paşa, to the Office of the Grand Vizier.
[74] Ibid. The term used in all the official correspondence is *"tedabir-i hakimane ile işin geçiştirilmesi"*.
[75] Ibid. This last sentence in the draft memorandum was crossed out. These cancelled sentences in draft memoranda are actually very interesting because they provide insights into the official mind.

governor openly stated that "these conversions are the result of fear of attacks and will not look good to friend or foe". The Porte replied: "The said conversion of the Christian villages is due to a reason and that is their fear of the assaults of the Kurds. In this case you are to make clear that mass conversions are not permitted (*müctemian ihtidaların caiz olmadığı*). You are also instructed to defend them from attack and prevent undesirable events."[76]

The formula of "not looking good to friend or foe" (*yar ve ağyara hoş görünmemek*) is an obvious reference to foreign consuls, missionaries, etc. A few days later the vilayet of Sıvas similarly reported the following:

Today some 2,000 Kurds attacked the town of Divriği and started looting the goods of the Christians. So far 23 Armenians have been killed and some 500 people, men and women, have applied by a petition through their village elders to become Muslim of their own free will and to be circumcised. If the Kurds do not listen to reason, it will be necessary to use armed force against them. ... The conversion of 500 people at once is likely to draw attention and this will not have good results at the moment.[77]

The reference to "drawing attention" and "not having good results just now" was, again, a clear reference to potential foreign observers. The answer by the Porte left no doubt about this:

You have reported that some 500 people have applied to convert. For this to be accepted by the government would mean that it would be shown by subversive elements as the result of fear and as such it is not acceptable politically. You are to tell the applicants that their conversion can only be accepted after order has been restored.[78]

The phrase "not acceptable politically" is all-important here; this is clearly a reference to the fact that these conversions were political acts, which the "subversive elements" (i.e, Armenian committees, missionaries, etc.) would use, and as such would have political repercussions in the shape of diplomatic pressure.

Sıvas continued to be a flashpoint. Two days later the governor reported that in the town of Darende some 200 Armenians had applied to convert to

---

[76] BOA A.MKT MHM 638/32, 23 Teşrin-i Evvel 1311 / 5 November 1895; 27 Teşrin-I Evvel 1311 / 9 November 1895, the governor of Erzurum, Rauf Paşa, reply by Special Commission of Ministers. Tercan is today a sub-prefecture of the vilayet of Erzincan. Hınzıri (or Hınzoru) is today a village in Erzincan called Tanyeri/Pınarlıkaya. See Nuri Akbayar, *Osmanlı Yer Adları Sözlüğü* (Dictionary of Ottoman Place Names).

[77] BOA A.MKT MHM 660/35, 4 Teşrin-I Sani 1311 / 17 November 1895, telegramme from the governor of Sıvas, Halil Paşa, to the Grand Vezier.

[78] İbid., 5 Teşrin-i Sani 1311 / 18 November 1895, the Sublime Porte to the vilayet of Sıvas.

Islam and "were applying every day to the government offices". They had been turned away according to official instructions.[79]

An observation is in order here. The reference to "people applying every day to have their conversions accepted" refers to the official conversion procedure in force in the Ottoman Empire referred to in Chapter 1. In times of extreme crisis, such as the massacres of the 1890s, an Armenian village that had offered to become Muslim, but had not yet been accepted, would be in a dangerous state of limbo, making the villagers even more of a target for their enemies, who could accuse them at any time of insincerity or, even worse, potential apostasy.

In some cases, out of desperation, in order to force the hand of the government, Armenians even declared that they had been circumcised. On 12 November 1895 it was reported from the vilayet of Mamüretülaziz that the Armenians from the village of Perri had "performed their own circumcisions" (*kendü kendilerine hitanlarını icra eyledikleri*). Yet this did not prove good enough. The Porte replied: "This matter results from two reasons. One is the fear of the attacks of the Kurds; the other is to enable them at a later date to complain to the foreigners that they were converted by force. ... They are to be told that if they still want to convert individually when order is restored the matter will be considered according to the proper procedure and precedent."[80]

On 27 November the vilayet of Bitlis reported that "all the men and women" in three villages attached to the kaza of Genc – Mezan, Erzif, and Tanimaveran – had applied to convert. The answer from Istanbul was almost copied verbatim from the telegramme just quoted: "The official acceptance of mass conversions by Armenians will cause this to be seen as forced conversion. ... If they apply again when order has been restored, the matter will be considered according to proper procedure and precedent. Until then the matter should be passed over with wise measures as ordered in the imperial *irade*."[81]

In some cases the conversion issue comes up in what seem to be quite mundane circumstances. On 27 December the Mutasarrıf of Dersim asked

---

[79] Ibid., 7 Teşrin-i Sani 1311 / 20 November 1895, the vilayet of Sıvas to the Sublime Porte.

[80] BOA A.MKT.MHM 657/24, 30 Teşrin-I Evvel 1311 / 12 November 1895, the governor of Mamuretülaziz, Amirî, to the Sublime Porte; 31 Teşrin-I Evvel 1311 / 13 November 1895, the Sublime Porte to the governor of Mamüretülaziz. Mamüretülaziz is present-day Elazığ. Perri is the present-day *bucak* of Akpazar. See Tahir Sezen, *Osmanlı Yer Adları* (Ottoman place names, BOA publication).

[81] BOA A.MKT. MHM 619/24, deputy governor of Bitlis, Ömer Paşa, to the Sublime Porte, 14 Teşrin-i Sani 1311 / 27 November 1895. The Sublime Porte to the vilayet of Bitlis.

the following question: "[W]hat is to be done about people who were previously Armenian when they were fiancéed and now want to marry as Muslims?" The problem arose because of the official refusal to recognize Armenian conversions, which was holding things up bureaucratically. Another related issue was that neo-Muslim Armenians were demanding that they be registered as Muslims and, as such, that they be exempt from the military service tax, the *bedel-i askeri*. At this point, the issue of "voluntary" conversion being carried out "without any coercion, force or pressure" is stressed and repeated so many times (verbatim three times within two paragraphs) that it seems particularly suspicious. The reason given to prove how "voluntary" these conversions were is instructive: "The fact that these conversions were carried out after the restoration of order and after their villages were attacked by Kurds and the Kurds dispersed, shows that they converted only because they had found the true religion".[82] Apparently, fear of a repetition of Kurdish attacks as a motive for conversion did not occur to the writer of the report, who was just that bit too eager to stress that the Armenians had experienced a spiritual enlightenment.

Another case of dubious spiritual enlightenment is a petition presented by the Armenians of the *kaza* of Koyulhisar in Sivas. It is worth quoting in total as it is a particularly poignant example of the plight of a desperate people:

We are Armenians from Koyulhisar and our lives and property have been spared thanks to our beloved Padişah. Fifteen days after the disturbances some of us, of our own accord, decided to accept Islam. Now the local government is insisting that we become Armenian again, but we did not convert out of fear or pressure. We saw that this was the true faith may Allah grant eternal life to our glorious Padişah, amen. Until now everybody was free to belong to any confession they wanted. Has this permission been revoked? If our Islam had been due to fear, all of us would have converted. But some of us have remained Armenians. Please for the sake of Allah and our Sultan send us reliable officials who can investigate our behaviour and what is in our hearts. They will see that we converted of our own free will and register us accordingly in the population and property registers. Because when we travel here and there our commercial papers and our identity papers state that we are Armenians, but in our hearts and in our dress we are Muslims. This causes awkward questions. We are presenting this petition in Armenian because the Muslims will not write it for us. In short, may the state hang us if it pleases, we

---

[82] BOA A.MKT.MHM 658/10, 10 Receb 1313 / 27 December 1895, the vilayet of Mamüretülaziz Secretariat, no. 409, forwarding a copy of a report from the *mutasarrıf* of Dersim. "[M]ahza hidayet-i rabbani üzerine kabul-ü Islamiyet etmiş oldukları".

are willing and we will not turn our back on Islam. (*Devletimiz bizi idam etsün ırazıyız Müslümanlığımızdan vaz geçmeyiz*)[83]

The Vali adopted a rather bleak view of the petition and pointed out that two women from the same area had recently reverted to Christianity "after firmly declaring for Islam". He acknowledged the official order that "extreme care [was] to be taken in the matter of conversions" and recommended that no action be taken "until the weather improves", when the petitioners could be summoned to Sıvas for questioning.[84]

CONVERSIONS AS FALLOUT OF MASSACRE

In fact, most of the conversions that come up in the dispatches were reported *after* the ostensible restoration of order, or at least after the worst of the massacres were over. The *kaza* of Pütürge in Mamüretülaziz reported on 1 January that "some one hundred Armenian and Nestorians, men and women, from the Şirvan village of Amirdun have converted to Islam and, summoning circumcisers, performed their circumcisions". Similarly, in the district (*nahiye*) of Kerker and in the village of Keferdiz in Van and "several other villages", Christians had converted and "renewed their marriages, performed their circumcisions, and it is heard that they are praying five times a day in places where there are mosques". The report repeated that they were fully aware of the order to "avoid the official acceptance of mass conversions as this will imply fear of attacks by the Kurds", yet pointed out that in none of these cases had the Christians officially applied to have their status recognized; they were simply living as Muslims, and the matter was coming up only because of bureaucratic hiccoughs such as marriages, demands for exemption from the *bedel*, or cases like "two Armenians who were members of the *kaza* Administrative Council who are unable to perform their duties". The *kaymakam* of Pütürge, apparently quite a resourceful official, had taken it upon himself to carry out a secret investigation; "through spies sent into their midst it has been ascertained that they do not intend to renege on Islam". He pointed out that in some areas all but a small minority had converted and that "because this *kaza* is inhabited by savage and nomadic Kurds and

[83] BOA A.MKT. 661/34, 11 Mart 1312 / 24 March 1896, the vilayet of Sıvas to the Sublime Porte, enclosing a petition signed by eleven residents of Koyulhisar and written in Turkish using Armenian characters. My thanks to Rober Koptaş for reading the original. Koyulhisar is now a *kaza* by the same name in the vilayet of Sıvas.

[84] Ibid., 20 Nisan 1312 / 3 May 1896, the Vali of Sıvas, Halil Paşa, to the Sublime Porte.

we do not have the necessary military force [but] ... are doing our best to keep order [we request urgent instructions]."[85]

Ostentatious religious observance, grown men arranging for their own circumcision, couples renewing their marriage vows – all of these seem to be indications of conversion as a result of fear or at least severe pressure. The official's reference to the "savage Kurds" in the area also points in this direction, and the implication in the report is that the local forces were unable to secure the safety of the neophyte Muslims.

Reports of conversions continued to pour in. On 9 January 1896 the governor of Mamüretülaziz wrote that "During and after the recent troubles quite a few people singly and in groups presented and continue to present petitions to have their conversions recognized and to have their *bedel* cancelled. According to the present orders we have done our best to make them change their minds and to delay proceedings".[86]

The Armenian Patriarchate in Istanbul did not fail to protest to the authorities. In a communication dated 15 January, the Patriarch declared:

[It has been reported that] fifteen Christian villages in the *nahiye* of Eğin in the vilayet of Mamüretülaziz, as a result of the recent terrible events, fearing for their lives, have converted to Islam. They even became circumcised and converted their church, which had been looted, into a mosque. The signed declaration that was sent by the *müdür* of the place, to the effect that they accepted Islam of their own free will was signed because they feared for their lives.

The Patriarch made it quite clear that there was nothing voluntary about these conversions, which had taken place "[i]n the said areas of Anatolia [where] hitherto unseen oppression and cruelty, insults to Christianity and efforts to convert Christians have been witnessed". He declared that he had received this information in an official letter written to the Patriarchate. Nor was the worst over; even though the necessary orders had been sent, it was reported that "the extraordinary fear and terror caused by the recent terrible events continues to reign and the victims still feel threatened." The Patriarch demanded that the conditions be made propitious for the eventual return to Christianity of these people,

---

[85] Ibid., 19 Kanun-u Evvel 1311 / 31 December 1895, the vilayet of Mamüretülaziz forwarding a report from the *kaza* of Pütürge (today a Municipality (*ilçe*) by the same name of the city of Malatya). Amirdun may well be the present-day İmrun in the centre of Pütürge. Keferdiz is the present-day village of Doğanyol. My thanks to Professor Jelle Verheij for these place names.

[86] BOA A.MKT. MHM 658/10, 23 Receb 1313 / 9 January 1896, the governor of Mamüretülaziz, Rauf Paşa, to the Sublime Porte.

"in keeping with the principle of the freedom of religion".[87] The Porte duly asked the governor of Mamüretülaziz to explain what was going on and asked why they had accepted the conversions in question. The vilayet replied that the *kaymakam* of Eğin had indeed disregarded official instructions and had accepted the petition of the Armenians to convert, but that there had been no coercion and that the statement about the church being converted to a mosque was false. The governor admitted that "many Armenians had been applying singly or in groups and in fact getting themselves circumcised, we have been obeying the official order to delay matters".[88] The Patriarchate repeated its demands a month later: "Reports from the Armenian church Metropolitans (*Marhasa*) in the area continue to come in to the effect that many Armenians, laymen as well as priests, fearing for their lives in the recent terrible events, are showing themselves as Muslims. We demand that rapid and effective measures be taken which will guarantee their safety if they return to their own faith".[89]

It seems that although the Porte issued orders that Armenian conversions were not to be accepted, some Ottoman officials actually had different views and did not hesitate to express them. On 15 January the governor of Van, Şemseddin Paşa, reported that although, as per instructions, he had been turning down Armenian conversion applications, he now felt that "because the Armenians here live in mixed villages with Kurds and therefore have a natural familiarity with Muslims, this inclines many of them naturally to convert to Islam". He went on to point out that this was "causing great anxiety to the Armenian leaders", and that he had therefore accepted the recent applications for conversion of twenty-one Armenian men and women.[90] However, this was not looked upon favourably by Istanbul. A special commission of the Council of Ministers replied to the governor's telegramme: "Although according to the principle of the freedom of religion, no objection can be made to individual conversions and their acceptance according to established practice and precedent,

[87] Ibid., 29 Receb 1313 / 15 January 1896, memorandum from the Patriarch of the Armenian *millet*, Mağakya Ormanyan, to the Sublime Porte, no. 255.
[88] Ibid., 3 Kanun-u Sani 1311 / 16 January 1896, cipher telegramme from the Sublime Porte to the vilayet of Mamüretülaziz; 12 Kanun-u Sani 1312 / 25 January 1896.
[89] Ibid., 10 Şubat 1312 / 23 February 1896.
[90] BOA Y.A RES. 85/12 2 Şubat 1312 / 15 February 1896, the governor of Van, Şemseddin Paşa, to Yıldız Palace.

group conversions will lead our enemies to claim that the Muslims are converting the Christians by force."[91]

The claim by the governor that Armenians were "naturally inclined" to convert because they lived cheek by jowl with Kurds was clearly disingenuous, and served to camouflage the fact that most Armenians who converted were doing so not out of some suddenly discovered affinity for their Muslim neighbours, but because they were afraid of them. Nonetheless, the reference to "the principle of the freedom of religion", both in the memorandum of the ministers and in the letter of the Armenian Patriarchate, is important because it shows that the idea of the Tanzimat period was at least kept alive as a polite fiction.

Indeed, the fact that the Armenians of the area did not live in anything resembling peace and harmony is borne out by the official correspondence. On 2 January the British embassy complained to the Porte that some seventy Armenians from the districts of Ispayrıt and Hizan in the vilayet of Bitlis had fled to the monastery on the island of Akhtamar on Lake Van. The embassy claimed that this was because they feared for their lives as they were the only survivors from thirty-three villages who had not been killed or forced to convert. The embassy asked that they be permitted to remain in Akhdamar.[92] The governor of Van, Nazım Paşa, who was Şemseddin Paşa's predecessor, reported that the Katogigos of Van had asked for a guarantee of safe conduct for these people, some 120 souls. But their remaining in Van was not desirable, and they should be sent back to Bitlis "because they are not of the people of this province". However, the governor admitted that "although instructions to this effect were sent to the local authorities, it has not been possible to convince them to go back."[93] The matter did not end there. On 4 January the governor of Bitlis, Ömer Paşa, wrote a long telegramme that is very important as an indicator of the official mind-set. The Paşa declared that the claim of the British embassy was totally baseless and that "the 6,000 Armenians living in the *kaza* [of Hizan] continue to live there according to their religion and in all security". He pointed out that the problem in the area was "entirely

---

[91] Ibid., 13 Ramazan 1314 / 3 Şubat 1312 / 16 February 1896, the minutes of a meeting of the Special Commission of the Council of Ministers.

[92] BOA A.MKT MHM 619/35, 20 Kanun-u Evvel 1311 / 22 January 1896, translation of a memorandum of the British embassy. Ispayrıt is today a region in the vilayet of Bitlis. Hizan is today the *kaza* of Aşağıkarasu in Bitlis. See *Osmanlı Yer Adları* (Ottoman place names), BOA Publication 2001.

[93] Ibid., 21 Kanun-u Evvel 1311 / 3 January 1896, cipher telegramme from the governor of Van to the Sublime Porte.

the work of a famous Armenian subversive", a certain Dilboş. Ömer Paşa declared that Dilboş did not hesitate to attack and kill Muslim and Christian alike without distinction, and that the Armenians attempting to flee to Akhtamar were in fact fleeing Dilboş. "Otherwise there is no reason for good Muslims living in this area since centuries in peace and harmony with Christians who always freely practiced their religion, to suddenly start behaving in a manner so reprehensible to our August Master."[94] After providing a classic example of blaming the victims, the governor went on to declare: "[I]f the claim of the British Embassy [that people were being converted by force] were true this would not be confined to sixty or so Armenians out of some 6,000 population and it would not have been possible for some sixty Armenians to get past so many Kurds who are in the area and escape to Akhdamar". Thus, the governor was arguing, the Kurds would have done a proper job and not left a single Armenian. As to those Armenians who did convert: "In Hizan a few villages of Armenians did convert of their own free will and applied to the authorities to have their conversions recognized. This was not done and they continue to live as Muslims, have the *ezan* chanted and pray five times a day. It is this that has been used by the Armenian subversives who seize upon the least excuse to slander the Sublime State." The governor added that since Akhatamar was "virtually a home of subversion", the refugees should not be allowed to swell the numbers there.[95]

Two days later Ömer Paşa was to clarify the position even further:

[According to the latest information received from the kaymakam of Hizan] 2,006 men and 1,015 women making a total of 3,211, the majority in 54 villages of Armenians, have made it known that they have accepted Islam of their own free will. Some of the people of the said villages kept their own faith. This shows that the claim of the Embassy is entirely baseless. Because if the Armenians were supposedly invited to embrace Islam and if those who refused were killed, all the remaining Armenians in these villages would have been dead and even those going to Akhtamar would have been killed.

The governor could not resist adding, "[T]hose misinforming the Embassy are a few well known missionaries who are in fact the ones who are after converting people".[96] Apparently there was nothing unusual about the fact that 3,021 people should suddenly become enamoured of Islam and

---

[94] BOA A.MKT.MHM 619/35, 22 Kanun-u Evvel 1311 / 4 January 1896, cipher telegramme from the governor of Van, Nazım Paşa, to the Sublime Porte.
[95] Ibid.
[96] Ibid., 24 Kanun-u Sani 1311 / 6 January 1896. It seems that the Paşa could not add.

seek the true path "of their own free will" when they were surrounded by hostile Kurds.

THE ABDUCTION OF WOMEN

The fact that this "free will" was often the result of terror was borne out by the efforts that were subsequently made by some foreign consuls to rescue women who had been abducted during the massacres and forced into marriage. Well before the massacres, the abduction of Armenian women by Kurds was a frequent occurrence in the region that often went unpunished. As early as 1878 Bogos Natanyan was to write : "The greatest amusement of the men called the *ağas* is to amuse themselves by outraging the honour of Armenian women. ... When they are unable to get the woman they want, they persecute her husband. They are protected by the local officials."[97] A case that became symbolic of the government's proclivity to ignore the abduction cases was the case of Musa Bey. In 1889 a prominent Kurdish sheikh from Muş, Musa Bey, abducted a young Armenian girl, Arménouhie, who was forced to convert and take the name Gülizar. Musa Bey was summoned to Istanbul and put on trial, becoming something of a public hero. The case attracted the attention of the foreign diplomatic community and became something of a cause célèbre. Arménouhie was restored to her family, but Musa Bey was acquitted, causing outrage in the Armenian and foreign communities.[98] A large portion of the correspondence of Gustave Meyrier deals with this issue: "Yesterday they brought back six women, none of them wanted to go back to her family. I know and I have living proof at hand that these unfortunates behave like this because they are threatened with death by the Kurds and they have no confidence in the protection of the authorities." He was to propose that rather than lodging these women in Muslim homes where they were subject to threats, they should be handed back to their religious leaders and kept in the church while the investigation was going on.[99] A

---

[97] Yarman, *Palu, Harput, Çarsancak, Çemişkezek, Çapakçur, Erzincan ve Civar Bölgeler. Raporlar*, p. 190.

[98] Armenouhie Kevonian, *Les noces noires de Gulizar* (Paris, 1993). To this day Musa Bey's trial serves as subject matter for apologetic works that see his trial as an instance of "the usual enmity and interference of foreigners": see Musa Şaşmaz, *19. Asrın Davası. Kürd Musa Bey'in Yargılanması* (The case of the century: The trial of Kürd Musa Bey) (Niğde, 1997), p. 123.

[99] Meyrier, *Les Massacres de Diarbekir*. Gustave Meyrier to Paul Cambon, 12 March 1896, p. 85. My translation.

few days later Meyrier was to report that a nine-year-old girl had been brought in, a Syriac Catholic who refused to go back to her community. When the bishop of the Syriac Catholics intervened, the governor, Enis Paşa, "publicly reminded him of the Salonica affair where two Consuls had been killed in similar circumstances and said he could not expose himself to similar inconveniences. I take this as a personal and direct threat." This statement about the killing of two Consuls in Salonica in similar circumstances was indeed perceived as a threat by the French and British embassies, which protested energetically to the Porte.[100]

Enis Paşa was to come as close as possible to having his knuckles officially rapped, and he was asked in rather stern terms: "In order for there not to ensue anything untoward and likely to cause murmurings please clarify if such a conversation did or did not take place."[101] Enis Paşa replied: "Christian women who had been dispersed here and there during the troubles are being recovered and handed back to their families or religious leaders." There was a problem, however: "[S]ome of these have become Muslim of their own free will and married Muslims and are now firmly declaring that they will not accept either their families or Christianity".[102] Enis Paşa then went on to recount the conversation he had with the Syriac bishop. Apparently just as the Armenian Metropolitan and the bishop were visiting with him, a group of girls and women were brought in from the surrounding villages. They were questioned in the presence of the Metropolitan and the bishop and declared that "they would in no circumstance return to their families or churches". At this point the bishop had intervened in the case of the Syriac girl, who was insisting that she was Muslim and a legal adult. The bishop stated that because she was a child her testimony was not valid and that she should be returned to her community. It is at this point that the conversation takes an interesting turn:

I told the Bishop that we also did not approve of the likes of her remaining Muslim and that the reason why we did not officially carry out their conversions was precisely in order for them to be able to return to their previous religions now or later. But nor can it be acceptable, given the times and the circumstances, to drag

---

[100] Ibid., p. 175. This was discussed as the "grievous Salonica incident" in Chapter 2 of this volume.

[101] BOA A.MKT.MHM 637/16, 13 Mart 1312 / 26 March 1896, cipher telegramme from the Sublime Porte to the vilayet of Diyarbakir. "*Sızıldı*" (murmuring, lamentation) was one of the most common Ottoman euphemisms for "trouble from foreigners".

[102] Ibid., 14 Mart 1312 / 27 March 1896, the Vali of Diyarbakir, Enis Paşa, to the Sublime Porte.

such a person by the arm and hair to the church, when they are openly and in front of witnesses declaring that they are Muslims. This is also against the principle of religious freedom (*hürriyet-i mezhebiye*) that my government has always defended, and touches upon the matter of national feelings (*hissiyat-ı milliye tokunur*). From small matters such as this big problems may arise, particularly as public excitement has only just been appeased and efforts are being made to assure its continuity.[103]

This is a very cleverly formulated position. The reference to the official line not to accept mass conversion is mentioned, ostensibly keeping the door open for an eventual return to Christianity, although it was highly unlikely that a terrorized young person would find the courage to take such a step.

The issue of the abduction of women also had a specific gender dimension. Very often, in addition to fear, shame would have been the reason why many of these women would refuse to go back to their communities, as a loss of virginity in these circumstances would have condemned them to lifelong stigmatization and ended their marriage prospects. Forced conversion was therefore much more traumatic for women because it involved institutionalized rape under the cover of "marriage" to their abductors.[104]

What is most remarkable was the Paşa's reference to "religious freedom", which was very clearly a polite fiction in this context, not to say a travesty. Even more striking is his reference to "national feelings" because it gives away the nature of the massacres as a manifestation of "national feelings", implying that a provocative act could once again enflame them, leading to further massacre. Even so, he makes no admission of mentioning the Salonica affair directly, stating only that "great problems could arise from small matters".[105]

The British embassy continued to put pressure on the Foreign Ministry, claiming that "over one hundred Christians remain in the hands of the Kurds and are afraid to reveal their true religious inclination because of fear".[106] The ministry also relayed information from the British embassy to the effect that the commission that had been sent to recover Christian women had brought sixteen such women to Diyarbakır on 11 March: "Because they were

---

[103] Ibid.

[104] For a discussion of "sexual humiliation used to intimidate the Armenian community" during the genocide of 1915, see Katherine Derderian, "Common Fate, Different Experience: Gender-Specific Aspects of the Armenian Genocide, 1915–1917", *Holocaust and Genocide Studies* 19 (2005), 1–25. Although this article deals with a later period, the experiences of Armenian women in the 1890s must have been very similar.

[105] BOA A.MKT.MHM 637/16. Meyrier, *Les Massacres de Diarbekir*, p. 86.

[106] BOA A.MKT.MHM 637/16, 28 Mart 1896 / 10 April 1896, the foreign minister, Tevfik Paşa, to the Sublime Porte, Foreign Ministry Chancery no. 292.

threatened by death by the Kurds who had abducted them and by the Muslim population, they said they did not want to go back to their families and did not trust the local authorities to protect them. ... These threats led them to change their minds [about declaring for Christianity]".[107]

Meyrier repeatedly told his ambassador that the Ottoman authorities in Diyarbakır were deliberately blocking his efforts to reunite abducted women with their families. "Their situation is indeed lamentable; in all this morbid affair, they deserve the most compassion."[108] Meyrier reported further that the abducted victims were threatened "not only by their ravishers but also by other Muslims". He had sent one Muslim and two Christians into the villages around Diyarbakır to rescue the victims of abduction, but they had been largely unsuccessful; "it seems many murders have been committed in the villages for similar reasons". The consul had given the delegation a list of some hundred names; they had returned with only one woman and her daughter. The delegation was sure that the Kurds hid the victims and sometimes even transported them from one village to another.[109]

The British vice consul in Diyarbakır, C. M. Hallward, was to sum up: "In all about 8,000 appear to have been killed in the vilayet, and 25,000 turned Moslem. Upwards of 500 women and girls have been abducted. ... I give these figures for what they are worth and subject to correction. ... The general belief is that the whole thing was organized by Ennis Paşa, the Vali, in concert with some of the leading Moslems".[110] Meyrier had already identified some of these "leading Muslims", including Cemil Paşa, "ex-governor of Yemen known for his fanaticism", and Arif Efendi, a local leader of the Kurds. At the behest of the embassies, the Porte was obliged to send a commission of enquiry to Diyarbakır, led by Abdullah Paşa, one of the Sultan's ADCs and one of the few Ottoman officials about whom the diplomats had anything good to say.[111] Meyrier stated, "Abdullah Paşa knows that the tension in the area is kept up by them".[112] Abdullah Paşa reported that it was indeed Cemil Paşa and Arif

---

[107] Ibid., 16 Mart 1312 / 29 Mart 1896, the foreign minister, Tevfik Paşa, to the Sublime Porte, Foreign Ministry Chancery no. 117.

[108] Meyrier, *Les Massacres de Diarbekir*, 20 March 1896, pp. 175–9.

[109] Ibid., 21 March 1896, p. 179.

[110] Vice Consul Hallward to Consul Cumberlach, 17 March 1896, *British Blue Book: Turkey 1896*, as cited in Meyrier, *Les Massacres de Diarbekir*, pp. 215–16.

[111] Walker, *Armenia*, p. 147. The chief dragoman of the British embassy, Adam Block, referred to Abdullah Paşa as "a fairly straight man".

[112] Meyrier, *Les Masacres de Diarbekir*, p. 171.

Efendi who had spread the rumour during Ramazan that "all the Christians were going to be massacred and that this was an order of the Sultan". Abdullah Paşa was particularly scathing about Arif Efendi: "[A]lthough the imperial instructions that the said people be scolded and told that measures will be taken if they do not mend their ways, will work on Cemil Paşa, no amount of advice can effect Arif Efendi who is known for his bad behaviour . . . and is after increasing his influence and glory by provoking further disturbances". Accordingly, Abdullah Paşa advised that Arif be exiled "as an example to others of like mind".[113] The Porte, however, considerably softened the punishment and instructed Abdullah Paşa that "Arif Efendi not be exiled but that it be suggested to him that he remove himself temporarily to Mosul".[114] On 24 March, Abdullah Paşa asked permission to end the commission and return to Istanbul as "peace and order reigns again and we have seen the end of Ramazan without any trouble".[115] Meyrier felt that this issue of abducted girls and women was something that had broken Abdullah Paşa: "Abdullah Paşa, who at the beginning had taken this matter to heart, told me lately that he was discouraged and he no longer wanted to occupy himself with it. He has certainly received orders from his superiors which have changed, if not his mode of thought, at least his mode of action".[116]

Meanwhile, Enis Paşa, far from being held responsible for the massacres, remained at his post despite the various promises that the French and British embassies extracted from the Porte that he would be dismissed. The French embassy actually told Meyrier that the Council of Ministers had suggested to the sultan that he be replaced.[117] Evidently Enis Paşa had the sultan's support because he was still in place well after the Inspection Committee left Diyarbakır. Moreover, he continued to deny the British claims that a large number of Christians were still being held by Kurds and to report on cases of "women and children who were dispersed here and there during the troubles and are now being recovered and turned over to their families". He reported on 17 April that two women and two boys had been brought in from the kazas of Eğin and Garb; they had declared

[113] BOA Y.A HUS 347/58, 23 Şubat 1311 / 8 March 1895, the Committee of Inspection to the Sublime Porte.
[114] Ibid., 23 Ramazan 1311 / 10 March 1896, the Sublime Porte Receiver's Office to Grand Vizier Rıfat Paşa.
[115] BOA Y.A HUS 348/52, 11 Mart 1312 / 24 March 1896, the Committee of Inspection to the Sublime Porte.
[116] Meyrier, *Les Massacres de Diarbekir*, p. 183.
[117] Ibid., Jules de La Bouliere to Gustave Meyrier, 27 February 1896, p. 184.

that they were Christians and been handed over to their families. One of the women, who had a six-year-old child with her, "had insisted that she was a Muslim even after she had been put in an empty room with her brother". Presumably the brother was to try to dissuade her.[118] As late as the summer of 1896, Enis Paşa continued to hold his post. Again responding to an accusation of the British embassy that he was carrying out forced conversions, he confidently declared that "these are the slanders of enemies" (müfteriat-ı bedhahaniyeden).[119]

MASS CONVERSION AS A DIPLOMATIC ISSUE

No doubt Enis Paşa would have counted the foreign consuls among his "enemies". One of the most celebrated cases of forced conversion and subsequent return to Christianity was that of the Armenians of Birecik, near present-day Urfa. This case also became a cause célèbre like that of Şeyh Musa as it developed into an international diplomatic crisis involving the British, French, and Russian governments. On 3 March 1895, it was reported that a sizeable population (some 200 households) of Armenians had converted to Islam in Birecik, in south-east Anatolia. The Ottoman government had therefore consented to send a mixed commission of enquiry to the area, consisting of two officials from the vilayet of Aleppo and the dragoman of the British embassy, Fitzmaurice.[120] The commission had interviewed leaders of the convert community, who were named as "ex-Gregorians Haçik Efendi, now called Mehmet Şakir Efendi, and Abos Efendi now called Şeyh Müslim Efendi, ex-Catholic Hacıbekuzan Efendi now called İbrahim Efendi". The leaders of the community openly stated that "the recent events had caused them to fear for their lives, and that was why they became Muslim". They also promised that they would not convert back to Christianity once the danger was over. Moreover, "the conversion of the church which they had made into a mosque was done entirely at their own expense, and they had no intention whatever of

---

[118] BOA A.MKT.MHM 637/19, 4 Nisan 1312 / 17 April 1896, Enis Paşa to the Sublime Porte. The fact that this particular woman had a six-year-old child shows that she had "married" some six years previously, probably making it impossible for her to return even if she wanted to. The child would have been born some years before the massacres.

[119] BOA A.MKT.MHM 637/33, 1 Temmuz 1312 / 14 July 1896, Enis Paşa to the Sublime Porte.

[120] BOA Y.A HUS 352/1, 18 Şubat 1311 / 3 March 1895, the Sublime Porte, Office of the Grand Vizier, report prepared by Accountant of the Evkaf of Aleppo Ali Rıza, President of the Court of Aleppo Mustafa, Dragoman of the British Embassy, Fitzmaurice.

converting it back to a church". The Armenians interviewed were then asked to sign a report written by the commission. The report recorded that "the community had not been subjected to any pressure or force in accepting Islam but had only acted out of fear of recent events, being obviously in a state of great distress and poverty after the recent calamities and the sacking of their property". On 28 May the Vali of Aleppo was asked his opinion on the matter. The Ottoman governor reiterated that the Armenian converts had converted "only because they feared for their lives" (*sırf muhafaza-i hayat maksadına müsteniddir*). He pointed out that the state had two options. The first was to allow the Armenians to remain where they were and revert to Christianity; if it took this option, it was necessary to "execute some of those Muslims who had taken part in the killing and looting, in order to frighten the [rest of the population]". This would work, however, only for the urban areas. Those in the countryside would still not be able to circulate among the Kurdish tribes who were their neighbours, "which is in fact the very reason for their insistence on the sincerity of their conversion". The second option was to move the converts somewhere far from Birecik, so that when they re-converted back to Christianity, their Muslim neighbours would not know that they were apostates.[121]

What I have called a dangerous state of limbo for all new converts was remarked upon by Fitzmaurice:

As the legal formalities necessary on conversion to Islam had not yet been performed, the government refused to recognize them as such before demanding instructions from Aleppo; and, as the population were still menacing in their attitude, and reproached them with insincerity in their newly-adopted faith, to prove their sincerity, in the face of threats, the Armenians proceeded to convert their church into a mosque, which they called 'Hamidieh Mosque' after His Imperial Majesty the Sultan; some of them took a second wife, went through the rite of circumcision. ... They now all wear turbans, and are apparently most zealous in their attendance at the mosque and in the other observances of their newly adopted religion. ... A declaration of Christianity by them at the present would be most dangerous.[122]

Fitzmaurice, for his part, was convinced that the massacres and conversions were the work of the central government and the local authorities. "In the final massacre, faced with a Moslem mob crying 'Our Padishah has

---

[121] Ibid.
[122] Vice-Consul Fitzmaurice to Sir P. Currie, 5 March 1896, House of Commons Parliamentary Papers. *Turkey*, no. 5 (1896), *Correspondence Relating to the Asiatic Provinces of Turkey*, pp. 4–5.

ordered that the Armenians be massacred, and that no Christians are to be left in the country', the Ottoman official and reserve soldiers who had turned up in early December stood aside".[123] From Birecik Fitzmaurice travelled to Urfa, the scene of the most severe massacres, where, he said, 8,000 Armenians had been killed in two days, half of them burnt alive in the cathedral.[124]

Fitzmaurice returned to Istanbul in April but was back in Birecik on 30 May as part of the Birecik Commission of Enquiry that the sultan had agreed to form. He also claimed to have persuaded at least some of the Armenian converts who had converted "under the influence of terror" to return to Christianity, and to demand the protection promised by the sultan. But in the villages he was not so successful as "he found them too fearful".[125] This is also borne out by the Ottoman sources. The vilayet of Aleppo reported on 10 September 1896 that in Urfa, "the majority (*kısm-ı azamı*) of the 1,000 Armenians who had converted to Islam, having seen the return of peace and order, have returned to their old faith. The remnants insist on remaining Muslims. The English official Fitzmaurice seems satisfied with this outcome and is preparing to leave."[126]

It appears that by the summer of 1897 fear still ruled, but the worst was over, and a shade of normality had returned. There is a very interesting paper trail relating to the conversion to Islam and potential return to Christianity of the Armenians in the *sancaks* of Sason and Genc in the vilayet of Bitlis. On 11 August, the Foreign Ministry was informed that in Genc a total of 105 households in 12 *nahiye*s had made it known that they had converted during the "troubles of 1895" and now wanted to return to their original faith, but were afraid to do so. Some of the Armenians who had reverted back to their original faith had complained that the population officer (*nüfus müdürü*) of Genc, a certain Haydar Efendi, had tampered with the registers, and by increasing the ages of male children was now demanding that they pay an extortionate amount of military exemption tax (*bedel i askeri*). In reaction, the Armenians had stated that they were going back to Islam.[127] What is remarkable here is that

---

[123] G. R Berridge, *Gerald Fitzmaurice (1865–1939), Chief Dragoman of the British Embassy in Turkey* (Leiden, 2007), p. 27.
[124] Ibid.
[125] Ibid., pp. 28–30.
[126] BOA Y.A HUS 359/6, 28 Ağustos 1312 / 10 September 1896, the vilayet of Aleppo to the Sublime Porte.
[127] BOA A.MKT. MHM 620/50, 29 Temmuz 1313 / 11 August 1897, the foreign minister, Tevfik Paşa, to the Sublime Porte, Foreign Ministry Secretariat no. 1969.

the Armenian Islamo-Christians felt that they were in a position that was at least safe enough to enable them to bargain with the state. One week later the vilayet of Bitlis reported that "all the Christians who had converted to Islam during the troubles have now returned to their old faith without suffering pressure of any kind". It was further reported that the Armenians who had claimed that they were being unfairly taxed also claimed to be part of the "unregistered population" (*nüfus-u mektume*).[128]

In response to the declaration that they would return to Islam, the Vali of Bitlis was to blandly declare: "It is entirely up to them to decide whether they want to become Muslims or remain as Christians ... but it has been determined by the Ministry of Finance that they are to pay the *bedel* from the date of their birth to the date they became unregistered population". In other words, the state was telling them that they were responsible for their tax arrears as Christians even if they turned Muslim. In the event, the people in question remained Christians.[129] Despite the evident tension, the official fiction was kept up. On 8 November the Foreign Ministry wrote that "The claim of the British Embassy that the Christians who converted during the troubles were now afraid to return to their old faith because of the attitude of the Kurds, is entirely unfounded." The minister declared, "[T]he 900 Christians in the *kaza* of Genc have since reverted back to their old faith and are practicing their religion in complete peace and security".[130]

It appears that the fallout of 1895 was to last a long time. On 26 April 1902 the British embassy was to report that twelve families amounting to seventy-five souls in the village of Çatal, *kaza* of Andırın, vilayet of Aleppo, "who had been forced to accept Islam to save their lives during the troubles", had applied to return to their original faith. The embassy claimed that they had been prevented from doing so by the local authorities, who were forcing them to have their children circumcised and to marry their daughters to Muslims.[131]

---

[128] Ibid. "Nüfus-u Mektume" was an official category that we have seen earlier in several similar contexts.

[129] Ibid., 5 Ağustos 1313 / 18 August 1897, the Vali of Bitlis, Ömer Paşa, to the Sublime Porte.

[130] Ibid., 26 Teşrin-i Evvel 1313 / 8 November 1897, the Foreign Ministry to the Sublime Porte, no. 2931.

[131] BOA A.MKT. MHM 654/10, 13 Nisan 1318 / 26 April 1902, the Sublime Porte to the Ministry of the Interior. Andırın is today a sub-prefecture of Kahramanmaraş.

CONCLUSION

The conversions of the Armenians in Anatolia during these fateful years were entirely a survival tactic, as indeed is indicated by the fact that many went back to their original faith once the danger was over. Some, however, appear to have remained committed, even zealous Muslims. In an oral history interview preserved at the Armenian Research Centre, Garabed Bandazian declared the following:

"Did any Armenian in Perri become a Turk before 1915?"

"As far as I remember, three families became Turks during the 1895 massacre, Urachian, Mazmanian, and Booloutian."

"How did the Armenians look upon these people? Did they hate them?"

"The Armenians did not resent them. Even though they had become Turks, they were still with the Armenians. They still had the Armenian spirit – During peaceful times they did not go to the mosque or carry out their custom of getting washed several times a day. But when the fear started, they would go to the spring and obviously wash their hands before they went to the mosque to pray, so they wouldn't show they were Armenians."

"What happened to them in 1915?"

"Nothing happened to them."

"Because they had become Turks?"

"Yes, they became fanatical Armenian haters. And we heard that one of the Mazmanian sons ... and one of the Urachian sons, massacred many Armenians in Perri. To save their skin, they wanted to show that they were dedicated Turks and would kill Armenians. That's the kind of Armenians who became Turks and preserved their Mohammedanism."[132]

The issue of mass conversions of Armenians is obviously linked to the whole vexed question of whether the massacres were ordered, inspired, or encouraged by the sultan and his government. Even if most of the evidence pointing to official complicity or official inspiration is circumstantial, it is nonetheless substantial. François Georgeon, in what amounts to the only recent political biography of Abdülhamid II, gives a very balanced assessment. Georgeon contends that to view the sultan as "avenging himself against the Armenians" for forcing him into reforms that he did not want to carry out goes against "the extreme prudence in foreign and domestic policy that he manifested

---

[132] ARC. [GEN 44] Interview with Garabed Bandazian (May 8 1980), born on 27 November 1907 in the city of Perri in the vilayet of Charsancak (now Akpazar in Tunceli). Although it is clearly not possible to extrapolate on the basis of this one example how many Islamized Armenians fit this pattern, the fact that the interview subject mentioned specific families and individuals suggests that life stories of this sort had become part of the historical memory of the generation that grew up hearing them.

during his long reign".[133] Also, there were in fact whole regions that escaped the massacres through the energetic actions of some local authorities. The actual massacres were carried out by "the Muslims of eastern Anatolia, notables, dervishes, *ulema*, and the sheikhs of Kurdish tribes". All of these elements were terrified "by the spectre of an independent Armenia" where they would become " immigrants" (*muhacir*, as it happened in the Balkans. That was why the massacres "spread like shockwaves" immediately after the announcement of the acceptance of the reforms by the sultan. Various sources also attest to the fact that provocative sermons were preached in mosques after Friday prayers, spreading the rumour that the reforms amounted to the granting of independence to the Armenians.[134] A newspaper published by the Kurdish opposition to Abdülhamid claimed that he had pardoned murderers and included them in the ranks of the Hamidiye. The leading article commented:

Let us consider what disasters have befallen the people, how much blood has been spilt how many homes ruined as the result of the bloody oppression and murderous policies of His Imperial Majesty. . . . Had the Kurd previously suffered at the hands of the Armenian? No! What evil had befallen the Armenian at the hand of the Kurd? None![135]

Christopher Walker, based on his research in the British consular records, states unequivocally, "That they were the orders of Abdul Hamid there can be no doubt." The fact that troops took part in the massacres and that they began and ended with a bugle call is cited as further proof of official complicity.[136] Enflamatory sermons by mollahs of doubtful provenance, some amounting to "veritable calls to murder", would explain why many of the massacres occurred on Fridays.[137] Often local officials like Enis Paşa at Diyarbekir were involved in aiding and abetting the massacres. Many of the goods plundered from Armenian shops would later turn up at the homes of senior officials.[138] Dragoman Fitzmaurice, for his part, was convinced that the massacres occurred at a signal from the sultan: "No direct orders had been issued . . . but clear hints had come down from

---

[133] François Georgeon, *Abdulhamid II le sultan calife* (Paris, 2003), p. 293.
[134] Ibid., p. 294.
[135] *Kurdistan*, no. 26, 14 December 1900. This is a newspaper published in Cairo primarily by the sons of the famous Kurdish leader Şeyh Bedirhan Bey. My thanks to Rezzan Karaman for this reference.
[136] Georgeon, *Abdulhamid*, p. 294. Christopher Walker, *Armenia*, pp. 146, 157.
[137] François Georgeon, *Abdulhamid II*, pp. 294, 295; Hüseyin Nazım Paşa, *Ermeni Olayları Tarihi* (Istanbul, 1997), vol. 1, pp. 94, 100.
[138] Gustave Meyrier, *Les Massacres de Diarbekir*, p. 130.

Yıldız that 'it would be desirable to give the Armenians a good lesson'. In an Oriental country, he said, this was all that was needed."[139] Rev. W. A. Wigram, who travelled in the area soon after the massacres occurred, was convinced that they were carried out on the orders of the centre:

Diarbekr [sic] in 1895 was one of the centres of the Armenian massacres, and as many as 2500 perished in this place alone. ... The massacre was undoubtedly prompted by the government of Constantinople; but their agents were the fanatical Kurds who swarm in the slums of Diarbekr. ... That the massacre was political and not religious was proved by the fact that the Syrian Christians (who are also numerous in Diarbekr) did not suffer to anything like the same extent as their Armenian co-religionists. The crowd of refugees who sought sanctuary in the Jacobite cathedral were not molested. ... But the very fact that the distinction was made between Armenians and Syrians, is sufficient to indicate that in this instance the mob was under some sort of control.[140]

Although there is no evidence of a direct order on the part of Abdülhamid to massacre Armenians, the ultimate responsibility rests on him as head of state:

The extent of Abdülhamid's direct complicity in the full spectrum of the massacres is ... unclear. ... It may well be that the sultan was not always precisely informed about the extent and proximate cause of of the massacres in the provinces. ... This is not to absolve him of guilt, since he bore the primary responsibility of inculcating the athmosphere of anti-Christian, Islamic chauvinism in which the massacres took place.[141]

When Said Paşa, ex-foreign minister and sometime Grand Vizier, took refuge with the British embassy in 1895, "firmly convinced that the Sultan intended to deprive him of liberty if not of life", he was to confide openly in the British ambassador: "The Sultan's complicity in the Sassoun massacres received full confirmation from him, and he quoted a statement made by His Majesty that the Armenian question must be settled not by reform but by blood. 'At first' he said, 'I did not understand his meaning. I thought he referred to war with a foreign Power, but I find he meant massacre'".[142]

[139] G. R. Berridge, *Gerald Fitzmaurice*, p. 25.
[140] Rev. W. A Wigram, *The Cradle of Mankind. Life in Eastern Kurdistan* (London, 1922), pp. 34–6.
[141] Donald Bloxham, *The Great Game of Genocide*, p 55.
[142] Roy Douglas, "Britain and the Armenian Question 1894-7", *The Historical Journal* 19 (1976), 113–33. Douglas cites Salisbury Papers, Christ Church, Oxford, Currie to Salisbury, 11 December 1895 (Salisbury, A/135 fos. 249–56).

The fact that the massacres actually ceased abruptly, even if the state of terror continued, strongly implies that they were not simply acts of spontaneous cruelty: "If we regard the atrocities as the mere sadistic cruelty of a half-mad tyrant, or an expression of Moslem fanaticism, [if] the massacres could be explained in either of these two ways, there was no way of stopping them at all. Evidently, they must be seen as deliberate acts of policy." Abdülhamid was to tell the British ambassador, Sir Philip Currie, in 1897 that "the Armenian question" was "finally closed".[143]

Indeed, there was nothing essentially "Eastern" or "oriental" about the Hamidian massacres and the mass conversions of the period. What was perceived as a thorn in the side of the state had to be torn out or at least pruned down. The target was no dubious "Armenian peasant Renaissance", as argued by Robert Melson, but rather a segment of the population that was perceived of as potentially disloyal or treacherous.[144] The aim was thus to render them ineffectual; in this sense killing them or converting them (provided the conversion was permanent) achieved the same result. What Eldem has claimed to be the Hamidian state's position vis-à-vis the Armenians after the Ottoman Bank raid can also be transposed to the massacres and mass conversions: "If we accept that this position of 'terror against terror' was the position of . . . Yıldız, it represents a serious departure from the legalist, bureaucratic and reconciliatory tradition of the Tanzimat. Even so it is an understanding where, ideology, *realpolitik*, and manipulation are dominant , and as such, it is in a strange and terrifying way, more 'modern'".[145]

How can we contextualize the issue of mass conversions during the Hamidian massacres, and how do they differ from conversion policies and practices that we have seen in the previous chapters? In what way does the story of the conversion of the Armenians during the Hamidian era differ from the pattern seen before under the Tanzimat State? The most obvious difference was that the complicated and detailed conversion procedure that we saw in the previous chapters was not put into practice. In none of the cases just cited was there any reference to a witness declaring that the conversions were voluntary, of a priest being present, or of the family of the convert being given the opportunity to dissuade them. Also,

---

[143] Ibid.
[144] Robert Melson, "A Theoretical Inquiry into the Armenian Massacres of 1894–1896", *Comparative Studies in Society and History* 24 (1982), 481–509. See also Robert Melson, *Revolution and Genocide: On the Origins of the Armenian Genocide and the Holocaust* (Chicago, 1992), p. 69.
[145] Eldem, "26 Ağustos", p. 146.

the previous regimes and the Hamidian regime itself had no qualms about accepting the most bogus of conversions, as seen in Chapter 4. The key seems to be the official policy that individual conversions were permissible but that mass conversions were not to be accepted. There are several remarks that can be made on this conjuncture. The ostensible reason for the state's refusal to accept mass conversions was that, at some later date, at the first opportunity, the Armenians would "complain to the foreigners" that they had been forced to convert. Even if this reason is taken at face value, it still means depriving the Armenians of a last desperate measure of defence against being massacred. The official documentation openly stated on all occasions that the reason for the conversions was "fear of the Kurds" (*ekrad'dan havf ve haşiyetleri*), because when an Armenian village converted, but their conversion was not accepted officially, they were in that very dangerous state of limbo where they were at the mercy of the Kurds and other Muslims who were looking for the slightest excuse to fall upon them. To take a cynical view, this would suit the state because, on the one hand, they could claim to the observers on the spot, like the foreign consuls or missionaries and their superiors in Istanbul, that they had nothing to do with it and that the mass conversions and previous or subsequent massacres were the result of popular outrage that they could not control. On the other hand, their interests would be served, either through the Armenians becoming genuine Muslims or by their eventual decimation by the Kurds. Moreover, telling the Armenian potential converts "You may convert individually once order has been restored" seems disingenuous at best when there was a very real chance that they would not live that long.

Dragoman Fitzmaurice certainly did not nourish any illusions about the actual conversions being the result of "free will":

I would beg here to point out and it is a distinction upon which the Turkish authorities may lay great stress, that the Moslems did not with axes in their hands invite the Christians to choose between the alternatives of Islam or death. They simply showed and proved their determined resolve to massacre all Christians, and the latter, to save their lives, accepted Islamism. It is the subtle logical distinction between objective and subjective. The alternatives offered by the Mussulmans were not Islam or death, whereas the only alternative left to the Christians were those of death or Islam. So that the Armenians, to save themselves from certain death, became Mussulmans of their own free will, if, indeed, people under such terrible circumstances can in any way be considered as free agents possessing a free will.[146]

---

[146] Vice Consul Fitzmaurice to Sir P.Currie Birejik, 5 March 1896, *Turkey*, no. 5 (1896), 3.

The deliberate delay in the conversion formalities also seems to be reprehensible from the standpoint of Islamic jurisprudence. In an earlier period, at least in one instance, the Şeyhülislam's office (*fetvahane*) had issued an official *fetva* denouncing the negligence of officials who declined to accept a conversion:

> [I]f any individual from among the infidels presents himself before any governor, ruler or officer or even anybody from the humble folk, saying 'make me a Muslim and initiate me in the faith', if he was to receive the answer 'I do not know' or 'go to so-and-so', this is verily the greatest of sins. ... This delay and neglect is against Şeriat rulings and deserves divine retribution.[147]

Indeed, just what was meant by "individual" or "isolated" (*münferid*) conversions is a moot point. Who decided on the conversion? It would seem that heads of families would make the decision or, as in the case of the Birecik Armenians, community leaders. How many heads, or heads of families, had to be counted for the act to qualify as an acceptable conversion? It must also be borne in mind that the various references in the documents to the Armenians "converting freely and without pressure" almost always occur right after a reference to their converting "out of fear of the Kurds", which puts an entirely new face on the idea of free will. It appears that – to Hamidian officialdom, at least – fear of recent massacres or of their probable repetition amounted to free will. In at least one case, the Armenians were said to be converting *after* the immediate danger had passed because their villages had already been hit, and this was held as proof of the genuineness of the conversion. In another case the converted Armenians were told that even if they converted they would still be responsible for extortionist tax arrears. The frequent reference to grown men having themselves circumcised, in what were most likely to be primitive hygienic conditions, and this still not qualifying as a legitimate conversion, also seems to point in the direction of official complicity. The repeated references to Armenians "applying every day" to have their conversions recognized, to renew their marriage vows, must surely indicate a serious degree of desperation that the state was choosing to ignore. References to "natural inclinations to convert" because of proximity to Muslims as a genuine motive for conversion appear to be highly cynical. Open admission that Armenian claims to forced conversion were baseless because if the Kurds wanted to they

[147] BOA. A MKT 86/42, 15 Receb 1263 / 24 June 1847. *Fetva* from the Şeyhülislam's office regarding a breach in the procedure of conversion on the part of the *kaza* council of Şehirkoy and the *eyalet* of Niş.

would not have spared any of them, comes as close as possible to an official admission of complicity. The official attitude in relation to the abduction of Armenian girls and women is also highly suspect; in particular, the mention of the provocation of "national feelings" if one interfered too much with the abductors strongly implies that some degree of official approval was extended to the acts that had led to the inflaming of "national feelings".

Robert Melson has drawn attention to the distinction that must be made between the policies of Abdülhamid and the subsequent policies of the Young Turks:

Sultan Abdul Hamid II had no intention of exterminating the Armenians or destroying the Armenian millet as such. The main reason why total genocide was not perpetrated by the Ottoman regime in 1894–1896 was its commitment to Islam, to the millet system, and to restoring the old order. Abdul Hamid was not a revolutionary. ... The Porte was able to go along with or to help perpetrate massacre, but it was not willing to go so far as to destroy the Armenian millet.[148]

The Young Turks, on the other hand, made it their policy to deliberately and systematically exterminate the Armenians. In this genocidal context, conversion and its acceptance or rejection by the authorities was to take on a very different hue. When Talat Paşa ordered the deportation of converted Armenians in 1915 "because no importance should be placed on these conversions which are fake and temporary", he was not speaking the language of the imperial old order; he was speaking the terrifying language of the future.[149]

[148] Melson, *Revolution and Genocide*, p. 69.
[149] Taner Akçam, *Ermeni Meselesi Hallolunmuştur* (Istanbul, 2008), pp. 297–8.

Conclusion

We began by asking what was specific to the nineteenth-century Ottoman state in the acts of conversion and apostasy, and offered the hypothesis that what made them specific to the time was their overlapping with the age of National Revival movements. The previous chapters have examined the question across a period spanning the pre-Tanzimat era, the Tanzimat state, and the Hamidian state. The failure of the Tanzimat state was inevitable given the fact that it was "too little, too late" as far as the non-Muslim *reaya* were concerned and given the increase in pressure from the West. The Hamidian state, turning in on itself and emphasizing Islam, came to consider non-Muslims as expendable or even, as in the case of the Armenians, dangerous. In each of the previous chapters the questions of conversion and apostasy were examined as the expression of a dialectic between European pressure on the grounds of supposed humanitarianism, on the one hand, and the desire to maintain Ottoman sovereignty, on the other. As to the state's policy on the very desirability or undesirability of conversion, it seems possible to trace a pattern that resonated with the historical conjuncture. During the period of the Tanzimat State proper (1839–76) conversion and even more apostasy, sometimes one immediately following the other, were seen as undesirable acts – causing the "imperial headache", increasing social tension, and bringing down the wrath of the foreigner. In the case of the "coming out" of the crypto-Christians, the Porte feared that this would be the thin end of the wedge causing an avalanche of apostasy. It felt that it had to take measures that would prevent this and yet keep its pledges of religious freedom. As to the illustrious career converts of the failed revolutions of Europe, their conversions were a matter of convenience at best, and an embarrassment at worst. The Armenian converts of the 1890s were seen as the undesirable side effects of the massacres and were not to be trusted as they could later complain to the foreigners that they had been forced to convert, which was indeed the case.

These concluding comments are intended to flag some of the salient points that emerge from the story.

ON THE LANGUAGE OF OTTOMAN OFFICIALDOM

At this point some methodological considerations concerning the language of Ottoman officialdom are in order.[1] Many of the reports, cipher telegrams, and memoranda that were used in this book were meant to be "in house" and, as such, destined only for the eyes of a limited number of officials. Even so, Ottoman officialdom spoke elliptically and euphemistically, and it is precisely this wording that is invaluable as a window into the official mind. For instance, Enis Paşa, the Vali of Diyarbakır, would always refer to Armenian women who had been abducted by Muslims and forced to convert to Islam during the massacres of 1895 as "Armenian women who were dispersed here and there during the troubles" (*zaman-ı iğtişaşda öteye berüye dağılmış olan Ermeni kadınları*), thus entirely removing the agency of the abductors.[2] Similarly, when the minister of police, Hüseyin Nazım Paşa, referred to "classes of the population who intervened in the restoration of order" (*asayişin iadesinde müdahil olan sınıf-u ahali*), albeit as an undesirable event, he meant the massacring mob.[3] When the Vali of Sıvas reported that "today some two thousand Kurds have killed twenty-three Armenians. Some five hundred Christians now want to convert to Islam of their own free will", the bland and unquestioning use of "free will" strongly implies that conversion as a survival tactic came to be seen as "free will" by Ottoman officialdom.[4] Or when it is reported that "the many sticks that are being made in the carpentry and basket weaver shops in the city [Istanbul] should be

---

[1] I discuss some aspects of this in the *The Well-Protected Domains*; see the section "The Symbolism of Language" in Chapter 1. For a more recent study, see Maurus Reinkowski, "The State's Security and the Subjects' Prosperity: Notions of Order in Ottoman Bureaucratic Correspondence (19th Century)", in Hakan Karateke and Maurus Reinkowski (eds.), *Legitimizing the Order: The Ottoman Rhetoric of State Power* (Leiden, 2005), pp. 195–212.

[2] BOA A.MKT MHM 637/16, 4 Mart 1312/27 March 1896, vilayet of Diyarbekir to the Sublime Porte.

[3] Hüseyin Nazım Paşa, *Ermeni Olayları Tarihi* (The history of the Armenian events) (Ankara, 1998), vol. 1, pp. 94, 45.

[4] BOA A.MKT 660/35 4 Teşrin-i Sani 1311/17 November 1895, the Vali of Sivas, Halil Paşa, to the Sublime Porte.

confiscated and they should be forbidden to make more." This document can appear quite innocuous to the untrained eye – that is, until we look at the date, 13 November 1896, only a few months after the Kum Kapı massacres of 26 August, when sources reported that the massacring mob had been bearing similar sticks and cudgels, issued by the police, as some sources contend.[5] Ottoman officials in the provinces often told the sultan what they thought he wanted to hear, nor were they above downright lies.[6]

The language of conversion narratives also follows the political climate of the times. During the Tanzimat they speak of the need to act in accordance with the "requirements of the times" (*icabatı asriyyeye göre münasib*) or acts that would "damage the trust of the *reaya*" (*insilab- emniyet-i reayayi mucib*), or, "avoiding the Imperial Headache" (*tas'di-i Âli'yi mucib olmamak*). Another thing the Porte could not abide was the occurrence of untoward events that "would not look good to friend and foe" (*yar ve ağyara hoş görünmemek*). By "friend and foe" the Ottomans usually meant foreigners of one stamp or another.[7] During the Hamidian period the bureaucracy would speak in terms of "correction of the beliefs" (*tashih-i akaid*), or "confusing the minds of simple people" (*sade dil ahalinin tağşiş-i ezhanı*), or "the results of the deceptions of the Armenian subversives" (*Ermeni mefsedlerinin asar-i iğfalleri*).[8] During the Second Constitutional period following the Young Turks revolution of 1908, one often finds references to acts of conversion and/or apostasy that somehow "are not in accordance with the age of the constitution" (*asr-i meşrutiyete yakışmaz muamele*), or acts not in keeping with "the felicitous age of Freedom" (*asrı dilâra-i Hürriyet*).[9] The spirit of the age is thus reflected in the language of the documents. Yet there is also a sub-current that is discernible to the trained eye. The illiterate peasant lad of twelve who declares before witnesses that he "had for some two years been contemplating converting to Islam" because he had "become convinced of the purity and brilliance of the One True Faith" (*Islamın nezafet ve revnakı*) is almost certainly having words put into his mouth. The

---

[5] BOA.Y.A HUS 362/35 31 Teşrin-i Evvel 1316/ 13 November 1896. On the motif of "uniform sticks", see Edhem Eldem, "26 Ağustos 1896 'Banka Vak'ası' ve 1896 'Ermeni Olayları'". See, for example, Christopher Walker, *Armenia*, p. 167, who refers to the mob bearing "clubs, similar, carefully shaped".

[6] Abdülhamid Kırmızı, *Abdülhamid'in Valileri*, pp. 105–109.

[7] See Chapter 1 of this volume.

[8] Selim Deringil, *The Well Protected Domains*, Chapter 1; Hüseyin Nazım Paşa, *Ermeni Olayları Tarihi*.

[9] BOA DH.ID 133/1 28 Haziran/ 12 July 1912.

declaration of his conversion as "entirely a result of his desire for salvation" is also highly suspect.

Similarly, the repetition ad infinitum of the formula that "no sort force or coercion" (*bir güna cebr ve ikrah*) was being used in the conversion process, or the formula that is repeated throughout this book, that all the converts were converting "of their own free will and desire" (*bit' tav ver' rızâ*), even in highly dubious circumstances – these are clearly formulaic codifications for what were at the very least irregularities. Another term that should be noted is the term "somehow" (*her nasılsa*). This was a term that was used regularly in Ottoman official parlance when the scribe wanted to refer to an event that was somehow embarrassing yet had to be mentioned, such as the occurrence of an apostasy or some form of gross negligence on the part of an official.

Another aspect of the official language is that constantly repeated orders "not to do something" are a fairly certain indication that the practice or act in question is in fact taking place. In most of the examples mentioned it is a case of according the reality with polite fictions.

THE POLICY OF POLITE FICTIONS – PROMISES, SECRETS, AND FACE-SAVING

In this book I have referred to "polite fictions" on several occasions. It would not be too much of an exaggeration to say that the late Ottoman Empire was based on a policy of polite fictions. When real coercive power to enforce its policies did not exist, as was often the case, the centre had to reach a *modus vivendi* with local power holders, vested interests, and even the humble peasantry, the *reaya* and the Muslims. In this context, when a new system of rule, the Tanzimat State, was being put into place, the centre had to negotiate. As brilliantly put by Harry Harootunian: "[Nationalist] history's primary vocation has been to displace the constant danger posed by the surplus of everyday life, to overcome its apparent 'trivia', 'banalities' and untidiness in order to find an encompassing register that will fix the meaning".[10] In other words, nationalist history has no time for the "untidiness" of polite fictions as it "tries to fix meaning".

We began with what I called the Tanzimat State. According to the Eastern Question paradigm, the "tidy" received wisdom was that the Tanzimat reforms were the result of foreign pressure on a small cadre of

[10] Harry Harootunian, "Shadowing History: National Narratives and the Persistence of the Everyday", *Cultural Studies*, 18 (2004), 181–200.

Ottoman bureaucrats.[11] As to the homegrown Turkish version, it was almost single-handedly the work of Mustafa Reşid Paşa.[12] Although that paradigm has been more or less demolished in the more recent literature, there are still some important grey areas that have been overlooked. The most important aspect of the Tanzimat was that it made *promises*. It was not a process that was undertaken willingly and enthusiastically by the Ottoman élite, but once it was under way, they knew there was no turning back. It is worthwhile here to quote İlber Ortaylı *in extenso* as his work is still seminal for our purposes.

'Ottoman westernization turned its face to the West, not out of admiration, but out of necessity. Let us not forget that Cevdet Paşa, the statesman who appears to be the most conservative figure of the Tanzimat, was one of the leading lights in the westernization of the administrative structure. Finally, this unnamed process of westernization was much more the result of an internal decision rather than a result of outside pressure. The sources that are very often used by our modern historians to prove foreign pressure are the memoirs of megalomaniac foreign ambassadors who claimed to run the empire. Although these are important sources, they are inadequate and sometimes deceiving historical documents'.[13]

In Chapter 2 we have indeed seen the extent of Stratford Canning's "megalomania", as he did not hesitate to lecture the Caliph of Islam on the finer points of Islamic doctrine. On the other hand, we have also seen that the same Caliph and his government were obliged to send a "secret order" to the provinces outlawing the official execution of apostates, knowing full well that an open declaration could undermine the very basis of sultanic/Caliphal legitimacy. Here the polite fiction was that the decision was entirely the initiative of the sultan and his government and in no way the result of foreign pressure. Nonetheless, once given, the Sultan's word was a word of honour and had to be taken extremely seriously. No less a personage than the Şeyhülislam Arif Hikmet Efendi came to consider the matter a question of "national honour" (*namus-u milli*). Yet later in the century, during the Armenian Crisis discussed in Chapter 5, the Vali of Diyarbakır, Enis Paşa, would have a very different take on "national honour". For him, writing in 1895, national honour was the honour that would be impinged upon if the Armenian women abducted by good Muslims were to be taken from them. Here the polite fiction was that these women had converted voluntarily and were content with their lot.

[11] M. Anderson, *The Eastern Question* (New York, 1966).
[12] Reşat Kaynar, *Mustafa Reşit Paşa ve Tanzimat* ... (Ankara, 1985).
[13] İlber Ortaylı, *İmparatorluğun En Uzun Yüzyılı*, p. 25.

It has been pointed out earlier that the common mistake is to lump the Tanzimat Rescript of Gülhane of 1839 together with the Reform Edict of 1856. The Tanzimat Rescript was largely homegrown and was a synthesis of Islamic statecraft and Western concepts of the rule of law and enlightened despotism. However, the promises of religious freedom that were made in the Reform Edict of 1856 *were* indeed largely the result of foreign pressure and were seen as such by the Ottoman élite themselves. Let us recall at this point the memorandum penned by Reşid Paşa himself where he bemoaned the fact that his successors, Âli and Fuad, "gave away too much too quickly". As put by Cevdet Paşa in his folksy euphemistic style, "they sliced too thick" (*bol doğradılar*).[14] Here too the polite fiction was that the edict was entirely the result of sultanic magnanimity and concern for the well-being of his subjects.

The promise of religious freedom would also cause some people, like the crypto-Christians, the Kromlides, and the Istavri, to take the state at its word and "come out" openly, declaring that they had been Christians all along. The aim was to avoid conscription. This proved to be a miscalculation because the Porte balked at the prospect of many more such folk emerging from the woods and mountains, and some indeed did, as was seen in Chapter 3. Moreover, as was seen in the case of the Kromlides of Trabzon, their "secret" faith was something of an "open secret" as they were among the most prominent people in their area.

The Ottoman state in the nineteenth century was prepared to go quite far in tolerating such opens secrets, and relegating them to the domain of polite fiction, as long as the persons in question loyally served the state, or at the very least did not make trouble. Such was the case of the people discussed above as "career converts". It was very clear that the conversions of some of them were very nominal, not going very far beyond having a Muslim name and wearing the *fez*. General György Kmetty was also Ismail Paşa while he was in Istanbul, but went back to being Kmetty when he was in London. The polite fiction was that Ismail Paşa was a highly decorated Muslim Ottoman officer who had fought with distinction in the Crimean War. In reality, he was a Hungarian aristocrat who lived in London and commuted to Turkey whenever there was a war with Russia. Some of the career converts did not convert at all but allowed their Muslim hosts to think that they had; either way, this polite fiction allowed all parties to save face and to proceed on that basis. In most of these cases of career conversion, it is unlikely that any of the converts worked on losing their previous identity even after becoming well

---

[14] Cevdet Paşa *Tezakir*, vol. 1, *Tezkere* (Memorandum), no. 10, 74.

and truly Muslims, some even to the point of being circumcised. The Hungarian or Polish converts of 1849 remained Hungarian or Polish even after they had "turned Turk", even while loyally serving their new sovereign, some into the second generation.

ON "FREE WILL AND CONSCIENCE"

The other important issue that has to be touched upon in these concluding remarks is the issue of "free will", which comes up in many of the cases featured in this book. It is quite safe to say that in the late Ottoman Empire conversion was not unconditionally encouraged, and apostasy was not ruthlessly stamped out. Indeed, it seems doubtful whether the state actually *wanted* new converts during the Tanzimat State period. They only muddied the waters and caused the "Imperial Headache". According to the official policy, what was to be done with apostates was nothing worse than displacement. The state more or less instructed its officials to look the other way if they "happened to escape during the journey". It has occurred to me that this may have been a euphemism for murdering them. However, after examining hundreds of documents I have come to the conclusion that this was not the case. The reason is the fact that by the early to mid-nineteenth century, people were traceable. When a young Armenian girl who had converted under dubious circumstances and then gone back to Christianity was shipped off to Istanbul under escort, the Armenian Patriarchate wanted to know just when they departed and when they arrived. Therefore, two scenarios could apply here; the polite fiction would apply that she had escaped, but in fact she either went to live someplace where her chequered past was unknown or not a problem, like a big city, or was indeed safely delivered to her destination and often even provided with some employment or charity.

Yet, even in official documents with their "proper" guarded wording, one thing that immediately stands out is the oft-repeated formula that the convert was acting "of his own free and conscience" and that no force or coercion was applied. This is repeated so frequently that it gives rise to the suspicion that force or "persuasion" *were* indeed applied. This suspicion is compounded by the fact that many of the cases in the archival records concern young people. The obvious difficulty here is that there is often no actual proof in the documentation that force was applied, the obvious exception being the conversions during the Armenian massacres of the 1890s. In those cases, when the local authorities spoke of the people of an Armenian village "converting of their own free will", what was at issue was a matter of life and death, and conversion being used as a strategy of survival. This whole tragic episode puts an entirely new face on the idea of free will, as was remarked upon by the British dragoman Fitzmaurice: "[T]he Armenians, to save themselves from certain death, became Mussulmans of their own free will, if, indeed, people under such terrible circumstances can in any way be considered as free agents possessing a free will."[15]

The challenge facing the local authorities in more mundane cases was that they were being asked to pass judgement on something that was nearly impossible to quantify, that is, sincerity. Not only were they, more often than not, confronting local resistance to state prying, but the spectrum of conversions from "voluntary" to "forced" was extremely broad. Force did not necessarily come in the shape of a sword or an axe, and "voluntary" conversion could well be the result of incremental pressure and/or promises of reward. On the other hand, forced conversion, especially of young children, could become "voluntary" with the passage of time as the child became socialized in an Islamic context. In cases where one of the parties in a marriage converted to Islam and the other did not, the latter-day practice of allowing the children to choose their religion when they came of age was not as humanitarian a measure as it seems at first glance, the child being very unlikely to change the religion that he or she had been brought up in. Very often the child or young person converting would be in a position of some sort of dependency on their "patron", either as a servant attached to the household or as a concubine. The whole issue of concubinage offers up another can of worms. Seen as slavery in the West, this could lead to the clash of two socio-legal systems, as we saw in the case of Fazlı Bey and his servant in Chapter 2. In the case of the Stavriote of Ak Dağ Maden the relationship was reversed; there it was a Christian (or crypto-Christian) family that was causing the conversion to Christianity of the young Muslim servant boy in their household.

In the archival sampling that I have used for this study, young people or children of both genders are overrepresented. Although the source materials do not overtly declare it, there is a very real "smell" of sexual abuse, or at least of molestation.[16] Take the case of the boy who is approached by a

---

[15] See Chapter 5 in this volume.

[16] Carlo Ginzburg, "Checking the Evidence: The Judge and the Historian", in James Chandler, Arnold I. Davidson, and Harry Harootunian (eds.), *Questions of Evidence: Proof, Practice and Persuasion across Disciplines* (Chicago & London, 1994), pp. 290–303. In suggesting this as a distinct possibility, I have tried to heed the warning of Ginzburg of the need to use a "specific interpretative framework".

Halil Ağa on board a ship with the "promise of a reward", who "remains silent" and whose silence is taken as implied consent to convert while aboard ship, but who changes his mind as soon as he reaches port; or the young Armenian girl who suddenly decides to become a Muslim after being taken to the public baths by her adult Muslim neighbours; or the ten-year-old Serbian girl in Niş who is abducted and converted, whose family claim that she had been "bewitched", to mention a few – all of these cases give off the same "smell". The authorities may well have smelt it, too, as they time and again issued orders banning the conversion of young children. The frequent references to "avoiding loose talk" also point in the same direction.[17] Of course, there is nothing ambiguous about the abducted Armenian women and girls of the massacres; yet even here, the fiction (in this case not even polite) of free will is repeated time and again. Free will in conversion could indeed be exercised, despite opposition from the religious community, to enable a marriage that would otherwise be forbidden by prohibitively close blood ties. Conversion to Islam was the only way Christian blood relatives of a certain closeness of kinship (first cousins, perhaps) could marry.[18] Similarly, a Christian or Jewish girl, with no likelihood of a dowry and with diminishing marriage prospects, may well have exercised genuine free will in converting in order to marry a Muslim.

Free will also had to be coupled with the legal right to exercise it, particularly in the case of minors or young people. The struggle over the bodies and souls of these young people was carried out on the issue of the legal age of discernment. If the conversion was contested by the family or community of the convert, their last line of defence was that the convert was not of the age to be able to exercise free will.

It will be recalled that the issue of minimum age had also been linked to the issue of free will in the debate in 1879 between the Council of State (*Meclis-i Vala*) and the Christian Patriarchates. The Orthodox Patriarchate had asked for a definitely set minimum age, whereas the council had argued against this, stating that it was against the principle of the freedom of conscience.[19]

Free will could also cut both ways. After the Reform Edict of 1856, the missionaries thought that the Muslims could exercise their free will and

---

[17] See Chapter 1 in this volume.
[18] BOA DH.MKT 829/60 27 Kanun-u Evvel 1319 / 9 January 1903, the vilayet of Yanya to the Ministry of the Interior, dealing with the conversion and elopement of a young Greek couple.
[19] See Chapter 1 in this volume.

become Christian. The Ottomans soon put them right about that. Their position on this was quite unequivocal; free will did not extend to propagandizing against the dominant faith of the land.[20]

Denationalization, Devaluation, and Secularization

It seems that in matters of conversion and apostasy two counter-currents were at work in the late nineteenth- and early twentieth-century Ottoman state. On the one hand, conversion became a very socially and politically charged issue as it overlapped with the birth and rise of Romantic Revival nationalism in the Balkans and Anatolia. Therefore, conversion and the consequent abandoning of a religious community were seen as *denationalization*, which could have explosive consequences, as we have seen in cases like the "grievous Salonica Affair" of 1876. On the other hand, we can talk about a definite *devaluation* process whereby conversion and/or apostasy cases went from being strident, soul-wrenching, diplomatic crisis creating, potentially murderous affairs, to a routine police matter. The matter-of-fact tone with which the conversion and apostasy cases are reported in the Ministry of Police records bear witness to this. "So and so, a German subject, had converted to Islam" – not a glorious victory for the Last Revealed Religion, but just one more suspect that the Istanbul police have to keep under surveillance. Even during the Armenian massacres of the 1890s, the eventual return of some of the Armenian converts to their original faith, once the danger was over and the situation was stabilized, came to be accepted as a routine development. Similarly, the open declaration of the Kromlides and the Stavriote that they were Christians did not provoke massacres or mass disturbances, as often happened during earlier periods. It will be recalled that the British consul in Trabzon actually commented on the "extreme indifference with which all Mahomedans talk of the intended change". Similarly, when the Hemşinli attempted to return to their original faith, they were foiled not by the coercive power of the state but by a clever stratagem of the "*hocas* from Of", who told the government officials that if the Hemşinli should be allowed to go back to their original faith, so should they, as they too were the descendants of converts.

The whole Ottoman stratagem of creating the category of *tanassur* (converts to Christianity) is also an indication of the devaluation of conversion and apostasy. It is highly likely that, as apostates, the Kromlides,

---

[20] See Chapter 2 in this volume.

the Hemşinli, and the Stavriote would have faced much more dire consequences if they had declared themselves in earlier centuries. In the same vein, the fact that for over ten years Ali Nuri and Bogos Asfaryan could be the same person in a small place like Tokad indicates that Bogos/Ali was a "public apostate" who, far from being put to death, was allowed to accumulate a serious fortune.

Moreover, the illustrious Hungarian and Polish *paşas* were able to operate in Istanbul and in London under Muslim and Christian personas, respectively. Nobody seems to have made any enquiries as to whether they were in fact circumcised, and it may even have been considered the height of indiscretion to do so. The fact that Richard Guyon was buried in the British military cemetery in Istanbul, even though he was officially Hurşid Paşa, bears this out. It is inconceivable that the Ottoman embassies in, say, London or Paris could have been unaware of the ambivalent identity of these men. They were, after all, decorated Ottoman officers who no doubt attended embassy functions.

In Chapter 3 we have seen that in the mid-1890s the Population Registration Bureau regularly dealt with individuals who, having converted to Islam, now applied to return to their original faith. Such was the case of Aleksi from Yanina, who had become Hüseyin in 1887 and in 1893 applied to become Aleksi again. The same document mentions that there was an Armenian in the same position.[21] Although their wish was not always granted, apostasy had become a mundane bureaucratic procedure. In the case of some of them, the problem arose not because of the blasphemous act of apostasy, but because of the fact that it had not gone through "proper channels" and had not been registered. Another indication of the devaluation of conversion/apostasy is the almost passing mention of the apostasy of the Stavriote "not being recognized" officially by the Ministry of Justice and Religious Sects. The implication is that apostasy was now a legal category recognized by the state, as in the case of the Kromlides who became *tenassur-u rum*. Indeed, the term *"tanassur ve irtidad"* – literally, "to Christianize and apostatize" – seems to set them apart from straightforward apostates, who are called simply *"mürted"*.

Ali Riza/Kevork, the local businessman from Diyarbakır who had gone bankrupt and converted "in order to solve his difficulties" in 1912, is also a good example of devaluation. When conversion did not allow him to write off his debts, he had decided to go back to his old faith. He was "frequently applying to the government offices to have his apostasy recognized". It

[21] See Chapter 4, n. 14, in this volume.

sounds like Ali Riza/Kevork was applying to have a very routine affair regularized, almost as if he were applying to register a house sale.[22]

In a similar vein, as early as 1850 Hacu and Asib could "secretly pay *cizye*" while ostensibly living as Muslims as a way of proving, in case of necessity at a later date, that they had been Christians all along. They thus took out a form of re-insurance enabling them to dodge the conscription officer or the tax collector.[23]

Another aspect of the devaluation process are conversion narratives like that of Bishop Harutyun and General Bem, which are also a vivid illustration of Ottoman weakness. In vivid contrast to the "symbolic victories" and the public flouting of the conversion of distinguished figures such as the Orthodox priest, Mehmed of Athens, who converted in front of Ahmed I (1603–17), or the Hungarian İbrahim Müteferrika who became famous for founding the first Ottoman printing press in the eighteenth century, Bishop Harutyun is treated almost as an embarrassment and is hidden away in an obscure post translating newspapers. Similarly, Bem/Murad Paşa is sent to Syria; his wish to remain in the Balkans and fight the Russians is ignored as it would be seen as a deliberate provocation.[24]

This devaluation was accompanied by a *secularization* of the conversion process. The whole bureaucratization process starting with the Tanzimat made the conversion ceremony almost a civil rather than a religious occasion. The fact that the conversion formalities were carried out in a sitting of the local council, the presence of the priest in the secular council together with the *kadi* to bear witness that the conversion was voluntary, the rule that the next of kin be allowed to try to dissuade the convert, the issuing of a conversion certificate, the subsequent obligation to have the conversion registered at the Ministry of Justice and Religious Sects, and even the publication in the newspapers of reports of conversions – all these are a far cry from the private declaration of the *shahada* that binds the individual to Allah, or the ritual submission at the feet of the sultan during the imperial hunt.[25]

The next stage was the abolition of the official execution of apostates from Islam in 1844. Even if this was done in a very circuitous manner and was occluded by the deliberate obfuscation of the wording of the note

[22] See Chapter 3, n. 109, in this volume.
[23] See Chapter 3, n. 134, in this volume.
[24] Tijana Krstic, "Illuminated by the Light of Islam", pp. 54, 59, 61.
[25] Baer, *Honored by the Glory of Islam*, pp. 185–203.

given to the ambassadors, what was understood to be a fundamental principle of Islam was nonetheless breached. It was now possible to think the unthinkable, that a Muslim might, of his or her "free will and conscience", embrace another faith. Although this did not happen in anything like the proportions that the missionaries hoped for and the Muslims feared, it was still technically legal for a Muslim to convert to Christianity. Even Abdülhamid would tell Layard as much when they were discussing the case of Ahmet Tevfik Efendi. What he objected to, he told the ambassador, was not that Ahmet Tevfik might have converted to Christianity, for "there was freedom of religion in his domains", but that he had actively worked towards encouraging other Muslims to convert.[26]

The entire Reform Edict of 1856 dealt with the issue of "freedom of religion" and was rightly seen as a threat by the Muslim population, who were now, as the popular saying went, "forbidden to call an infidel an infidel" (*gâvura gâvur demek yasak*).

The Nationality Law of 1869 changed the practice whereby any non-Muslim converting to Islam on Ottoman soil was considered an Ottoman citizen. Now each case was to be considered on its own merits. The connection of religious identity and civic identity – or rather, the privileging of civic identity over religious identity – was a further dimension of the secularization process. The ban on Ottoman non-Muslim women marrying non-Ottoman Christians and Jews was inspired by the similar ban on the marriage of Sunni Muslim Ottoman women to Shiites from Iran.

It will be remembered that in the discussions at the Porte over the issue of the property rights of those who had lost or given up Ottoman citizenship, it was the religious officials who had come down on the side of the inalienability of the income from property and its inheritability by the heirs of one who had lost Ottoman citizenship. In stark contrast, the secular officials had overridden them and openly declared that the confiscation was a purely punitive and preventive measure. Although the non-Muslim population were being targeted here, it is still significant that *raison d'etat* carried the day over the Şeriat. Even the practice of ostensibly allowing children from mixed broken marriages to choose their religion upon reaching maturity, rather than always giving custody to the side that converted to Islam, can be seen as part of the same process. Although it was unlikely that a child reared in one faith would opt for another upon reaching maturity, the official declaration that they would have a choice and not

---

[26] Azmi Özcan, Tufan Buzpınar, "Tanzimat, Islahat ve Misyonerlik", p. 75.

be automatically handed over to the parent who was a Muslim was clearly a step towards secularization.

Finally, in 1913, a law was passed clearly declaring that conversion to Islam did not mean automatic Ottoman citizenship. Citizenship was no longer required to carry the baggage of religion.

We have also seen how the category of "unregistered population" (*nüfus-u mektume*) became a very useful way of solving the problem of a dubious or contested identity, since the person did not legally exist until he or she had been registered and given identity papers. Therefore, the category of "unregistered population" became a very convenient catch-all pool for regularizing potentially thorny cases of apostasy and/or conversion and, as such, further contributed to the secularization of the conversion process. In fact, we saw earlier that the Mutasarrif of Amasya in 1912 protested that it was "disturbing that the rejection of the greatest of revealed religions should be reduced to a mere administrative matter".[27] He was quite right, that was exactly what was happening. The only thing that apostates had to do to qualify as "unregistered population" was to bring a certificate from their patriarchate (or rabbinate) testifying that they were hitherto unregistered, making absolutely no mention of any conversion or apostasy; they were then registered as new entries in the population registers, as was done for other hitherto unregistered persons, and were given an Ottoman identity certificate, anonymity thus being assured.

What I have called the devaluation and secularization process did not represent by any means a total defusing of apostasy and conversion as volatile material when yoked to nationalism. The two seem to have been parallel developments. When acts of apostasy or conversion had little or no symbolic value, or when they occurred quietly and individually, they became routine matters. The apostates evoked hatred and fear when they became the living, walking *symbols* of the potential *unravelling* of the community. Particularly as the act of apostasy overlapped with de-nationalization, the threat that the apostate posed was that of a possible *precedent*. If Dimitri could do it, so could Yannis, or Eleni or Krispina. For Muslims, it was even worse; something that had been unmentionable until 1844 or 1856 was now, apparently, not only spoken of but, albeit in rare instances, actually happening. If Ahmet could become Aleko, or Mehmed could become Yani, and live to tell the tale, when rumours abounded about what the Alekos and Yanis (or the inverse, the Mehmeds and the Ahmeds) were doing to their opposite numbers in the unseen spaces of the nationally

---

[27] See Chapter 3, n. 113, in this volume.

imagined countryside, it was no longer a question of faith, it became a question of survival; hence the need for the exemplary punishment of the apostate/convert.

The other important aspect of most of the cases of conversion and/or apostasy that became explosive issues was that they were *public*. Ussama Makdisi's brilliant study of the case of As'ad Shidyaq, the Maronite who became an evangelical Protestant, has shown that what made As'ad's situation particularly dangerous was not the simple fact of apostasy, which was bad enough, but the fact that he made a point of declaring his heresy *publicly*.[28] Makdisi draws attention to the polite fictions of Ottoman society and how they worked in a Lebanese context. People converted from Islam to Christianity, technically becoming apostates, but this was done discreetly and quietly. When it was a case of someone converting to Islam, the issue was not blown up into a victory for Islam; rather, the new convert was quietly taken into the fold.[29] What made Shidyaq so potentially dangerous was that he flew in the face of the polite fictions. Similarly, the Bulgarian girl who converted to Islam in Salonica in 1876 became willy-nilly a public figure and a public issue because, like Shidyaq, she came to symbolize a deadly threat to the established order. When the act of conversion or apostasy breaks boundaries, trips wires that coincide with crises or tensions in the broader context – when Stephana becomes Ayşe three days after the Bulgarian uprisings just north of Salonica – that is when the explosion occurs. Even at a more subdued level, when a young Greek boy in an obscure town in Anatolia is converted in dubious circumstances, the case can go right up to the Patriarchate in Istanbul, who can actually warn the Porte that such matters "could cause coldness and enmity between the communities".[30]

On the other hand, the process of devaluation of conversion/apostasy could take place when the convert/apostate had little or no value as a symbol. The obscure German engineer Hans, who became Emin, had no symbolic value and did not pose a threat even if he remained Hans in his daily practices. Nor did the ex-*honvéd* Hungarian General Kmetty, who became İsmail Paşa but who continued to frequent the London season as Kmetty. They both had only utilitarian value. Even Ahmed Tevfik Efendi, who had committed what amounted to a cardinal crime, aiding in the publishing of tracts that were supposed to entice believers away from

[28] Ussama Makdisi, *Artillery of Heaven*, p. 203.
[29] Ibid., p. 120.
[30] See Chapter 1, n. 78, in this volume.

Islam, could be quietly pardoned and ignored as he disappeared into ignonimity because he was no longer a symbolic threat; he was no longer a potential unraveller. To stretch the point a trifle, even the Armenians who quietly "went back" to their original faith after the bloodletting of the 1890s never had any symbolic value because the pogroms themselves had been brutal but entirely political acts. What could be a tripwire in one particular historical conjuncture could well go unnoticed in another. The bankrupt Armenian businessman converting to Islam in order to escape his debts in, say, 1880 may well not draw any undue attention, but if he were to make the same demand in the mid-1890s he might well get a very different reception.

Symbolic Boundaries and Negotiated Identities

Much of what has been discussed in this book revolves around what Anthony Smith calls the "inner worlds" and "symbolic boundaries" of nations, which, he claims, modernists have not given the emphasis they deserve.[31] Speaking as a modernist, I would submit that Smith misses one very important thing: some symbolic boundaries could be changeable according to the historical context. What defined "us" one day could become useless and even dangerous the next when it is easily applied to "them". The fact that the Serbs, Croats, and Bosniaks speak pretty much the same language did not prevent them from killing each other. But some symbolic boundaries are indeed immutable. Circumcision is a very good example, because it was the ultimate marker. General Bem underwent circumcision despite the advice of his Turkish hosts, who pleaded with him to wait for his wounds to heal, because "he wanted to become a true Muslim".[32] The other illustrious Hungarians in Vidin did not follow his example. Yet we know from the documents that at least some of the Hungarian refugees were indeed circumcised in subsequent years. It may well be the case that there was a choice, to cross the ultimate boundary line or not. Furthermore, the Armenians in Chapter 5 had themselves circumcised out of desperation as a means of forcing the state to recognize their conversions, thus saving their lives. A particularly poignant case came up in 1915, when an Armenian presented himself in Bolu in central Anatolia actually pretending to be circumcised and claiming to be a Muslim. The Mutasarrıf of Bolu wrote, "[U]pon inspection it was seen that he had tied a

[31] Anthony Smith, *Ethno-Symbolism and Nationalism*, pp. 18, 25, 40, 49.
[32] See Chapter 4, n. 34, in this volume.

string around his reproductive organ and when the string was cut it became clear that he was entirely uncircumcised".[33] Evidently this person was trying to keep his "symbolic boundaries" open, thus avoiding the death marches.

Jessica Coope's Cordoba Muslims of the ninth century refused to work alongside Christians because they were uncircumcised and therefore ritually polluting.[34] Linda Colley's English captives of the 1780s in India, who feared that they would be forced to convert to Islam, "feared for their foreskins". As put by one of them who had actually been forcibly circumcised, "I lost with the foreskin of my yard all the benefits of a Christian and Englishman, which were and ever shall be my greatest glory".[35]

Thus, the of acts conversion or apostasy could be seen as something *shameful*, something one does not like to talk about, like having a rape in the family or someone convicted of murder. Tannus Shidyaq, As'ad's elder brother, completely ignored his brother's conversion when he wrote what he claimed to be a definitive history of the great families of Mount Lebanon. Tannus did not hate his brother and had tried to save him. He made the omission because As'ad's conversion to Protestantism did not fit the official line; as put by Makdisi, "He became complicit ... in expunging his brother's memory for the coherence of the 'truthful' history that he narrated".[36]

There is hardly any mention in the official Hungarian historiography of the Hungarian heroes of the 1848 Revolution who "turned Turk" or at least appeared to do so for a good part of their lives. The official Hungarian narrative that celebrates and commemorates the "martyrs of 11 October", the Hungarian patriots who were executed by the Austrians, is almost entirely silent on the "Turkish episode" of their brothers in arms. Is this because it is more honourable to die a martyr than to live as a "Turk"?[37]

I have examined how the historical context affected state conversion policies and their interface, survival strategies and/or personal negotiations of identity and accommodation on the part of individuals. Thus, this is not

---

[33] BOA DH.EUM. 2 Şb 51/12/2, 6 Mart 1334 / 29 March 1915, the Mutasarrıf of Bolu Mustafa to the Ministry of the Interior. My thanks to Sait Çetinoğlu for this reference.

[34] Jessica Coope, *The Martyrs of Cordoba: Community and Family Conflict in an Age of Mass Conversion* (Lincoln and London, 1995), p. 82.

[35] Linda Colley, "Going Native, Telling Tales: Captivity, Collaboration and Empire", pp. 170–93. The person in question was a navy ensign, hence the naval terminology.

[36] Ussama Makdisi, *Artillery of Heaven*, p. 201.

[37] Hungarian school textboks hardly mention Bem's Turkish episode and his conversion to Islam. My thanks to Szabolcs Pogonyi for this information.

a book about religion per se but is more concerned with how conversion and apostasy were used as a *negotiating space* by various actors – the state, Muslim subjects, non-Muslim communities and individuals, foreign powers trying to further sum-zero interests, refugees from political persecution, and plain opportunists. This negotiating space was by no means some kind of safe haven or sanctuary. Conversion and apostasy tales, as was seen, often occurred in situations of dire stress or even mortal danger. But negotiation there was, whether it be the negotiation of identity, divorce, custody of children, livelihood, political rights, or material well-being, not necessarily in that order. Moreover, the spectrum of negotiations can be extremely broad. It can range from the inveterate gambler converting to Islam hoping to escape his gambling debts, to the terrorized Armenian for whom conversion is a last card to play to save himself and his family. The negotiation process, therefore, often takes place between highly unequal parties. The negotiation space can also be used by people who do not even know they are negotiating, like children who run away from their parents' beatings and take refuge with a Muslim neighbour, claiming they want to convert. Similarly, a mistreated Christian or Jewish wife may seek the divorce she might otherwise not be granted by converting to Islam. Negotiation could be carried out literally, as in the case of the Kromlides, who felt that they would get a better "deal" as open rather than crypto Christians. Similarly, the Shparataks of Albania actually shopped around for the religion that would give them the best strategic advantage.[38]

One could argue that the concurrent development of intensification and devaluation in matters of conversion and apostasy occurred precisely *because* of the overlap with nationalism. On the one hand, the conversion of our apocryphal goatherd became a symbol of de-nationalization and therefore volatile material. On the other hand, as it came to be seen as a secular rather than a religious betrayal, it went from being a metaphysical cataclysm to being a political problem. The likelihood of conversion – and apostasy – coming to be seen as an unraveling of the political rather than the religious community led to the concurrent intensification of political conflict, but as it became more and more common, or at least more openly talked about, devaluation of its significance as a religious matter occurred. Ultimately, in 1915, even those Armenians who had converted to Islam were not spared from the death marches; their destruction was clearly a political, not a religious decision.

---

[38] See Chapter 3 in this volume.

There are very few, if any, spiritual athletes in the pages of this book. The figures who emerge from the documents are mostly people who sought to manipulate, bend, outwit, collaborate with, or become invisible to a system of power that was, itself, making up the rules as it went along. One will search in vain for Willam James's "self" who, "hitherto divided and consciously wrong inferior or unhappy, becomes unified and consciously right superior and happy, in consequence of its firmer hold upon religious realities".[39] Nor do any of the cases studied fit the neat "seven stages" of the conversion process as outlined by Lewis Rambo and Charles Farhadian.[40] The context in which they occur differs greatly from the colonial context studied by Gauri Viswanathan, and the difference is not only the obvious fact that here the power relationship is reversed, the ruling class being Muslim.[41]

The aim of the present study is not to serve as a corrective to blatant nationalist distortion, but it is perhaps more an invitation to think about nuances, grey areas, innuendos and what I have called "polite fictions". The unsaid as well as the said, the endless repetitions that give off bad smells, the polite jargon that talks of displacement and dispossession. The continuous references to acts that are supposed to be voluntary but appear just that bit "too voluntary". Things happening that are simply not supposed to happen and things not happening when every standard historical source tells us that they should.

---

[39] William James, *The Varieties of Religious Experience: A Study in Human Nature* (NewYork, 2002), p. 210.
[40] Lewis R. Rambo and Charles E. Farhadian, "Converting: Stages of Religious Change", in Christopher Lamb and M. Darrol Bryant (eds.), *Religious Conversion: Contemporary Practices and Controversies* (London and New York, 1999), pp. 23–4.
[41] Gauri Viswanathan, *Outside the Fold: Conversion, Modernity and Belief* (Princeton, 1998).

Bibliography

Primary Sources

Başbakanlık Osmanlı Arşivi (BOA), Prime Ministry Ottoman Archives,
İstanbul

A.MKT MHM	Sadaret Mektubi Mühimme
A.MKT	Sadaret Mektubi
A.MTZ.CL	Sadaret Mümtaze Cebel-i Lübnan
A.MKT.UM	Sadaret Mektubi Umumi
BEO Bab-ı	Âli Evrak Odası
CEVDET TASNIFI	Adliye
DH.ID	Dahiliye Irade Dahiliye
DH.MKT	Dahiliye Mektubi
DH.MUI	Dahiliye Muhaberat-ı Umumiye
DH.EUM.THR	Dahiliye Emniyet-i Umumiye Tahrirat
DH-HMŞ	Dahiliye Nezareti Hukuk Müşavirliği
DUIT	Dosya Usulü İradeler Tasnifi
HH	Hat-ı Hümayun
HR.SYS	Hariciye Siyasi
HR/MTV	Hariciye Mütenevvi
MV	Meclis-i Vükela
IMM	Irade Mesail i Mühimme
İRSM	İrade Rüsumat
ANZD	Sadaret Nezaret ve Devair
HR.MKT	Hariciye Mektubi

Y.A HUS   Yıldız Arşivi Hususi Maruzat
Y.A RES   Yıldız Arşivi Resmi Maruzat
YEE   Yıldız Esas Arşivi
Y.MTV   Yıldız Mütenevvi Maruzat
Y.PRK. UM   Yıldız Perakende Umumi Maruzat
ZB   Zabtiye Nezareti

National Archives, London

TNA, FO 195/1107, The National Archives, Foreign Office

Official Publications

Düstur (Register of Ottoman Laws) 1. Tertip. İstanbul Matbaa-i Amire 1299 (İstanbul Imperial Press 1882), vol. 1, 4–7.

House of Commons, *Correspondence Respecting Protestant Missionaries and Converts in Turkey, Presented to both Houses of Parliament by Command of Her Majesty 1865*. House of Commons Parliamentary Papers Online 2005, www.parlipapers.chadwyck.co.uk.

House of Commons. Parliamentary Papers. Turkey (1896). *Correspondance Relating to the Asiatic Provinces of Turkey*.

Hüseyin Nazım Paşa, *Ermeni Olayları Tarihi* (The history of the Armenian events) (Ankara, 1998), vols. 1–2.

Milli Tetebbu`lar Mecmuası (Journal of National Studies), vol. 1, no. 3, Temmuz–Agustos (July–August) 1331 (1915).

Osmanlı Belgelerinde Ermeni İsyanları 1878–1909 (Armenian uprisings according to Ottoman documents) (Ankara, 2008, 4 vols.). Official publication, Turkish State Archives.

Pallas Lexicon (in Hungarian), (Budapest, 1893), vol. 2, p. 580.

"Protestant Milleti Nizamnamesi" (The regulations of the Protestant millet), *Düstur*, I. Tertib, vol. 1 (İstanbul: Matbaa-i Amire, 1856), 652–4.

Redhouse, Sir James, *A Turkish English Lexicon* (Beirut, 1974 [1894]).

Redhouse Sözlüğü, Türkçe–İngilizce (Redhouse Turkish–English Dictionary) (İstanbul, 1979).

Sami, Şemseddin, *Kamus-uTurki ...* DerSaadet 1317 (İstanbul, 1901).

Sezen, Tahir, *Osmanlı Yer Adları* (Ottoman Place Names), BOA publication (İstanbul, 2001).

Published Material

Abu Manneh, Butrus, "The Islamic Roots of the Gülhane Rescript", in Abu Manneh, *Studies on Islam and the Ottoman Empire in the 19th Century (1826–1876)* (İstanbul, 2001), pp. 73–97.

Abu Manneh, Butrus, "The Sultan and the Bureaucracy: The Anti-Tanzimat Concepts of Grand Vizier Mahmud Nedim Pasa", in Abu Manneh, *Studies* on Islam and the Ottoman Empire in the 19th Century (1826–1876) (İstanbul, 2001), pp. 161–80.

Adanır, Fikret, and Faroghi, Suraiya (eds.), The Ottomans and the Balkans: A Discussion of Historiography (Leiden, 2002).

Addison, James Thayer, The Christian Approach to the Moslem (New York, 1942).

Adıyeke, Nıikhet, "Osmanlı Millet Sistemi uygulamasında gelenekçiliğin rolü" (The role of traditionalism in the application of the millet system), Düşünen Siyaset (Ağustos Eylül, 1999).

Adıyeke, Nuri, "Multi Dimensional Complications of Conversion to Islam in Ottoman Crete," in Antonis Anastasopoulos (ed.), Crete and the Eastern Mediterranean 1645–1840 (Rethymno, 2008), pp. 203–209.

Adrianopoulou, Konstantina, "Alexander Mavroyeni Bey: The Nineteenth Century Reforms and the Young Turk Revolution from the Writings of a Neo-Phanariot Ottoman Bureaucrat", M.A. thesis, Boğaziçi University, 2004.

Afifi, Mohamed, "Reflections on the Personal Laws of Egyptian Copts", in Amira El Azhary Sonbol (ed.), Women, the Family and Divorce Laws in Islamic History (Syracuse, NY, 1996), pp. 202–15.

Akarlı, Engin Deniz, The Problem of External Pressures, Power Struggles, and Budgetary Deficits in Ottoman Politics under Abdulhamid II (1876–1909), unpublished Ph.D. dissertation, Princeton University, 1976.

Akarlı, Engin Deniz, The Long Peace: Ottoman Lebanon 1861–1920 (Berkeley and London, 1993).

Akbayar, Nuri, Osmanlı Yer Adları Sözlüğü (Dictionary of Ottoman place names) (İstanbul, 2004).

Akçam, Taner, A Shameful Act: The Armenian Genocide and the Question of Turkish Responsibility (New York, 2006).

Akçam, Taner, Ermeni Meselesi Hallonmuştur (The Armenian Question has been resolved) (İstanbul, 2008).

Alder, Lory, and Dalby, Richard, The Dervish of Windsor Castle (London, 1979).

Aleksov, Bojan, "Adamant and Treacherous Serbian Historians on Religious Conversions", in Pal Kolsto (ed.), Myths and Boundaries in South-Eastern Europe (London, 2005), pp. 158–90.

Alpay, Sahin, "Bir Osmanlı Vikingi. Herr Gustaf Noring ya da Ali Nuri Bey" (An Ottoman Viking: Herr Gustaf Noring or Ali Nuri Bey), Tarih ve Toplum 2 (1984), 70–3.

Anderson, Benedict, Imagined Communities: Reflections on the Origins and Spread of Nationalism (London, 1991).

Anderson, Margaret Lavinia, "Down in Turkey Far Away: Human Rights, the Armenian Massacres, and Orientalism in Wilhelmine Germany", The Journal of Modern History 79 (2007), 80–111.

Anderson, Mathew, The Eastern Question 1774–1923: A Study in International Relations (London and New York, 1966).

Andić, Fuat, and Andić, Stephen, The Last of the Ottoman Grandees: The Life and Political Testament of Âli Paşa (İstanbul, 1996).

Andreadis, Yorgo, Gizli Din Taşıyanlar (Those with a secret religion) (İstanbul, 1999). Originally published as Oi Klostoi (Thessaloniki, 1995).

Anscombe, Frederick F., "Islam and the Age of Ottoman Reform", *Past and Present* 209 (2010) 160–89.

Arnakis, George, "The Greek Church of Constantinople and the Ottoman Empire", *The Journal of Modern History* 24 (1952), 235–50.

Artinian, Vartan, *Osmanlı Devleti'nde Ermeni Anayasası'nın Doğuşu 1839–1863* (The birth of the Armenian Constitution in the Ottoman Empire) (İstanbul, 2004).

Aslantaş, Selim, *Sırp İsyanları 19. Yüzyılın Şafağında Balkanlar* (The Serbian uprisings: The Balkans at the dawn of the 19th century) (İstanbul, 2007).

Augustinos, Gerasimos, *The Greeks of Asia Minor: Confession, Community, and Ethnicity in the Nineteenth Century* (Kent, Ohio & London, 1992).

Baer, Marc, "Islamic Conversion Narratives of Women: Social Change and Gendered Religious Hierarchy in Early Modern Istanbul", *Gender and History* 16 (2004), 425–58.

Baer, Marc, *Honored by the Glory of Islam: Conversion and Conquest in the Ottoman Empire* (Oxford, 2008).

Balivet, Michel, *Romano Byzantine et Pays de Rum Turc. Histoire d'une espace d'imbrication Greco-turque* (İstanbul, 1994).

Barkan, Ömer Lütfi, "Osmanlı İmparatorluğu'nda bir iskan ve kolonizasyon metodu olarak Vakıflar ve Temlikler I: Istila Devrinin Kolonizatör Türk Dervişleri ve Vakfiyeler" (The Vakif and Temlik as a method of colonization in the Ottoman Empire: The Colonizing Turkish Dervişes and the Vakfiye of the expansion period), *Vakıflar Dergisi* 2 (1942), 22–53.

Barret, Thomas M., "Lines of Uncertainty: The Frontiers of the Northern Caucasus", in Jane Burbank and David L. Ransel (eds.), *Imperial Russia* (Bloomington, 1998), pp. 148–74.

Behar, Cem, "Sources pour la demographie historique de l'Empire Ottoman. Les *tahrirs* (denombrements) de 1885 et 1907", *Population* 1–2 (1998), 161–78.

Behar, Cem, "Qui Compte? Recensements et statistiques demographiques dans l'Empire ottoman, du XVIe au XXe siècle", *Histoire & Mesure* 13.5 (1998), 135–46.

Berridge, G. R., *Gerald Fitzmaurice (1865–1939): Chief Dragoman of the British Embassy in Turkey* (Leiden, 2007).

Beydilli, Kemal, *Recognition of the Armenian Catholic Community and the Church in the Reign of Mahmud II* (Cambridge, MA, 1995).

Bilmen, Ömer Nasuhi, *Hukuku İslamiyye ve İstilahatı Fıkhhiyye Kamusu* (The encyclopedia of Islamic law and *Fikh* rulings) (İstanbul, 1969), vol. 4.

Bliss, Rev. Edward Munsell, *Turkey and the Armenian Atrocities: The Reign of Terror: From Tartar Huts to Constantinople Palaces* (Philadelphia, 1896).

Bloxham, Donald, *The Great Game of Genocide: Imperialism, Nationalism, and the Destruction of the Ottoman Armenians* (Oxford, 2005).

Bona, Gábor, *The Hungarian Revolution and War of Independence of 1848–49* (New York, 1999).

Boratav, K., Ökçün, G., and Pamuk, Ş., "Ottoman Wages and the World Economy", *Review* 8 (1985), 379–406.

Bozkurt, Gülnihal, *Batı Hukuku'nun Turkiye'de benimsenmesi* (The adoption of Western law in Turkey) (Ankara, 1989).

Braude, Benjamin, and Lewis, Bernard, *Christians and Jews in the Ottoman Empire: The Functioning of a Plural Society* (New York, 1982).

Breuilly, John, *Nationalism and the State* (Manchester, 1993).

Burbank, Jane, and Ransel, David L. (eds.), *Imperial Russia: New Histories for the Empire* (Ann Arbor, MI, 1998).

Bryer, Anthony, "Nineteenth Century Monuments in the City and Vilayet of Trebizond: Architectural and Historical Notes", *Archeion Pontou* 29 (1968–69), 12–44.

Bryer, Anthony, "The Crypto-Christians of the Pontos and Consul William Gifford Palgrave of Trebizond", *Deltio Kentrou Mikrasiatikon Spoudon* 4 (1983), 17–34.

Bulliet, Richard W., *Conversion to Islam in the Medieval Period: An Essay in Quantitative History* (Cambridge, MA & London, 1979).

Campbell, Sir G. M. P., "The Races, Religions and Institutions of Turkey", *The Eastern Question Association: Papers on the Eastern Question*, no. 4 (London, 1877).

Celalettin Paşa, "Türklerin Aslı" (On the origins of the Turks), *Edebiyat-ı Umumiye Mecmuasi*, no. 31 (2 June 1917), 12–25.

Çelik, Zeynep, *The Remaking of Istanbul: Portrait of an Ottoman City in the Nineteenth Century* (Berkeley, 1993).

Çetin, Osman, *Sicillere Göre Bursa'da Ihtida Hareketleri ve Sosyal Sonuçları 1472–1909* (Conversion movements in Bursa according to the court records and their social consequences) (Ankara, 1994).

Cevdet, Paşa, *Tezakir*, ed. Cavit Baysun (Ankara, 1986), vol. 1, p. 12.

Clayer, Natalie, *Religion et Nation chez les Albanais XIX–XX e Siècles* (İstanbul, 2002).

Colley, Linda, "Going Native, Telling Tales: Captivity, Collaboration and Empire", *Past and Present*, no. 168 (August 2000), 170–93.

Colović, Ian, *Politics of Identity in Serbia: Essays in Political Anthropology* (New York, 2002).

Coope, Jessica, *The Martyrs of Cordoba: Community and Family Conflict in an Age of Mass Conversion* (Lincoln and London, 1995).

Cromer, the Earl of, *Modern Egypt* (London, 1911).

Curl, James Stuart, *Kentsal Green Cemetary: The Origins and Development of the General Cemetery of All Souls, Kentsal Green London 1824–2001* (London, 2003).

Dadrian, Vahakn, *The History of the Armenian Genocide: Ethnic Conflict from the Balkans to Anatolia to the Caucasus* (Providence, RI & Oxford, 1995).

Daily News, The, 14 May 1855, www.batteryb.com/Crimean_War/biographies/genguyon.htm

Davison, Roderic H., "Turkish Attitudes Concerning Christian Muslim Equality in the Nineteenth Century", *American Historical Review* 59 (1954), 844–64.

Davison, Roderic, "Turkish Attitudes Concerning Christian-Muslim Equality in the Nineteenth Century", in Roderic Davison, *Essays in Ottoman Turkish History 1774–1923* (Austin, TX, 1990), pp. 45–67.

Davison, Roderic, "The Advent of the Principle of Representation in the Government of the Ottoman Empire", in Roderic Davison, *Essays in Ottoman and Turkish History 1774–1923* (Austin, TX, 1990), pp. 96–111.

Dawkins, R. M., "The Crypto-Christians of Turkey", *Byzantion* 8 (1933), 247–75.

de Nerval, Gerard, *Oeuvres complètes* (Paris, 1984), vol. 2.

Demir, Fevzi, "Osmanlı Kimliği Üzerine Osmanlı'nın Son Tartışması: Osmanlı'da Hüviyet Cüzdanı nasıl olmalı?" (The last discussion on Ottoman identity by the Ottomans: What should the Ottoman identity card look like?), *Kebikeç* 10 (2000), 245–51.

Derderian, Katherine, "Common Fate, Different Experience: Gender-Specific Aspects of the Armenian Genocide, 1915–1917", *Holocaust and Genocide Studies* 19 (2005), 1–25.

Deak, Istvan, *The Lawful Revolution: Louis Kossuth and the Hungarians, 1848–1849* (New York, 1978).

Deringil, Selim, "The Invention of Tradition as Public Image in the Late Ottoman Empire", *Comparative Studies in Society and History* 35 (1993), 3–29.

Deringil, Selim, "Ottoman to Turk: Minority-Majority Relations in the Late Ottoman Empire", in Dru Gladney (ed.), *Making Majorities: Constituting the Nation in Japan, China, Korea, Malaysia, Fiji, Turkey and the US* (Stanford, CA, 1998), pp. 217–26.

Deringil, Selim, *The Well-Protected Domains: Ideology and the Legitimation of Power in the Ottoman Empire 1876–1909* (London, 1998).

Deringil, Selim, "'There Is No Compulsion in Religion': Conversion and Apostasy in the Late Ottoman Empire, 1839–1856", *Comparative Studies in Society and History* 40 (2000), 547–75.

Deringil, Selim, "'The Armenian Question Is Finally Closed': Mass Conversions of Armenians during the Hamidian Massacres of 1895–1897", *Comparative Studies in Society and History* 51 (April 2009), 344–71.

d'Eszlary, Charles, "L'emigration Hongroise de Louis Kossuth en Turquie entre 1849–1850", *VI Türk Tarihi Kongresi* (Ankara, 1967), pp. 430–50.

Dimitrov, Strashimir, *Pradegovar in Osmanski Izvori za islymizatsionnite protesi* (Sofia, 1990).

Donia, Robert J., *Islam under the Double Eagle: The Muslims of Bosnia and Hercegovina 1878–1914* (New York, 1981).

Duguid, Stephen, "The Politics of Unity: Hamidian Policy in Eastern Anatolia", *Middle Eastern Studies* 9 (1973), 130–55.

Dumont, P., and Georgeon, F., "Un bourgeois d'Istanbul au debut du XXeme siècle", *Turcica* 17 (1985), 127–88.

Dündar, Fuat, *İttihat ve Terakki'nin Müslümanları İskan Politikası 1913–1918* (The Committee of Union and Progress and its policy of Muslim resettlement) (İstanbul, 2001).

Dündar, Fuat, *Modern Türkiye'nin Şifresi* (The code of modern Turkey) (İstanbul, 2008).

Durham, Edith M., *High Albania* (London, 1909).

Dutton, Yasin, "Conversion to Islam: The Qur'anic Paradigm", in Christopher Lamb and M. Darrol Bryant (eds.), *Religious Conversion:*

Contemporary Practices and Controversies (London and New York, 1999), pp. 151–66.

Düzdağ, Ertuğrul, *Ebussud Efendi Fetvaları Işığinda 16. Asır Türk Hayatı* (Sixteenth-century life in Turkey in the light of the fetvas of Ebussuud Efendi) (İstanbul, 1972).

Džaja, Srećko M., "Bosnian Historical Reality and Its Reflection in Myth" in Pal Kolsto (ed.), *Myths and Boundaries in South-Eastern Europe* (London, 2005), pp. 106–29.

Ekmečić, Milorad, *Stvaranje Jugoslavije 1790–1818* (Belgrade, 1989).

Eldem, Edhem, "26 Ağustos 1896 'Banka Vakası' ve 1896, 'Ermeni Olayları'" (26 August 1896 'Ottoman Bank Incident' and the 'Events of 1896'), *Tarih ve Toplum* 5 (2007), 113–46.

Eldem, Edhem, "İbrahim Edhem Paşa Rum Muydu?" (Was İbrahim Edhem Paşa a Greek?), *Toplumsal Tarih* 11 (October 2010), 2–12.

Encyclopaedia of Islam (Leiden, 1965), vol. 3, pp. 736–8.

Enhegger, Robert, "Evangelidos Misailidis ve Türkçe Konuşan dindaşları" (Evangelidos Misailidis and his Turcophone co-religionists), *Tarih ve Toplum*, 9 (1988), 177, n. 2.

Erdem, Hakan, *Slavery in the Ottoman Empire and Its Demise 1800–1909* (London, 1996).

Erdem, Hakan, "'Do Not Think of the Greeks as Agricultural Labourers': Ottoman Responses to the Greek War of Independence", in Faruk Birtek and Thalia Dragonas (eds.), *Citizenship and the Nation-State in Greece and Turkey*, (London, 2005), pp. 67–88.

Fahmy, Khaled, *All the Pasha's Men: Mehmed Ali, History and the Making of Modern Egypt* (New York, 1997).

Finkel, Caroline, *Osman's Dream: The Story of the Ottoman Empire 1300–1923* (London, 2005).

Fawaz, Leila, *Occasion for War: Civil Conflict in the Lebanon and Damascus in 1860* (Berkeley, 1994).

Findley, Carter, *Ottoman Civil Officialdom* (Princeton, NJ, 1989).

Fine, John, *The Early Medieval Balkans: A Critical Survey from the Sixth to the Twelfth Century* (Ann Arbor, MI, 1987).

Fotiadis, Konstantinos, *Piges tis istorias tou kryptochristianikou provlimatos* (History of the Crypto Christian Question) (Thessaloniki, 1997).

Gábor, Egressy, *Törökörszági Naplo 1849–1850*. www.terebess.hu/keletkultinfo/index.html.

Garo, Armen, *Bank Ottoman* (Detroit, 1990).

Georgeon, François, *Abdulhamid II. Le sultan calife* (Paris, 2003).

Ginio, Eyal, "Childhood, Mental Capacity and Conversion to Islam in the Ottoman State", *Byzantine and Modern Greek Studies* 25 (2001), 90–119.

Ginzburg, Carlo, "Checking the Evidence: The Judge and the Historian", in James Chandler, Arnold I. Davidson, and Harry Harootunian (eds.), *Questions of Evidence: Proof, Practice and Persuasion across Disciplines* (Chicago and London, 1994), pp. 290–303.

Girard, Rene, "Generative Scapegoating", in R. G. Hammerton-Kelly (ed.), *Violent Origins: Ritual Killing and Cultural Formation* (Stanford, CA, 1987), pp. 73–148.

Gladstone, W. E., *The Bulgarian Horrors and the Question of the East* (London, 1876).

Gradeva, Rossitsa, and Kuneralp, Sinan, *On Love, Religion, and Politics: Salonica (1876) and Ruse (1910)*. Unpublished manuscript.

Greene, Molly, *A Shared World: Christians and Muslims in the Early Modern Mediterranean* (Princeton, NJ, 2000).

Guleserian, Papgen (Papgen A. Atoragits Gatoghigos Medzi Dan Gilio), *Badmutyun Gatoghigosats Giligio (1441-en minchev mer orere)*, 2nd ed. (Antilias, Lebanon, 1990).

Gülsoy, Ufuk, *Osmanlı Gayrımüslimlerinin Askerlik Serüveni* (The military service adventures of the Ottoman non-Muslims) (İstanbul, 2000).

Gündüz, Ali, *Hemşinliler: Dil-Tarih-Kültür* (The Hemşin: Language, History, Culture) (Ankara, 2002).

Haçikyan, Levon, *Hemşin Gizemi* (The Hemşin mystery) (İstanbul, 1997).

Hamlin, Cyrus, *Among the Turks* (New York, 1878).

Hanioğlu, Şükrü, *Bir siyasal düşünür olarak Abdullah Cevdet ve Dönemi* (Abdullah Cevdet as a political thinker and his time) (İstanbul, 1981).

Hanioğlu, Şükrü, *The Young Turks in Opposition* (New York and Oxford, 1995).

Hanioğlu, Şükrü, *Preparation for a Revolution: The Young Turks 1902–1908* (Oxford, 2001).

Hanioğlu, Şükrü, "The Collapse of the Ottoman Empire and the Present Kurdish Problem", *Zaman*, 22–3 November 2007.

Hanioğlu, Şükrü, *A Brief History of the Late Ottoman Empire* (Princeton, NJ, 2008).

Harootunian, Harry, "Shadowing History: National Narratives and the Persistence of the Everyday", *Cultural Studies* 18 (2004), 181–200.

Hasluck, William, *Christianity and Islam under the Sultans* (Oxford, 1929), vols. 1–2.

Herzl, Theodor, *The Complete Diaries of Theodor Herzl* (London, 1960).

Hitchins, Keith, *The Rumanian National Movement in Transylvania 1780–1849* (Cambridge, MA, 1969).

Hoare, M. A., *The History of Bosnia: From the Middle Ages to the Present Day* (London, 2007).

Hobsbawm, Eric, *The Age of Empire* (London, 1987).

Hobsbawm, Eric, *Nations and Nationalism since 1780* (Cambridge, UK, 1990).

Hobsbawm, Eric, and Ranger, Terence (eds.), *The Invention of Tradition* (Cambridge, UK, 1983).

Hurewitz, J. C., *Diplomacy in the Near and Middle East: A Documentary Record 1535–1914* (Toronto, London & New York, 1956), vol. 1.

Hüseyin Nazım Paşa, *Hatıralarım. Ermeni Olaylarının İçyüzü* (My memoirs: The inside story of the Armenian incidents) (İstanbul, 2003 [1924]).

İbnülemin, Mahmud Kemal İnal, *Son Sadrazamlar* (The last Grand Viziers) (İstanbul, 1982), vol. 1, pp. 4–29.

Imber, Colin, *Ebu's Su'ud: The Islamic Legal Tradition* (Stanford, 1997).

İnalcik, Halil, "Ottoman Methods of Conquest", *Studia Islamica* 2 (1954), 103–29.

İnalcık, Halil, *The Ottoman Empire in the Classical Age, 1300–1600* (London, 1973).

İnalcık, Halil, "The Status of the Greek Patriarch under the Ottomans", *Turcica* 21–2 (1991), 411.

İnalcık, Halil, *Tanzimat ve Bulgar Meselesi* (The Tanzimat and the Bulgarian Question) (İstanbul, 1992).

James, William, *The Varieties of Religious Experience: A Study in Human Nature* (New York, 2002).

Janin, R., "Musulmans Malgre Eux, Les Stavriotes", *Echos D'Orient* 15 (1912), 495–505.

Janossy, Denes A., *Great Britain and Kossuth* (Budapest, 1937).

Jennings, Ronald, *Christians and Muslims in Ottoman Cyprus and the Mediterranean World 1571–1640* (New York and London, 1993).

John, Hutchinson, *Nations as Zones of Conflict* (London, 2005).

Kantarcı, Şenol, *Ahmed Rüstem Bey* (İstanbul, 2009).

Karateke, Hakan, *Padişahım Çok Yaşa! Osmanlı Devletinin Son Yüz Yılında Merasimler* ('Long live the sultan!' Ceremonial in the last century of the Ottoman Empire) (İstanbul, 2004).

Karateke, Hakan, and Maurus Reinowski (eds.), *Legitimizing the Order: The Ottoman Rhetoric of State Power* (Leiden, 2005).

Karpat, Kemal, "Kossuth in Turkey: The Impact of the Hungarian Refugees in the Ottoman Empire 1849–1851", *Hungarian Heritage Review* 6 (March 1990), 18–23.

Kaynar, Reşat, *Mustafa Reşid Paşa ve Tanzimat* (Mustafa Reşid Paşa and the Tanzimat) (Ankara, 1954).

Kemikli, Bilal, *Şair Şeyhülislam, Arif Hikmet Beyefendi. Hayatı Eserleri ve Şiirleri* (The Poet Şeyhülislam, Arif Hikmet Efendi: His life, works and poetry) (Ankara, 2003).

Kenanoğlu, Macit, *Osmanlı Devleti"nde Fikir ve İnanç Hürriyeti* (Freedom of faith and thought in the Ottoman Empire), unpublished paper, 2002.

Kenanoğlu, Macit, *Osmanlı Millet Sistemi. Mit ve Gerçek* (The Ottoman millet system: Myth and reality) (İstanbul, 2004).

Kevorkian, Raymond, *Le Genocide des Armeniens* (Paris, 2006).

Kırlı, Cengiz, "Balkan Nationalisms and the Ottoman Empire: Views from Istanbul Streets", in Antonis Anastasopoulos and Elias Kolovos (eds.), *Ottoman Rule and the Balkans, 1760–1850: Conflict, Transformation, Adaptation.* Proceedings of an international conference held in Rethymno, Greece, 13–14 December 2003.

Kırmızı, Abdülhamid, *Abdülhamid'in Valileri. Osmanlı Vilayet İdaresi. 1895–1908* (Abdülhamid's governors: Provincial administration in the Hamidian state) (İstanbul, 2007), pp. 105–109.

Kitromilides, Paschalis, "'Imagined Communities' and the Origins of the National Question in the Balkans", in Paschalis Kitromilides, *Enlightenment, Nationalism, Orthodoxy: Studies in the Culture and Political Thought of South-Eastern Europe* (Aldershot, 1994), pp. 149–52.

Kitromilides, Paschalis, "Orthodox Culture and Collective Identity in the Ottoman Balkans during the Eighteenth Century", in his *An Orthodox Commonwealth. Symbolic Legacies and Cultural Encounters in South-Eastern Europe* (Aldershot, 2007), pp. 131–45.

Klein, Janet, *Power in the Periphery: The Hamidiye Light Cavalry and the Struggle over Ottoman Kurdistan*, Ph.D. dissertation, Princeton University, 2002.

Kolsto, Pal (ed.), *Myths and Boundaries in South-Eastern Europe* (London, 2005).

Köse, Ali "İhtida", *Islam Ansiklopedisi: Türk Diyanet Vakfı*, vol. 21, p. 555.

Kristić Tijana, "Illuminated by the Light of Islam and the Glory of the Ottoman Sultanate: Self-Narratives of Conversion to Islam in the Age of Confessionalisation", *Comparative Studies in Society and History* 51 (2009), 35–63.

Lamb, Christopher, and Bryant, M. Darrol, *Religious Conversion: Contemporary Practices and Controversies* (London and New York, 1999).

Lane-Poole, Stanley, *The Life of the Right Honourable Stratford Canning, Viscount Stratford de Redcliffe: From His Memoirs and Private and Official Papers* (London, 1888), vol. 2.

Latka, Jerzy S., "Polonya Mültecileri ve Yeni Fikirler" (Polish refugees and new ideas), *Tarih ve Toplum* 10 (July 1991), 23–37.

Levtzion, Nehemiah, "Toward a Comparative Study of Islamization", in Nehemiah Levtzion (ed.), *Conversion to Islam* (New York, 1979), pp. 24–37.

Lewy, Reuben, "The Social Structure of Islam", in *Orientalism: Early Sources* (London and New York, 2004), p. 123.

Lienhardt, P., "The Interpretation of Rumour", in J. M. H. Beattie and R. G. Lienhardt (eds.), *Studies in Social Anthropology: Essays in Memory of E.E. Evans-Pritchard* (Oxford, 1975), pp. 45–67.

Lowry, Heath, "The Ottoman Renaissance: The Conqueror's Dream", *Cornucopia* 34 (2004), 28–9.

McCarthy, Justin, *Death and Exile: The Ethnic Cleansing of Ottoman Muslims, 1821–1922* (Princeton, NJ, 1995).

Magnus, Philip, *Gladstone: A Biography* (London, 1963).

Makdisi, Ussama, *The Culture of Sectarianism: Community, History and Violence in Nineteenth Century Ottoman Lebanon* (Berkeley, 2000).

Makdisi, Ussama, *Artillery of Heaven: American Missionaries and the Failed Conversion of the Middle East* (Ithaca and London, 2008).

Mardin, Şerif, "Center-Periphery Relations: A Key to Turkish Politics?", *Daedalus* 17 (1972), 169–90.

Mardin, Şerif, *Religion and Social Change in Modern Turkey: The Case of Bediuzzaman Said Nursi* (Albany, 1989).

Mayer, Philip, "Witches", inaugural lecture, Rhodes University, 1954, in Max Marwick (ed.), *Witchcraft and Sorcery: Selected Readings* (Bungay, 1982), pp. 54–70.

Mazower, Mark, *The Balkans: A Short History* (New York, 2002).

Mazower, Mark, *Salonica: City of Ghosts* (London, 2004).

Meeker, Michael E., "Greeks Who Are Muslims: Counter Nationalism in Nineteenth Century Trabzon", in David Shankland (ed.), *Archeology,*

Anthropology and Heritage in the Balkans and Anatolia: The Life and Times of F. W. Hasluck 1978–1920 (Istanbul, 2004).

Menage, Victor, "The Islamization of Anatolia", in Nehemiah Levtzion (ed.), *Conversion to Islam* (New York, 1979), pp. 42–58.

Meyrier, Gustave, *Les Massacres de Diarbekir. Correspondance diplomatique du Vice-Consul de France*, presentée et annotée par Claire Mouradian et Michel Durand-Meyrier (Paris, 2000).

Milutinović, Zoran, "Sword, Priest and Conversion: On Religion and Apostasy in South Slav Literature in the Period of National Revival", *Central Europe*, 6 (2008), 17–46.

Minkov, Anton, *Conversion to Islam in the Balkans: Kisve Bahası Petitions and Ottoman Social Life 1670–1730* (Leiden, 2002).

Molho, Anthony, "Jews and Marranos Before the Law: Five Mediterranean Stories", *GRAMMA* 6 (1998), 13–30.

Mouradian, Claire, *L'Arménie* (Paris, 1995).

Mouradian, Claire, "Aperçus sur l'Islamization des Arméniens dans l'Empire Ottoman: le cas des Hamchentsi/Hemşinli", presented at the conference Conversion to Islam in the Mediterranean World, Rome, 4–6 September 1997.

Nalbandian, Louise, *The Armenian Revolutionary Movement: The Development of Armenian Political Parties through the Nineteenth Century* (Berkeley, Los Angeles, and London, 1975).

Nazir, Bayram, "Macar özgürlük savaşçısı Osmanlı Murad Paşa'sı, Jozef Bem'in Ölumu üzerine bir tekzip yazisi" (A declaration of denial regarding the death of Josef Bem, Hungarian freedom fighter and the Murad Paşa of the Ottomans), *Toplumsal Tarih* 12 (1999), 32–4.

Nazir, Bayram, "Lajos Kossuth'u Kıtahya'dan kaçırma girişimleri" (Attempts to abduct Lajos Kossuth from Kıtahya), *Tarih ve Toplum* 36 (2001), 15–19.

Nazir, Bayram, *Osmanlıya Sığınanlar. Macar ve Polonyali Multeciler* (Those who took refuge with the Ottomans: The Hungarian and Polish refugees) (İstanbul, 2006).

Neamtu, Gelu, and Bolovan, Ioan, *The Revolution of 1848–1849 in Transylvania* (Cluj Napoca, 2004).

Neumann, Cristoph K., *Araç Tarih amaç Tanzimat. Tarih-i Cevdet'in Siyasi Anlamı* (History as a tool, Tanzimat as the aim: The political meaning of Cevdet's history) (İstanbul, 1999), p. 194.

Nirenberg, David, *Communities of Violence: Persecution of Minorities in the Middle Ages* (Princeton, NJ, 1996).

Norris, H. T., *Islam in the Balkans* (Columbia, SC, 1993).

Ortaylı, İlber, *Tanzimat'dan Sonra Mahalli İdareler (1840–1878)* (Local government after the Tanzimat) (Ankara, 1974).

Ortaylı, İlber, *İmparatorluğun en Uzun Yüzyılı* (The longest century of the empire) (İstanbul, 1983).

Ortaylı, İlber, "Osmanlı Imparatorluğu'nda Askeri Reformlar ve Polonyalı Mülteci Subaylar" (Military reforms in the Ottoman Empire and the Polish refugee officers), in Ortaylı İlber, *İmparatorluğu'da İktisadi ve Sosyal Değişim Makaleler* (Ankara, 2000), 185–91.

Ortayli, İlber, *Zaman Kaybolmaz*. *İlber Ortaylı Kitabı* (Time is not lost: The İlber Ortayli book. Interviews with İlber Ortayli) (İstanbul, 2006).

Osman Nuri, *Abdülhamid-i Sani ve Devr-i Saltanatı* (Abdulhamid the Second and his reign) (Istanbul, 1327/1909).

Özbek, Nadir, "Anadolu Islahatı, 'Ermeni Sorunu' ve vergi tahsildarlığı 1895–1908" (Anatolian reform, the 'Armenian Question' and the system of tax collection), *Tarih ve Toplum*, no. 9 (Winter 2009), 1–19.

Özcan, Azmi, and Ş. Tufan Buzpınar, "Church Missionary Society İstanbul'da. Tanzimat, İslahat, Misyonerlik" (The Church Missionary Society in Istanbul: The Tanzimat, reform and missionaries), *İstanbul Araştırmaları* 1 (1997), 63–79.

Özçelik, Selahittin, "Osmanlı İç Hukukunda Zorunlu bir Tehir (Mürted Maddesi)" (An obligatory postponement in Ottoman domestic law: The apostasy matter) *OTAM* 11 (2000), 347–438.

Özel, Oktay, "Muhacirler, yerliler ve gayrımüslimler. Osmanlı'nın son devrinde Orta Karadeniz'de toplumsal uyumun sınırları üzerine bazı gözlemler" (Immigrants, locals and non-Muslims: Observations on social harmony in the central Black Sea in the last days of the Ottomans), *Tarih ve Toplum* 5 (2007), 93–112.

Pamuk, Şevket, *The Ottoman Empire and European Capitalism 1820–1913* (Cambridge, UK, 1987).

Peters, Rudolph, and De Vries, Gert J. J., "Apostasy in Islam", *Die Welt des Islams* 17 (1975–76), 1–25.

Petrov, Milen V., "Everyday Forms of Compliance: Subaltern Commentaries on Ottoman Reform, 1864–1868", *Comparative Studies in Society and History* 46 (2004), 730–59.

Pivany, Eugen, "Hungarian American Historical Connections", in Edmund Vasvary, *Lincoln's Hungarian Heroes* (Washington, DC, 1939).

Radusev, Velkov E., E. Siljanova, M. Kalicin and A. Radusev, *Sources Ottomanes sur le Processus d'Islamisation aux Balkans (XIV–XIX siècles). Traduction des documents* (Sofia, 1990), pp. 33–4.

Rambo, Lewis R., and Farhadian, Charles E., "Converting: Stages of Religious Change", in Christopher Lamb and M. Darrol Bryant (eds.), *Religious Conversion Contemporary Practices and Controversies* (London and New York, 1999), pp. 23–4.

Reinkowski, Maurus, "The State's Security and the Subjects' Prosperity: Notions of Order in Ottoman Bureaucratic Correspondence (19th Century)", in Hakan Karateke and Maurus Reinkowski (eds.), *Legitimizing the Order: The Ottoman Rhetoric of State Power* (Leiden, 2005).

Reinkowski, Maurus, "Hidden Believers, Hidden Apostates: The Phenomenon of Crypto-Jews and Crypto-Christians in the Middle East", in Dennis Washburn and Kevin A. Rheinhart (eds.), *Converting Cultures: Religion, Ideology and Transformations of Modernity* (Leiden and Boston, 2007), pp. 409–33.

Richter, Julius, *A History of Protestant Missions in the Near East* (Edinbugh and London, 1910).

Riis, Carsten, *Religion, Politics, and Historiography in Bulgaria* (New York, 2002).

Roberts, Ian W., *Nicholas I and the Russian Intervention in Hungary* (London, 1991).

Roudometof, Victor, *Nationalism, Globalisation and Orthodoxy: The Social Origins of Ethnic Conflict in the Balkans* (Westport, CT, 2001).

Salibi, Kamal, *The House of Many Mansions: The History of Lebanon Reconsidered* (London and Los Angeles, 1988).

Sapkidi, Olga, "Family Structure in the Pontos", *Encyclopedia of the Hellenic World*, vol. 1: Asia Minor, www.ehwr.gr.

Şaşmaz, Musa, *19. Asrın Davası. Kürd Musa Bey'in Yargılanması* (The case of the century: The trial of Kürd Musa Bey) (Niğde, 1997).

Saydam, Abdullah, "Müslüman olan Macar-Leh Mültecileri Meselesi" (The affair of the Hungarian and Polish refugees' conversion to Islam), *Toplumsal Tarih* 4 (1995), 21–32.

Saydam, Abdullah, "Kütahya'a Mülteci bir Cumhurbaşkanı: Louis Kossuth" (A refugee head of state in Kütahya: Louis Kossuth), *Tarih ve Toplum* 28 (1997), 5–14.

Saydam, Abdullah, *Osmanlıların Siyasi İlticalara Bakışı ya da 1849 Macar Leh Mültecileri Meselesi* (The Ottoman attitude to political asylum or the Hungarian and Polish refugees of 1849), off-print from *Belleten* 161 (1997), 339–85.

Schick, Irvin Cemil, "Christian Maidens, Turkish Ravishers: The Sexualization of National Conflict in the Late Ottoman Period", in Amila Baturović and Irvin Cemil Schick (eds.), *Women in the Ottoman Balkans: Gender, Culture, and History* (New York, 2007).

Scott, James C., *Weapons of the Weak: Everyday Forms of Peasant Resistance* (New Haven, CT, 1985).

Seton-Watson, Robert W., "The Era of Reform in Hungary", *Slavonic and East European Review* 21, part 2 (1943), 32–54.

Shukri, Ahmed, *Mohammedan Law of Marriage and Divorce* (New York, 1966).

Simonian, Hovan H., "Hemshin from Islamization to the End of the Nineteenth Century", in Hovan H. Simonian (ed.), *The Hemshin: History, Society and Identity in the Highlands of North-East Turkey* (London and New York, 2007).

Skendi, Stavro, "Crypto Christianity in the Balkan Area under the Ottomans", *Slavic Review* 26 (1967), 227–46.

Skendi, Stavro, *Balkan Cultural Studies* (New York, 1980).

Smith, Anthony D., *Ethno-symbolism and Nationalism: A Cultural Approach* (Abingdon and New York, 2009).

Spira, György, *The Nationality Issue in the Hungary of 1848–1949* (Budapest, 1992).

Stark, Freya, *The Journey's Echo: Selections from Freya Stark* (London, 1933).

Stone, Frank Andrew, *Academies for Anatolia* (Lanham, New York, and London, 1984).

Strauss, Johann, "Ottoman Rule Experienced and Remembered: Remarks on Some Local Greek Chronicles of the Tourkokratia", in Fikret Adanir and

Suraiya Faroghi (eds.), *The Ottomans and the Balkans: A Discussion of Historiography* (Leiden, 2002), pp. 200–22.

Subaşı, Turgut, "The Apostasy Question in the Context of Anglo-Ottoman Relations", *Middle Eastern Studies* 38 (2002), 1–34.

Suny, R. G., *Looking towards Ararat: Armenia in Modern History* (Indianapolis, 1993).

Sumner, Charles, *White Slavery in the Barbary States 1853* (Boston, 1853).

Somel, Akşin, "The Problem of Crypto-Christians in Albania during the Hamidian Period", in *South East Europe in History: The Past, the Present and the Problems of Balkanology* (Ankara, 1999), pp. 117–24.

Süreyya, Mehmed, *Sicil-i Osmani* (Istanbul, 1983), vol. 2, pp. 395–6.

Tarhanlı, İştar, *Müslüman Toplum 'laik' Devlet: Türkiye'de Diyanet İşleri Başkanlığı* (Muslim society 'secular' state: The history of the Diyanet) (İstanbul, 1993).

Tashnadi, Edit, "18–19 Yüzyılda Osmanlı'da Macar Mültecileri" (Hungarian refugees in the Ottoman Empire in the eighteenth and nineteenth centuries), *Tarih ve Toplum* 36 no.215 (November 2001), 71–5.

Terminassian, Anahide, *Nationalism and Socialism in the Armenian Revolutionary Movement* (Cambridge, MA, 1984).

Tevfik, Mehmed, *Cok Yasa! Csok Jasa! Yadigar-i Asr-i Abdulhamid Han* (Long live! Memento of the century of Abdulhamid Han) (İstanbul, 1294).

Thesprotou, K., and Psalida, A., *Geographia Alvanias kai Hellenismou* (Janina, 1964).

Todorova, Maria, "The Ottoman Legacy in the Balkans", in Carl L. Brown (ed.), *Imperial Legacy: The Ottoman Imprint on the Balkans and the Middle East* (New York, 1996).

Todorova, Maria, *Imagining the Balkans* (New York, 1997).

Todorova, Maria, "Conversion to Islam as a Trope in Bulgarian Historiography, Fiction and Film", in Maria Todorova (ed.), *Balkan Identities: Nation and Memory* (London, 2004).

Toledano, Ehud, *State and Society in Mid-nineteenth Century Egypt* (New York, 1990).

Toumarkine, Alexandre, "Ottoman Political and Religious Elites among the Hemshin", in Hovan H. Simonian (ed.), *The Hemshin: History Society and Identity in the Highlands of North East Turkey* (London, New York, 2007), pp. 98–117. pp. 102–5.

Trencsényi, Balćzs and Kopećek, Michael (eds.), *Discourses of Collective Identity in Central and Southeast Europe: Texts and Commentaries* (Budapest and New York, 2006).

Trotsky, Leon, *The War Correspondence of Leon Trotsky: The Balkan Wars 1912–13* (New York, 1993).

Turner, Victor, *Dramas, Fields and Metaphors* (Ithaca, 1974).

Tzedopoulos, Yorgos, "Public Secrets: Crypto-Christianity in the Pontos", *DELTIO* 16 (2009). Journal of the Centre for Asia Minor Studies, Athens.

Uzun, Ahmet, *Tanzimat ve Sosyal Direnisler, 1841 Nis Isyani Uzerine ayrintili bir Inceleme* (The Tanzimat and social resistance: A detailed study of the 1841 Nis uprising) (İstanbul, 2002).

Uzunçarşılı, İ.H., *Osmanlı İmparatorluğu'nun İlmiye Teşkilatı* (The scholarly establishment in the Ottoman Empire) (Ankara, 1965).

Uzunçarşılı, İ. H., *Midhat Pasa ve Taif Mahkumlari* (Midhat Pasa and the convicts of Taif) (Ankara, 1985).

Vambery, Arminus, *Travels in Central Asia: A Journey from Teheran across the Turcoman Desert on the Eastern Shore of the Caspian to Khiva, Bokhara and Samarkand. Performed in the Year 1863* (London, 1864).

Vambery, Arminius, *Arminius Vambery: His Life and Adventures by Himself* (London and New York, 1883).

van Bruinessen, Martin, *Agha Shaikh and State: The Social and Political Structures of Kurdistan* (London, 1992).

Varkongy, Agnes, "Rakoczi's War of Independence and the Peasantry", in Janos M. Bak and Bela Kiraly (eds.), *From Hunyadi to Rakoczi: War and Society in Late Medieval and Early Modern Hungary* (New York, 1982).

Vasvary, Edmund, *Lincoln's Hungarian Heroes: The Participation of Hungarians in the Civil War 1861–1865* (Washington, DC, 1939).

Verheij Jelle, "Les frères de terrre et d'eau: Sur le role des Kurdes dans les massacres arméniens de 1894–1896", *Les Cahiers de l'autre Islam* 5 (1999), 225–76.

Viswanathan, Gauri, *Outside the Fold: Conversion, Modernity and Belief* (Princeton, NJ, 1998).

Walker, Christopher, *Armenia: The Survival of a Nation* (Chatham, Kent, 1991).

White, Luise, "Telling More: Lies, Secrets and History", *History and Theory* 39 (2000), 11–22.

Wigram, W. A. *The Cradle of Mankind: Life in Eastern Kurdistan* (London,1922).

Yarman Arsen, *Palu, Harput, Çarsancak, Çemişkezek, Çapakçur, Erzincan ve Civar Bölgeler. Raporlar* (Palu, Harput, Çapakçur, Erzincan and neighboring areas: Reports).(Istanbul, 2010). Translated from Armenian by Arsen Yarman and Sirvart Malhasyan.

Yasamee, F. A. K., *Ottoman Diplomacy: Abdülhamid II and the Great Powers 1878–1888* (İstanbul, 1996).

Yosmaoğlu, Ipek, "Counting Bodies, Shaping Souls: The 1903 Census and National Identity in Ottoman Macedonia", *IJMES*, 38 (2006), 55–77.

Young, George, *Corps de Droit Ottoman*, vol. 2 (Oxford, 1905).

Zhelyazkova, Antonina, "Islamization in the Balkans as an Historiographical Problem: The Southeast European Perspective", in Fikret Adanir and Suraiya Faroghi (eds.), *The Ottomans and the Balkans: A Discussion of Historiography* (Leiden, 2002), pp. 244–5.

Zurcher, Eric-Jan, "The Ottoman Conscription System in Theory and Practice", *International Review of Social History* 43 (1998), 439–40.

Index

Lightning Source UK Ltd.
Milton Keynes UK
UKOW06f1903180616

276557UK00008B/199/P